# Video Over IP:
# A Practical Guide
# to Technology
# and Applications

# Video Over IP:
# A Practical Guide
# to Technology
# and Applications

Wes Simpson

AMSTERDAM • BOSTON • HEIDELBERG • LONDON
NEW YORK • OXFORD • PARIS • SAN DIEGO
SAN FRANCISCO • SINGAPORE • SYDNEY • TOKYO

Focal Press is an imprint of Elsevier

**ELSEVIER**

Acquisitions Editor: Angelina Ward
Project Manager: Jeff Freeland
Assistant Editor: Rachel Epstein
Marketing Manager: Christine Degon

Focal Press is an imprint of Elsevier
30 Corporate Drive, Suite 400, Burlington, MA 01803, USA
Linacre House, Jordan Hill, Oxford OX2 8DP, UK

∞ Recognizing the importance of preserving what has been written, Elsevier prints its books
on acid-free paper whenever possible.

**Library of Congress Cataloging-in-Publication Data**
Application submitted

**British Library Cataloguing-in-Publication Data**
A catalogue record for this book is available from the British Library.

ISBN-13: 978-0-240-80557-3
ISBN-10: 0-240-80557-7

For information on all Focal Press publications
visit our website at www.books.elsevier.com

06 07 08 09 10   10 9 8 7 6 5 4 3 2

Printed in the United States of America

# DEDICATION

This book is dedicated in loving memory of my sister Lyn and my uncle Rufus.

*"Even the death of friends will inspire us as much as their lives .... Their memories will be encrusted over with sublime and pleasing thoughts, as monuments of other men are overgrown with moss; for our friends have no place in the graveyard."*

*–Henry David Thoreau*

# TABLE OF CONTENTS

# INTRODUCTION

The field of video transport is constantly evolving. As new technologies emerge, they are put to work in transporting video signals. This has been true for radio, coaxial cable, microwave, satellite, and optical fiber, and will also be true for the Internet Protocol, or IP. This latest step in the path of evolution may be the most important yet, because IP allows so many different types of video, audio, and data formats to be transported economically to any corner of the globe.

Several recent technology trends have combined to make video transport over IP networks useful for a wide variety of applications today.

- *Transition to Digital Video:* Video production has almost completely migrated from analog to digital technology during the past 20 years, and today even reaches into the home with digital camcorders, digital television displays, and digital broadcasts from terrestrial, satellite, and cable television providers. One result of this change is that video signals no longer need to be transported on specialized analog networks but can now take advantage of the wide range of digital technologies that are available.

- *Advances in Video Compression:* Compression technology has rapidly evolved from the first MPEG–1 standard in 1991 to today's Advanced Video Codec for MPEG–4 and the latest Windows Media codec, both of which have been made public in the past two years. Compression means that acceptable video signals can be sent over networks with limited capacity, including those that serve many households and most businesses around the world.

- *Growth in IP Network Capacity:* The rapid growth of Internet traffic (by a factor of 10,000 in the decade up to 2003[1]) and the widespread adoption of broadband access lines (passing the 100-million line mark worldwide by the end of 2003[2]) mean that the IP network capacity needed for video transport has reached critical mass.

Together, these developments have made it technically and economically feasible to deliver high-quality video content to a huge number of viewers over IP networks.

As with any technology, users have many different choices for video transport, with a wide range of confusing acronyms, standards, and applications. This book will help you make sense of all this information, help you understand how this technology works, and, most importantly, help you choose which technology is right for your application.

Many people who have a great deal of knowledge about video technology have limited understanding of networking, and vice versa. This book spans this gap, because successful video over IP deployments require good planning in both the networking and the video technology areas. As we will see, decisions that are made in one area can have a great impact on the other. This book will help experts in both fields gain some insight in new areas, and it will serve as an ideal starting point for readers who are new to both fields.

1. A. M. Odlyzko. "Internet Traffic Growth: Sources and Implications," in *Optical Transmission Systems and Equipment for WDM Networking II*, B. B. Dingel, W. Weiershausen, A. K. Dutta, and K.-I. Sato, eds., Proc. SPIE, vol. 5247 (2003): 1–15.
2. World Broadband Statistics: Q4 (2003) © Point Topic Ltd. 2004.

## PURPOSE OF THIS BOOK

There are two main purposes of this book. First is helping the reader to understand the wide range of technologies that are available for video transport over IP networks. Second is helping the reader to figure out which technology is right for a given application. Along the way, we'll look at a number of real-world examples that show how people have successfully used IP technology for a wide variety of purposes.

Video content can be moved across an IP network in literally dozens of ways. Although the thought of postage-stamp-size, jerky video springs to mind when many people hear the words "Internet video," in reality, broadcast-quality, high definition video can be sent over the Internet. There are many different applications for IP video, including surveillance, videoconferencing, video to the home, corporate training, and professional video production, to name a few. Video can be sent over public networks, private networks, optical networks, and pretty much any other network that can handle IP packets, and these networks have reached the maturity levels needed to allow interoperability between these networks. Much of this video is serving a solid business purpose, whether it is paid for by advertising, subscriptions, or sponsored by companies seeking to improve productivity or reduce costs. As we will see throughout this book, there are enough different ways to move video content over an IP network to satisfy virtually any application.

With all this variety, it can be hard to pick out the right solution. To help that process, we'll spend a lot of time analyzing the benefits and drawbacks of the technologies that we discuss. In particular, we'll try to look at why a technology might be suited for an application and what the alternatives are. Because there are so many variables from one network to another, we'll try to avoid specific recipes. The goal is to give each reader the information needed to make intelligent choices and to focus on the important factors for each application.

One thing that we will try to avoid in this book is the often mind-numbing description of all the different bits and bytes that make up each of the different protocols and standards. There are lots of free, public domain sources for this information, and, frankly, they don't tell a reader much about how a protocol is used or its applications. Instead, in this book we'll look at the big picture and focus on how a protocol works and why it may (or may not) be suitable for a particular purpose. In this way, we'll be able to serve the 90% or more of the reading audience who will never need to write a line of code nor diagnose a data circuit with a protocol analyzer, but who need to know how to get the results they need through the use of video over IP technology.

## INTENDED AUDIENCE

This book was written for a variety of audiences, including

- *End Users*, particularly those who might say: "I have video; I have an IP network; so can I use this network to transport my video?" Many times, video projects need to be driven by end users, because they will reap the benefits. However, it is important to realize that video can use a significant amount of network resources, and many system administrators are understandably cautious about adding video to a network that is already busy with other tasks. This book will have served its purpose if end users feel comfortable in talking to system administrators about the issues and trade-offs that need to be discussed prior to video deployment.
- *Video Professionals*, some of whom have had little or no exposure to the world of data networking (aside from the dubious joys of e-mail and text based pagers). A number of the technologies that are available today for transporting high-quality video over IP networks were simply not available five years ago, or, if they were, had a prohibitive price tag. Thanks to the relentless march of technology, a great deal of data networking technology has become useful and cost effective in the broadcast video world. This book aims to provide video professionals with the information they need about IP networking to make informed decisions about how and why to deploy this powerful technology.
- *Computer and Telecom Networking Professionals*, who know that video transport has always been a capability of their network

but have not had an easy way to learn about this sometimes-daunting field of video transport. With all of the new technologies that have come onto the market, video transport has become much less of a burden for data networks and the people who manage them. This book is intended to both serve as an introduction to modern video technology and to familiarize readers with many of the different tools that are available for video transport.

- *Service Provider Staff*, who are often faced with trying to understand and support customers with a wide variety of different networking needs. As video over IP networking becomes more affordable and popular with users, many different departments in a large service provider need to become familiar with video, including sales, marketing, and technical support staff. This book provides a solid introduction into many of the necessary concepts, and could serve as the basis for an effective training course.

- *Investors and Managers*, who want to get a good overview of the technologies in this market but want to avoid becoming overwhelmed with technical details would also find this volume helpful. As a bonus, sections of several chapters are devoted to discussions of the financial considerations that surround the decisions about whether or not to deploy video networks.

Overall, people at several different levels (entry-level technical, system administration, purchasing/sales, managerial, and executive) in a variety of organizations (manufacturing, services, government, and carriers) would benefit from this book.

## HOW TO READ THIS BOOK

Not every reader will need to read every chapter of this book to benefit from it. The first seven chapters cover the basic technologies and applications for video over IP and form a good core of information for all readers. The remaining chapters focus on more specialized topics; readers should feel free to pick and choose the topics that they find of interest. The following descriptions of each chapter should help readers navigate through the book:

Chapters 1 and 2 provide an overview of video transport in terms of technology and applications. Highlights include a discussion about the usefulness of the public Internet for video transport near the end of Chapter 1 and a peek at the economics of video services in Chapter 2. Most readers should benefit from reading these chapters, because they help set the stage for many of the applications we will be talking about in the rest of the book.

Chapter 3 is intended for readers who need an introduction to video. It explains a number of terms that will be used throughout the book and in any meaningful discussion about video technology. Folks who have a good background in video technology can safely skip this chapter.

Chapter 4 focuses on the many different forms of video and audio compression, including some that many folks (even those in the video field) may not have been exposed to. Because compression is so important to video over IP applications, readers are urged to carefully review this chapter.

Chapter 5 covers the essential elements of IP technology. Readers with more than a basic understanding of IP networking can bypass this material with impunity.

Chapter 6 covers the fusion of video and networking technology, particularly in the area of protocols for video transport. These are some of the key underlying technologies involved in video over IP, and are significantly different in application and behavior from standard data networking protocols. Most readers will benefit from this discussion, because these protocols have a big impact on the behavior of video streams and the networks that carry them.

Chapter 7 begins with a discussion of a number of different IP packet transport technologies. It also examines the ways in which network impairments can affect video traffic, which can be quite different from the effects on data traffic.

Chapter 8 talks about streaming, which is one of the most popular technologies for delivering video over IP. In this chapter, we will discuss how true streaming is differentiated from some very clever imposters. We'll also talk about the corporate giants of video streaming technology and look at their technology.

Chapter 9 goes into multicasting and why it is so desirable for delivering video to multiple users at the same time. We'll see why it is also one of the biggest headaches for system administrators. This chapter lays out the arguments, both for and against, the use of multicasting for video signals.

Chapter 10 focuses on videoconferencing, which has a unique set of requirements and a unique set of technologies to meet those requirements. In it, we'll cover the several important aspects of videoconferencing, including the need for low delay networks and equipment. Folks who need to send video only one way can safely skip this chapter.

Chapter 11 focuses on content ownership and security. This is important both for users who own their own content and for those who obtain content from others.

Chapter 12 discusses ways that private networks and virtual private networks can be used to provide secure transport for valuable content. This information will be important to anyone who needs to send video from one location to another.

Chapter 13 looks at a very popular application for video over IP: video to the home. Some unique technologies in this area can have a powerful impact on the technical and economic success of a mass deployment. Readers who are interested only in corporate video can safely skip this chapter.

Chapter 14 looks at how video content can be transported as data files. Because many of these files are staggeringly big and difficult to manage, several service providers have gone into business specifically to support this application. We'll look at some of the tools and techniques that have been developed to manage video file transport.

Chapter 15 looks at network administration and some of the unique management concerns involved in controlling video networks. We'll look at some of the key functions of a video network management system, and we'll discuss an example of a system that is used to manage a distance-learning network.

## Video User Checklist

Throughout this book, we will develop a video user checklist, which we will add to at the end of each chapter. This list tries to capture all of the key issues that need to be considered when planning a video network deployment. By reading this list and trying to provide suitable answers to the questions, readers will be able to anticipate and think through many of the issues that will arise during a system deployment. Although the complete list may appear to be a bit daunting at first, time spent working with it could highlight issues that are much easier to deal with before a project begins. (Remember the old rule of thumb: One day of planning can save one week of implementing a network.)

The checklists from all the individual chapters are gathered into one easy-to-read location at the back of this book in Appendix C. Readers are encouraged to copy this list and use it whenever they need to plan or evaluate a video-networking project.

## ACKNOWLEDGMENTS

I would like to take this opportunity to thank many of the people who have provided me with encouragement and support during the writing of this book. My editor, Angelina Ward, and my Project Manager, Jeff Freeland, have helped immeasurably in bringing this book into being. Becky Golden-Harrell, Assistant Editor, has helped me survive a number of pressing deadlines. My publisher, Joanne Tracy, has been a valuable source of insight, inspiration, and thoughtful opinions. MJ Drouin did a fantastic job as the principal reviewer; this book would not be half as good as it is without her tireless support and meaningful suggestions. Other reviewers, including Brad Medford, Lloyd Lacassagne, and Fred Huffman, have provided many useful comments and critiques. A number of companies and organizations have also graciously permitted me to include real-world examples of current technologies and applications; their contributions are included as case studies in a number of chapters. Merrill Weiss, the editor of this series, who has been a valuable reviewer, was instrumental in making it possible for me to go on this fantastic (and somewhat grueling) adventure. And finally, I would like to thank my wife Laurie, who has been incredibly supportive of this idea, and who has graciously put up with the long hours, missing weekends, and abbreviated vacations that were necessary to make this book a reality.

Wes Simpson, June 2005
wes.simpson@gmail.com

# 1

# OVERVIEW OF VIDEO TRANSPORT

Transporting video signals is a round-the-clock business throughout the world today. Whether for entertainment, education, or personal communication, we now live in a world where we are constantly exposed to video content in many different forms. The scale and scope of the technologies and systems that are used to gather and deliver all of this content are quite amazing. For example, over 1 billion viewers around the world saw the final match of the 2002 FIFA World Cup™ tournament.

As Internet Protocol (IP) technologies for video transport continue to mature, more and more of the video delivery process will take place over IP networks. This change will ultimately include all phases of video content creation and delivery, beginning right at the video camera and ending at a home viewer's video display. As we will see throughout this book, there are many different areas of the video industry that will be affected by IP technology.

In this chapter, we will look at the primary methods that are used today for delivering video signals to viewers around the world. Then we'll discuss some of the main technologies that are used in telecom-munications networks, including ATM and IP protocols. We will also investigate some of the issues surrounding video transport on the Internet. Finally, we will introduce our Video User Checklist, which we will be creating and expanding as we progress through the book. By the end of this chapter, you should be familiar with some of the common forms of video transport and some of the common types of telecom networks.

## VIDEO TRANSPORT TECHNOLOGIES

Television was invented for a single purpose: to transport moving pictures from one location to another. The very word "television" comes from the Greek word "tele," meaning "far off" or "distant," and the Latin verb "visio," meaning "to see." (The word "video" also comes from this same Latin root.) Hence, "television" means "seeing at a distance." Modern video transport technology is all about solving the same problem: how to send moving images to a viewer who is far away.

Today, users have many more video transport options than the pioneers of television had. With all these options comes a challenge: How does a user select the best way to transport video for each application? Many factors are involved in this choice, so there is not one single best answer for every user. Let's begin by looking at the many methods that are used for transporting video signals from source to user today.

### Broadcast TV

Many of us first encountered television in its original form—as a signal broadcast from a central tower, through the air over a dedicated channel, to a receiver equipped with an antenna located in our home. Let's look at some of the key components of a modern broadcast television system (see Figure 1-1).

The Master Control Room (MCR) is the operational hub of a modern television station. The MCR is the place where all the pieces of video content are put together and made ready for broadcasting to viewers.

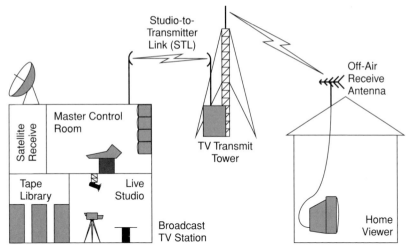

**FIGURE 1-1**   Broadcast Television System Diagram

Video content can come from a variety of sources—a local studio, a signal supplied by a broadcast network,[1] or from a videotape or video server. (As we'll see in Chapter 3, video content includes many things besides basic video and audio information.) Table 1-1 gives a small sample of the many functions that a modern television station must perform.

**TABLE 1-1**

Television Station Functions

- Collect video content from a variety of sources, including broadcast network feeds, advertising agencies, local television studios, and syndicated program distributors.
- Prepare the video content for broadcast by editing the material to fit into time constraints and adding local programming and advertising.
- Ensure that the broadcast signal meets all of the performance standards (such as operating frequency and peak radiated power) specified in the station's broadcast license.
- Make sure there is no "dead air," i.e., times when nothing is being broadcast.

---

1.   Somewhat confusingly, the term "network" has two different meanings for people with broadcast television or data communications backgrounds. In this book, we will try to use the term "broadcast network" whenever we are referring to the distributors of programming that operate in many countries, such as the BBC in the UK, ARD in Germany, or CBS in the United States. When we use the term "network" by itself or with another modifier, we are referring to a data, voice, or other type of telecommunications system.

A Studio-to-Transmitter Link (STL) is used whenever the Master Control Room is separated from the actual transmitter tower. The STL carries the television signal directly to the transmitter. An STL normally operates over a dedicated facility, usually a fiber optic or a microwave radio channel (or both, with one acting as a backup for the other). Microwave radio can be used where there is a direct line of sight available from the studio to the transmitter and where the required licenses can be obtained. Fiber optic links are more reliable than microwave radio links, but they require a fiber optic cable to be connected from the studio to the transmitter. These links can be owned by a local telephone company, other local utility, a municipality, or they can be owned by the television station itself.

At the transmitter, the signal is received from the studio (possibly over an STL) and then placed into a specific channel frequency band. For example, in the USA, Channel 2 occupies the radio channel frequencies between 54 and 60 MHz; Channel 30 occupies the frequencies between 566 and 572 MHz. The modulated signal is amplified to a high power level and fed into the broadcast antenna. The television signal then radiates from the antenna to viewers' locations.

At each viewer's location, an off-air receiving antenna collects the radiated signal and generates a very tiny output signal. This signal is then demodulated and decoded to recover the video and audio signals. These signals are then amplified many times over until they are powerful enough to drive the television set's display and loudspeakers. A significant amount of synchronization information is required by the television set to put the right image at the right location on the television screen at the right time; this sync information is also contained in the broadcast signal.

## Satellite Television

Satellites orbiting the earth are commonly used to receive signals from one earth location and send them to another. Satellites can also be used to broadcast a collection of television signals directly to viewers' homes. Both these applications are in widespread use today.

Satellite transmission of television programs has been used since the mid-1960s to send live programming from one continent to another. Broadcast networks began using satellites to send programming to local television stations and cable TV systems in the mid-1970s. At the same time, consumers started to install their own satellite-receiving dishes that enabled them to receive the broadcast network signals. In 1986, this market changed dramatically, as broadcast networks in the USA began to scramble their signals. This move forced viewers who had purchased their own systems to pay a monthly subscription fee in order to receive content. However, it wasn't until the late 1980s that satellite broadcasting to consumers really began, as exemplified by Sky television in the UK in 1989. This market became known as the direct-to-home (DTH) market, since satellite television service providers were transmitting their programs directly to the ultimate consumers, rather than to local television broadcast stations or cable television systems as in the past. This service is also commonly known as Direct Broadcast Satellite (DBS) service. Let's look at the key components of a typical Satellite DTH system (Figure 1-2).

An Uplink Facility transmits signals from the ground to a satellite, using a high power signal and a large diameter satellite dish. The Uplink Facility gathers video content from a variety of sources,

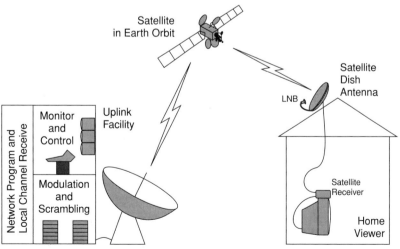

**FIGURE 1-2**   Direct-to-Home (DTH) Satellite Television System Diagram

including local television stations in various cities, specialized programmers (such as movie and sports networks), and many others. Because a single Uplink Facility can create multiple signals to be sent to one or more satellites (by means of a separate dish for each satellite) for rebroadcast over a large area, only one facility is needed to serve an entire continent (although some providers use multiple sites).

Satellites are positioned above the equator at a height of 22,300 miles, which causes them to orbit the earth once every 24 hours and thereby appear to be stationary above a fixed point on the earth's surface. Each satellite is equipped with multiple transponders, each of which receives a signal transmitted by an uplink, converts its frequency (so that the signal sent back to earth [downlink] is different and won't interfere with the signal that is sent up to the satellite [uplink]), amplifies it, and broadcasts the signals back to earth. Currently, a satellite transponder doesn't do any processing of the uplinked signal (other than amplification and frequency conversion), so a transponder can be used for basically any type of content, such as voice, video, or data. This permits a DTH broadcaster to change the types of services that are offered over time without changing the satellite.

One of the biggest changes in satellite broadcasting occurred in the second half of the 1990s. The conversion from analog to digital transmission allowed satellite service providers to put from 8 to 20 (or more) television channels on each transponder. Using more channels per transponder spreads the cost of the satellite transport over more channels and increases the number of channels that the DTH broadcaster can offer. One of the first satellite providers to offer exclusively digital satellite service was DirecTV, which began operation in 1994. To support digital transmission, additional equipment is needed at the Uplink Facility. Once the content is gathered, it must be digitized and compressed, so multiple video signals can fit into the bandwidth formerly occupied by a single analog channel. The signals are also scrambled so customers who have not paid the required programming fees cannot view them.

Each satellite TV customer must purchase and install a dish antenna. The antenna must normally be installed outdoors with a clear line of sight to the satellite, with no intervening buildings, branches, leaves, or other items. The dish must be installed at the correct elevation angle (up and down tilt) and azimuth (compass direction) to point directly at the satellite. The dish assembly contains a Low Noise Block (LNB) down-converter that receives the signal at the focal point of the dish and converts it to a signal that can be transmitted over coaxial cable to the satellite receiver located at the customer's television set. Table 1-2 lists the main functions of a satellite receiver.

## Cable TV

Cable television (CATV) can trace its origins to broadcast television beginning in the 1950s. Originally, the acronym CATV stood for Community Antenna (or Community Access) TV, and that was exactly its purpose—to allow a community of viewers to share a common antenna for receiving broadcast television signals. By sharing a common antenna that was located on a tall tower or a convenient hilltop, viewers could pull in signals from remote broadcast stations that would be impractical for them to receive on their own.

Since those days, CATV has made major strides into new areas, including subscription television (movie channels), pay-per-view, Video on Demand, and specialized interest channels, such as Spanish

**TABLE 1-2**

Satellite Receiver Functions

- Accept commands from the customer's remote control to determine which channel the customer wants to watch.
- Ensure that the customer has authorization to watch the selected channel (sometimes by means of a special identification card).
- Receive the signal from the LNB, and process it to recover the desired channel. This step may include descrambling the incoming signal.
- In most cases, the satellite receiver must be connected to a telephone line to permit the box to communicate with the DTH service provider's central computers.

For digital satellite transmission, the following functions must also be performed:

- Demodulate and demultiplex the digital data to select the correct digital stream.
- Remove any encryption that has been performed on the signal.
- Decompress the stream to create a video output that is fed to the customer's television set.

language programming and channels devoted exclusively to sports or weather. However, the video transport mechanism is essentially the same as that used by broadcast television—each video signal is placed onto a specific carrier frequency (TV channel), and transported into each subscriber's home via a coaxial cable in place of an antenna. Let's look at a typical CATV system (see Figure 1-3).

A CATV system can serve tens or hundreds of thousands of customers from a single Master Head End (MHE). The MHE is the central facility where video content is gathered from a wide variety of sources and made ready to transmit to viewers. Video feeds can come from local TV broadcasters (received at the MHE via an antenna or by means of a dedicated link from the TV station), from satellite feeds, from local programming sources (including educational and government institutions), and from pre-recorded content, such as advertisements.

Many CATV providers have started supplying some or most of their programming in digital format, for many of the same reasons as satellite and over-the-air broadcasters. First and foremost, digital video streams can be compressed to use network bandwidth more efficiently, allowing the transmission of multiple digital video channels in place of one analog channel. This improvement in efficiency

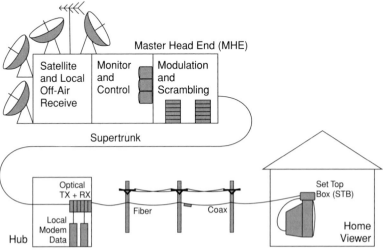

**FIGURE 1-3**  Cable Television System Diagram

becomes even more important as CATV providers seek to free up bandwidth that can then be used to provide other revenue-generating services, such as voice and data transport.

The techniques used to combine and organize the different digital video signals vary from one CATV provider to another. In Europe, many systems operate in accordance with standards published by the Digital Video Broadcasting (DVB) consortium. Many other techniques are used around the world, including some that are based on IP technology.

The functions of an MHE are very similar to those of a television station's Master Control Room (MCR) with three major exceptions:

- The MHE typically handles dozens or even hundreds of channels, whereas an MCR generally handles one or possibly a handful of channels. This both limits the amount of processing that is done to each video signal and increases the attractiveness of automation within an MHE.
- A portion of the channels processed by the MHE are typically scrambled or encrypted to prevent them from being watched by subscribers who have not paid the appropriate fees. Scrambling is very common for programming that requires monthly subscriptions or special payments, such as premium movie or sports channels, or pay-per-view video services that can be purchased by viewers from time to time. The technology that is required to manage this content is called a Conditional Access (CA) system, which controls the decryption and descrambling function of each subscriber's receiver device, commonly known as a Set Top Box (STB), see Table 1-3.
- In many cases (such as for pay-per-view movies or cable modem service), communications from subscribers back to the MHE or hub (see following paragraphs) is permitted. The MHE must process these return path signals to accomplish functions such as subscriber Internet access or for fulfilling orders for programming such as pay-per-view movies.

Just like standard TV broadcasting, each channel must be placed onto an individual RF channel before it can be sent out of the MHE. All of the channels are then combined into a broadband RF output, typically

**TABLE 1-3**

Set Top Box (STB) Functions

- Accept commands from a user's remote control to determine which channel the user wants to watch.
- Verify that the user has authorization to watch the selected channel.
- Receive the broadband signal from the coaxial cable network.
- Tune to the correct RF channel.
- If the channel is scrambled or encrypted, process the signal to create an unscrambled output.
- If the channel is digital, demultiplex and decode the digital information into an output suitable for the television display.
- Supply a video signal for display on the customer's television.

covering a range from 50 to 860 MHz. Some systems operate up to 1 GHz in frequency, with the higher frequencies generally reserved for data and voice services. (Note that when an MHE serves multiple areas with different channel configurations [or lineups] that a different output can be created for each individual area.) This broadband signal is then distributed to subscribers using a tree and branch type network that typically employs both fiber optic and coaxial cable, creating a Hybrid Fiber Coax (HFC) network.

From the Master Head End, a Supertrunking system is used to distribute the broadband signal to local hubs. Supertrunking may be either analog or digital, but is almost always fiber optic. Depending on the CATV system, processing may be done at the hubs to add local programming or to handle cable modem data.

From the hubs, the broadband signal is sent out to the distribution network. The distribution network can be fed directly by coaxial cables, or fiber optics can be used to cover part of the distance from the hub to the subscriber's home. Optical nodes receive fiber optic inputs and convert them to coaxial cable outputs for further distribution. Amplifiers are inserted into the coaxial cable path to amplify the signal and split it into multiple branches. Customers receive the broadband signal via coaxial cable either directly at their television sets or via STBs.

In many CATV systems, consumers are able to hook a "cable-ready" television set directly to the incoming coaxial cable. In this case, the tuner in the television set is responsible for selecting the correct channel from the incoming broadband signal. Many consumer video-tape recorders and DVD recorders are also equipped with cable-ready inputs. In many other cases, customers use a set top box (STB) to receive the broadband signal, particularly when digital transmission is being used. Key functions of a typical STB are given in Table 1-3.

## New Technologies

All of the technologies described in the preceding sections currently have hundreds of millions of subscribers around the world. However, some new technologies are gaining popularity. They include Fiber To The Premises (FTTP) and Digital Subscriber Line (DSL). Let's quickly review both of them.

*Fiber To The Premises (FTTP)* technology involves making a direct, fiber optic connection to each customer's home or business for telecommunications services. FTTP has long been a goal of many tele-phone companies and other service providers. These companies want to replace aging, limited-capacity copper wires with new, high-capac-ity optical fibers. This technology also goes by the names Fiber To The Home (FTTH) and Fiber To The Business (FTTB). Recent work on Passive Optical Networks (PONs) has created a new method for delivering video services to the subscriber.

In essence, a PON is an all-optical network with no active compo-nents between the service provider and the customer. The network is Optical because the path from the service provider to the customer is entirely made up of fiber optic and optical components. The network is Passive because there are no active elements (such as electronics, lasers, optical detectors, or optical amplifiers) between the service provider and the customer.

One key feature of a PON network is the use of an optical splitter near the customer premises, which greatly improves the economics of the system. In the case of one popular standard, up to 32 end customers can be served by one fiber from the service provider. A second key feature of a PON network is that the optical fibers and the optical splitter are configured to handle a wide range of laser wavelengths (colors) so that new services can be deployed on the network simply by changing the optics at either end of the fiber to handle new wavelengths of light. This gives a PON a great deal of flexibility for adapting to future customer needs. Let's look at how a PON system is constructed (see Figure 1-4).

The physical structure of a PON is specified in standards (such as G.983 from the International Telecommunications Union, or ITU). At the service provider, a single fiber is used to feed up to 32 homes. The splitter can be a single device, or it can be spread out (such as an 4-way splitter followed by a 8-way splitter on each leg). The maximum distance from the service provider to any of the 32 subscribers is specified to be 20 km, or about 12 miles.

Each customer must have an Optical Network Terminal (ONT; also known as an Optical Network Unit, or ONU) device installed. The ONT is responsible for taking all of the signals from the PON and converting them into electrical signals that can be used by the customers' devices. The ONT also converts data being sent by the customer into optical signals that are sent back over the PON to the service provider. In general, the ONT operates using power supplied by the customer, by connection to normal commercial power. In the event of a power

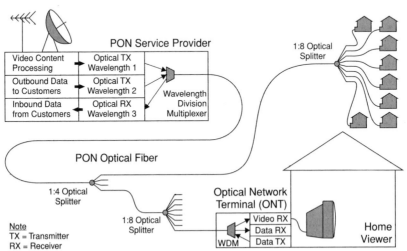

**FIGURE 1-4**   Fiber To The Premises (FTTP) Using 6.983 Passive Optical Network (PON) System Diagram

outage, the ONT must have a method to power itself (i.e., a battery) if it is required to support emergency communication.

The system shown in Figure 1-4 uses three different wavelengths (colors) of light. Two wavelengths go from the service provider to the customers. One wavelength is normally used for a multi-channel video signal. A second wavelength carries data from the service provider to all the customers. A third wavelength carries data from the customers back to the service provider. At both the service provider and the customer ends of the fiber, specialized filters (called Wavelength Division Multiplexers, or WDMs) are used to separate the three colors of light.

Video in a G.983 PON can be as simple as an optical version of a normal CATV signal. At the customer's ONT (Optical Network Terminal), a simple circuit is used to convert the optical signal into an electrical signal. This signal can then be fed into a standard cable-ready television set or a set top box. One big advantage of this system is that customers may not need a set top box if they are not interested in scrambled, encrypted, or digital content.

Data in a G.983 PON system is multiplexed. From the provider, one stream that contains all of the data for all of the customers is created. Each customer's ONT receives and processes the entire incoming bit stream and selects the data for that customer. In the reverse direction, only one customer ONT can transmit at a time. So, each ONT must synchronize to the incoming bit stream and send data back only when given permission by the service provider. For data-intensive customers such as businesses, other wavelengths of light can be used to provide dedicated, high-speed links over PON optical paths.

A major advantage of PON technology is that it can supply very high bit rate data connections to each customer. Normal G.983 service supports aggregate bit rates from the service provider to customers of 622 Megabits per second (Mbps, or millions of bits per second) and 155 Mbps from the customers back. If all 32 users are running simultaneously at maximum speed, this works out to 19 Mbps that can be transmitted to each subscriber.

A major drawback of PON technology is that it requires the service provider to install a fiber optic connection to each PON customer.

This is not a big obstacle in new construction since the service provider would normally have to install copper cable to each new dwelling unit. Also, because the splitters can be installed close to customers, only one fiber needs to leave the service provider for each group of 32 customers. Still, the expense of replacing a large installed base of copper cabling with optical fiber and supplying each user with an ONT can be a very large investment for existing customers.

*Digital Subscriber Line (DSL)* technology has become popular with service providers and many customers because it offers a way to use existing copper, twisted pair telephone lines for carrying high-speed data. Many consumers are aware that they can purchase DSL service for Internet access. Some service providers also offer video content that is delivered using DSL service. Let's look at how a DSL system can be constructed (see Figure 1-5).

All DSL systems have to make a trade-off between speed and distance. That is, longer distances must operate at lower bit rates, because losses in the cable increase as the frequency of the signal (bit rate) increases. (As technology improves, these limits change, but designers still need to make compromises.) To help keep distances down, a service provider will typically install DSL equipment in Remote Terminals (RTs), which are located between the provider's main offices and customers.

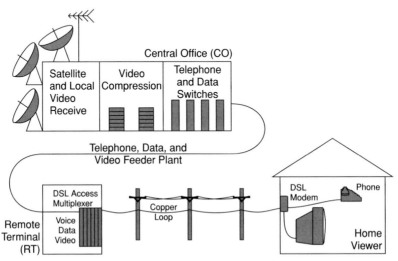

**FIGURE 1-5**   Digital Subscriber Line (DSL) System Diagram

The Central Office (CO) is the main hub for services. This is the place where the telephone switch is located, which handles normal telephone traffic. (A commonly used acronym is POTS, which stands for Plain Old Telephone Service.) The CO is also normally the place where connections are made to the Internet and where video services are processed prior to distribution.

Customers who are located close to the CO can be fed directly from copper pairs that terminate in the CO. More distant customers are typically served by an RT. Fiber optics are commonly used to send the signals from the CO to the RT; this is called the Feeder Plant. In the Feeder Plant, voice, video, and data signals often travel over different transmission equipment. This is mostly due to the fact that the Feeder Plant for voice signals was installed well before the video and data feeders, and has limited capacity. Feeders for video and data services are generally installed alongside existing voice feeders, and typically carry much higher rate data signals.

Each RT provides direct copper connections to each customer in the RT serving area. In general, an RT is installed to supply voice services using digital copper or fiber optic feeder connections, and standard copper telephone cables are used to connect to the customer. When DSL service is installed, a Digital Subscriber Line Access Multiplexer (DSLAM) is also placed into the RT (or in a CO for directly fed customers). The DSLAM takes the video and data signals from the feeder and selects the correct ones for each customer. Then, the DSLAM generates the DSL signals and places them onto the pair of copper wires (or local loop) leading to each home.

Every DSL customer must install a DSL modem. The modem receives the DSL signals from the DSLAM and converts them into the proper form for the customer's other devices, such as a PC, a data router, or a television set. The modem also takes data signals from the customer and transmits them back to the service provider. Table 1-4 lists some of the more common types of DSL services that are available.

One big advantage of a DSL system is that it uses the existing wires that already run to homes and businesses for telephone service. Another advantage is that the DSL circuits are normally designed to

**TABLE 1-4**
Common Types of Digital Subscriber Line (DSL) Services

- Asymmetric DSL (ADSL) operates at speeds up to 8 Megabits per second (Mbps, or millions of bits per second) from the CO to the customer (downstream), and up to 800 kilobits per second (kbps, or thousands of bits per second) from the customer to the CO (upstream).
- G.Lite DSL (also known as Universal DSL) operates at speeds up to 1.5 Mbps downstream and up to 512 kbps upstream. One advantage of G.Lite is that the splitter required on ADSL circuits to separate voice and data signals is not required for G.Lite.
- High-speed DSL (HDSL) operates symmetrically (same speed upstream and downstream) at a rate of 1.544 or 2.048 Mbps, and is mostly used to provide services to businesses.
- Very high-speed DSL (VDSL) operates at bit rates from 4 to 50 Mbps downstream and 1.5 to 2.3 Mbps upstream.
- xDSL collectively refers to the above standards as a generic term.

To put this all into perspective, dial-up modems normally operate at a maximum speed of 56 kbps today. Note that the actual bit rates that can be achieved on a DSL circuit are highly variable and depend on many factors including the length of the subscriber's loop and the amount of noise or interference present on the line.

fail gracefully, so that if a customer loses power or the DSL equipment fails, then normal telephone calls can still be made.

A disadvantage of DSL services for video is that very few video signals can be sent down a DSL line. Typically, these technologies are restricted to one video content stream per television set or other video device. This also requires every consumer television set or other video-receiving device (VCR, digital recorder, etc.) to be equipped with a set top box (STB). Each time a customer wishes to switch the program that is being viewed, the DSLAM must switch to send out a different video stream. The STB is responsible for accepting channel change commands from the viewer and sending them to the DSLAM. The STB is also responsible for receiving the digital video signal from the DSLAM and converting it into the correct output for the user's video display.

## Dedicated Networks

In the world of television, movie, and video production, special-purpose links are used to transport video. Table 1-5 lists several advantages of dedicated networks for corporate users.

**TABLE 1-5**

Advantages of Dedicated Video Networks

- Extremely large bandwidths as needed for uncompressed video signals (such as those described in Chapter 3).
- High-quality transport with extremely low error rates, allowing original content to be transported with essentially no degradation.
- Compatibility with video formats that are used in video production, including feeds from studio-quality cameras and professional editing systems, making it easy for video producers to use these services.
- Privacy, since many of these links operate over dedicated facilities that are extremely difficult for malicious users to access.
- Reliability, because these networks are normally isolated from traffic created by other users.

Of course, all these advantages come at a price—monthly rental fees that frequently run over $1,000 per month per dedicated video link for local service in major US cities. Plus, these networks are not very flexible—installation fees normally apply, and installation lead times can sometimes exceed a month or more (although they are often more rapidly deployed than comparable-speed data circuits). However, for high-end users (television stations and broadcast networks), these links are extremely valuable and widely used.

Coaxial cable was used for the first dedicated networks. An amplifier was needed every few thousand feet to make up for losses and distortions that occurred in the cable. Each circuit was installed by the service provider and then adjusted to achieve the required end-to-end performance. Periodically, the adjustment process needed to be repeated, as the amplifier components aged and as the coaxial cable degraded over time. A few coaxial circuits are still in use today, but they continue to be replaced with optical fiber.

Microwave radio technology was a big step forward for dedicated video networking. With this technology, a service provider could install a circuit simply by placing equipment at each end of the link, provided there was a clear line of sight from one end to the other. Point-to-point links can extend for tens of miles (or dozens of kilometers). A repeater can be used to receive and re-transmit the signal for longer distances or to skirt obstacles. Most of these links supported analog video signals, and many have been retired recently to free up radio spectrum or because they have been replaced by fiber optics.

Satellite networks are used heavily by television broadcasters, both for gathering content and for distributing it to local broadcasters. When content is being gathered, remote locations take turns in transmitting their content to a satellite, which retransmits the signal to the main studio. (By using only a single transponder, the broadcaster's rental costs for the satellite are minimized). This method is commonly used for live events in remote locations, such as sports arenas. In many cases this content is scrambled to prevent unauthorized viewing of the unedited video feeds. For distribution, the main studio transmits a signal to a satellite that rebroadcasts the signal to multiple local television stations. Much of this content is also scrambled. In many cases, content is sent to the local stations in advance of when it is needed for broadcast and then simply stored locally and "played out" at the appropriate time.

Fiber optic links for video services first gained widespread acceptance in the 1980s and today form the majority of dedicated video networks. Originally, only analog video network interfaces were offered. Today, many service providers have moved to support digital video interfaces as well. Fiber optic links can run over long distances (over 100 km between signal regenerators) and provide many services (including non-video services) on a single fiber. Fiber optic links also offer much lower error rates than other technologies. Terminal devices have become very inexpensive over the past decade, which helps keep service provider costs down. Drawbacks include the need to connect fibers to both signal source and destination, and the inability of some end devices to share fibers with other types of equipment. Also, many service providers offer these services only on a local basis; long-distance video transport is generally done over telecom networks.

## TELECOM NETWORKS

Many different types of telecom networks are in use around the world today, and most of them can be used for transporting video signals. In fact, it's not at all unusual for one type of network traffic (e.g., IP) to be transported over another type of network (e.g., SONET) at some point in a long-distance circuit. So, it's important to have some understanding about each of the network types and how they can affect video traffic. Let's look at some of the most commonly used networks.

Table 1-6 summarizes much of the data in the following four sections.

## PDH

For a challenge, try pronouncing the first word of "Plesiochronous Digital Hierarchy," which is abbreviated PDH. This very nasty looking word has a fairly simple meaning—it means "nearly synchronized."

**TABLE 1-6**

Telecom Standards Comparison

| | PDH | | ISDN | | | | |
|---|---|---|---|---|---|---|---|
| Bit Rate | USA | Europe | USA | Europe | SDH | SONET | Voice Channels |
| 64 kbps | DS0 | E0 | | | | | 1 |
| 144 kbps | | | BRI | BRI | | | 2 |
| 1.544 Mbps | | | PRI | | | | 23 |
| 1.544 Mbps | T1/DS1 | | | | | | 24 |
| 2.048 Mbps | | E1 | | PRI | | | 30 |
| 34.368 Mbps | | E3 | | | | | 480 |
| 44.736 Mbps | DS3/T3 | | | | | | 672 |
| | | | | | | | Payload Rate |
| 51.840 Mbps | | | | | | STS-1 | 50.112 Mbps |
| 155.520 Mbps | | | | | STM-1 | OC-3/STS-3 | 150.336 Mbps |
| 622.080 Mbps | | | | | STM-4 | OC-12/STS-12 | 601.344 Mbps |
| 2.48832 Gbps | | | | | STM-16 | OC-48/STS-48 | 2405.376 Mbps |
| 9.95328 Gbps | | | | | STM-64 | OC-192/STS-192 | 9621.504 Mbps |

Commonly Used Video Rates
Videoconferencing: 128 kbps to 768 kbps
Compressed Video: 2.5 Mbps to 15 Mbps
Uncompressed Video: 270 Mbps, 1.485 Gbps

kbps – kilobits (1,000 bits) per second
Mbps – Megabits (1,000,000 bits) per second
Gbps – Gigabits (1,000,000,000 bits) per second

More technically, two circuits are considered Plesiochronous if their bit rates fall within a strictly limited tolerance range. By far, the most common PDH signal in North America is a T1 (also known as a DS1), which operates at a bit rate of 1.544 Mbps (+/− 50 parts per million [ppm], or roughly 77 bits per second). This is enough capacity to carry 24 voice channels each operating at 64 kbps, plus overhead. In Europe, the corresponding signal is commonly called an E1, which operates at 2.048 Mbps (+/− 50 ppm) and has the capacity to carry 30 voice channels (also at 64 kbps each) plus overhead. Moving up in speed, the next most popular speed in North America is a DS3 (or T3), which operates at 44.736 Mbps and carries 28 DS1's, equivalent to 672 voice channels. In Europe, the E3 rate is used, which operates at a speed of 34.368 Mbps and carries 16 E1s, equivalent to 480 voice channels. Higher speed PDH interfaces have been defined, but they are not commonly used today because they have been replaced by SONET/SDH standards (see the following section describing SONET/SDH).

Occasionally, you might see a reference to a circuit called a DS0 in the USA or E0 in Europe. This is simply a single voice channel, which operates at 64 kbps.

PDH standards are still very important today, even though a lot of new technology has been developed. T1, E1, DS3, and E3 rates are still with us because of the huge installed base of networking equipment with these interfaces, and because SONET and SDH networks operate at higher rates (see the following section). Most service providers offer circuits at these bit rates to customers anywhere in their service areas. Also, these bit rates make sense for a lot of voice and data applications (and even for a few video ones) because they are relatively inexpensive. So, it is likely that PDH circuits will be with us for quite some time to come.

## ISDN

The Integrated Services Digital Network (ISDN) was developed in the early 1980s as a replacement for analog telephone service. Two subscriber interfaces were defined—the Basic Rate Interface (BRI) and the Primary Rate Interface (PRI). An ISDN link is made up of Bearer

(B) channels and Delta (D) channels. B-channels are each 64 kbps and are used to carry user data. D-channels come in different speeds and are used to carry the control and signaling information that is necessary to set up and maintain a connection. A BRI has two B-channels and one D-channel that operates at 16 kbps for a total of 144 kbps. The PRI speed depends on its location. In North America, a PRI has 23 B-channels and one D-channel that operates at 64 kbps, for a total of 1.544 Mbps, including overhead. In Europe, a PRI has 30 B-channels and one D-channel that operates at 64 kbps, for a total of 2.048 Mbps, including overhead.

ISDN circuits can be dedicated or dial-up circuits. Dedicated circuits are similar to most other network connections—an always-on, fixed-bandwidth network link. Dial-up circuits allow temporary connections to be made from one ISDN device to another by use of special network connection procedures, which are similar to those used in placing a normal voice telephone call.

ISDN lines have some video transport applications. The H.320 video-conferencing standard (see Chapter 10) uses ISDN lines for call setup and video transport. Also, some businesses use PRI lines for data traffic and Internet access, and low bit rate IP video signals can flow over these links.

## SONET/SDH

The Synchronous Optical NETwork (SONET) standard in North America and the Synchronous Digital Hierarchy (SDH) standard in Europe ushered in a new era in network speed and flexibility. Based on fiber optic technology, these networks can operate at speeds ranging up to (and beyond) 10 Gbps. What's more, SONET and SDH networks have a common set of bit rates that allow many pieces of equipment to change from one standard to the other.

Because it is easier to understand, let's look at the SDH standard first. The basic SDH building block is an STM-1, which stands for Synchronous Transport Module-1. An STM-1 operates at 155.52 Mbps and can contain a huge variety of different payloads. Mappings, or schemes for constructing payloads, are available for voice signals, data signals (including ATM and IP, see the following section), video signals, etc. STM-1 signals can be combined to form higher speed interfaces, including STM-4 (622.08 Mbps), STM-16 (2.48832 Gbps), and STM-64 (9.95328 Gbps). Even higher speeds are possible in the future.

Now let's look at the more confusing world of SONET. The basic building block is the STS-1 (Synchronous Transport Signal), which operates at 51.84 Mbps. Please don't rush out and try to order a circuit or buy a piece of equipment with this kind of interface because they basically don't exist. The reason is that carriers recognized that the STS-1 rate is very close to the DS3 rate, and there wasn't much incentive to introduce new technology with so small an increase in bit rate. So, instead, basically everyone agreed to use the STS-3 rate of 155.52 Mbps. (Note that this is exactly the same bit rate as an STM-1 in the SDH.)

Again, please don't rush out and try to buy an STS-3 because these circuits have a much more popular name—OC-3 (for Optical Carrier 3). You see, the folks who designed SONET (Bellcore) decided that there should be a different name for the optical interface (OC) and the electrical signal format (STS). So, if you order an OC-3 from your local carrier, you should, in a few weeks time, get a pair of fibers, one to transmit and one to receive data at 155.52 Mbps.

Higher speed links are also available. OC-12 operates at 622.08 Mbps, OC-48 at 2.48832 Gbps, and OC-192 9.95328 Gbps. Even higher speeds, such as OC-768, will become common in the future. Again, notice that there is a match between some OC signal rates and STM rates. The concept of the STS is important for only one reason—data inside an OC-x is organized into frames based on the STS-1. So, an OC-12 is basically made up of 12 independent STS-1 signals, each operating at 51.84 Mbps. For higher speed data, such as uncompressed digital video operating at 270 Mbps (see Chapter 3), you need to use the concatenated form of the signal, denoted by adding a lowercase "c" to the signal name. A "concatenated" signal combines the STS-1 signals into a single, high-speed payload envelope. So, to move a 270 Mbps signal, you would need to use an OC-12c signal.

Virtually all long-distance telecommunication networks operate on SONET/SDH backbones today. This has been caused by the growth of fiber optic technology and by service providers who require their vendors to adopt these standards for what is, essentially, new construction. So, chances are pretty high that, if you are running a signal over a large geographic area or connecting to the Internet, your data will flow over a SONET/SDH network. This is true even if you are using other signal types, such as PDH, ISDN, ATM, or even IP, because there are widely used standards for inserting all of these types of signals into SONET/SDH networks.

## ATM

Asynchronous Transfer Mode (ATM) was developed to provide a high-speed digital telecommunications network. Originally created to be a broadband form of ISDN, ATM has become quite popular with carriers for a wide variety of services. ATM is particularly well suited for video transport because it allows carriers to set up and manage very high performance connections for users.

The core concept of ATM is a "cell," which contains 48 bytes of data and 5 bytes of control and routing information, for a total of 53 bytes in a cell. Terminal devices accept user data, break it up into 48-byte chunks, and then add the 5 bytes of header information. The way that the data is broken up depends on the application, so, in ATM, we have a number of different ATM Application Layers (AALs) that are defined for different uses. They differ in the amount of error handling performed by the network, the amount of bit rate variation that is present in the network, the price of the network services, and in other ways that are beyond the scope of this book. Suffice it to say that both ends of a network must be configured to use the same AAL for each signal. Also note that there are several choices of AAL that can be used for signals such as video, with AAL-1 and AAL-5 being the most popular.

Because ATM is a connection-oriented system, before any data can flow across the network, a connection must be established between the source and the destination for the data. This connection establishes a specific route for the data called a Virtual Circuit (VC). Note that the process of establishing a VC requires stacks of software in the terminal devices and in each piece of network equipment along the route of the signal. Once the VC is fully established, data can flow. Software is also required to handle cell errors and to re-establish connections when failures occur, or when a new VC needs to be set up. The ATM network adapters also need to remove any timing changes that are made to the video signals caused by the ATM network.

Data goes through a process called Segmentation to break it up into ATM cells. This process also adds the header information that is required to route the cells to their destinations. The resulting cells are combined with cells from other data sources to form an outgoing signal, and passed into the ATM network. At each stop along the network, the header of each cell must be examined to determine to which VC the cell belongs, and the contents of the header must be processed to make it ready for the next hop along the route for the data. At the far end of the network, cell headers are removed, cell data is extracted, and the data reassembled into the original format.

The real beauty of ATM for video traffic is the ability to reserve bandwidth from one end of the network to another and the ability to make sure that certain types of time-sensitive traffic (such as video) have a higher priority over other types of traffic. This helps ensure that each of the cells makes it through the network intact and (usually) in the same order in which they were sent. These properties make it very easy for end devices to smoothly and reliably send and receive video.

Service providers are heavy users of ATM within their own networks, even for non-ATM data (lots of IP traffic is carried over ATM facilities within carriers). The biggest benefits of ATM for a carrier are the abilities to control the amount of bandwidth used by each customer, to ensure that data from different customers are kept separate, and to ensure that adequate bandwidth exists across the entire data path from source to destination.

The biggest drawback of ATM for most users is cost. First, the user must purchase an ATM multiplexer to format the data into cells. ATM devices can be quite expensive in comparison to IP devices, due, in part, to the large amounts of software required to set up and manage connections. Each user must lease an ATM access link from a carrier at each end of the data circuit. Furthermore, many carriers charge for actual network usage on the ATM links, rather than the flat-rate services that are common on IP links. All these factors combine to make ATM transport typically more expensive than other services, such as IP.

## IP

Internet Protocol (IP) is a standard method for formatting and addressing data packets in a large, multi-function network, such as the Internet. A packet is a variable length unit of information (a collection of bytes) in a well-defined format that can be sent across an IP network. Typically, a message such as e-mail or a video signal will be broken up into several IP packets. IP can be used on many different network technologies, such as Ethernet LANs and wireless Wi-Fi links.

- To help illustrate the functions of IP, an analogy might be useful. For folks who live in the USA, use of the US Postal Service requires the sender to put a destination Zip Code on each piece of mail that is sent out. (If you leave the Zip Code off, the Postal Service staff might be nice enough to put one on for you, but generally, they just send your letter back to you.)

There are rules for assigning IP addresses, and their format is precisely defined. There are many excellent references on this, so we won't go into detail here. Certain IP addresses are reserved for special purposes such as multicasting (see Chapter 9).

- It is the same with Zip Codes—the first two digits indicate the state (or part of a big state), the third is the region within the state, and the last two indicate the local post office.

IP is connectionless, which means that each packet can be sent from source to destination along any path that happens to be available. Each packet is handled individually; that is, the network is not required to always select the same path to send packets to the same destination. This can easily result with the packets being received in a different order than they were sent.

- In the US mail, each letter is handled individually. At each sorting location, the Zip Code of the destination address is examined on each letter. The sorter's function is to choose any available method (airplane, truck, etc.) to move the letter along toward its destination. If a particular method is full to capacity, another method will be chosen. This is why two letters mailed on the same day from the same location to the same recipient may not arrive on the same day.

IP packets are variable in size. The length of each packet is included in the header information. Contrast this with ATM, where each cell is fixed in length.

- Of course, mail messages can be of different sizes as well.

IP has some functionality for controlling which packets get priority when congestion occurs, called Differentiated Services (DiffServ). This allows certain packets to be flagged as having high priority and others as low priority.

- In the US mail, letters and parcels can also be assigned a priority, as in First Class, Bulk Rate, Express Mail, etc.

A number of different video transport standards operate on IP networks, as we shall see in this book. Applications range all the way from low resolution, low frame rate applications like webcams to high definition television and medical images. IP technology is incredibly widespread, and a huge variety of video technologies use IP. So, it is paramount that users, technologists, and service providers understand how video works on an IP network. That is a topic that we will explore in great depth in the rest of this book.


## THE INTERNET

The Internet is a worldwide network that provides IP-based communication services for a wide range of users and applications. One of the most familiar uses of the Internet is the World Wide Web, which can be accessed through web browsers essentially everywhere on the planet. The Internet also supports e-mail, file transfer, and many other applications. In this book, we will use "Internet" with a capital "I" when we are referring to this enormous, public network.

Many users would like to be able to transport high-quality video signals over the Internet. However, due to some serious limitations, the Internet may not be suitable for most users most of the time. Let's take a look at both the advantages and the disadvantages of the Internet for video.

## Advantages

Two big advantages top the list of reasons why so many users would like to be able to send video over the Internet—ubiquitous availability and low cost.

Connections to the Internet are available throughout the world, and today there are hundreds of millions of regular Internet users. The Internet even reaches to Antarctica but not yet to the South Pole (at least not on a round-the-clock basis). Of course, the quality and speed of the connections vary greatly by location. Overall, the Internet has many more connections than even the largest private or government network in existence.

The cost of sending data over the Internet is transparent to most users. A monthly fee for access through their Internet Service Provider (ISP) is all that most users pay. Of course, website hosting is more expensive but still a relative bargain. Both of these costs are but a fraction of the cost that would be incurred to construct a private network with dedicated facilities to each customer in a worldwide video IP network.

## Disadvantages

Unfortunately, the Internet is not an ideal place for video traffic. There are no foolproof methods for making sure that video streams flow smoothly and reliably.

High-performance video generates a large number of packets that must arrive properly at the destination to accurately re-create the original signal. Impairments can occur when packets are missing, arrive out of order, or simply get bunched up or separated along the transmission path. (Methods to reduce the impact of these impairments are available, but they can be costly.) Because the Internet is shared among so many users and because its function is dependent on the interaction between so many different networks, congestion or delay can occur in many places. The total effect of all these impairments makes high-performance video transport very difficult on the Internet.

Overall, it is possible to transport video content over the Internet, and we will discuss several examples in this book. However, users must be prepared to deal with the shortcomings of the Internet, and understand that many video applications will work best on specialized or private IP networks.

## REVIEW AND VIDEO USER CHECKLIST

In this chapter, we looked at many different ways to transport video. We discussed the three most popular methods for delivering programming to consumers: terrestrial broadcasting, direct-to-home (DTH) satellite broadcasting, and cable television (CATV). We examined a couple of new technologies that can also be used for consumer delivery: Passive Optical Networks (PONs) and Digital Subscriber Line (DSL). We also glanced at dedicated video networks that are commonly used in the video production/content creation market, as well as for delivering video to broadcasters. Next, we looked at some popular telecommunication networks, including PDH, SONET/SDH, and ATM. We concluded with a brief look at the basics of IP networks, and discussed some of the advantages and disadvantages of using the Internet for video transport.

Throughout this book, we will be discussing many of the different aspects of video transport over networks. Most of these issues affect the choices that users need to make in order to achieve success with video networking. To help guide the discussion, we will be creating a checklist of information that users should gather before beginning a video transport project. Following are some of the topics that will make up our checklist.

## Chapter 1 Checklist Update

❏ *Source of Content:* Who will be supplying the content? Who owns the content? Are there any restrictions on use of the content? Can only certain users view the content? Will the content need to be protected against copying?

❏ *Type of Content:* What types of scenes are included in the content? How much detail is there? How much motion is present? Does the detail level of the content need to be preserved for the viewer?

❏ *Content Technical Requirements:* Does the content come from film, videotape, or a live camera? Is there a synchronized audio track? Is there more than one audio track (second language, commentary)? Is there any data that is included with the content, such as closed captioning, V-chip data, or program descriptions? Are there any limits mandated by the content owner on the amount or type of compression that can be used?

❏ *System Funding:* How will the content be paid for? How will the network usage be paid for? Will payments be required from each viewer? Will advertising be used?

❏ *Viewer Profile:* How many users will be viewing the content? Where will they be located? What equipment will they use to view the content?

❏ *Network Capabilities:* What bit rates will the network support? Will the network support multicasting? What security features does the network offer? Who owns the network?

❏ *Performance Requirements:* How much delay will be acceptable in this application? What video and audio quality levels will users accept? Will all users get the content at the same time? Will users be allowed to pause, rewind, and fast-forward the content? What is the financial impact of a service interruption?

A more detailed list appears at the back of this book in Appendix C. In each chapter, we will be adding to this checklist as our discussion covers more topics.

# 2

# VIDEO TRANSPORT APPLICATIONS

Many different types of users have benefited from video transport technology. Let's look at some familiar and some not-so-familiar applications. In this chapter, we will discuss some interesting ways in which people have had success with video transport.

## ENTERTAINMENT

Lots of people use television solely as a means of entertainment. This multi-billion dollar industry depends on efficient, reliable video transport for many functions. First, let's look at the important distinction between contribution, distribution, and delivery networks in broadcast television networks (see Figure 2-1).

*Contribution networks* are used to gather content that will be used in a television program. These networks are configured as many-to-one, funneling content from a variety of sources into a central location for producing a program.

*Distribution networks* are used to transmit finished content to various program delivery providers including over-the-air broadcasters, cable television (CATV) providers, and direct-to-home (DTH) satellite companies. These networks are usually configured as one-to-many, spreading content from a master source to tens or hundreds of delivery service providers.

*Delivery networks* are used to transmit content to the final viewers by many different means, including broadcast, satellite, CATV, DSL, IP, and other types of networks.[1] This transport takes place in real time, that is, delivering the same content at the same time to all viewers in a service area for immediate viewing. Delivery networks are configured as one-to-many, and the number of viewers can range from a few hundred to many millions.

Contribution, distribution, and delivery networks have all been successfully implemented over IP networks. As we shall see in the following sections, each type of network has unique performance requirements.

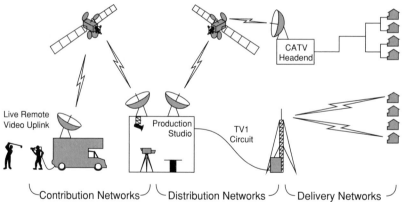

**FIGURE 2-1** Broadcast Television Contribution, Distribution, and Delivery Networks

---

1. Several standards organizations have chosen to call this portion of the signal delivery chain "emission." We will use the term "delivery" in this book, because when IP networks are employed for this function, the signal is never truly "emitted" from the network.

## Contribution

In the mind of a television producer, the mission of a contribution network is clear. The mission is to deliver the highest possible quality video to the production studio, while staying within budget. Quality is important because video content can go through many different processing steps before it is ready for broadcast. These steps can include editing, color-correction, special effects, voice-overs, audio enhancement, logo insertion, digital compression, and others. All of this processing may be done at a single location, or the video content may need to be moved among several locations. It is not uncommon for a piece of content to undergo 100 processing steps before it is ready for broadcast. Each processing step can affect the quality of the finished video, and defects in the source material can become magnified in each successive step.

Various types of programming can emphasize different aspects of quality. News programs, for example, emphasize timeliness—the only thing worse than low-quality news video is late or missing news video. In contrast, scheduled live events such as awards shows or public celebrations can be planned in advance, so quality expectations are higher. Essentially perfect video is demanded for any content that will become part of a program that is being produced for broadcast at a later date. If errors occur in content being recorded for future use, that content can usually be retransmitted if necessary.

Different techniques can be used to increase the quality of a contribution network. Whenever feasible for live broadcasts, producers like to deploy a redundant network, with both a main and a backup circuit. In many cases, one service provider carries the main circuit and another provider carries the backup. Producers also like to use dedicated networks that have been specially constructed just for video transport. In the USA, dedicated video circuits are available from a large number of local service providers. They are commonly called "TV1" circuits by the carriers. TV1 circuits operate in one direction, and are specifically designed to transport analog video and audio signals. More carriers are also starting to offer TV1-like circuits for transporting digital signals (such as the uncompressed 270 Mbps digital video signal that we will discuss in Chapter 3).

Long-distance transport is frequently handled with compressed video that is transported over telecom networks.

One particular challenge for a contribution network occurs when a live interview is to take place. A typical setup involves a live announcer located in a broadcast studio and an interviewee in a remote location, possibly in another country. For the interview to work well, the time delay must be strictly controlled. If the delay becomes too long, both people will have difficulty since there will be an uncomfortable pause from the time when one person ends speaking until the other person begins. To keep the delays reasonable, producers can choose to avoid satellite links, if possible, and to avoid using video processing equipment that produces long delays.

Another concern for contribution networks is security, particularly for high-value content such as sporting events. Broadcasters (and certainly movie studios) don't want their raw, unedited content made available to unauthorized parties. (Note that news organizations place less of a premium on security, and will sometimes share live feeds between different broadcasters.) Raw content can contain material that is unacceptable for broadcast and may also contain proprietary subject matter. Most producers want some assurance that their unedited content will not fall into the wrong hands or be viewed by the public before a finished product is produced.

## Distribution

The mission of a distribution network is to send high-quality content to every contracted delivery provider for the lowest cost possible. Quality is a significant concern, because the video content may need to be processed prior to the final content delivery, even if the processing is simply temporary storage of the content and insertion of local advertisements. Cost is also a significant concern, because even a small recurring cost per station can mount up quickly if the signal needs to be delivered to hundreds of stations. Reliability also plays a role, since a service interruption can cause many viewers to change channels during a live program, or require resending programs that are to be aired in the future.

Satellite technology is very often used for distribution. By sending its main signal (known as a "feed") by way of a satellite, a broadcast network can distribute video to many stations simultaneously. This same feed can also be received by other signal distributors, including CATV operators, direct-to-home satellite services and providers offering other forms of video distribution to homes, businesses, hotel rooms, college dormitories, etc. A big advantage of satellite technology is that the cost to the broadcast network for an additional receiver is zero. Any antenna that is within the satellite's coverage area can receive its signal.

Reliability is also a concern for a broadcaster. The loss of one frame of video (which lasts a fraction of a second) during a 30-second advertisement can mean that the broadcaster will not get paid for that advertisement. To ensure reliability, many broadcasters employ redundant networks. One way to achieve this is to use two or more satellites that have overlapping coverage areas. Another way is to use two different distribution technologies, such as satellite and terrestrial fiber optic networks.

## Delivery

The delivery network is that last step in the content distribution chain, where content is delivered to viewers. As we discussed in Chapter 1, several different technologies can be used to accomplish this task. Cost of the delivery network is the main concern; even a tiny cost per viewer can add up quickly for millions of viewers. Reliability is also important, although the amount of work that can be done in this area is tightly constrained by cost. Video quality needs only to be high enough to prevent viewers from switching to another program.

Cost concerns have a heavy impact on the decision about delivery methods. For an average prime time program (generally between 7 p.m. and 11 p.m. each night) in the USA, a television advertiser will have to pay less than one cent per viewer for a 30-second advertisement. Other times of day, the rates are even lower. This money needs to pay for the programming, the costs of the provider's operation, and the costs of distribution. Clearly, these costs leave a very small amount of money to pay for a delivery network.

## Sports and Gambling

A very popular form of video entertainment is a live sporting event such as football (two different sports in Europe and the USA, but both big businesses). Some of these events are broadcast free over the air. Others are on pay television channels, which receive a monthly fee from subscribers. Still others are available only to viewers who have paid a fee to view a single game or event (pay-per-view). Also, don't ignore video used for gaming (also known as wagering, betting, gambling, or punting) purposes. Live sports and gaming events place a unique set of burdens on a video network.

One of the key differences between sports and regular entertainment television is the need for timeliness. Long delays from the field of play to reception of a signal by a home viewer can cause viewer dissatisfaction. If the signal is used for wagering, long delays can be a financial nightmare for a gaming establishment.

Another key difference between sports and most other types of programming is the need for a very flexible contribution network. Since sporting venues are typically used only a few hours per week and the location of key events changes from town to town, flexibility is key. The good news is that sporting events can be planned well in advance, so that for major events specialized production vehicles can be set up on site a few days ahead of time.

Sports fans also demand a high level of reliability, particularly for events where they have paid for viewing rights. Viewers may demand refunds of their viewing fees if the broadcast is interrupted, even for a short time. This need for reliability extends from the delivery to the contribution networks. Since the number of professional sports venues is fixed, some fiber optic network service providers have installed direct links to many of these locations. This allows broadcasters to use fiber optic lines for their main contribution video feeds. Many broadcasters will still use satellite circuits as a backup contribution network.

Distribution and delivery costs are as important for sports broadcasts as they are for pre-recorded entertainment programs. Even the most-watched sports broadcast in the USA, the Super Bowl, generates only a few dollars of advertising revenue per viewer during a four-hour broadcast. Out of this revenue, the network must pay hundreds of millions of dollars to the football league to get permission to carry the broadcast and then pay millions more for producing the program. In addition, the contribution network from the venue to the broadcaster's production facility can also cost tens of thousands of dollars to set up and operate. When all is said and done, the costs of distribution and delivery must be on the order of a few cents per subscriber.

Content security may also be required in a distribution network for sports events. Content security is usually provided by some kind of scrambling and encryption that is inserted by the broadcaster. For instance, in pay television systems, only authorized viewers who have paid their monthly fees or pay-per-view fees will be given access to the broadcast. Each viewer will typically have a device (such as a set top box or a satellite receiver) that will receive authorization codes from the broadcaster. These codes can then be used to decode the signal. Contrast this with conventional entertainment that will end up as a free broadcast. In this case, broadcasters do worry about security on the contribution side and may also have protection on the distribution side, but not in the delivery network.

## Advertising

Although advertising may or may not be considered entertainment by viewers, it is a big part of the equation for entertainment television. Special networking challenges abound in the creation and playback of advertising content.

First, it is important to understand that advertising video is much more heavily processed than normal content. Since advertisers typically pay huge sums of money to broadcast each 30-second commercial, they want to make sure that every second counts. The amount of editing time and production cost for a 30-second spot can exceed that of some 30-minute programs.

Virtually all advertising is pre-recorded. This basically removes the need for live video transport during the production process. However, video transport can be involved in many other aspects of advertising.

One very important aspect of advertising production is client review and approval. Clients may wish to review the ad creation process at each step along the way. These steps can include concept review, raw film/video review, rough edit review, special effects or animation review, audio review, and final review. Some brave clients may wish to review only the finished ad. Either way, video transport links can be used to deliver content to the client, thereby eliminating the need to travel to the ad agency. Ad agencies and clients can save time and get same-day decisions by using video transport instead of express shipping videotapes. A network for delivering advertisements to clients for review may be expensive to set up and operate, but the resulting productivity gains from closer collaboration may help to offset these expenses.

Video transport also plays a role in delivering advertisements for broadcast. Advertisers use many different strategies for planning their ad campaigns. Some ads may need to be delivered nationally, others to a particular region, and yet others to a very limited local audience. To implement their marketing strategies, advertisers select specific delivery providers that will broadcast each ad. National networks, local broadcast stations, national cable or DTH networks, and local cable television operators all can feed ads to different size audiences. Video networks can play a role in delivering advertisements to all of these different providers. Special-purpose video servers are generally located at each facility; they can be preloaded with ads and then triggered to play back each ad at the appropriate time in an outgoing video stream.

Since most ad content is pre-recorded and because quality requirements are very high, file transfer is the preferred method for transport of advertising video. A simple definition of a file transfer is the use of a protocol that ensures the correct delivery of every bit of a media file. Errors detected by the receiver are either corrected or a fresh copy of the corrupted data is requested from the sender. This is explained in more detail in Chapter 14.

## INTERACTIVE VIDEO

Video content is considered interactive when the viewer can affect the content while it is being displayed. The form of the interaction can vary. Videoconferencing, whereby two or more people can view each other live on a video connection, is one of the most familiar applications of interactive video. Several others will be discussed in the following sections. We'll go into much greater detail on videoconferencing in Chapter 10.

An important distinction: In the following sections, we will not discuss interactivity where it applies strictly to controlling the playback of pre-recorded content. This includes functions like pausing, rewinding, or fast-forwarding through video content that is being delivered over a network from a central server. While this is a form of interactivity, the viewer cannot truly interact with the content, but only control when it is played back. Instead, in the following sections, we will discuss applications in which the viewer actually can affect the content of the video that is displayed.

### Videoconferencing

Although it is loved by some and hated by many, videoconferencing is a powerful tool for business. A videoconference is simply a telephone call with video added on, so that participants can see each other as well as hear each other. In its most basic form, a videoconference room can be built with a camera, a microphone, and a video display for each participant. A network connects the participants and allows each participant to view and hear the others, although not necessarily all the others at the same time. In a well-designed system, participants can carry on a meeting as if they were sitting around a conference table.

Limiting end-to-end time delay is very important in a videoconference. This delay is measured from the time when a signal is captured by the camera at one end of the link until it is displayed at the other end of the link. Long delays make it difficult to carry on a natural conversation. When people talk, they naturally pause when they anticipate that the other person might have something to say. If the

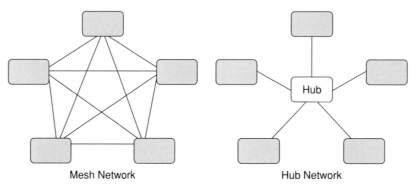

Mesh Network                          Hub Network

**FIGURE 2-2**   Mesh and Hub Videoconferencing Networks

other person does not begin speaking right away, then the first person might begin another thought or sentence. Long delays make this interaction difficult, because people must wait for the signal to return to see if the other person has decided to begin speaking. Although limiting the time delay sounds easy, this can be very difficult to do in practice.

Network configurations can vary but generally fall into two categories: mesh networks and ones where a hub is used (see Figure 2-2).

- In a mesh network, the video/audio/data stream from each user is sent to every other user's location. Once there, all the signals can be displayed using multiple video images. Alternatively, each user can select one of the signals to view.
- When a hub is used, a central device (often called a multipoint control unit; see Chapter 10) receives the signals from each user, performs processing, and sends a dedicated signal out to each viewer. The processing can vary, but one popular scheme is to give each viewer a mix of all the audio signals and a video image of the person who is speaking (or making the most noise).

## Telemedicine

Telemedicine involves using networks to allow a physician in one location to practice medicine in another location. There has been a lot of hoopla surrounding the idea of using remote control robots to do surgery over the Internet, but there are many more down-to-earth examples of using current technology for telemedicine that are benefiting patients today. Here are a few examples:

- Teleradiology, where images from X-rays, CAT scans, MRI scans, etc., are sent to a radiologist at a distant location for interpretation. This has even been done around the globe to let a radiologist working normal daylight hours in India support a US hospital for middle-of-the-night emergencies. While radiologists primarily use still images, motion (video) images are becoming more common.
- Telepathology, where a pathologist inspects tissue samples from a remotely located patient. Frequently, the pathologist will need to take control of the sample imaging tools (such as a microscope) to complete the diagnosis. For this to work, the round-trip delay needs to be kept very short, to make it possible for the pathologist to correctly operate the controls of the imaging device.
- Telepsychology, where video-, audio- and/or text-based interaction is used to provide mental health treatment for distant patients. This technology can be used for a variety of purposes, including patient screening, case management, therapy, and crisis intervention. Telepsychology can be particularly helpful for patients who are geographically isolated or physically disabled.

Network reliability is essential to most telemedicine applications. Because physician and patient time is valuable, the network needs to be operational whenever it is needed. Private or dedicated networks often can be used to achieve this goal.

Privacy of patient data is also very important. Many countries have strict rules about maintaining the privacy of patient communications and data. Physicians are very serious about ethics and would not be willing to use a telemedicine system that did not adequately ensure the confidentiality of patient information. To ensure privacy, many telemedicine systems are implemented using private networks that operate on private facilities or on dedicated bandwidth in a shared network. Efforts also can be made to remove patient identification from clinical data files so that non-medical, patient-related data (address, telephone number, etc.) isn't transmitted over the telemedicine network.

An interesting example of telemedicine in action occurred on the Eastern Montana Telemedicine Network. A US Navy Reserve otolaryngologist based in Billings, Montana, Dr. Sheri Rolf, uses a videoconferencing system to "see" patients at the LeMoore Naval Base in southern California from her office in Montana. The application uses video-enabled viewing scopes that allow the doctor to observe patients' ears, noses, and throats during appointments that occur several times per month. This application allows Dr. Rolf to fulfill her duty requirements without needing to travel to the base in southern California. Figure 2-3 shows the basic layout of this network.

## Distance Education

Distance education includes a wide range of technologies that are used to provide instruction to students who are physically separated from their instructors. This instruction can be live or pre-recorded, it can be interactive or one-way, and it may or may not involve the use of a telecommunications network. (An example in which a network is not needed would be a student viewing a lecture on a CD-ROM or videotape.) Distance education has been used successfully in applications ranging from primary school through advanced

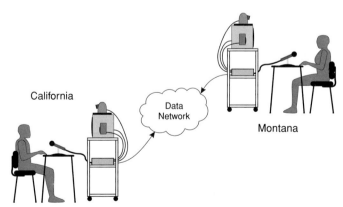

**FIGURE 2-3**  Telemedicine Videoconferencing Application

graduate school, as well as in corporate training and adult/continuing education programs.

One large segment of the distance education market is commonly called Interactive Distance Learning (IDL). IDL takes place when students receive live instruction from a teacher, and are able to interact with the teacher to respond to teacher questions and to ask questions of their own. Many of these systems employ two-way video and audio links, although systems that use only text or audio in one or both directions are also used.

Video and audio delay must be carefully managed in an IDL system. Long delays make communication more difficult, since participants must pause longer than they would in a normal conversation to wait for the other parties to begin speaking. In some IDL systems, the instructor is given remote control of a movable camera with the ability to zoom in on individual students; with excessive delay, this function can become difficult to operate. A widely recognized maximum delay for each direction in a two-way videoconference is 400 milliseconds (800 milliseconds for a complete round trip), with a preferred limit of no more than 150 milliseconds delay in each direction.

Video and audio quality is also important to maintain. Use of high-quality cameras and microphones is essential. Since most IDL operates using compressed digital video, performance of the compression equipment can also impact the video quality. Interestingly, the need for high-quality video goes up for younger students, who tend to be more easily distracted by video artifacts and less disciplined in their classroom behavior. Generally, compression technologies such as MPEG–2 and higher speed versions of H.323 (see Chapter 4 for details on these) are preferred over low-resolution systems. In the future, MPEG–4 and H.264 will likely gain a significant portion of the market.

Echo cancellation is also important in IDL networks. An echo canceller operates by making sure that people who are speaking do not hear their own voices transmitted back to themselves after traveling through the network. (For a more detailed explanation of echo cancellation, see Chapter 10.)

## Telejustice

Telejustice provides the services of courts and lawyers to distant clients. It is normally used for routine court matters such as bail hearings and arraignments. Telejustice has also been used occasionally during actual trials, in which defendants or witnesses require special safety or security precautions. Governments find telejustice systems to be a low-cost substitute for the expense of guarding and transporting prisoners from a jail to a courthouse for simple legal proceedings that may take only a few minutes.

The single most important feature of a telejustice network is privacy. Very strict rules in the USA and elsewhere require communications between lawyers and their clients to be held strictly private. Accordingly, these systems are almost always implemented on private networks, without any connection to the Internet.

## NARROWCASTING

Narrowcasting is best thought of as broadcasting to a small audience. It involves transmitting program content that may be of interest to only a few select people who are spread over a network. For our purposes, we will focus our discussion of narrowcasting to applications in which the communications take place in one direction only, i.e., from the source to the viewer. Applications offering two-way communications are considered to be interactive and are covered in the previous section of this chapter. Table 2-1 lists some of the many different types of content that are applicable to narrowcasting.

**TABLE 2-1**

Common Uses for Narrowcasting

- Shareholder meetings
- Executive speeches
- Corporate training
- Sales presentations
- Internet radio and video entertainment
- Traffic cameras
- Security and "spy" cameras

Many different types of technology can by used for narrowcasting. Low-quality video can be created with a low-cost webcam and a desktop PC that produces a tiny video window that updates once every few seconds. High-quality video can be achieved with a hardware-based video encoder that can send full-screen video with full motion over a high-bandwidth network. And, of course, there are a variety of solutions in between. We will discuss many of these technologies for narrowcasting throughout this book.

An important distinction needs to be made between three different methods that are used for narrowcasting: live streaming, on-demand streaming, and download and play. Table 2-2 gives a definition of each of these terms. But first, we need to understand the concept of streaming.

**TABLE 2-2**

Methods for Narrowcasting

- *Live streaming* happens when the video content appears on every viewer's display at the same time. Technically, every viewer is sent a copy of the same video stream simultaneously. Note that the displays of any two users may not be perfectly synchronized because of the variation in network delays and in the amount of buffering of the video data that occurs in each display device. Even if the content is pre-recorded, we will consider it a live stream by this definition if each user must view the content at the same time that it is being sent.
- *On-demand streaming* happens when users can request that video content be streamed to them when they want to view it. In this case, the content is still streamed to each user, but each user gets to choose when to begin and end the stream (and possibly rewind or fast-forward the stream as well). On-demand streaming is popular with viewers because they can control when they watch the content. It is also popular with content owners because the video information is never stored in complete form on the customer's device, thereby making piracy (somewhat) more difficult.
- *Download and play* uses storage (memory or hard disk) inside a viewer's device to receive a file of audio/video content that is sent from a central server. Once the content file is received, it can then be displayed (played) by the viewer's device. One advantage of using download and play is that the content can be played at a rate that is significantly different from the speed of the network connection. This allows users with dial-up Internet connections to successfully watch full-screen versions of movie trailers on their PCs, provided they are willing to wait for the download. A disadvantage of using download and play is that the user's device needs to have enough storage available to hold the entire file. Also, some content owners may not approve of download and play, because it results in a copy of the content becoming resident on every user's storage device prior to viewing.

Streaming is a process for sending video and audio content to a user as a smooth flow of data that is watched immediately, just like watching a network television broadcast. When streaming isn't used, the entire file of video/audio content must be sent to the user before viewing can begin. A useful analogy is to think about a Just-In-Time manufacturing system, in which parts are delivered to the assembly line just when they are needed, thereby removing the need for piles of parts at each workstation. Similarly, when content is streamed, it avoids the need for the viewing device to gather (download) the video content before playback begins. We'll talk a lot more about streaming in Chapter 8.

Now, let's look at some of the applications of video streaming.

## Shareholder Meetings

As public companies move to create a level playing field for all classes of shareholders, more opportunities are provided for small shareholders to participate in yearly or quarterly meetings. Narrowcasting is an effective way of doing this, because it allows shareholders who are interested in these meetings to participate without traveling to the meeting location.

In the past, these meetings sometimes were made available to shareholders using a telephone conferencing service. Shareholders were given a special number to dial, and they were connected to a telephone conference bridge to receive the audio from the meeting. This technology can get expensive since either the shareholders or the companies must pay for the telephone calls to the bridge. Also, specialized conference bridges would have to be reserved to accommodate a large number of potential callers. With narrowcasting technology implemented over the public Internet, communications costs can be reduced, although enough servers need to be set up to generate streams for each listener. Some of these servers can also simultaneously record the content that is being sent out so that the content can be made available for on-demand streaming after the end of the meeting.

Audio quality is one of the most important features of a shareholder meeting. Most of the information being presented is in audible form, even if it has already been distributed in written form. In particular, during meetings to discuss quarterly results, company management takes questions from Wall Street analysts who follow their stock. Since most of these questions come over telephone lines, good audio quality will ensure that both parties will be audible to the shareholders.

## Executive Speeches

Executive speeches (or what I like to call "ego-casting") are commonly used by senior company executives to communicate with employees. All types of material can be covered, from discussions of company results to awards presentations to ways of dealing with a crisis. The speeches can be directed to all employees or just to certain groups of people.

Live streaming is a popular method for narrowcasting an executive speech. A key factor in many of these speeches is ensuring that as many employees as possible receive the information at the same time. Many companies can use their own private networks to distribute the live stream directly to employees equipped with PCs and can greatly reduce network bandwidth requirements if their networks are enabled for multicasting. Multicasting uses network equipment such as routers to make copies of the stream for each user, removing the need to send an individual stream to each viewing device (see Chapter 9 for details). For employees who do not have PCs, hardware devices can be used to receive the stream from the network and display the content on a normal television.

High video quality is an important requirement for executive speeches. Executives of large corporations often feel that they need to portray a certain image, and a poor-quality video speech is a good way to damage one. Since private networks can be used for distributing the streams, high-quality, high-bandwidth streams (such as MPEG–2 or MPEG–4; see Chapter 4) often can be used. For employees who are not attached to the corporate network, a low-resolution, low-bandwidth version of the stream can be created and distributed over the Internet, or just the audio portion of the stream can be sent.

## Corporate Training

Many modern corporations are using video training to enhance the skills of their workforce, to improve quality and productivity, and to cut costs. Video training can remove the need for specialized trainers to travel to each company location simply for the purpose of delivering the same training presentation repeatedly. Instead, these trainers can focus on creating new content, and employees can view the training when and where they choose. Overall, video training can be a great way to improve corporate performance.

All three types of narrowcasting technology described previously are used for corporate training. Live streaming is used when multiple employees all need to be trained at the same time or for special events. On-demand streaming is used for classes delivered at each student's convenience. Download and play is used for remote or mobile users with low-bandwidth connections.

## Sales Presentations

Narrowcasting can be used effectively to give information about a wide range of products and services to prospective customers. The presentations can be standardized for a wide range of viewers, or they can be custom tailored for an individual customer. Any of the different types of narrowcasting technologies can be used.

An important consideration in designing video content for prospective customers is to understand the great variations in network capacities and display devices, because of the wide varieties of external customers' networks. Creators must be careful to make sure that they either produce content that is playable across many platforms and networks or produce several versions of the content to accommodate different viewer capabilities. Contrast this with the environment for executive speeches and corporate training, where network environments and viewing devices can be standardized within a corporation.

## Internet Radio and Video Entertainment

Although entertainment over the Internet has followed the boom-and-bust cycle of the industry at large, a significant amount of content is still being delivered to paying customers every day. Plus, a huge amount of free content is available, much of which is free of the issues associated with illegal copies of copyrighted content.

Content owners have a lot of impact on how audio and video content is provided over the Internet. Digital Rights Management (DRM) is an all-encompassing term that covers many different aspects of how content can be controlled, as listed in Table 2-3, and described in greater detail in Chapter 11.

Particularly for paid content, a big technical issue in Internet entertainment is ensuring that viewers have permission to view the content they have requested. The DRM system needs to make sure that unauthorized copies are not made, or, if they are, that they cannot be played.

Another big issue in Internet entertainment is ensuring that the quality of the video and audio content is acceptable to the user. Acceptability depends on a number of factors, including the amount of motion in the video, the resolution (number of picture elements or pixels; see Chapter 3) of the video frame, the type of content (live sports, news reports, weather forecasts, animation, movies, etc.), how much the viewer has paid for the content, and other factors. Interestingly, tests have shown that a relationship exists between

**TABLE 2-3**

Functions of Digital Rights Management

- Content encryption or scrambling
- Encryption key distribution
- User storage management
- User playback tracking and limitation
- Content labeling
- License management

audio and video quality—higher quality audio makes viewers perceive that the video quality is higher as well. Of course, user perceptions can also be affected by a number of network factors, particularly the speed of the user's connection to the Internet and any congestion that occurs between the content provider and the user. Overall, it is important for content providers to make sure to carefully manage user quality perceptions.

## Security and "Spy" Cameras

Security and "spy" cameras are a common feature of modern life. They are used to provide surveillance of a large number of public spaces, including airports, streets, and shopping malls. Security cameras are also used to monitor private property, such as banks, casinos, and industrial plants. These cameras provide a number of benefits, including crime prevention, safety monitoring, and improved response times in emergencies. Small-scale installations, with a single camera and a recording device, are almost a fixture in businesses operating late at night, such as convenience stores and gasoline (petrol) stations.

In a traditional security camera installation, a television camera sends a video signal over a cable directly to a video monitor. This simple setup gave rise to the common term Closed Circuit Television (CCTV) because the camera and display form a closed electrical circuit for the video signal. Early installations used a security guard or other person to watch multiple video displays to determine whether anything was happening on any of the screens. Improvements have been made over time through the addition of devices to record the video and to automatically detect movement within a camera image and alert a guard. Security cameras are increasingly being connected to data networks for a number of reasons, as shown in Table 2-4.

Some additional hardware is required to connect a camera to a data network. First, the video signal needs to be converted into digital form and then compressed to take up less network bandwidth. Display devices must also be adapted to display the digital video signal. In many cases, this can be a desktop PC with video-viewing software. Alternatively, a digital video decoder can be used to create a signal for a standard video monitor. Any networking hardware must have enough capacity to

**TABLE 2-4**

Security Camera Data Network Benefits

- Multiple cameras can share a single data network cable or link, which can dramatically lower the costs of installing cables for a large or geographically spread-out network.
- Several viewing stations can be set up, each of which can view video content from the same cameras. This setup might be useful, for example, in monitoring highways; one monitoring station can be set up at each local police station for local sections, and another at a central traffic and maintenance office that manages the entire roadway.
- The need for video switching equipment is greatly reduced or eliminated, because each viewer can pick from any of the signals on the IP or other data network simply by choosing the right video source address on the data network.
- The video network can be shared with other data applications such as remote sensors or remotely controlled equipment. Any such sharing needs to be done carefully to make sure that the data traffic and the video traffic don't interfere with each other.
- Commercial telecommunications networks can be used as a backbone for large networks. This setup can help reduce or eliminate the need to construct a dedicated video network over fiber optic or other facilities.

handle the bandwidth demands of the video signals. Fortunately, many products perform video adaptation for networks, and some surveillance cameras even have networking hardware built right in.

Security camera installations have some unique features relative to other video networks. Audio transport is not needed in many cases, or it is limited to a subset of the total collection of cameras. However, in many cases, networks need to transport other types of data. This can include data that comes from remote locations to a central facility, such as fire alarms, smoke detectors, or intrusion sensors. The network can also be used to send out commands to the remote devices, such as rotating or zooming cameras, or unlocking doors for authorized visitors. Low-cost units for connecting these devices to a data network are readily available.

Many security camera systems use endless loop recording. In this system, new video content is constantly being recorded over the oldest, previously recorded content. The term "endless loop" came directly from the way the first systems worked, by recording onto a videotape that had been specially modified to be in a continuous loop. (This is very similar to the 8-track audiotapes that were popular with consumers in the 1970s in the USA.) Unfortunately, because the tapes are constantly moved past the video recording head, they become heavily worn after a few weeks of service. This wear makes it difficult to see the image actually recorded on the tape. Technology has been introduced that uses digital storage (computer memory or hard disk) to perform this same function with much more repeatable video quality. With networked digital video, it is relatively easy to make an automatic endless loop recording of all the video flowing over a network. Also, if information such as time of day is recorded along with the video signal, users can quickly retrieve and view the content they desire.

## THE TRUE MEANING OF "REAL TIME"

Real time is a common thread in discussions about video. For our discussion, we will use "real time" to refer to any activity performed with content that takes the same amount of time to complete as the duration of the content. For example, if sending a 27-minute program over a video network takes 27 minutes, then we would call that network a "real-time" network. Other examples of real-time activities include television broadcasts, recording of a live studio news program, or a videoconference.

Real time is a very important concept to understand. If an activity needs to take place in real time, then the amount of time that it takes is equal to the duration of the content. The content does not need to be stored inside a playback device; it can simply be displayed as it comes in. Basic television sets don't have any kind of memory, because they don't need it—all the programming they receive is delivered in real time. Table 2-5 gives a few examples of video applications that typically occur in real time.

It is also important to distinguish between hard real time and soft real time. For our purposes, we will use the following definitions:

*Hard real time* is an application in which success or failure depends on a low-delay video transport system. For example, a videoconference cannot take place if the video link is not up and running, with minimal delay. Hard real time is required whenever live events are being broadcast (sports, awards shows, etc.) and whenever interactivity is needed.

**TABLE 2-5**

Real-Time Video Examples

- Radio and television broadcasting (including over-the-air, CATV, and satellite)
- Contribution networks for live events (such as sports or news)
- Videoconferencing
- Video streaming
- Highway surveillance
- Consumer videotape or video camera recording

*Soft real time* is any application that needs to occur in real time, but it can be interrupted or delayed without creating complete failure of the application. For example, television networks frequently distribute syndicated programs (game shows, daytime dramas, etc.) to television stations during times when the satellites (or other video network) are not being used for other broadcasts. These transmissions are typically made as a real-time video signal so that each television station can simply set up a videotape recorder to receive the program. If this transmission is interrupted or if a particular station's tape deck breaks down, then the application won't fail as long as the program can be re-delivered (possibly by another means) before the program is supposed to be broadcast.

A number of video applications happen in non-real time. For example, some videotape recorders can operate in faster-than-real time, allowing 30 minutes of content to be copied from, say, an editing system to a tape deck in 15 or 7.5 minutes (for 2 × and 4 × faster than real time). In other cases, transmissions can be made in slower-than-real time. This will occur when some kind of bottleneck occurs in the video transmission system that makes it infeasible or uneconomical to send the video in real time. One example of this is given in Chapter 14, where low-cost file transfer networks are used overnight to send advertisements to clients for approvals. Another example is a download and play video transport system, as discussed earlier in this chapter.

It is also important to distinguish between "real-time" and "live" events. Any event that is broadcast live is also being broadcast in hard real time. However, many broadcasts that occur in real time are not live. For example, all of the programming coming from a local broadcaster is delivered in real time, but very little of this content is live (the exceptions are usually limited to news programs and sports coverage).

The concept of real time is important for two reasons. First, as we discussed previously, video streaming is a real-time activity and must be supported with hardware that can deliver a stream to each destination in real time. Second, video compression equipment (which takes video content and makes it easier to transport over a network, and will be discussed in Chapter 4) can be sorted into two broad categories: real time and non-real time. Real-time equipment tends to be more expensive because many of the key compression functions need to be implemented in specialized hardware in order to make sure that all the required tasks are completed quickly enough to keep up with the incoming video signal. In contrast, non–real-time compression tends to be done using general-purpose computing hardware (such as a PC) and through the use of software. In general, if real-time compression is not required for a particular application, then non–real-time systems can be used to either reduce cost, increase quality, or both. Note that many real-time streaming applications use video that has been previously recorded (such as Hollywood movies) and compressed using non–real-time systems.

## VIDEO TRANSPORT ECONOMICS

Many different benefits can be used to justify the costs of installing video transport systems. Broadly speaking, they can be sorted into two areas: revenue enhancement or cost reduction. Sometimes, both can come into play. Table 2-6 lists some of the ways that companies have justified their use of video transport networks.

### Video Content Costs

Before a video transport system can be used, there needs to be content to move across the network. There are many different kinds of ownership models, but one of the most common is the ownership of entertainment content by television networks. For anyone who is

**TABLE 2-6**

Video Transport Network Business Benefits

*Revenue Enhancement*

- Sell video content on a pay-per-view or a subscription basis
- Provide in-depth information to customers
- Increase effectiveness of sales presentations, and improve company sales
- Provide customers with interactive video help services
- Provide demonstrations of merchandise

*Cost Reduction*

- Improve productivity
- Develop employee skill and provide cross-training
- Increase customer and employee retention
- Reduce travel costs for customers, employees, and training staff

interested in the video delivery business, it is important to understand the costs of obtaining the necessary content.

Content can generally be obtained inexpensively from local broadcast stations, partly because of the need for those stations to reach local viewers who generally don't receive their programming via over-the-air broadcasts. For many other channels of programming, particularly those that are carried only on CATV and direct-to-home satellite systems, the delivery system operators pay monthly fees to the programmers. Table 2-7 lists some of the fees charged per subscriber per month for popular cable TV channels in the USA in 2003.

**TABLE 2-7**

Sample Fees for Cable TV Programming

| Network Name | Fee Per Subscriber Per Month |
| --- | --- |
| ESPN | $1.76 |
| Fox Sports | 1.16 |
| TNT | 0.78 |
| USA | 0.40 |
| CNN | 0.38 |
| Nickelodeon | 0.34 |
| FX | 0.32 |
| TBS | 0.23 |
| MTV | 0.23 |
| ESPN2 | $0.20 |

*Source:* Kagan Research, LLC; used with permission.

Together, these fees total $5.80 per subscriber per month. Since most of these channels are part of the basic offerings provided by CATV and DTH providers, these costs need to be paid out of the subscriber basic fees. For many delivery providers, these fees range from $15.00 to $30.00 per month, for anywhere from 20 to 50 channels. All told, it is easy to see how programming content costs can consume upwards of one-third to one-half of a delivery provider's revenues.

## Consumer Video Business Modeling

Supplying video content to consumers can be a very lucrative business. After all, broadcasters and cable television operators have been doing it for years. Table 2-8 lists and explains some of the many factors that contribute to the costs of these systems.

**TABLE 2-8**

Consumer Video Cost Factors

- *Government Permits and Franchise Fees:* These fees are paid to local governments in exchange for the rights to construct and operate a video delivery service. (Note that over-the-air broadcasters pay license fees in order to use the radio spectrum.) Some portion of these fees can be paid up front, and some are paid on an annual basis. Typically, the recurring fees are calculated as a percentage of the service revenue.
- *Rights of Way:* Payments may be required to gain physical access to private property for installing a cable or placing a wireless transmitter or receiver. These payments can be lump sum, recurring, or a combination of the two.
- *Government Mandates:* These can range widely, but it is very common for local governments to require local service providers to offer public access channels and television coverage of local government meetings. Some service providers even furnish free services to local schools, which can be used for distance learning.
- *Network Equipment and Cable Purchases:* The cost of these purchases can be a significant expense because they must include equipment to gather programming from a variety of sources (such as satellites and local broadcasters), format video for distribution, control subscriber access, transmit and receive video signals, and support and bill customers. Even in a relatively small network, costs of cabling can also be substantial.
- *Installation Labor:* Installation labor usually comes in two phases: first, the cost to deploy the common equipment in each served area, and then the cost to connect or disconnect individual customers. This separation makes sense because the "take rate" (the percentage of actual customers out of the total pool of potential customers) typically starts low and increases over time as more people decide to subscribe to the service.

**TABLE 2-8** (*Continued*)

- *Cost of Capital:* Large sums of money are typically required to fund a video network that covers thousands of subscribers, and this money needs to come from somewhere. The cost of capital is either the interest on money borrowed from a bank or the return that is promised to investors in the operation. Calculations about how many subscribers are needed to reach the breakeven point are critical to include in a business plan.
- *Consumer Marketing:* Consumers need to be convinced that any new service is going to be worth the cost. Even with a compelling set of services, a successful marketing plan can take months or years to persuade a large percentage of the target audience to become subscribers. Marketing costs will tend to be high when a system is new and decline somewhat over time, but this should be budgeted as a permanent, ongoing expense.
- *Cost of Programming:* It is absolutely critical to understand these costs, because they can easily eat up half of the consumer revenue from selling video service. Fortunately, these fees tend to be based on the number of actual subscribers, and so they will be low when the take rate is low. Staff will also be required to manage content ownership rights and to ensure that the content is being delivered as specified in the content usage contracts.
- *User Guides:* Many modern video delivery services can have hundreds of channels of programming available. For viewers to be able to find the channels that they want to view, some form of program guide needs to be made available. This is often done electronically, with the listings display on the viewer's television set. Of course, like anything else, the guide needs to be configured and maintained, which costs money.
- *Customer Service and Order Entry:* Once a consumer decides to place an order, the value of professional, efficient order entry staff cannot be underestimated. Some providers use special paid programming events (concerts, sports, etc.) to help pay for the cost of their customer service staff.
- *System Maintenance:* Due to human nature and mother nature, repairs and changes to service are part of doing business. Many providers also deploy system upgrades from time-to-time, adding new services or new programming, or both. This continual expense must be budgeted, even for a brand new installation.

Many new service providers explicitly go after "triple-play" services, where each consumer is offered video, voice (telephony), and data service all from a single supplier. This strategy can work well, particularly if consumers are dissatisfied with their current suppliers. Many carriers offer package discounts to customers who purchase two or three of the triple-play services. Although the actual cost savings to the provider for offering a triple-play is debatable, there is no doubt about the marketing benefits of this approach.

## REVIEW AND CHECKLIST UPDATE

In this chapter, we looked at some of the applications of video transport. We began with entertainment, by defining the difference between contribution, distribution, and delivery networks. We discussed the differences in performance and cost that is required by these three applications. We also glanced at live sports, gaming, and advertising, and saw how their requirements differ from other types of programming. We discussed a number of applications of interactive television such as videoconferencing, telemedicine, distance learning, and telejustice. We covered narrowcasting and the use of both pre-recorded and live video to serve applications such as shareholder meetings, executive speeches, training, entertainment, and security cameras. We defined hard and soft real time, and discussed their differences. Finally, we looked at some of the factors that can impact the business case for a video delivery network. One major cost, which is easy to overlook, is the cost of programming. For DTH and CATV systems, programming costs can easily consume one-third or more of the service provider's revenues.

### Chapter 2 Checklist Update

❏ If the application is entertainment television, determine if the network will be used primarily for contribution, distribution, or delivery.

❏ If the network will be used for contribution, determine the amount of processing that will be done to the video after the transport. As a rule, when more processing is done, higher-quality source video is needed. Consider using lightly compressed or uncompressed video signals for feeds where lots of post-production will be done.

❏ If the network is to be used for distribution, make sure that all categories of delivery providers can be reached as required by the application. Also, make sure that the network is reliable enough to handle this class of traffic.

❏ If the network is to be used for delivery, determine the number of subscribers that will be served simultaneously. Make sure that the chosen delivery system can scale up to this number. Also, consider the costs that will be incurred to equip each new viewer.

❑ For interactive video, make sure that the video quality is high enough to suit the application and that the delay is low. Generally, lower delay is more important than video quality, except for applications that require high image fidelity (e.g., telemedicine).

❑ For narrowcasting, determine if live feeds will be required, or if content can be stored and then streamed. If live feeds are required, then real-time video compression equipment will also be needed.

❑ For live narrowcasting, determine how many viewers will be served simultaneously, and select a mechanism to create an adequate number of streams for all the viewers.

❑ Determine if the application requires hard real time, or if soft real time or non-real time will be adequate. Also determine if real-time compression will be needed.

❑ When creating a business plan for a video delivery system, make sure that all the key factors are analyzed. Pay close attention to costs for obtaining necessary permits and the costs of controlling the ownership rights.

❑ Make sure that the costs of programming are included in any video delivery system business case.

# 3

## VIDEO BASICS

A basic understanding of video and audio signals will make our discussions of video transport much easier to comprehend and to put in context. Readers with significant video experience may choose to skip reading this chapter, but be advised that we will be covering some terminology that will be used in much of the remainder of this book. By the end of this chapter, readers should have a good understanding of the different types of analog and digital video signals, should have gained some background about audio and other signals that can accompany video signals, and should have had a brief look at some of the different ways in which video and audio signals can be switched.

## PIXELS, LUMA, SCANNING, AND CHROMA

Any discussion of video needs to start with the definition of some basic terms, and our discussion will be no different. We'll briefly introduce each term and then explain each one in more detail in the following sections.

A *pixel* is a single picture element in a digital video image; it is the building block for all forms of digital imaging, including both still photography and video.

*Luma* is the portion of a video signal that represents the brightness of each pixel. Maximum luma is used for an all-white pixel, and minimum luma is a black (or off) pixel.

*Scanning* is the process used in a video signal for capturing, storing, transporting, and displaying the luma and chroma values of each pixel. Scanning puts the information for each pixel in a specific order so that all types of video equipment can determine the information that belongs to each pixel.

*Chroma* is the portion of a video signal that represents the color of each pixel. Colors are intended to range over the full spectrum of the human visual system, from red through green and blue, in any combination.

Each of these terms is defined in greater depth in the following sections.

## Pixels

As our society becomes ever more video and computer literate, the concept of a pixel becomes useful in more and more applications. Computer displays, digital cameras, document scanners, and many other devices are specified in terms of pixels. Digital video images are also described in terms of pixels, so it is important to get a good understanding of this concept.

A pixel is the smallest possible picture element that can be represented by a digital image. Each pixel can be thought of as a single tiny dot of color that represents a portion of an image. If you magnify any digital image sufficiently, you will see that it is made up of thousands or millions of these tiny dots, each of which is a single pixel. This is true whether the image has been photographed by a digital camera (still or video), captured by a digital scanner (or facsimile machine), displayed on a digital monitor (television or computer), printed on a digital printer, or created by graphics software inside a computer or a video game console.

A pixel is similar in concept to a single character out of a page of text, or a single byte of data on a computer's hard drive. Taken by itself, a pixel doesn't carry very much information (and neither does a single character of text or a single byte of data). However, when a pixel is combined with thousands or millions of other pixels, a very realistic image can be created. As the number of pixels in an image increases, so does the amount of detail that can be represented in the image, because each pixel represents a smaller portion of the overall image.

Like a character of text or a byte of data, each pixel has a value. This value represents the pixel's color (or hue) and the pixel's intensity (or saturation). For a still image, the value for each pixel is fixed. For a motion image, such as a video, the values for each pixel are updated many times per second. For television systems in North America and Japan, the information for each pixel is updated just about 30 times per second; in much of the rest of the world, each pixel on a television screen is updated 25 times per second.

In addition to its value, each pixel also has a location. This location is defined in both the vertical dimension (up and down the image) and the horizontal dimension (across the image from left to right). All of the pixels for an image must be sent in the correct order to a display device so that each one ends up at its assigned location on the video display. This order proceeds from left to right across the display, and from the top to the bottom of the screen. We will discuss this process (called "scanning") in more detail shortly.

Pixel displays can be formed in many different ways. In a traditional television or cathode ray tube (CRT) display, each pixel is a small group of dots of phosphor. The phosphor dots give off light when hit by an electron beam (or cathode ray). The brightness of the glow depends on the intensity of the electron beam; the more intense the beam, the brighter the phosphor glows. The main function of all the high-voltage electronics in a conventional TV set is to control the movement and the intensity of the electron beam. For color television, the smallest possible pixel is made up of three different colored phosphor dots, one red, one blue, and one green, as shown in Figure 3-1.[1]

Liquid crystal displays (LCDs) use liquid crystals (chemicals that can be used to block or pass light based on an electrical signal) and a light source to create a viewable image, either directly on a glass sheet or by projecting the light onto a screen. Plasma displays use electron beams and phosphors just like a CRT, except that each pixel has its own microscopic beam source. Large outdoor displays can use thousands upon thousands of light emitting diodes (LEDs, just like the ones used as power indicators on electronic devices) in three different colors to create an image.

## Luma

The luma (or luminance) portion of a video signal contains information about the brightness or intensity of a video signal as perceived by

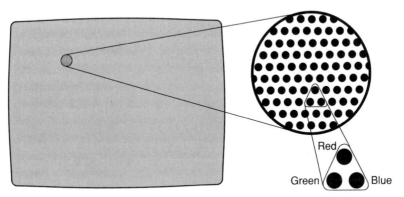

**FIGURE 3-1**   Typical Phosphor Dot Pattern on a Television Display

---

1.   It is possible for a pixel in an image to cover several pixels in a display. This commonly happens, for example, when a high-resolution display (such as an SVGA computer display) is used to display a low-resolution image (such as a Video Graphics Adapter, or VGA, image). But, we are getting ahead of ourselves here.

the human eye. Pixels with a high luma value appear brighter to a viewer than pixels with a low luma value.

The luma signal carries a significant portion of the information contained in a video signal. The human visual system is very sensitive to changes in brightness of an image, and much of the information carried in the fine details of the image is due to changes in brightness, not color. One example of this would be an image of a person's hair: All of the strands of hair are essentially the same color, but the fine detail of the image is contained in the patterns of light and dark that show the boundaries of each strand of hair. If the luma signal becomes degraded, then the overall quality of the video image suffers, particularly in any portion of the image that contains fine details.

An easy way to actually observe just the luma portion of a video image is to modify the settings of a television set to remove all the color from the signal. This can be accomplished by placing the "color" control to the minimum possible value (on some TV sets the color control is an actual knob; on others this setting is accessed through an on-screen command menu). The resulting image, which appears to be black-and-white, is a good approximation of the luma portion of a video signal.

The luma signal is a legacy of the original black-and-white television transmission systems. (Technically, old television should be called gray-scale or monochrome, not black-and-white, because the televisions could generate black pixels, white pixels, or any shade of gray in between.) When color television broadcasts began, virtually the entire installed base of televisions was monochrome, so the luma signal was retained in the video signal for use by these sets. However, the luma signal continues to have important uses to this day, which we will now discuss.

As we discussed earlier, the human visual system is very sensitive to closely spaced differences in the brightness of an image and, as it turns out, less sensitive to closely spaced changes in the color of an image. This attribute of vision has been taken advantage of in most modern color video systems, which use different methods to represent the luma portions of video images than the methods that are used to represent the color (or chroma) portions of the image. This is true for all broadcast video formats, as well as for all of the most widely used video compression systems. We'll go into this in more detail in the discussion of chroma later in this chapter.

So, as we have seen, the luma signal has some important applications, both as a result of the evolution of television and as a result of the properties of human vision. In the next section, we will look at the other key aspect of a video signal—the concept of scanning.

## Scanning

A video signal must contain all of the picture information that needs to be sent to each pixel to form an image. One way of doing this would be to broadcast a separate signal to each pixel. However, since a basic television image has more than 300,000 pixels, that would be impractical. Instead, the pioneers of television developed the concept of scanning.

*Scanning* is a technique wherein the luma and chroma values for a whole row of pixels are captured, stored, delivered, and/or displayed in sequential order, followed by the luma and chroma values for the next row below (see Figure 3-2). Scanning always works from left to right on the display, so the leftmost pixel is scanned first, and the

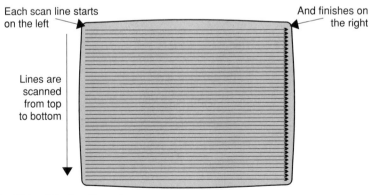

**FIGURE 3-2**   Video Display Scanning

rightmost pixel is scanned last for each horizontal line or row. In a video signal, at the end of each line, a short horizontal "blanking interval" is inserted, which allows time for the cathode ray to be turned off and moved back quickly to the left side of the display to begin creating the next line on the display. Even though other types of displays don't need them, essentially all video signals still contain blanking intervals for backward compatibility and to indicate when one horizontal line stops and the next begins.

A video signal is sent as a sequence of horizontal scan lines, one after the other. Each scan line contains the picture data for one row of pixels. If we were to look at the waveform of one scan line and see how it changes over time, we would get something that looks like Figure 3-3. In this diagram, brighter pixels are represented by higher level signals, and darker pixels are lower level.

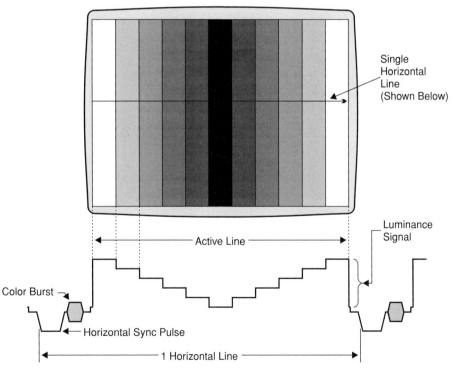

**FIGURE 3-3** Horizontal Scan Line, Showing Sync Pulse

To make scanning work properly, accurate synchronization is required. A little before the picture data in each horizontal scan line is a *horizontal synchronization* pulse, as shown in Figure 3-3. This pulse occurs at exactly the same time before the start of the first pixel signal on every horizontal line. The display is responsible for detecting these pulses and making sure that each line on the display is aligned so that vertical objects in the image (which are made up from pixels on many different horizontal lines) appear vertical on the display.

The video signal also contains information that indicates which horizontal line is the first one to be drawn across the display. This information is called *vertical synchronization*, and it works by placing specially formatted horizontal lines into the signal. The display recognizes this pattern and is then able to place the first horizontal scan line on the top row of pixels on the display.

## Chroma

The chroma portion of a video signal carries the information that is needed to create a color image. This signal works in conjunction with the luma signal described earlier; neither one alone is adequate to produce a normal full-color, full-resolution video image.

Color televisions differ from black-and-white in that each pixel has three colored phosphor dots in place of one white phosphor dot. The colors are red, green, and blue, because basically all the colors that the eye can see can be represented by a combination of these three colors. In LCD displays, each pixel is made up of three individual liquid crystals, each having a different colored light source (created with colored filters). In a plasma display, each colored dot gets its own electron gun. In a large format LED display, each pixel is made up of three different colored LEDs.

Now, the astute reader will probably be thinking: "OK, so all we have to do is send one signal to all the red pixels, another to all the green pixels, and a third to all the blues, right?" These readers would be right in a many circumstances, including essentially all computer displays. But, for television broadcast applications, there is a significant downside: The amount of radio spectrum that would be consumed by transmitting separate R, G, and B signals would be three times that of a comparable black-and-white broadcast. This isn't a problem for a 2-meter cable from a computer to a display (just add some wires and a few pins on the connectors). This is a big problem for the crowded airwaves in a city like New York.

So, once again, the pioneers of television did something very clever—they devised a way to use the luma signal that they already needed to broadcast for the monochrome television sets. They did this by first combining the R, G, and B signals into the luma signal by figuring out how the human eye perceives color. They called this new signal the Y signal, because it was different from R, G, and B. Since our eyes are most sensitive to the color green, the G signal is the largest contributor to the Y signal. The R and the B signals are also contained in the Y signal, but with less weighting. Then, the difference between the B signal and the Y signal was calculated, to give a blue color difference signal, called B-Y, or $P_B$, or parallel blue color difference signal. (Technically, it's not pure blue, but it's blue enough for our discussion.) Similarly, R-Y, or $P_R$, was calculated to be the parallel red color difference signal.

An interesting characteristic of the human visual system is that the resolution of our color perception system is lower than the resolution of our brightness perception system. Color television takes advantage of this: The chroma signals can be sent with less detail than the luma signal and still give a very pleasing picture to our eyes. In addition, the amount of resolution varies depending on the color of the image. This fact led to the development of two other color difference signals: I and Q. The I signal is used to model colors where the eye is very sensitive to color differences (in the orange part of the color spectrum), and the Q signal is used to model colors where the eye is less sensitive to color differences (in the purple part of the color spectrum). So, by using the color difference signals and sending them at lower resolution, the amount of extra broadcast spectrum needed to broadcast color television can be greatly reduced.

But, the developers of color television still weren't satisfied. So, they decided to squeeze the color difference signals into the same 6 MHz broadcast channel that they used for the original television signal.

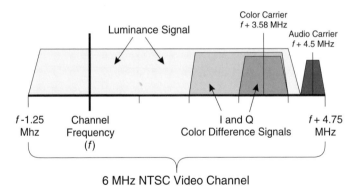

**FIGURE 3-4**   RF Spectrum of NTSC Color Video Signal

They did this by taking the two color difference signals and modulating them onto an RF carrier operating at 3.58 MHz (in North America—other frequencies are used elsewhere), also known as the color carrier. Then, they combined the luminance and the chrominance signals into one spectrum, giving us the composite color television that we use today. Note that the Q signal is sent with less bandwidth than the I signal because the accuracy for the I signal can be less than that for the Q and still give a pleasing image to the eye. Figure 3-4 shows the resulting RF spectrum for a composite video signal that would be broadcast in North America using the National Television System Committee (NTSC) color system.

## TYPES OF VIDEO

Video signals come in many different flavors. This has occurred for three main reasons:

- *Different functional requirements*: Sometimes, video quality needs to be preserved at the highest level, no matter the cost. A good example is the growing use of advanced computer workstations to create special effects for cinematic movies. In other cases, quality can be compromised to make video signals affordable to the masses, as done in broadcast television and the popular VHS home videotape format.

- *Changing limits of technology*: Techniques that are feasible today were not possible even 5 years ago. Incredible advances have been made since the 1920s, when the first experimental television systems were developed. The beauty (or curse, depending on your perspective) is that standards developed 50 years ago are still being used today.
- *Different development locations*: North America and Europe were the primary locations of video technology development in the early days of television. These two regions have long had different video standards, and the differences continue to this day. In the past few decades Japan has also emerged as a major center of video technology development; many of the videotape and camera signal formats in use today were designed completely by or in conjunction with Japanese companies.

All of these factors have combined to create many different types of video signals, each of which has benefits and drawbacks. Numerous companies derive a significant amount of revenue from supplying the video production industry with devices to change video signals from one standard to another. Let's look at a few selected varieties of video.

## Composite Video

A composite video signal contains all of the information required to form a full-motion, full-color image on a television screen. A composite signal is normally sent on a single coaxial cable between devices such as a videotape player and a television set. (Many consumer systems use a yellow connector cover and are labeled "video" on the device.) Composite video signals are also used for normal analog television broadcasts, and in this case they also contain audio information.

Several different composite color video standards are used around the world:

- *NTSC* video is used in North and Central America, Japan, South Korea, Taiwan, most portions of South America, the Caribbean, and several other countries, including the Philippines. Video signals using this standard contain 525 horizontal lines that are each transmitted 29.97 times per second, and use a 3.58 MHz color carrier frequency. NTSC stands for National Television System Committee, which was active in the USA in the early 1940s and again in the early 1950s.

- *PAL* video is used in most countries in Europe, and many in Africa, the Middle East, Asia, and part of South America. Germany, China, India, and the UK all use the PAL system. Video signals using this standard contain 625 horizontal lines that are each transmitted 25 times per second, and use a 4.43 MHz color carrier frequency.[2] PAL stands for Phase Alternating Line, which describes the way the color carrier signal changes with each horizontal line of video.

- *SECAM* video is used in France, countries of the former Soviet Union, North Africa, and a number of other countries. Like PAL, SECAM video signals contain 625 horizontal lines that are each transmitted 25 times per second. The main difference between SECAM and PAL is the method for transmitting the chroma signals, which is much too technical for us to care about here. SECAM stands for the French name of the standard: SEquential Couleur Avec Memoire (which means "sequential color with memory" in English).

- **Note:** It is technically possible to use any color standard with either of the two frame rates (29.97 or 25 frames per second). However, the vast majority of NTSC signals operate at 29.97 frames per second, and the vast majority of PAL and SECAM signals operate at 25 frames per second. For readers who work with the exceptions (and for those who work with SECAM), I hope you can excuse the occasional lapse into using NTSC and PAL as shorthand for the two different frame rates.

Compounding the issues for PAL and SECAM are a variety of broadcast formats, which are given letter designations such as B/G, D, I, and others. These letters have to do with the size of the broadcast channel allocated to each television station and the characteristics of the video and audio modulation. Fortunately, because there are so many different standards, most PAL television sets have been designed to accept a range of different formats.

---

2.  In Brazil, television broadcasts use the 525 line/29.97 frames per second standard, but use the PAL color system. Other exceptions can exist but are relatively rare.

Composite video has been used since the dawn of the television era. Over-the-air broadcasts contain a composite video signal and an audio signal (more on audio later in this chapter). Many consumer grade television sets have composite video inputs, which can be connected to other consumer devices such as VCRs, camcorders, cable TV set top boxes, and game consoles. Those television receivers that don't have these inputs can receive a composite signal once it has been modulated onto a TV channel (normally channel 3 or 4 in the USA) and connected to the television's antenna input connector. As with any video format, composite video has a number of benefits and drawbacks, which are discussed in Table 3-1.

## S-Video

S-video signals are similar to composite video signals, with one crucial difference. In S-video, luma and chroma information are carried on different wires. This is why an S-video cable has four pins: one pair for the chroma signal (I+Q for NTSC, U+V for PAL) and another pair for the luma (Y) (plus an outer shield, for those quibblers in the audience). See Figure 3-5 for an illustration of these connectors.

S-video can be found on a number of consumer video devices, including many recent television receivers, DVD players, digital camcorders, and high-end VCRs, particularly those with S-VHS (Super

**TABLE 3-1**

Advantages and Disadvantages of Composite Video

*Advantages*

- Huge number of display devices available throughout the world
- Low-cost signal sources and recorders, such as VCRs
- All the required video signals are on a single conductor, so cables and switches can be simple and inexpensive.

*Disadvantages*

- The chroma and luma signals can interfere with each other, causing some degradation in the displayed image.
- The wide variety of composite standards drives up complexity for video producers.
- Television displays need sophisticated signal processing devices, called comb filters, to separate the luma and chroma signals in order to produce a high-quality image.

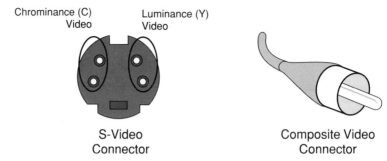

**FIGURE 3-5**   S-Video and Composite Video Connectors

VHS, or Super Video Home System) capability. Other devices that are used for digital video may have S-video output connectors, including digital set top boxes for CATV, digital satellite receivers, and some video interface boards for PCs.

In general, for point-to-point consumer and semi-professional applications, S-video should be used whenever feasible in place of composite video. S-video avoids two steps in the manipulation of the video from a source: first, combining the chrominance and luminance signals in the signal source, and second, separating the chrominance and luminance signals in the display device. Both steps can affect the quality of the composite signal, although the impact may be slight. Table 3-2 shows some of the advantages and disadvantages of S-video.

**TABLE 3-2**
Advantages and Disadvantages of S-Video

*Advantages*

- Many modern consumer devices have S-video inputs and/or outputs.
- Separated chrominance and luminance signals can give better picture quality.

*Disadvantages*

- Cabling and connectors are slightly more complicated than for composite video; video switches require two signal paths for each video signal.
- S-video format is still closely related to composite, so wide variety of video standards (NTSC, PAL, etc.) still need to be accommodated.

## Component Analog Video

Component analog video offers benefits over composite and S-video. Because different color signals are carried on different sets of conductors, processing of the signals is kept to a minimum. The two main flavors of component video are as follows:

- *RGB* component video uses one conductor for each of the three main video component signals: red, green, and blue. Each signal carries a full resolution image, with data for every pixel. (Remember that each pixel in a color television display has three different colored elements, one each of red, green, and blue). To form a white pixel, all three signals are set to maximum intensity. RGB component video requires the least amount of processing inside a display because the video information is compatible with the signals that drive the three different color inputs for the display.
- *YUV* or $YP_BP_R$ (also known as Y R-Y B-Y) component video signals use three signal paths: one for a luminance signal (Y) and one for each of two color difference signals (U and V or $P_B$ and $P_R$). As in composite video, the Y signal contains information from all three color channels (red, green, and blue) and is formed by combining different amounts of each color. The two color difference signals have the advantage of requiring less bandwidth than the Y signal, which is used to advantage in digital video signals, as we will discuss later in this chapter.

Both RGB and YUV/$YP_BP_R$ signals require three or more signal paths, depending on the method chosen for sending the synchronization signals. Three main standards exist:

- *Sync on Green* (or on Y) requires three signal paths. This method uses one of the three signals (typically the Green signal or the Y signal) to carry the horizontal and vertical synchronization information.
- *Separate Composite Sync* uses a fourth signal path to carry the synchronization data, including both the horizontal and the vertical synchronization. Don't confuse the use of the term "composite" here with the composite video signal described previously; in

this case, it simply means a combination of the sync signals, with no picture information at all.

- *Separate Horizontal and Vertical Sync* uses a total of five signal paths: one for each color signal, one for horizontal sync, and one for vertical sync. This system is used by virtually all computer monitors and was part of the original Video Graphics Adapter (VGA) de facto standard.

Table 3-3 shows some of the advantages and disadvantages of component analog video.

## High Definition Video

High definition video (also known as High Definition Television, or HDTV) offers much more detail in video images because it uses many more pixels than standard video. These added pixels allow much larger video displays to be used without the loss of sharpness that can come from simply enlarging a standard definition video signal.

Another feature of HDTV signals is that they utilize a different aspect ratio for the video image. For normal television signals (and many common computer displays, including VGA, SVGA, and XGA, as shown in Table 3-7 later in this chapter), the aspect ratio is 4:3, meaning that the video image is 4 units wide by 3 units high. For most HDTV signals, the aspect ratio is 16:9, which is one-third wider than 4:3. (Don't take the larger numbers to mean that the video display is

**TABLE 3-3**

Advantages and Disadvantages of Component Analog Video

*Advantages*

- Highest possible quality analog video
- Suitable for editing and post-production use in professional applications

*Disadvantages*

- Requires more cables (up to five for separate vertical and horizontal sync), thereby making cables and switches more complex and expensive
- Delay in each one of the signal paths must be identical to all the others—if one cable is longer or shorter than the others, then objects can display ghosts or color fringes on the screen

any larger; it's just easier to write 16:9 instead of 5.33:3.) The wider aspect ratio of HDTV was chosen in part to make it closer to the aspect ratios used in most films. Note that many video devices, such as DVD players, allow 4:3 content to be shown on 16:9 displays and vice versa; in many instances, the portions of the display that are not covered by the video image are simply sent as black sections of the screen.

The benefits of HDTV come at a price, both in terms of money and technology (see Table 3-4). HDTV signals don't really offer any benefit to viewers at small screen sizes, so HDTV displays tend to be large and costly. From a technology standpoint, the large number of pixels requires much more detail in the signal. This in turn causes the bandwidth of the signal to increase, making it impossible to send an HDTV signal in the same amount of spectrum as a standard definition signal without using some kind of compression. (Compression will be discussed further in Chapter 4.)

## Digital Video

Just like many other types of technology, video has leapt into the world of digital signals, and for good reason. Digital video signals can be created, recorded, copied, transported, and displayed with incredible fidelity. Minor noise and distortions that would degrade analog video signals have no impact on a digital signal.

**TABLE 3-4**

Advantages and Disadvantages of High Definition Video

*Advantages*

- Much more image detail, with many more pixels on display
- Some versions are suitable for use in creating cinema feature films.

*Disadvantages*

- Requires HDTV-compatible equipment throughout the production chain, including video cameras, videotape or video disk recorders, broadcast equipment, and video displays
- Uses compression to permit broadcasting within existing television broadcast channels, which can add considerable expense for both broadcaster and end customer

Within the world of professional video production, virtually all new equipment installed today is digital. Video cameras produce digital outputs. Digital tape recorders gather many different types of inputs and record them using high-quality digital techniques. Digital video displays can accept digital signals directly and display them. Video editing suites have also gone all-digital—every scrap of video content is converted into digital form and manipulated using software.

The most common form of digital video goes by a variety of names, including SDI, SMPTE 259M, 270 Mbit, CCIR 601, ITU-R BT.601, and sometimes D1 (although the latter is really a tape format and not a video signal format). This signal, which we will call SDI (Serial Digital Interface) in this book, operates at 270 Mbps and contains a single, component, serial, digital video signal. Amazingly enough, this format was designed to be compatible around the world, so both 625-line (PAL) and 525-line (NTSC) signals can be carried on data streams operating at the same rate. SDI is a component video format, so the signal is carried in three data streams: a luminance signal (Y) and two color difference signals (called $C_B$ and $C_R$ in digital form, but functionally equivalent to the color difference signals $P_B$ and $P_R$ discussed earlier in this chapter).

Each of these data streams is created by sampling one of the component video signals. The luma signal is sampled 13.5 million times per second, and each color difference signal is sampled 6.75 million times per second. As we saw previously, chroma signals can be processed at lower resolution than luma signals and still provide a pleasing image, but they still need to be sampled at fairly high rates for video production purposes. At these rates, for every four luma samples, there are two $C_R$ samples and two $C_B$ samples, which gives this pattern the name 4:2:2. Also, each sample can be either 8 bits or 10 bits according to the standard, but most applications today use 10 bits per sample. At 10 bits per sample, the luma signal generates 135 Mbps (13.5 million samples per second at 10 bits per sample), and the two color difference signals generate 67.5 Mbps each, for a total of 270 Mbps for a video signal. To keep track of the vertical and horizontal synchronization, some of the samples are converted into special codes that are different from any of the permitted video codes. Between the samples that are used for active video (i.e., in those parts of the video signal that would be used for horizontal and vertical blanking in an analog signal) is space for ancillary data; this can be any number of things, including digital audio signals (see the section on digital audio later in this chapter).

There is also a high definition serial digital signal, commonly called SMPTE 292M, or HD-SDI (High Definition Serial Digital Interface) that operates at 1485 Mbps, which is more than five times the data rate of the SDI signal. Just like SDI, HD-SDI uses 10-bit samples and half as many color difference samples of each channel as compared to the number of luminance channels. The reason for the difference in bit rate is the much higher number of pixels in high definition video. Systems using HD-SDI are readily available, as are systems that use compressed HD digital video.

Some other digital video formats are used, such as DV, DVC, DVCAM, and others, and are often based on consumer videotape formats. Many of these formats are compressed signals and used primarily by video camera and videotape recorder manufacturers. Also, a number of editing systems can work with these video formats. A popular mechanism for transporting many of these signals over short distances between devices is IEEE 1394, also known as FireWire. Because of the variety of these signals and because these formats can be converted easily into SDI signals to work with other equipment and for MPEG compression, we won't discuss them in detail in this book.

SDI signals are used in a number of applications. One of the most important is as a standardized input for MPEG compression devices. As we will see in Chapter 4, MPEG compression uses component video (luma and the two color difference signals) as a source format. Many MPEG compression units will accept SDI inputs directly and then process them internally. Other MPEG devices will accept other forms of video, such as analog composite, and internally convert the signals to SDI (or the closely related parallel version of SDI, known as SMPTE 125M) before beginning the compression process. Table 3-5 shows some of the advantages and disadvantages of digital video.

**TABLE 3-5**

Advantages and Disadvantages of Serial Digital Interface (SDI) Video

*Advantages*

- Very robust signal; small variations in signal amplitude or noise, can be ignored by the digital format
- Easy to transport and switch inside a production facility
- A wide variety of equipment is available for use in all applications, including cameras, recorders, switchers, editors, displays, special effects units, and many other types of gear.
- Many converters are available for handling the changes to and from SDI and composite, component, or other analog video formats.
- Related signals, such as digital audio or program-related data, can be embedded into the SDI signal for ease of transport and switching.

*Disadvantages*

- Requires SDI-compatible equipment on both ends of each connection
- Much of the equipment that handles SDI is considered professional level and can be expensive.
- High bit rate signals (270 Mbps for standard definition, 1485 Mbps for high definition) can be difficult and expensive to transport over wide area networks.

## VIDEO FIELDS AND FRAMES

Whenever we need to discuss motion imaging, we will end up talking about frames. Very simply, a frame is a single still image out of the sequence of images that make up a motion image. A field is a portion of a frame; in interlaced video, two fields, each with half the horizontal lines of the total image, form a single frame. We will discuss interlaced video in more detail in one of the following sections.

## Frame Rate

Anyone who has ever looked at the film used in a movie projector knows that the film contains a series of still pictures. Each picture is slightly different from its predecessors, and when the pictures are shown to a viewer in rapid succession, the viewer perceives the image to be moving (hence the familiar term "moving pictures"). The images in a movie camera are captured at the rate of 24 images each second, or 24 fps (frames per second). A movie camera operates by moving unexposed film into position, opening the camera's shutter to allow light from the lens to form an image on the film, closing the shutter, and then advancing the film.

A television camera operates in a similar way. Instead of film, an electronic image sensor is used. Each pixel on the image sensor captures a signal that depends on the intensity of the light that hits it. In a modern digital camera, these signals are read out as a series of digital numbers, which are strung together to create a digital video stream.

Each time a complete image (every pixel on the image sensor) is captured and read out, a complete video frame is said to have occurred. In television, two main frame rates are used: 25 and 29.97 frames per second (fps). It is technically possible to use either frame rate with any color system (NTSC, PAL, or SECAM). However, the vast majority of NTSC video uses 29.97 fps and both PAL and SECAM almost always operate at 25 fps.

## Frame Height

If you want to provoke a debate, ask a photographer, a printer, a videographer, and a computer graphics specialist to define the term "resolution." You'll probably get a different answer from each one. Since we don't want to get into the middle of this argument, we are going to try to avoid using the term "resolution." Instead, we are going to talk about the height of a video frame in lines.

A video frame is made up of a number of horizontal lines of video, stacked vertically up and down the video image. The frame height is just the count of the number of lines in the visible portion of the video signal. An NTSC signal has 525 horizontal lines, of which approximately 40 are not visible. This gives an NTSC signal a frame height of about 485 lines. Note that the value 40 is not fixed; different kinds of equipment will give an active picture frame height that can range from 480 to 486 lines. A PAL or SECAM signal has 625 horizontal lines, of which approximately 50 are not visible, giving a PAL signal a frame height of about 575 lines. Again, the quantity 50 is not fixed, and the visible picture in PAL can range from 574 to 576 lines.

The astute reader now probably wants to know the purpose of these 40 or 50 "unused" lines, and the answer is quite simple. One major function of these lines is to provide synchronization for the video display in the vertical direction (also known as vertical sync). That is, a special vertical sync pattern is inserted into some of these "unused" lines that identifies the first horizontal line of the video signal so that the display can correctly position the image. The vertical sync signal doesn't take up all of these lines, and the remaining lines are used to allow enough time for the beam in a CRT to perform a vertical retrace, or move from the bottom of the display back to the top. We call these 40 or 50 lines the Vertical Blanking Interval (VBI) because they are turned off or "blanked" so that they don't appear on the video display during the retrace interval. The VBI can be used for lots of other interesting stuff, like closed captioning and teletext, which we will discuss later in this chapter.

Let's go back to the topic of resolution for a moment. In video, we define resolution as being the number of lines of alternating black and white that can be seen on the display. A sample pattern for testing vertical image resolution is shown in Figure 3-6A. As a practical matter, the number of lines that can actually be resolved is about 30% less than the number of horizontal scan lines used by the camera. So, a PAL image with 576 visible horizontal lines has a useful vertical

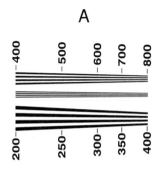
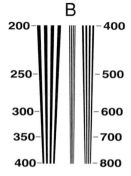

**FIGURE 3-6** Vertical and Horizontal Resolution Test Patterns

resolution of about 400 lines, and an NTSC image with 485 visible horizontal lines has a useful vertical resolution of about 330 lines.

## Horizontal Resolution

Well, if you thought we had fun talking about frame height and vertical resolution, then you will really enjoy our discussion of horizontal resolution because it gets even more complicated. Simply put, horizontal resolution is a count of the number of alternating black and white lines that can be distinguished going across a display horizontally. See Figure 3-6B for an illustration of a test image for horizontal resolution.

Horizontal resolution is measured in terms of Lines per Picture Height (or LPH). This measurement relates the horizontal resolution of an image to the height of the image in lines. Since a standard 4:3 aspect ratio image is 1.33 times as wide as it is high, the number of lines that can be resolved in the horizontal direction must be divided by 1.33 to get the actual resolution in LPH.

All sorts of factors affect the amount of horizontal resolution in an image, and the amount can vary greatly from one technology to another. For example, the digital format (SDI) that is used for video production uses 720 pixels for the active video picture in each horizontal line for both 625-line (PAL) and 525-line (NTSC) systems. This is not the actual resolution—because it is further constrained by the circuits that are used to process the signal. These factors bring the actual horizontal resolution of the digital SDI signal down to about 455 LPH.[3] In comparison, Super-VHS has a horizontal resolution of 300 LPH, and standard VHS has horizontal resolution of about 190 LPH. So, as you can see, there is a great deal of variation in performance of the different technologies.

A number of different frame heights and widths are used in video compression, which we will cover in Chapter 4. They have different

---

3.  Michael Robin, *Television in Transition* (St-Laurent, Quebec: Miranda Technologies, 2001): page 67.

**TABLE 3-6**

Image Sizes Commonly Used in Video Compression[4] (width in pixels × height in lines)

| | |
|---|---|
| 720 × 576 | PAL (625-line) Full Resolution |
| 720 × 480 | NTSC (525-line) Full Resolution |
| 704 × 576 | 4CIF[5] |
| 352 × 576 | PAL (625-line) Half-D1 Resolution |
| 352 × 480 | NTSC (525-line) Half-D1 Resolution |
| 352 × 288 | CIF[6] |
| 176 × 144 | QCIF[7] |

uses that are described in Table 3-6. Note that the horizontal measurements are given in pixels, which, as we shall discuss in Chapter 4, is what matters for most compression systems.

## Computer Image Resolution

The computer industry has adopted a significantly different meaning for the term "resolution." If a computer image is said to have a resolution of 640×480 (standard Video Graphics Adapter, or VGA), it will have an active picture size that is 640 pixels wide by 480 pixels high. Table 3-7 shows the image height and width for a number of popular computer graphics formats.

**TABLE 3-7**

Popular Computer Graphics Image Sizes (width in pixels × height in pixels)

| | |
|---|---|
| 640 × 480 | VGA |
| 800 × 600 | SVGA |
| 1024 × 768 | XGA |
| 1280 × 1024 | SXGA |
| 1600 × 1200 | UXGA |

---

4.   All of these image sizes have a 4:3 aspect ratio, and they are all standard definition and below (i.e., not high definition).

5.   Resolution equal to four times that of CIF (see following footnote).

6.   CIF stands for Common Intermediate Format, often used in both PAL and NTSC videoconferencing systems.

7.   Resolution equal to one Quarter CIF Resolution.

## Progressive and Interlaced Scanning

Now, let's look at yet another facet of video that has caused a great deal of confusion for people starting out in the video business. This is the use of two different methods of horizontal scanning: progressive and interlaced. In progressive scanning, every horizontal line in the image is scanned sequentially from the top of the image to the bottom. In other words, in each frame line 1 is scanned first, followed by line 2, then line 3, and so on. Figure 3-7A illustrates a progressively scanned image.

Interlaced scanning is different. In interlaced scanning, first only the odd-numbered lines of the frame are scanned in order from the top to the bottom of the image. Then, the even-numbered lines are scanned from top to bottom. In other words, in each frame line 1 of the image is scanned first, followed by line 3, then line 5, etc., all the way to the bottom of the image. Then, once these are done, scanning starts over again at the top of the images with line 2, then line 4, line 6, etc. The first set of scan lines is called the Odd Field, and the second set is called the Even Field. So, for a video image that is running at 25 fps, interlaced scanning actually provides 50 fields per second—25 odd ones and 25 even ones. Figure 3-7B illustrates the concept of interlaced scanning.

Progressive scanning is used pretty much universally for computer graphics displays, primarily because it is easier to calculate shapes

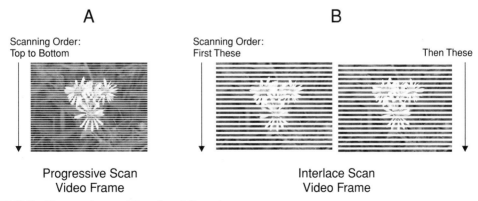

**FIGURE 3-7**  Progressive and Interlaced Scanning

and create moving images with software. However, it has one big drawback for television broadcasters: Progressive scanning requires a lot of bandwidth, since a complete image needs to be sent to the display often enough to prevent the image from flickering on the display. (More on flicker shortly.) This is no problem with the short cable that runs from a computer to a monitor, but it is a huge problem for broadcasters who must fit their television signal into the radio spectrum that they have been given.

To understand why interlaced video is used, you need to understand something about the human visual system and a concept called persistence. Persistence is the eye's natural tendency to retain an image for a short period of time after light hits it. Persistence allows you to enjoy movies and television because the eye and the brain naturally blend a series of rapidly changing still images together to give the illusion of motion.

Persistence lasts only a short time, and if the frame rate of an image is too low, then viewers will perceive that the image is flickering (i.e., small, rapid changes in image brightness). For most people, this limit is around 50 images per second. Movies, which are filmed at 24 fps, get around this problem by projecting each frame of the film on the screen two (or sometimes three) times. Television signals use interlacing to update the screen twice for each frame—first the odd field is displayed (the odd numbered horizontal lines), and then the even field is displayed. Since half of the screen is updated with each field, and the field rate (50 per second for PAL and 59.94 per second for NTSC) is greater than the flicker threshold, the images appear to be free of flicker to most viewers.

So, interlacing helps broadcasters by reducing flicker and by reducing the amount of radio spectrum that the television signal occupies. Unfortunately, these benefits come at a price. An interlaced signal can have visual artifacts, and the signal can be more difficult to create with computer software. Some of the visual artifacts are caused by the delay between the time when the odd field is captured by the video camera and when the even field is captured. If an object is moving horizontally in the image, the two fields will have the edge of the object in two different locations. This causes the object to appear to have a jagged edge, which is particularly noticeable when the image sequence is paused and a single image is displayed (freeze frame).

Interlacing is part and parcel of both PAL and NTSC video, and will likely be with us for quite a while into the future. Even HDTV has both interlaced formats (in the USA, 1080i stands for an interlaced signal with 1080 horizontal lines) and progressive formats (in the USA, 720p stands for a progressively scanned signal with 720 horizontal lines).

## From Movie Film to Video Signal

A great deal of video content has been created using movie film over the years. One of the reasons that audiences can still enjoy television programs like *I Love Lucy* is that the shows were originally filmed, rather than produced directly for television. Lots of other content is created using film, including Hollywood releases, numerous documentaries, and many shows that are destined for syndication and release in multiple countries. About the only kind of video content that can't be shot using film are live shows, because the delay to shoot the film, develop it, and convert it to video would simply take too long. (That's not to say that many live broadcasts aren't also simultaneously filmed; this is a common practice for major sporting events and other high-profile live activities.)

The process of converting film content into video content is called "telecine." This would be a fairly straightforward process, were it not for the fact that the frame rates of film and video are different. Film runs at 24 fps, PAL and SECAM video at 25 fps, and NTSC video runs at 29.97 fps. This problem is very simply solved for 25 fps PAL and SECAM broadcasts: The movie is simply played at a rate of 25 fps. This has the side effect of reducing the time span of a movie by 4%, so a 100-minute movie takes only 96 minutes to broadcast. Note that the playback time of the audio signals also needs to be adjusted so that lip synchronization can be maintained.

For 29.97 fps NTSC broadcasts, the situation is more complicated. Because NTSC runs at a 25% higher frame rate than movies, simply speeding up the film rate won't do (it would be objectionable to viewers). So, an ingenious method called "3:2 pulldown" was created. In 3:2 pulldown, 2½ frames of video are created from every two frames of movie. This is easier to understand when you remember that 2½ frames of interlaced video are five fields. So, 3:2 pulldown operates by converting the first movie frame to three fields of video and the second to two fields of video. Then, the process repeats, with the next movie frame being converted to three video fields, and so on. Figure 3-8 illustrates how this process works.

Readers may have noticed that some kinds of video equipment for consumers include a feature called "inverse telecine" or "reverse 3:2 pulldown." This feature is useful for progressive scan displays, and basically what it does is remove the effects of the 3:2 pulldown process. In other words, this process creates a 24 fps video signal with no interlacing. Then, the line rate is doubled to 48 fps or increased to 72 fps prior to display. Note that this feature is geared for high-end video displays, with progressive scan capability, and (most of the time) component video or digital video inputs.

## TYPES OF AUDIO

Even though we talk a lot about video, everyone in the video business understands that you need to have audio to accompany your

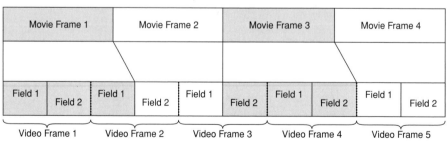

Frame Sequence of a Movie Film

Video Frame Sequence after 3:2 Pulldown

**FIGURE 3-8**   The 3:2 Pulldown Telecine Process

beautiful video images. And, to be sure, there is more than enough material to fill an entire book just on audio alone. However, since it is such an important part of video for business and entertainment purposes, it just wouldn't be right to have a book about video without discussing audio, at least a little.

## Analog Audio

Audio is what humans hear every day. Sound waves travel through air and reach delicate sensors located within the human ear. These sound waves can be created by a variety of sources, including the early morning thump of a garbage can on a sidewalk, the not-so-subtle tones of a co-worker in the next cubicle having an argument, or as the result of an electrical signal driving an audio loudspeaker. For our purposes, the term "analog audio" will mean the electrical signal that can be directly fed to a loudspeaker to produce a sound.

Analog audio signals cover a huge range of applications, ranging from the tiny signals generated by a phonograph (turntable) or a microphone up to the powerful signals needed to drive the loudspeakers at an outdoor concert. Fortunately, industry standards have been established to make it possible to connect different types of devices together, with relatively little pain and suffering. Most modern video equipment is designed to work with these standards, and even use the same style of connectors.

Analog audio outputs can be found on devices such as DVD players, CD players, videotape players, CATV set top boxes, and satellite receivers. Analog audio inputs can be found on stereo receivers, televisions, and audio or videotape recorders. In many cases, connectors will consist of a pair of round jacks, one red and one white (for stereo audio). Most personal computers provide audio outputs, and many provide audio inputs, although they tend to use different connectors than audio and video equipment.

The structure of an analog audio signal is very simple; it is simply an electrical representation of the position of the cone (or diaphragm) of a standard speaker. When the signal goes up, the speaker's cone moves out, and when the signal goes down, it moves back in. High-pitched sounds are created by rapid changes in the signal level that make the speaker cone vibrate rapidly; low-pitched sounds are represented by slower changes in the signal and slower movements of the cone. Sound volume increases with the amplitude of the signal: When the signal changes from a higher high to a lower low, the speaker cone moves over a greater distance, causing more sound pressure, and thus a louder volume, to be created.

Audio engineering has a number of challenges. Here are just a few:

- Sound levels won't sound proper if the source device and the destination device aren't correctly matched in terms of their electrical characteristics. They include balanced and unbalanced signals, impedance levels, and a host of other arcana.
- There are many different ways to set up and calibrate a specific sound level, so material recorded by one organization may need adjustment when it is transferred to another organization. One important parameter is the peak sound level that can be recorded without exceeding the limits of the device; different organizations use different limits.
- Each room, each set of speakers, and each collection of listeners can change the acoustics and the sound patterns for an audience. This is why audio professionals are on hand at many live music, theatre, and lecture events.
- Most important to video people, audio signals do not have their own built-in synchronization mechanism. This contrasts with video, which has lots of embedded vertical and horizontal synchronization information. One of the most difficult challenges of video transport is ensuring that audio and video signals remain in sync so that the lips and the voice of on-screen talent remain properly aligned.

## Digital Audio

Analog audio signals will always be with us, because ultimately in every sound system there has to be some method for creating air vibrations in a listener's ears. However, more and more audio signals are being converted to digital signals, and for good reason. Digital signals have the big advantage of being much more immune to noise than analog signals. For example, a low hum that may represent only 1% of the total signal amplitude will create a matching hum in an analog system, whereas in a digital system the hum can be ignored as long as it is low enough not to cause a digital "0" to be converted in to a digital "1."

Digital audio signals are becoming more common. One of the earliest ways that most folks were exposed to digital audio was through the introduction of the compact disc (CD) for audio. Once consumers saw the benefits, they were persuaded to migrate away from older, analog recording technologies such as phonograph records and pre-recorded audiocassette tapes. Other now-common digital audio devices include digital telephones and mobile telephones, MP3 recorders and players, and a wide variety of digital video devices.

Digital audio signals come in two main forms: compressed and uncompressed. For the time being we are going to discuss uncompressed signals. (We will cover compressed digital audio in Chapter 4.) In particular, we will discuss the Audio Engineering Society/European Broadcasting Union (AES/EBU) digital audio format, which is used throughout the professional video industry.

An AES/EBU digital audio signal is created by taking samples of an analog audio signal. Taking a sample involves measuring the audio signal and converting that measurement into a binary number. If each sample is measured with 16 bits of accuracy, the level can be determined to an accuracy of 1 part in 65,000. If each sample is measured with 24 bits of accuracy, the level can be determined to an accuracy of 1 part in 16 million. Greater accuracy means that less noise is introduced into the audio signal by the analog-to-digital conversion process (also called quantizing noise).

The rate at which the samples in AES/EBU are taken can also vary— from 32,000 times per second to 48,000 times per second. (Some newer professional systems offer sampling at 96,000 times per second, but they aren't in the AES/EBU suite of standards as of this writing.) Higher sampling rates are used to capture the higher pitched (high-frequency) sounds. As a rule of thumb (well supported in mathematical theory), the sampling rate needs to be at least twice the frequency of the highest pitched sound to be captured, and prefer-ably slightly higher. The three main sampling rates in use today are as follows:

- 32,000 samples per second, which is used for FM radio and other broadcast audio applications that have an upper frequency response limit of 15,000 Hz
- 44,100 samples per second, which is used for compact disc (CD) mastering
- 48,000 samples per second, which is used for professional appli-cations, including sound mastering for television and other applications

When you are thinking about digital audio, it is important to remem-ber that the bit rate of the resulting audio stream can be quite large. Since stereo audio is pretty much universally used, two samples are taken at each sampling instant: one for the left audio channel and one for the right. The AES/EBU format specifies that a 32-bit "subframe" is sent for each audio channel for each sample, regardless of the num-ber of bits in the sample (with 24-bit sampling there are 8 bits of over-head in each subframe, for a total of 32 bits). Thus, an AES/EBU signal that is running at 48,000 samples per second will result in a 3.072 Mbps (48,000 × 32 bits per subframe × 2 audio channels for stereo) digital audio signal. As we shall see in the upcoming chapters on video compression, 3 Megabits per second is enough capacity to carry a fairly decent compressed video signal and its associated com-pressed audio signal.

Digital audio signals can also be embedded into digital video signals, such as SDI. This makes life very simple in a video production envi-ronment, particularly in live video applications. Audio is embedded into an SDI stream in the portions of the stream that are reserved for ancillary data. The audio data is specially formatted to comply with the rules of the SDI signal, and then the two signals are combined by replacing some of the bits in the video stream with audio bits. To play the audio, you need to identify the ancillary data fields in the SDI sig-nal and then locate the audio bits. These are then copied out of the video stream and supplied as a digital audio signal. Audio embed-ding and extraction can be done without any degradation of either the audio or the video signal, because all of the processing is done digitally.

## Audio Formats on DVDs

As prices for DVD players fall, and more content becomes available, anyone working with video will, sooner or later, need to work with DVDs (Digital Versatile Disks, although many people think the acronym should be Digital Video Disk). With virtually all new Hollywood releases appearing on DVDs within months of their theatrical release, consumers are moving rapidly to purchase and install DVD players and home theater systems in their residences.

All DVD videodisks using the 525-line/29.97 fps format (the North American standard) must use at least one of two audio coding formats: either linear PCM audio or AC-3 compressed audio. Linear PCM audio is a form of uncompressed audio (described previously), with the following parameters:

- Sampling must be done at 48,000 or 96,000 samples per second.
- Sample resolution can be 16, 20, or 24 bits.
- A maximum of 8 audio channels is allowed (normal stereo occupies two audio channels).
- A maximum total bit rate of 6.144 Mbit/sec for an audio stream (multiple audio streams can be used, but the total cannot exceed the maximum DVD play out rate of 9.8 Mbit/sec).

Since a DVD is limited to 9.8 Mbit/sec total, and we generally want to have some video on a DVD, most disks use the AC-3 compressed audio format. This format, which has the trademarked name Dolby Digital®, is widely used. This format can contain 5.1 audio tracks, allocated as follows:

- Left and Right channels (similar to traditional stereo speakers)
- Center channel (speaker typically located with the video display)
- Left and Right Surround channels (speakers meant to be located alongside or behind the viewer)

- Low Frequency Effects channel, also called the ".1" channel, because it contains only a small fraction of the total sound spectrum. The LFE channel is typically fed into a subwoofer, which can be located anywhere in the viewing area because the low-pitched sounds it produces can usually be heard (and felt) throughout the viewing area.

We'll talk about how AC-3 compression works in Chapter 4.

## OTHER VIDEO SERVICES

In addition to standard audio and video content, television broadcasters and governments have been busy adding features and functions to television programming for a variety of purposes. In the following sections, we'll look at some of these other services that have been added to video broadcasts over the past couple of decades, including Secondary Audio Program (SAP), teletext, closed captioning, and the V-chip.

## SAP Audio

The Secondary Audio Program (SAP) channel was originally created in the USA to allow broadcasts to have a second language included with them. Recent changes, including a mandate by the Federal Communications Commission (FCC), have started moving the SAP channel toward being used for video description. Either way, SAP is an important part of video broadcasting standards.

Video description is a process whereby a trained speaker adds comments to a video program to assist visually impaired people in understanding the content of a video program. Comments could include descriptions of scenes, actions, actor's gestures or facial expressions, or any other material that would assist a viewer in understanding what is happening on the video screen. These comments are inserted during natural pauses in the audio content of the program. The FCC has mandated that the top local affiliates for the major broadcast networks provide at least 50 hours of programming with video description each calendar quarter, for either prime-time or children's programming. This video description will be combined with the normal audio of the program and transmitted using the SAP channel.

The technology for SAP audio is closely related to the technology used for normal audio. The SAP audio signal is modulated onto the same carrier signal that is used for normal monaural and stereo audio signals, albeit at a different frequency offset. This composite signal, containing mono, stereo, and SAP signals is combined with the video signal and then broadcast. These signals are carefully designed not to interfere with the accompanying video signals nor with the video signals of adjacent channels.

Inside the production or broadcast facility, SAP signals would be handled the same as any other audio signal, as either a baseband analog or digital signal. As a rule, the video descriptions would be created only after the final edit of the program has been made so that the exact timing for inserting the comments could be made with the finished video product. For storage and transmission, the SAP video descriptions would simply be treated as a third audio channel. When video compression is needed, SAP audio would simply be included as another audio channel and multiplexed into the overall video stream for storage, playback, or distribution.

## Teletext

Teletext was developed in the 1980s a mechanism to broadcast text information on a variety of subjects to mass audiences. This information could be put to a variety of uses, such as news, weather, local announcements, stock prices, sports scores, etc. Typically, this information would be displayed across the entire video window, with some bold colors and crude graphics thrown in for visual appeal. This information could be transmitted by standard television broadcasts and CATV systems by using data embedded in the VBI of any standard video program.

Teletext might not ever have come into existence had the World Wide Web been in existence. The concept was the same—allow customers to have timely access to information they wanted without requiring them to wade through a news program. Unfortunately, the limited speed of the information, coupled with the limited interactivity, prevented the service from catching on with audiences. Today, most of the bold experiments with teletext have been shut down, due in no small part to the costs of creating content for a medium with a small audience.

## Closed Captioning

Closed captioning provides a stream of text that can be shown on a display to assist viewers in understanding what is being said on-screen. Originally developed to help people with hearing impairments, closed captioning is also used frequently in loud environments, including noisy pubs and lounges. A great deal of broadcast video content contains closed captioning, due in part to governmental requirements.

Text for the captions is actually carried as a data stream in the VBI (Vertical Blanking Interval; see the description earlier) portion of the video signal. Text is represented as a string of binary bits, with logical ones and zeroes being carried as alternating high and low luminance signals. This data is carried in line 21 of the VBI, and, if you could see it on your video display, it would look like one horizontal line with a constantly changing pattern of white and black segments. Special decoder chips in the television tuner receive this data and generate characters that cover a small portion of the video display. This function is controlled by the viewer, who can select whether or not the captions are to be displayed. The viewer can also choose from among four different captions and four different text fields for display, although most programs contain data only in closed caption field 1.

Be careful not to confuse closed captioning with the text that crawls across the bottom of some broadcast news and finance programs. This text is inserted into the actual video image by the broadcaster and cannot be turned on or off by the viewer.

Also be careful not to confuse closed captioning with subtitles that are featured on some DVDs. Subtitles are designed for viewers with normal hearing who are watching a movie with dialog in a different language. As such, they do not include hints about the sounds in the content that could normally be heard through the sound track. For example, a closed caption might include notes on sound effects ("phone ringing," "footsteps") that would not be needed for subtitles. Note that the subtitle information in a DVD is not included in line 21 of the video; it is separately stored as user data on the DVD.

## Other VBI Services

Line 21 can also be used for other data services, including V-chip information in North America. V-chip data is required by the US and Canadian governments, and it provides ratings that indicate the intended audience for broadcast programming. In the USA, ratings range from TV-Y for content that is targeted for children through TV-MA for content that is intended to be viewed only by adults and may not be suitable for children under the age of 17. All televisions with screens exceeding 13 inches measured diagonally sold since mid-2000 in the USA must include the ability to decode the V-chip signal. These chips can also selectively block programs based on their rating. Line 21 also has a date feature that will automatically set the time and date on home customers' videocassette recorders (VCRs).

Other services can use the VBI as well:

- For example, some electronic program guide information is sent to televisions via data carried in the VBI.
- A popular system for programming home VCRs also broadcasts program schedule data in the VBI.
- Studio production equipment (video recorders, cameras, etc.) often use the VBI for carrying a time code that is used to precisely register when each frame of video is shot. This signal is known as the Vertical Interval Time Code, or VITC.
- Signals that are used for system testing and video quality assurance can also be inserted into the VBI.

## VBI Data and Compression

Many popular compression technologies, including MPEG, H.263, and others, do not process signals contained in the VBI unless specifically configured to do so. The reason is that most of the VBI is blank most of the time, and compressing a signal that doesn't contain any useful information would be a waste of processing power and bandwidth. In order to compress and transport VBI data, users typically need to configure their compression equipment to specify the line numbers and types of data that are being used.

## VIDEO AND AUDIO SWITCHING

Video signals are constantly being switched. Large broadcast production studios have video and audio switches that can accommodate hundreds or even thousands of inputs and outputs. Everyday broadcast and cable television is constantly being switched to perform functions such as changing from, say, a satellite feed to a tape player, or to insert a commercial for a local advertiser into a national program. Home and desktop viewers switch from video stream to stream as they "channel surf" from program to program. Because switching is so common, and because IP technology can offer some radically different switching architectures, we are going to look at video switching in a little more detail in the following sections.

A variety of technologies can be used for video switching:

- Baseband video and audio switches are used to connect analog video and audio signals.
- Digital switches handle digital video and digital audio signals.
- IP switches and routers can be used to handle video and audio signals that have been converted into Internet Protocol signals.

A note on terminology: Sometimes, baseband and digital video/ audio switches are called video/audio routers. In this context, the two words "switch" and "router" have the same meaning. In IP hardware, these two terms have different meanings (even though they have some overlapping functions). Switches are lower cost devices that perform a limited set of functions, primarily for local area networks. Routers are more software intensive, can include wide area network connections, and are programmed to do more sophisticated processing of IP packets. We'll discuss these functions more in later chapters.

## Baseband Switches

Baseband video is video in its raw, natural format. Most consumer videotape recorders record and play back using baseband video and audio. Countless video games have been sold that send baseband audio and video signals to televisions for display. Each baseband video signal requires its own cable, as does each baseband audio. (That's why VCRs and video games use three cables for output: one for video, one for left audio, and one for right audio.) Baseband switches need to handle each of these signals separately so that video outputs always get sent to video inputs, right audio outputs get sent to right audio inputs, etc. The industry term for a device that switches multiple signals at the same time is a "multi-layer" switch; each signal counts as a layer. For example, a switch that handles baseband video plus left and right audio would be a three-layer switch.

A small, three-layer baseband switch with 6 video ports and 12 audio ports could easily be found at a consumer electronics store. Larger switches, or those with more ports, are more commonly found at professional audio/video dealers. Very large switches, with 100 or more video ports and 5 layers of audio, would normally be specially ordered from a switch manufacturer. It is not unusual for a large broadcaster to have a 512-port, 5-layer switch that would connect an array of tape machines, satellite receivers, control room displays, and other video sources and destinations. Other, smaller switches might be installed at other locations around the broadcaster's facility to be used for other applications.

One drawback to baseband switches is the number of internal connections goes up exponentially as the number of ports goes up. A 256-port switch has four times as many internal connections points as a 128-port switch. As the number of ports goes up, the physical size of the switch also goes up. It is not unusual for large switches to occupy multiple equipment racks.

## Digital Switches

Digital switches operate on digital signals, such as SDI and HD-SDI. These signals can be routed using a single connection per signal, because they operate in a serial format.[8] Some of these switches can route both SD and HD signals, so it is up to the user to make sure that the signal types don't get mixed. As with baseband switches, digital switches can grow quite large—1000-port switches are available on the market.

Digital audio signals can be handled in two different ways in a digital switching architecture. One method is to use separate layers for the audio signals, similar to what is done on baseband systems. Another method is to embed the audio signals into digital video signals. Let's look at the benefits of each.

When audio signals are switched separately from video signals, a greater amount of switching equipment is required, since the number of signals increases. Since digital audio is almost always a stereo signal, it is normal to have two digital audio signals for each video, providing the same four audio channels as a baseband router. By not using embedding, the system provides more flexibility, because the audio signals can be routed to a different destination than the video signals. This method also saves the expense of providing audio embedding and extraction equipment for each signal.

When audio signals are embedded in video signals, only a one-layer switch is required, which can reduce both the cost and the size of the switch. Also, because the signals are tied together, the chance of mistakenly routing the video and audio signals to different destinations is greatly reduced. On the downside, it is necessary to embed all of the audio signals into the digital video signals. This can be done either using stand-alone embedding devices, or through the use of products such as tape decks that support embedded audio.

---

8.  Although the digital video standards include parallel interfaces, they are not normally used for switching, as the number of connections is too great (25 pins for standard definition, 93 pins for high definition).

## IP Switching

A new concept is appearing on the horizon for live video production environments: the use of an IP network for switching video and audio signals. In this type of a system, each digital video or audio signal is converted into a stream of IP packets and sent onto a local area network. Switching is performed using standard IP networking equipment. At each destination device, the incoming stream of IP packets needs to be processed to recover the video and audio signals. Generally, the receiving devices need to buffer and process the incoming signal to make sure that all of the video timing parameters conform to the proper specifications.

The spread of IP technology into the broadcast video space has been subtle but persistent. The first applications were for video file storage and retrieval, particularly for supporting digital video editing stations. From there, it was a small step to supporting live ingest, which is the process of taking live video content into the digital domain for storage in files on hard disks. Then, live-to-air output became feasible. As we will discuss in Chapter 13 about IPTV, home delivery of live video streams using IP technology is being done around the globe. This whole process has been driven in part by the continuing spread of high-performance computer workstations that are able to handle SDI and other video streams in real time. It is actually simpler to configure these workstations with a high-bandwidth networking card (such as Gigabit Ethernet) than it is to equip each station with a video and audio input and output cards.

One big advantage of using IP switching technology is that it can combine the functions of a number of other systems. Many different types of signals can be carried over IP, including digital video, digital audio, meta-data (data describing the video and audio signals), video files, system control data, intercom signals, and pretty much any other kind of signal used in a video production facility. When all of these functions are placed onto a single network, connections can be consolidated, network management can be simplified, and flexibility can be increased. Another advantage is the easy connection to wide area networks, many of which support IP traffic.

Of course, there are some downsides to the use of an IP network in place of more traditional video and audio switching systems. The main issue is the significant difference in timing between packet-based and circuit-based systems. In circuit-based systems, data is sent in a continuous flow, with a steady bit rate. Most video standards, including those for SDI and HD-SDI, are written around circuit-based signals and assume a constant bit rate and an unvarying system clock. In contrast, IP networks require all signals to be broken into packets, which are then sent over the network in a "best efforts" transport mode. At congestion points in the network, packets can become delayed as they wait for other packets to move through. This can cause the packets to arrive at their destinations with drastically different timing from the way they entered the network. This forces the destination devices to try to reconstruct the timing of the original signals, which can be a tricky process.

Another downside of IP-based switching systems is the fact that they rely on software-based processors to make the connections from one device to another. These devices (known as IP routers, not to be confused with video routers) often have lower overall reliability than the simpler baseband and digital switches. Plus, being software controlled, IP devices sometimes need to be taken off-line for software upgrades, etc. On the plus side, many of these devices have 1:1 redundancy, which allows them to keep operating in the event that a single hardware device fails. IP router manufacturers have made great progress in improving the reliability of their equipment, so this issue will become less significant as time passes.

One more downside is the relative lack (as of this writing) of traditional video production devices (e.g., cameras, tape decks, displays, etc.) that can use IP interfaces for video and audio signals. (**Note:** Many devices are equipped with IP connections, but they are mainly used for device status monitoring and control.) Adapters are available, but it can be an expensive nuisance to install them on a large collection of traditional equipment.

Overall, the trends are in place, and progress will be made toward more and more transport of production video over IP networks. Much of the work that is done in preparing video and audio content for broadcast will end up being done on workstations that are interconnected only with IP services. In the long run, as systems become even more reliable, it is possible that all video switching will move into the IP domain. We certainly aren't there today, but several forces are moving us in that direction.

## REVIEW AND CHECKLIST UPDATE

In this chapter, we looked at video and related signals, such as audio. Just like the history of television, we started out with a discussion of analog, composite, black-and-white television. We discussed color TV and the variety of different standards around the world. We also looked at different video signal types, including composite, S-video, component, SDI, and HD-SDI video. We covered the concepts of video fields, frames, and interlacing. Next, we spent some time defining a variety of different audio signals, including analog, digital, and multi-channel sound schemes. Then, we examined some of the signals that are carried in the Vertical Blanking Interval (VBI). Finally, we looked at baseband and digital switching technology and saw one way in which IP technology can be used in a video production environment.

### Chapter 3 Checklist Update

❏ Determine the type of video signal that will be used: NTSC, PAL or SECAM; composite, S-video, component, SDI or HD.
❏ Determine the audio signal type: analog, digital stereo, digital multi-channel.
❏ Make sure that video and audio sources and destinations are configured for the correct signal types and that appropriate cables are used.
❏ If 270 Mbps SDI signals are used, check to see if the signals are 625/50 (PAL) or 525/60 (NTSC), since they are not compatible, even at the SDI level.
❏ If SDI or HD-SDI signals are used, determine whether audio signals will be embedded.
❏ Find out about any required or optional services that are being carried in the VBI, particularly closed captioning, V-chip, or other government mandates.

❑ If compression equipment is to be used, make sure that any required VBI signals are processed.

❑ Make sure that any video or audio switches include enough conductors to handle all the required signals, such as multiple channels of audio.

# 4

# VIDEO AND AUDIO COMPRESSION

When video signals are transported over an IP network, they are most often compressed. In this context, compression means to reduce the number of bits that are required to represent the video image. Video technology users are free to choose whether or not to use compression for their video signals. However, it is important to understand that the choice of a compression method can sometimes mean the difference between success and failure of a video networking project.

Many communication systems that have become commonplace in the past few years depend on compression technology. For example, digital mobile telephones use compression to increase the number of users who can be served in a given area (by using less radio bandwidth per user) and to increase the amount of time that a mobile handset can be used between battery charges. Digital cameras use data compression to fit more pictures into a fixed amount of storage. MP3 players use compression to take files from audio CDs and make them small enough to fit into the memory of a portable player. Compression allows a 2-hour movie to fit onto a 4-inch DVD in place of a 12-inch video Laserdisc or an 812-foot (248-m) long VHS tape. Satellite television uses compression to place multiple video channels into the space formerly occupied by a single analog video channel, allowing hundreds of video channels to be distributed economically to viewers. An understanding of video and audio compression is essential to understanding and using modern video transport systems, including video over IP networks.

In this chapter we will begin by examining the reasons why compression is used and look at some of the factors that determine what form of compression is suitable for an application. Then, we will examine MPEG video compression, since it is one of the most popular technologies used for video and audio compression. After that, we'll discuss some of the other compression systems that are available for use with video and audio signals. Finally, we'll conclude with a look at some of the applications of video compression and discuss the licenses that are needed to use some forms of compression technology.

## COMPRESSION OVERVIEW

Compression technology is a continuing field of research. As better mechanisms are developed, more information can be carried in fewer and fewer bits. Plus, as processing power increases, these techniques can be implemented on ever faster, ever cheaper processors. So, compression is constantly being used in more and more applications. In this section, we'll look at the reasons for using compression, and the benefits and drawbacks of using it.

Figure 4-1 shows a simplified block diagram of a compression system. The input can either be a computer file, such as a document, an image, and/or a video/audio recording. Or, the input can be a continuous stream of data, such as a digital video or audio signal. Either way, this information is fed into the compression engine. The output of the compression engine is a second data file or data stream that is smaller (i.e., contains fewer bits) than the input file or stream. This output can be stored, or it can be transmitted over a network. Before the data file can be used, it must be restored to its original size, using a decompression engine. Note that a compression engine is often

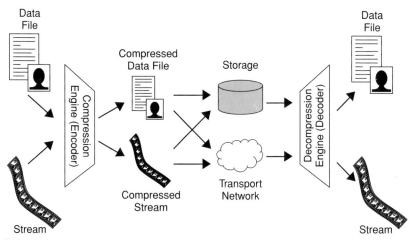

**FIGURE 4-1** Simplified Compression Block Diagram

implemented in a device commonly called an encoder, and the device housing the decompression engine is commonly called a decoder.

The goal of compression is to reduce the size of the incoming data file without removing useful information. In most real-world data files, some data patterns will repeat. For example, consider the data file that includes just the following sentence: "The job of compression is to remove redundant or unnecessary information." In most standard computer files, each character in this sentence would be represented by an 8-bit code, called ASCII. This code includes all of the uppercase and lowercase letters, the numbers 0 through 9, and special characters such as spaces and punctuation. There are a total of 73 characters including spaces and punctuation in the sample data file, which would occupy 584 bits using ASCII.

To make a compressed version of this sentence file, we need to analyze the data in the file. Figure 4-2 shows the result of this analysis.

The first two columns list all of the characters in the sample sentence and show the count for each character. Note that space is the most common character, with 10 occurrences. There are 9 occurrences of "o," 7 of both "e" and "n," and so on down to the final period that has

Sample Sentence Data File:
"The job of compression is to remove redundant or unnecessary information."

Standard ASCII

| Char. | Count |
|-------|-------|
| Space | 10 |
| o | 9 |
| e | 7 |
| n | 7 |
| r | 6 |
| s | 5 |
| l | 4 |
| a | 3 |
| m | 3 |
| t | 3 |
| f | 2 |
| c | 2 |
| d | 2 |
| u | 2 |
| T | 1 |
| h | 1 |
| j | 1 |
| b | 1 |
| p | 1 |
| v | 1 |
| y | 1 |
| . | 1 |

Fixed Length Code

| Char. | 5-bit |
|-------|-------|
| Space | 00000 |
| o | 00001 |
| e | 00010 |
| n | 00011 |
| r | 00100 |
| s | 00101 |
| l | 00110 |
| a | 00111 |
| m | 01000 |
| t | 01001 |
| f | 01010 |
| c | 01011 |
| d | 01100 |
| u | 01101 |
| T | 01110 |
| h | 01111 |
| j | 10000 |
| b | 10001 |
| p | 10010 |
| v | 10011 |
| y | 10100 |
| . | 10101 |

Variable Length Code

| Char. | 3/7-bit |
|-------|---------|
| Space | 000 |
| o | 001 |
| e | 010 |
| n | 011 |
| r | 100 |
| s | 101 |
| l | 110 |
| a | 1110000 |
| m | 1110001 |
| t | 1110010 |
| f | 1110011 |
| c | 1110100 |
| d | 1110101 |
| u | 1110110 |
| T | 1110111 |
| h | 1111000 |
| j | 1111001 |
| b | 1111010 |
| p | 1111011 |
| v | 1111100 |
| y | 1111101 |
| . | 1111110 |

73 characters at 8 bits per character (ASCII) gives a total file size of 584 bits

73 characters at 5 bits per character gives a total file size of 365 bits

48 characters at 3 bits per character and 25 characters at 7 bits per character give a total file size of 323 bits

**FIGURE 4-2**   Data Compression Analysis for Sample Sentence Data File

one occurrence. Also note that capital "T" is counted separately from lowercase "t."

Since there are only 22 different characters in this sample sentence, we can easily encode this data using 5 bits, which would allow up to 32 different combinations. The results of this are shown in the middle two columns of Figure 4-2. By doing this, we can compress the file from 584 bits down to 365 bits, which is a 37% reduction.

Can we do even better? Yes, by using variable length coding (VLC). In VLC, we use shorter bit patterns for more common characters and longer bit patterns for less common characters (readers who are familiar with Morse code will recognize this concept). Since we have 22 unique characters, we can use a 3-bit code (with 8 total combinations) to represent the most common characters. We'll save one of the combinations (111) to indicate a longer code is needed; we'll form those by adding another 4 bits to yield another 16 combinations. The results of this are shown in the right two columns of Figure 4-2. The 7 most common characters (space through "l") are each encoded with 3 bits. The less common characters are coded with 7 bits each—3 bits of "111" and then 15 other combinations. There are a total of 48 occurrences of the most common characters (10 space, 9 "o," 7 "e," etc.) and 25 occurrences of the less common characters (3 "a," 3 "m," etc.). This will result in a compressed file that is $(48 \times 3) + (25 \times 7) = 144 + 175 = 319$ bits, which is a reduction of 45% from the original file. (Plus, this reduction is lossless; see the discussion in the following section.) An even more efficient VLC scheme, called Huffman coding, would result in this file being reduced to less than half of its original size; this is why Huffman coding is used in MPEG.

In many real-world signals, there is a large amount of redundancy and unused bandwidth. Consider the audio signals resulting from a normal conversation. If both parties are each talking half of the time, then the signal from each party's mouthpiece will be meaningful only half of the time; the other half of the time the signal is carrying silence while that party is listening. Similarly, in a video image, many times a good portion of the image is identical to the image immediately preceding it, or immediately following it, or both. As we shall see, a compression engine can use this redundancy to greatly reduce the amount of data that needs to be stored or transmitted across a network.

## Lossy and Lossless Compression

Compression techniques can be broken into two broad categories: lossy and lossless. Lossless compression is used when it is important to preserve every bit of the original material. Lossy compression is used when it is important to maintain the meaning of a signal, but not every bit. Most of the commonly used video and audio compression systems are lossy.

Lossless compression does not remove any information from the source data. This is important in some applications, such as compressing a computer program to make it easier to download. If even one bit of the original is lost, then the program will probably not be usable. The lossless compression engine is designed to remove the redundancy in the source signal, but to do so in a manner that the decompression engine can completely re-create the original signal.

The biggest drawback to lossless compression is that it is not guaranteed to produce an output that is significantly smaller than the input. In fact, it is entirely possible to take a file and pass it through a lossless compression engine and end up saving only a small percentage of the original file size. (This author has experienced this very situation on a number of occasions.) This is not any fault of the compression engine; this simply means that the source file had very little redundancy that could be removed.

Let's look at how lossy compression could be applied to the sample sentence data file used previously in Figure 4-2. We could, for example, replace the word "remove" with the word "remov" and most folks would still be able to understand the sentence. Similarly, if we replaced the word "information" with the word "info," then more savings could be achieved. Some folks wouldn't even notice the difference if we substituted "unecesary" for the word "unnecessary." By making these three simple changes, we have removed 10 characters from the original file and "compressed" it by 13%. Since this form of compression would normally drive spell-checking software crazy, lossy compression is not typically used with text. However, it is a powerful tool for video and audio encoding.

For video and audio compression, lossy compression is normally used. In this situation, it is not possible to re-create a bit-for-bit copy of the original file once it has been compressed. Instead, the image (or sound) file that is produced by the decompression engine is meant to be similar in most key aspects to the source file. As the file becomes more heavily compressed, the amount of distortion increases, and more and more fine detail from the source is lost, but this is often deemed to be an acceptable trade-off. Figure 4-3F shows the result of excessive compression, which includes loss of detail and loss of the finer gradations in image brightness.

Analog Impairments ◀ | ▶ Digital Impairments

(A) Original Image

(D) With Macroblocking

(B) With Random Noise

(E) With Lost Data

(C) With Ghosting

(F) Excessive Compression

**FIGURE 4-3** Typical Image Impairments

## Perceptual Coding and Compression

Perceptual coding means taking advantage of the limitation of the human senses to make the perception of an image or a sound similar (or identical) to another. For example, in human hearing a loud sound at one pitch will hide (or "mask") any quieter sounds at nearby pitches. As we discussed in Chapter 3, the human vision system is better able to resolve differences in brightness than in color; this factor is one perceptual aspect that is exploited in modern video compression systems.

Design of a perceptual compression engine requires an understanding of human vision (or hearing) systems. This is not a cut-and-dried process; work is constantly under way to design algorithms that can create more pleasing results with fewer and fewer bits. To test these designs, it is necessary to have humans evaluate the results: If two designs create the same amount of image compression, and one appears better than the other to the evaluators, then that one is determined to be the better design. MPEG compression, both video and audio, relies on lossy, perceptual coding and lots of human perceptual testing.

## Benefits and Drawbacks of Compression

Compression provides a number of benefits and drawbacks for video signals. Table 4-1 provides a list of some of the key factors that can influence this decision.

## MPEG COMPRESSION TECHNOLOGIES

The Moving Pictures Experts Group has developed some of the most common compression systems for video around the world and given these standards the common name of MPEG. Not only did this group develop video compression standards including MPEG–1, MPEG–2, and MPEG–4, but it also developed audio compression standards, which we will discuss later in this chapter. This group continues to meet and to set new standards (which we won't discuss here), including work on MPEG–7 (a standardized means for describing audio

## TABLE 4-1

Benefits and Drawbacks of Compression

*Benefits*

- A compressed file will occupy less space on a disk drive or other storage medium than an equivalent uncompressed file. This enables users either to put more information in a given space or to use less space for a given file.
- Compressed streams can be transmitted over lower bit rate networks than uncompressed streams. This can often mean the difference between getting the stream to a user or not. For example, many remote company offices are connected by means of a data circuit operating in the range of 1.5 to 2 Mbps. Unless a digital video stream is substantially compressed, it will not fit into this circuit.
- More compressed streams can fit into a given bandwidth than uncompressed streams. This is particularly true for networks that have a fixed upper limit on bandwidth. For example, satellite transponders typically cannot exceed a fixed amount of bandwidth. As compression technology has advanced, more and more signals can be squeezed into the same amount of bandwidth.
- Lower capacity (and therefore less expensive) network connections can be used to send or receive compressed video content. Additionally, compression can lower storage costs by allowing more content to fit into a smaller space.
- More users can be simultaneously sent compressed streams than uncompressed streams. This is particularly true of servers that are used for Video-on-Demand services. Many of these devices have a limit on the amount of bandwidth that they can send at any given time; since each compressed stream occupies less bandwidth, more streams can be sent.
- A compressed signal can be sent faster than real time in a network that is configured for uncompressed signals. For example, networks that are configured to carry a 270 Mbps uncompressed serial digital video stream (see Chapter 3) are widely used in the video industry. If you were to take one of these signals and compress it to one quarter of its original bandwidth, it would be possible to transmit the entire signal over the network in one quarter the time.

*Drawbacks*

- Since most compression engines used for video and audio are lossy, the overall quality of compressed signals will be lower than the original uncompressed signal. Even though the compression engine has been designed to give a viewer the perception that nothing has been lost in compression, the fact remains that some information has been discarded in the compression process. While these losses are intended to be unnoticeable to a human viewer, the changes can be measured with the right equipment.
- Compression can introduce delay into a video or audio signal, at both the compression and decompression stages. This occurs because most video (and many audio) compression systems operate by looking at the differences between adjacent portions of the input signal, such as the changes from one frame to the next in a video signal. Since video frames occur at a rate of one every 33 milliseconds (for NTSC) or 40 milliseconds for (PAL), the incoming signal must be delayed when two or more frames are stored in memory while the differences are being calculated and the compressed video stream is generated.
- Compressed signals are more difficult to edit in their compressed form. In order for editing to take place, the signals typically need to be decompressed. This is particularly true for compression engines that have some video frames that rely on the data contained in adjacent frames (such as P frames and B frames in MPEG, discussed later in this chapter).

**TABLE 4-1** (*Continued*)

- Compression can be difficult on signals that have a lot of noise in them, such as static or other interference. When there is a lot of noise in a video signal (such as in the image in Figure 4-3B) that is being fed into a compression engine, the compression system has difficulty in identifying redundant information between adjacent video frames. Since most compression systems (including MPEG) depend on identifying and removing redundant information, noise can make this task more difficult (or even impossible) to accomplish. The result can be very disappointing, particularly when the signal is highly compressed.
- As a general rule, compression systems should not be concatenated; that is, signals should not be fed out of one compression/decompression system into another. Doing so will degrade the signal, because the losses that are introduced by the first compression will appear to be noise to the second compression (making the signal difficult to compress). Even if both compression systems use the same technology (i.e., MPEG–2), linking one system to another should be avoided whenever possible.
- Video compression requires many calculations to be done on the incoming digital video signal. If these calculations need to be done in real time (hard or soft), the burden on a processor can be very heavy, and not practical with many common desktop processors. Even decoding compressed video streams can severely tax general-purpose desktop machines. Special hardware accelerators are commonly used to provide the necessary computing power for video compression.
- Both the compression and the decompression engines for a given signal need to match in order for the overall system to work properly. The necessary data can be transmitted along with the compressed signal, but, failing this, care needs to be taken to match all of the key parameters. Here are some of the key parameters that need to be compatible between the encoding and the decoding engines:
  - Exact frame rate (e.g., 30 fps, 29.97, 25, etc.)
  - Interlaced or progressive scanning
  - Vertical image size (number of lines of resolution)
  - Horizontal image size (number of pixels in each horizontal line)

and visual content) and MPEG–21 (standards for describing content ownership and rights management).

MPEG standards have enabled a number of advanced video services. For example, MPEG–based DVDs (Digital Versatile Disks a.k.a. Digital Video Disks) are rapidly replacing the videotape as the preferred medium for viewing Hollywood movies in the home. Digital television, including digital satellite television and digital cable television, is based on the MPEG video compression standards. High definition (HD) television also uses MPEG technology. Also, much of the content for streaming media on the Internet is compressed using MPEG or closely related technologies.

Having an appreciation for how MPEG coding works can help users understand the trade-offs that make video compression work. Also, because there are so many different flavors of MPEG, it is important for users to know which ones are suitable for their applications. Finally, because MPEG compression engines can be adjusted in a variety of different ways, knowing what these terms mean can help users understand how to set up their equipment to best take advantage of the constraints of their applications.

In this section we will look at some of the basic technology that makes up the MPEG standards. Then we'll look at some of the common terminology that is used throughout MPEG video standards. We'll then look at what makes up the different compression standards, including the different profiles and levels. Finally, we'll summarize with a comparison of different MPEG technologies.

Appendix A provides a discussion of one of the key technologies used in video compression, particularly in MPEG. The explanation of this technology, called Discrete Cosine Transform (DCT), has been included for readers who, like the author, are interested in understanding the mechanisms behind some of the key advances in modern compression. For those readers who are not so inclined, this appendix can be skipped over with little loss of understanding of the other essential parts of the MPEG story. But for those who are interested, please read Appendix A.

## 4:2:0 and 4:2:2

When used in MPEG, the number sequences 4:2:0 and 4:2:2 have special meaning; they represent the relative resolution of the luma and the two chroma signals. Purchasers of MPEG compression devices will see both types of systems available. Generally, 4:2:0 devices are lower cost and will operate better on low-bandwidth networks. Also note that DVDs are encoded with 4:2:0 color resolution. Devices using 4:2:2 are generally preferred for higher quality contribution networks, because they are believed to represent image colors more accurately, at a cost of 33% more data for the video stream. Because 4:2:2 signals transmit more information for each picture, they do not perform as well on bandwidths below about 3–4 Mbps. Furthermore, 4:2:2 compression will show a benefit only if the source signal is very high quality—such as a signal coming from a professional quality video camera. So, the bottom line here is that 4:2:2 devices can provide better picture quality, provided the network bandwidths are relatively high, and the added expense of the equipment is justified by the application.

Let's look at what these two labels mean when we are talking about MPEG compression. Building on our discussion in Chapter 3, remember that chroma data can be sent at half the resolution of luma data. This applies to MPEG as well as uncompressed video signals. MPEG groups the pixels in each input image into a whole series of blocks, called macroblocks. Each macroblock in MPEG is 16 pixels wide and 16 pixels high (for a total of 256 picture elements), as shown in Figure 4-4. Inside each macroblock are four luma blocks (each 8x8 pixels) and either two or four chroma blocks.

In 4:2:0 systems, two chroma blocks are used in each macroblock: one for the red color difference signal ($C_r$) and one for the blue color difference signal ($C_b$). Each chroma block has 64 elements, with each

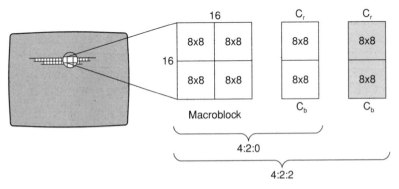

**FIGURE 4-4**   Macroblocks and Blocks in MPEG

element representing the color information from four of the original pixels.

In 4:2:2 systems, four chroma blocks are used in each macroblock: two for the red color difference signal ($C_r$) and two for the blue color difference signal ($C_b$). Each chroma signal has 128 elements, with each element representing the color information from two of the original pixels.

Some folks might argue that the label 4:2:0 would be more accurate if it were changed to 4:1:1 (four blocks of luminance info, one of red color difference and one of blue color difference), but that is not in the widely adopted standard that is MPEG. So, we will continue to talk about 4:2:0 and 4:2:2 signals in this book as well.

## I, P, B Frames and Groups of Pictures

Users of any MPEG system will quickly encounter a variety of frame types, including "I frames," "P frames," and "B frames," as well as the term "Group of Pictures." These terms all describe the way that picture data is structured in an MPEG stream or file. Since most compression devices will support a variety of frame types, it is important for MPEG system users to understand what these terms are and how the use of the different frame types will affect overall system performance. This section will help readers know what these terms mean and understand how these frame types are applied.

To begin, Table 4-2 gives some brief definitions of these terms; we will go into more detail shortly.

To understand why MPEG uses these different frames, it is illuminating to look at the amount of data that is required to represent each frame type. With a video image of normal complexity, a P frame will take 2–4 times less data than an I frame of the same image. A B frame will take even less data than a P frame—a further reduction by a factor of 2–5. Figure 4-5 shows the relative amounts of data for each frame type in a typical MPEG GOP.

**TABLE 4-2**

Definitions of Common MPEG Terms

- A *frame* is single image from a video sequence. In NTSC, one frame occurs every 33 milliseconds; in PAL, one frame occurs every 40 milliseconds. Note that in interlaced systems, a frame is made up of two fields: an odd and an even field. (See Chapter 3 for more detail.)
- An *I frame* is a frame that is compressed solely based on the information contained in the frame; no reference is made to any of the other video frames before or after it. The "I" stands for "Intra" coded, meaning that all the data used in the compression came from within the frame.
- A *P frame* is a frame that has been compressed using the data contained in the frame itself and data from the closest preceding I or P frame. The "P" stands for "Predicted," meaning that the frame data depends only on frames that have preceded it.
- A *B frame* is a frame that has been compressed using data from the closest preceding I or P frame and the closest following I or P frame. Note that a B frame cannot be predicted from another B frame; this is not allowed by the MPEG–2 standard, as the accumulation of errors would be too great. The "B" stands for "Bi-directional," meaning that the frame data can depend on frames that occur before and after it in the video sequence.
- A *Group of Pictures* or *GOP* is a series of frames consisting of a single I frame and zero or more P and B frames. A GOP always begins with an I frame and ends with the last frame before the next subsequent I frame. As we shall discuss later, this grouping makes sense because all of the frames in the GOP depend (directly or indirectly) on the data in the initial I frame.
- *Open GOP* and *Closed GOP* are terms that refer to the relationship between one GOP and another. A closed GOP is self-contained; that is, none of the frames in the GOP refer to nor are based on any of the frames outside the GOP. An open GOP uses data from the I frame of the following GOP for calculating some of the B frames in the GOP, as we will see in the following example.

To see how these different frame types work in practice, let's look at a sample GOP that could be used for a broadcast television signal, as illustrated in Figure 4-6. In our example, the GOP consists of 12 frames of video, which would last for four-tenths of a second in an NTSC system. The sequence of the frames is IBBPBBPBBPBB, which

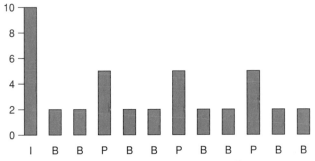

**FIGURE 4-5**  Relative Amounts of Data in Each MPEG Frame Type

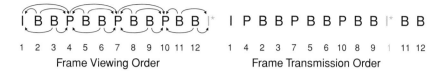

1  2   3   4   5   6   7   8   9  10  11  12        1   4   2   3   7   5   6  10   8   9     11  12

Frame Viewing Order                   Frame Transmission Order

*Note: The second I frame (shown in gray above) is the first frame of the next GOP.
B Frames 11 and 12 are based on this I frame because this is an Open GOP structure.

**FIGURE 4-6**  MPEG GOP Frame Viewing vs. Transmission Order

is read as an I frame, followed by two B frames, followed by a P frame, then two more B's, another P, two more B's, and a final P followed by two final B's. In a real television broadcast, this GOP would be followed by another GOP consisting of 12 more frames, and so on ad infinitum. This is an open GOP, meaning that the final two B frames are referenced to the I frame in the following GOP. This GOP has a length of 12, and what is sometimes referred to as a GOP pattern of IBBP. We will explain these concepts in more detail below.

Let's look at the frames that make up this GOP. The first frame of the GOP is always an I frame. This is by definition, but also for a much better reason. An I frame is the only kind of frame that can be decoded by itself without referring to any other frames. For the I frame in our sample GOP (Frame 1), the MPEG encoder (compression engine) performs a DCT on the entire frame and sends out the appropriate compressed video coefficients. At the decoder (decompression engine), the video frame can be completely re-created from this data. Both the encoder and the decoder do one other thing with this I frame: They both store a copy of the decoded I frame in local memory, because they will need this data for upcoming calculations.

The next frame to be encoded is the first P frame after the I frame, which is frame 4 in our example. (The encoder skips over the two B frames, numbers 2 and 3 in our example, because it doesn't yet have enough data to work on them. But don't worry; we'll get back to them very soon.) The encoder first subtracts the pixel values of the P frame from the pixel values of the last preceding I or P frame. In our example, the pixel values of frame 4 will be subtracted from the stored pixel values from frame 1. The resulting differences show the changes that have occurred in the image between frame 1 and frame 4, which are what the encoder will now go to work on. The encoder also looks to see if any portions of frame 4 are similar to any portions of frame 1, even if they have been relocated to a different location in the frame. If so, then the encoder measures the amount of movement. These measurements (called motion vectors) are sent to the decoder in place of the actual picture data to help reduce the amount of picture data that must be sent. The encoder then proceeds to compress the remaining pixel differences, using the DCT process. Note that this normally results in a much smaller data file than the DCT that was done for an I frame. This happens because the difference data normally contains much less data; at many locations in the frame, there may be very few differences between frame 1 and frame 4, and these areas will compress virtually to nothing when a DCT is applied. The encoder then sends this compressed difference data to the decoder. Again, both the encoder and the decoder do one more thing with this P frame: They both store a copy of the decoded P frame in local memory, because they will need this data for our next calculation.

Figure 4-7 illustrates the timing of the video data through the encoder and decoder. The first line of the diagram shows when the uncompressed video frames coming from the video source arrive at the encoder. The second line of the diagram shows when the data moves from the encoder to the decoder. The third line of the diagram shows when the video signal is sent out of the decoder.

The next frame to be encoded is the first B frame, or frame 2 of our example. This frame is to be encoded using bi-directional compression, which means that the encoder can look at an I or P frame that precedes this one, as well as an I or P frame that follows this one. Conveniently, the encoder has stored a decoded copy of frame 1 and a decoded copy of frame 4. Now, the encoder can go to work by first

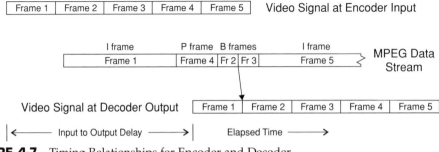

**FIGURE 4-7** Timing Relationships for Encoder and Decoder

subtracting the pixel data of frame 2 from the stored pixel values of frames 1 and 4. These difference signals can then be encoded using motion vectors and DCT, and then formed into the encoder output. As in the case of a P frame, the smaller the differences, the smaller the amount of data that has to be sent. This time, after the encoder has sent the data, any reference to frame 2 is deleted, because the encoder will not need this data again. However, we will still keep the data from frame 1 and frame 4 in memory, because we will need to use it again.

The next step is to encode the second B frame, which is frame 3 in our example. As before, the differences between this frame and the data from frames 1 and 4 are calculated, and the encoder output is created. Again, any references to frame 3 are deleted from the encoder, and the data from frame 4 needs to be kept on hand.

Let's pause for a moment and think about what has been happening in the decoder so far. First, the decoder received the data for frame 1, the I frame, which it was able to decode and send to the video display, while retaining a copy in memory for use in decoding the next three frames. Then, the decoder received the data from frame 4, the P frame, which needed to be decoded, but could not be sent to the video display yet, because frames 2 and 3 hadn't been decoded yet. So, the decoder places the decoded pixel information for frame 4 into storage. Then, the decoder receives the data for frame 2, the first B frame. As soon as this data is decoded (using the data stored locally in the decoder from frames 1 and 4), it can be sent to the video display. Similarly with the data for frame 3, the second B frame. As soon as this data is decoded, it can be sent to the video display. After this step is completed, the decoder can finally send the decoded data for frame 4 to the video display. However, the decoder isn't free to wipe its memory; it is still going to need data from frame 4 (a P frame) for processing the next three video frames.

The next frame to be compressed by the encoder is frame 7, the next P frame after frame 4. Since this is a predicted frame, the encoder will start by calculating the difference between pixel data of frame 7 and the stored pixel data of frame 4. (Note at this point, the encoder no longer needs to hold onto the pixel data from frame 1, so this data can be discarded.) Just like before, the difference signal is encoded using motion vectors and DCT, and the results are sent to the decoder. Now, both the encoder and the decoder change what they are keeping on hand—both will now change to storing copies of the decoded P frames 4 and 7 in local memory, because both devices will need this data for calculating the next frame.

As you might expect, the next step is to calculate and compress the difference data for the next two B frames, which are 5 and 6 in our example. As soon as this data is sent to the decoder, the encoder deletes it; as soon as the decoder displays the decoded data, it too deletes the data from frames 5 and 6.

Next, the encoder needs to process frame 10, which is the last P frame in the GOP. As before, the differences between frames 10 and 7 are calculated, and the compressed difference data for frame 10 is sent to the decoder. Then, the encoder reconfigures its local storage, getting rid of the data for frame 4 and keeping the data for frames 7 and 10. The encoder needs to calculate and send the compressed bi-directional difference data for the B frames 8 and 9.

Because this is an open GOP, the encoder needs to look ahead and get the first frame of the next GOP. This frame (which would be frame 1 of the following GOP) must be compressed as an I frame. When the compression is complete, the data can start being sent to the decoder, and it can be stored in the local memory of the encoder, along with the decoded data from frame 10 of the current GOP. Now, we are finally ready to compress the data for frames 11 and 12 of the current GOP, which are both B frames. The values of the B frames are calculated from the differences between frame 10 of the current GOP and frame 1 of the following GOP, and the values are sent to the decoder. Once these calculations are complete, the encoder can flush what remains in local storage of the previous GOP (frame 10) and start fresh with frames 4, 2, and 3 from the new GOP.

## GOP Length Selection

Selecting a suitable GOP length and GOP pattern can have a big impact on a video network. If the GOP is too short, then the encoded bit stream will occupy excessive bandwidth because of the increased number of I frames, or video quality will be decreased because I frames are less efficient at encoding information than P frames or

B frames. If the GOP is too long, then the video stream will be hard to work with and less tolerant to transmission errors. Since most MPEG–2 encoders allow users to select the GOP that they want to use, it is important to make an informed choice. In this section, we'll look at the relative benefits of short and long GOPs.

Before we go any further, let's make sure we all have the same understanding of the terms "short GOP" and "long GOP." A GOP is short when a small number of frames occur between successive I frames in an MPEG stream. In the shortest possible GOP, the stream is made up entirely of I frames, and thus the GOP is one frame. In a long GOP, many frames occur between successive I frames. There are no strict limits in some MPEG profiles for a maximum length GOP, but certain applications do have limits. For example, the DVD standards limit GOP length to 15 frames.

Unfortunately, there is no single answer as to which GOP length is the best; the choice depends on the user's application. Table 4-3 highlights these differences.

**TABLE 4-3**

Comparison of Long and Short GOPs

---

*Long GOP Benefits*

- As we have seen, I frames take more bits to encode accurately than P or B frames. When a long GOP is used, there are fewer I frames in the stream, so the overall bit rate is reduced.
- For a network with a fixed bandwidth, more video signals can be carried when each uses a long GOP to reduce overall bandwidth demands. This can benefit both terrestrial and satellite-based networks.

*Short GOP Benefits*

- When video images have lots of rapid scene changes (such as in action movies or music videos), a short GOP structure may create a better video image.
- In compressed video delivery systems (such as DSL or digital cable), short GOPs allow quicker channel change times, since it is easier for the decoder to find an I frame to begin the decoding process for a new channel.
- Accumulated errors that occur in an MPEG stream can be completely cleared out only when a new GOP is started with an I frame. With a short GOP, I frames occur more often, so errors are cleared out earlier.
- When streams are edited, many times it is necessary to make the cuts only at an I frame. With short GOP signals, I frames occur more often, so editing is easier and more precise.
- With noisy video sources, prediction errors can rapidly accumulate. Shorter GOP signals are less sensitive to noise, because few consecutive frames are based on predicted values.

---

No doubt some readers will be asking "Why not use mostly B frames and get the smallest amount of data possible"? The answer to this question is fourfold, as follows:

- A B frame can be predicted only from either I or P frames, according to the standard. Therefore, every sequence of video frames must include some I or P frames on occasion.
- Whenever one frame is predicted from another, some small errors will occur. When a frame is predicted based on another frame that has already been predicted, these errors can build on each other. As the number of generations increases, these errors will accumulate and make the resulting images unacceptable. The only way to clear out these accumulated errors is to transmit an occasional I frame.
- The process of editing a video involves stopping one sequence of video frames and starting another. When this happens in the middle of a GOP, B frames no longer make any sense, because one of the I or P frames that they were referenced to was replaced by the new stream. Traditionally, when editing is done, any new video scenes must begin with an I frame, so the encoder and decoder can clean out their buffers and start fresh. Newer technology is coming onto the market that lifts this requirement.
- In the event of an error in a MPEG video stream, the data that is needed to predict subsequent frames can become corrupted. Using the previous 12-frame GOP example, if frame 4 of the GOP is corrupted, and the image in frame 7 was predicted based on the data in frame 4, then frame 7 will also be corrupted. An error in frame 4 will also directly affect the B frames 2, 3, 5, and 6. This error can also be propagated throughout the rest of the GOP, as shown in Figure 4-8.

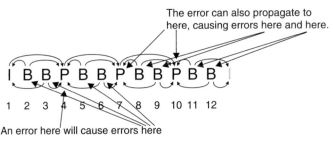

**FIGURE 4-8**   Effects of an Error in Frame 4 of the Sample GOP

## MPEG–1

MPEG–1 was the first standard developed for video compression by the Moving Pictures Experts Group. It was intended for use in creating video compact discs (CDs), which had some popularity in computer multimedia, but never completely caught on as consumer movie rental or purchase format. MPEG–1 is still in use today for a number of applications, including low-cost surveillance cameras and some web video applications. It is also interesting to note that MPEG–1 is allowed as a video compression method for DVDs, and many DVD players will play video CDs. Stand-alone and software-based MPEG–1 encoders are available for very reasonable prices from several sources.

MPEG–1 does not support interlacing, so standard full-resolution PAL and NTSC signals are not usable with MPEG–1. Instead, MPEG–1 uses a picture size of 352 pixels by 240 lines for NTSC (29.97 Hz) systems, and a picture size of 352 pixels by 288 lines for PAL (25 Hz) systems. Note that these figures are half the vertical and half the horizontal resolution of their full-frame, interlaced counterparts. Also note that these frame formats can be created by discarding all of the odd fields from an interlaced source and by removing half of the pixels in each remaining horizontal line. MPEG–1 also supports lower resolution images (such as QCIF, which is 176 pixels by 144 lines) and lower frame rates (such as 15 and 7.5 frames per second). These lower speeds are primarily used for lower quality real-time applications, such as live webcams and desktop videoconferencing.

MPEG–1 uses many of the techniques that are used in later standards such as MPEG–2 and MPEG–4. Some of these techniques include motion compensation, bi-directional frame coding, and many of the mechanisms to control the video stream, such as rate control and buffer management. MPEG–1 signals can also be decoded in real time inside a reasonably equipped desktop PC by means of a software decoder. This capability can be a great benefit for corporate video deployments, since it avoids having to install special video-processing hardware in user PCs. Table 4-4 lists some of the key advantages and disadvantages of MPEG–1.

Overall, MPEG–1 is a useful video format for a variety of applications. It can be of benefit to installations where a large number of

**TABLE 4-4**

Advantages and Disadvantages of MPEG–1

*Advantages*

- *Low Bit Rates:* MPEG–1 was designed for low bit rates, specifically the rates that can be achieved with an audio compact disc playing at normal speed (around 1.4 Mbps, with 1.15 Mbps for video and 0.25 Mbps for audio). At lower resolutions (such as QCIF), MPEG–1 can operate on data links well below 1 Mbps. Lower bit rates also allow multiple video signals to be carried using common data standards such as 10BaseT without overwhelming the network.
- *Good Interoperability:* The MPEG–1 standard has existed since the early 1990s and is very stable and mature. This means that most MPEG–1 applications can operate with each other with few problems.
- *Simple Decoder:* Because the decode function is relatively simple, an MPEG–1 decoder can be implemented in a reasonable performance desktop PC without the addition of special hardware.
- *Reduced Storage:* Because MPEG–1 operates at relatively low bit rates, the amount of data storage required per hour of recording time is relatively low. This allows more video to be stored on recording media such as CDs.
- *Widely Accepted:* MPEG–1 is essentially a subset of MPEG–2, so most of the millions of MPEG–2 decoders installed around the world today can be used for decoding MPEG–1 video, provided that the streams are formed into a format that these devices can understand.
- *Inexpensive:* Low-cost, real-time encoders are available for MPEG–1 systems, which can be deployed in a variety of locations. Software-based encoders are also available for non–real-time applications and for real-time applications on more powerful workstations.

*Disadvantages*

- *No Interlacing:* Established television standards such as PAL and NTSC use interlacing to give better perception of motion to viewers. MPEG–1 does not support interlacing, so video signals need to be converted to work with this standard. Fortunately, most MPEG–1 devices include the necessary converters.
- *Less Bandwidth Efficient:* MPEG–1 does not include some of the more advanced compression techniques that have been developed since the standard was finalized. This means that perceived video quality may be higher and stream bit rates may be lower with some of the more advanced standards that are now available and included in MPEG–4.
- *Quality Limits:* MPEG–1 was originally targeted at low bit rate applications, so high-quality and high bit rate encoders are essentially not available. In general, MPEG–1 is really suitable only for applications in which quality is a less important consideration than cost, as is common in surveillance applications.
- *Low Innovation:* Little new development effort is going into MPEG–1 devices, so the products that are currently on the market will not see many revisions or improvements in the future.

users need to be served, and cost control is major concern. MPEG–1 is a very mature standard, and there is little new product development in this area. Instead, new developments are primarily focusing on

MPEG–4, which has the potential to cover many of the applications in which MPEG–1 is currently used. However, it is likely that MPEG–1 will be with us for a number of years into the future.

## MPEG–2

MPEG–2 is the predominant standard for MPEG video today. It is used in a wide variety of applications, including digital TV production and broadcasting, high definition television, satellite television, and cable television. Each day, thousands of hours of MPEG-2 video are recorded, processed, and played back by television broadcasters around the world. Millions of hours of MPEG–2 recordings are sold to the general public each day in the form of DVDs. Thousands of PCs with MPEG–2 playback capability are sold each week, and the installed base of MPEG–2 devices continues to grow.

MPEG–2 offers some significant advances over MPEG–1. MPEG–2 supports interlacing, so standard NTSC and PAL signals can be supported at full resolution. It supports a variety of different resolutions and performance profiles, so a wide variety of applications, including HD television, can be accommodated. MPEG–2 supports multiplexing of a number of video and audio streams, so applications like multi-channel satellite television become possible. MPEG–2 also supports five channel audio (surround sound) and the Advanced Audio Coding (AAC) standard, neither of which are available in MPEG–1.

One of the key concepts that needs to be understood in MPEG–2 are the various profiles and levels that are available for encoding. Selecting the correct profile and level for a particular application can have a great impact on system cost. Higher profiles and levels add to the complexity of encoders and decoders, can require more bandwidth, and can significantly increase overall system cost. System implementers are encouraged to read through the following discussion and get a basic understanding of which profiles and levels are appropriate for their applications.

The term "level," when used in the context of an MPEG–2 performance specification, refers to the maximum picture size that can be supported. Four levels are defined (in order from lowest to highest resolution): Low, Main, High 1440, and High. Here are brief definitions of each level:

- *Low* Level refers to picture sizes up to a maximum of 352 pixels by 288 lines, just like MPEG–1.
- *Main* Level refers to the main picture sizes used in standard definition television, i.e., a maximum of 720 pixels on each of 576 horizontal lines. Note that normal NTSC resolutions will be somewhat lower than these limits; typical values will be 720 pixels on 480 lines.
- *High 1440* Level doubles the vertical and horizontal resolution of the Main Profile and so offers 1440 pixels on each of 1152 lines.
- *High* Level expands the High 1440 Level to widescreen high definition, by supporting a 16:9 aspect ratio (in place of 4:3 for normal Main Profile signals). This increases the maximum number of pixels per line to 1920 but leaves the line count maximum at 1152 lines.

MPEG–2 also supports a variety of different performance profiles, which specify the types of techniques that the encoder can use in compressing the video. As the profile increases, the cost and complexity of both the video encoder and decoder increase. However, the video quality normally also increases, so trade-offs need to be considered. The six MPEG–2 profiles, in order from least complex to most complex, are Simple, Main, 4:2:2, SNR, Spatial, and High. Here are brief definitions of each profile:

- *Simple* Profile does not allow B frames, so only I and P frames can be used by the encoder. This reduces the complexity of the encoder and decoder. This profile may also be useful for low delay applications, since the delays that are required for calculating B frames are eliminated.
- *Main* Profile is intended to be useful in a wide variety of applications. It supports all the different resolution levels and is the most commonly used profile for most applications. Note that the color space for this profile is 4:2:0. DVDs are authored following the Main Profile at Main Level specifications.
- *4:2:2* Profile was developed after most of the other profiles were developed when it became apparent that there was a need for a

profile that supported 4:2:2 color handling without all of the other features and functions required by the High Profile. It is now used in video production, post production, and network transmission for contribution signals.

- *SNR* (Signal to Noise Ratio) Profile introduced the concept of having two different video streams for one video signal: a basic stream that carried most of the picture data and a helper stream that could be used for enhanced noise performance. When the two streams were split, only devices that were capable of handling the helper stream would receive it, thereby saving processing power and bandwidth in those devices that could not process the helper stream. This capability has not been widely applied in MPEG–2 for most television broadcast applications. However, the concept of having a normal stream for most decoders, and a helper stream to support better noise performance when conditions permit, has been replicated with non-MPEG–2 streams that are sent over the Internet.

- *Spatial* Profile uses the same concept of splitting the stream, but the split is intended for a different application. In the Spatial Profile, the input signal is high definition. The Spatial Profile encoder creates two output streams: one at standard definition and a helper stream that contains the extra data that is needed by a HD display. With this pair of streams, standard definition decoders would process only one stream, and HD decoders would process both. This profile is not commonly used.

- *High* Profile, which offers the capabilities of both the SNR and the Spatial Profile, is the most complex MPEG–2 profile defined. High Profile was also the only profile that supported the 4:2:2 color resolution before the 4:2:2 Profile was defined. Encoders and decoders that support all of the functions required by the High Profile are significantly more complex (and more expensive) than Main Profile encoders and decoders. High Profile has found uses in high definition video.

When profiles and levels are being specified, it is customary to abbreviate the names of the profiles and levels, and join them with an "at" (@) sign. For example, Main Profile at Main Level would be abbreviated "MP@ML" and read "Main Profile at Main Level." High Profile at Main Level would be abbreviated "HP@ML." Also note that not every combination of profile and level is permitted; for

| | Simple Profile | Main Profile | 4:2:2 Profile | SNR Profile | Spatial Profile | High Profile |
|---|---|---|---|---|---|---|
| High Level 1920x1152 | | 4:2:0 80 Mbps | | | | 4:2:0 or 4:2:2 100 Mbps |
| High 1440 Level 1440x1152 | | 4:2:0 60 Mbps | | | 4:2:0 60 Mbps | 4:2:0 or 4:2:2 80 Mbps |
| Main Level 720x576 | 4:2:0 15 Mbps No B Frames | 4:2:0 15 Mbps | 4:2:2 50 Mbps | 4:2:0 15 Mbps | | 4:2:0 or 4:2:2 20 Mbps |
| Low Level 352x288 | | 4:2:0 4 Mbps | | 4:2:0 4 Mbps | | |

Maximum Picture Resolution: High ↑ Low

Low ◄————————————► High
Profile Complexity

**FIGURE 4-9**  Summary of Supported MPEG–2 Profiles and Levels

example, High Profile at Low Level is not permitted. Figure 4-9 shows the allowed profiles and levels, along with information about the permitted color resolution options (4:2:0 or 4:2:2) and the maximum supported bit rate of the video elementary stream for each combination.

MPEG–2 is widely used throughout the professional video recording and broadcast market for good reasons. It is a stable standard, and many devices, including specialized semiconductors, are in their third or fourth generations. There is a large pool of talented people who have worked with MPEG–2 and who are familiar with the technology's strengths and limitations. Table 4-5 lists some of the key advantages and disadvantages of MPEG–2 technology.

Overall, MPEG–2 is a well-defined, stable compression system that is used throughout the world for professional quality video. Because of its flexibility and power, not to mention the huge installed base of equipment, it will continue to be a popular standard for quite a while into the future.

**TABLE 4-5**

Advantages and Disadvantages of MPEG–2

*Advantages*

- *Flexible:* MPEG–2 has the flexibility to be able to support a wide variety of applications, so chances are there is a version of MEPG–2 that will fit almost any application.
- *Widespread:* There is a huge installed base of MPEG–2 equipment in the world, particularly decoders. There are literally hundreds of millions of set top boxes, digital satellite receivers, and DVD players installed in consumers' homes that can decode MPEG–2 signals.
- *Highly Integrated:* A number of highly sophisticated MPEG–2 encoder and decoder devices are available as custom semiconductors. As a result, new equipment is easier to design, and significant cost reductions can be achieved.
- *Stand-alone Encoders:* Low-cost, stand-alone MPEG–2 encoders are available from a number of sources that can be used to create compressed video streams in real time. A number of these devices have direct network interfaces, including 10/100BaseT Ethernet links.
- *Software:* Various software tools are available for producing MPEG–2 streams using general-purpose PCs. With sufficient processing power and memory, a PC can be used to create an MPEG–2 stream in real time. However, for many applications, such as program editing and production, real-time performance is not necessary, and even moderate performance PCs can create MPEG–2 compressed video files for later playback.
- *Infrastructure:* A wide variety of equipment is available on the market for handling many different functions with MPEG–2 streams. These functions include statistical multiplexing, bit rate converters, telecom and IP network adapters, and more. These devices can make it easier to design and deploy a complete video network.
- *Test Equipment:* Diagnostic tools and equipment for analyzing MPEG–2 encoder and decoder designs and for diagnosing system failures are also readily available.

*Disadvantages*

- *Complexity:* Because MPEG–2 has so many different profiles and levels, it is very common to find that specific hardware and software implementations support only a few of the possible combinations. This can cause problems for system implementers, who need to verify that all of the technology that is used will interoperate.
- *High Bandwidth:* MPEG–2 streams for full-resolution, full-motion video (i.e., standard NTSC or PAL video signals) typically operate at speeds above 2 Mbps. When audio and other related signals are added, it becomes difficult to use some of the lower speed telecom interfaces that are widely available (1.544 Mbps in North America and 2.048 Mbps in much of the rest of the world). MPEG–2 streams for HD video can also easily exceed the speed of a normal 10BaseT Ethernet link. Costs to use networks with larger bandwidths can add significantly to the recurring cost of an MPEG–2 network.
- *Processing Power:* Software-only decoders for MPEG–2 exist, but, depending on the profile/level used and the incoming bit rates, they can be difficult to run without the addition of a hardware accelerator to a desktop PC. Adding an accelerator can drive up the cost and complicate the deployment of networks that are intended to deliver video streams to a large number of desktops.

**TABLE 4-5** *(Continued)*

- *Performance Limitations:* MPEG–2 standards have been in existence for over a decade, and a great deal of work has been done to optimize the performance of all the pieces in the chain from the source to the ultimate user. During this time, the amount of bandwidth needed for a typical video stream has dropped significantly. However, continued dramatic improvement is not likely in the future, and MPEG–2 performance levels will probably remain close to the levels that have already been achieved. Newer protocols, such as MPEG–4 with a wider variety of compression tools available, will be necessary to increase performance and bandwidth efficiency.
- *Video Only:* All of the encoding and data representation standards for MPEG–2 are based on video images. Mechanisms to support advanced video concepts such as overlaid text and animation are not present, meaning that the MPEG–2 encoder has to work very hard to encode the text-based information that crawls across the bottom of many popular news and sports channels. In contrast, new standards such as MPEG–4 have the ability to process these data types more efficiently and obtain boosts in coding efficiencies.

## MPEG–4

MPEG–4 is a much more recent product of the standards process, the first version having become formally approved in 2000. As would be expected, MPEG–4 incorporates a whole range of new technologies for video compression that have been developed in the past decade. All of the necessary support technology for MPEG–4 system (such as custom semiconductors) is being developed to allow MPEG–4 to be widely deployed. As of this writing, many of these technologies are still being developed or are in their first generation, so it would be reasonable to expect a considerable number of new product introductions in the coming years.[1]

Many new compression techniques have been introduced since the development of MPEG–2. They include ways to encode not only video but also other objects that can be displayed to viewers, such as text or animation. In addition, the cost of processing power has continued to drop, making it cost effective to put more capabilities into a

---

1. Many readers may be curious about the lack of an MPEG–3 video standard. In fact, there was originally a working group set up to develop a standard for multi-resolution encoding. This group's work was completed before the work on MPEG–2 was completed, so it was simply incorporated into the MPEG–2 standard. Readers should be careful not to confuse the MPEG audio coding standard called Layer III, often abbreviated as MP3, with the non-existent MPEG–3 standard.

decoder chip that may be deployed in millions of set top boxes. By taking advantage of these advances, the designers of MPEG–4 have enabled higher quality video images to be generated using less bandwidth than the best MPEG–2 products on the market.

MPEG–4 achieves many of its advances in compression efficiency through the introduction of new video objects. These objects can be created by the encoder from original raw picture data, or they can be created as completely new objects that are overlaid on top of other picture data. An example of the latter could be a computer-generated map used to show weather data in a news broadcast. In MPEG–2, the only choice would be to treat the pixels that make up the map as part of the overall image and encode the changes that happen in the map using the standard video compression algorithms available to MPEG–2, such as DCT. In contrast, in MPEG–4, the computer-generated map could be treated as a separate video object from the rest of the scene, and it could be processed independently. In the latter case, if the map needs to change (say to pan to a new part of the map or to zoom in), then simple commands could be sent to the decoder telling it how to manipulate the map. This technology gives MPEG–4 many more ways to represent picture data and greatly improves the efficiency with which pictures can be encoded.

Several other technological advances have been incorporated into MPEG–4. The size of each macroblock is no longer fixed, so small ones can be used in areas of the image that are finely detailed. This also permits larger blocks to be used and encoded with fewer bits if the pixels in portions of the image are very similar. Another innovation is the use of fractal compression, which is a mathematical alternative to DCT that is useful for some types of images. Finally, MPEG–4 allows B frames to be based on other B frames, reducing the need for P frames and lowering the overall bandwidth requirement.

One key aspect of MPEG–4 technology is the ability of the decoder to assemble an image from multiple types of source material. A composite image that is being shown to a user can combine elements from both natural and synthetic sources. Natural sources are devices such as video cameras and audio microphones that capture input from the natural world. Synthetic sources are those that are generated through computer graphics or other means. Take, for example, a sports broadcast. The broadcaster might want to supply an on-screen scoreboard, add some graphics to comment on the current match and report on other matches occurring at the same time, and insert the local station identifier. In MPEG–2, all of these separate elements would be combined together at the broadcaster's facility and then compressed and transmitted to the viewers, who would all watch the same composite image. In MPEG–4, by contrast, each element would be generated separately and then transmitted as separate data units inside the MPEG–4 stream. The decoder at each viewer's location would process each of the different signal elements and then combine them prior to display to the user. In our example, once the format of the scoreboard was established, the score could be transmitted as a single number for each team. This is tremendously more efficient from the perspective of data transport: It is far more bandwidth efficient to send simple score numbers than to send brightness and color data of dozens or hundreds of pixels that make up the scoreboard image. Synthetic image technology provides two main benefits:

- Each user can be given control over the items that are being displayed. If, for example, the user doesn't want the score to be displayed, then the decoder can be instructed to simply not display the scoreboard. Or, if the user wants and the broadcaster permits, the user can move the scoreboard to another part of the screen or change its appearance.
- Much less bandwidth is consumed when synthetic signals are sent as compared to natural signals. This is due primarily to the innate complexity of natural signals and the need to accurately reproduce the pixels that make up a natural image.

To get a slightly better understanding of the MPEG–4 standard, let's look at four different types of objects that are coded:

- A still texture object (called a sprite) is an object that is flat on the video screen and does not change with time. A classic example would be a background, such as a distant mountain or the front of a building. Sprites can move with respect to the video frame, such as when the camera is panned or zoomed. The big advantage of a sprite in terms of compression is that the image data for the sprite can be sent once and then manipulated. Using our background example, much less data is required to tell an

MPEG–4 decoder that the background has shifted left by three pixels than would be required to update every macroblock in an MPEG–2 scene by the same change.

- A video object is a texture that changes with time. Video objects are encoded similarly to MPEG–2 video, except that they don't necessarily cover the entire screen. There are some improvements in the calculation methods, so lower bit rates can be achieved while maintaining the same picture quality. Video objects can also have defined shapes and can move around the screen over time.

- A mesh object is a two-dimensional or three-dimensional object that changes with time. The object is in the form of a surface, which can be covered with a texture. Mesh objects are very convenient for representing objects in scenes that may move or change with time. For example, an automobile driving through a scene could be represented as a three-dimensional mesh. As the auto moves through the screen, the shape of the image can change, say as the auto turns a corner. For compression, this is highly efficient—it is much simpler to send instructions on how to move, rotate, and distort an object than it is to track the changes that must be made to hundreds or thousands of pixels that would otherwise be needed to represent the object. Note that this technique applies mainly to computer-generated, rather than camera-originated images.

- MPEG–4 also has special constructs to support face and body animation. The concept is to take still images of people and transmit motion vectors for these people in lieu of complicated motion images. Again, the concept is to greatly reduce the amount of data that needs to be transmitted to create realistic scenes. Since a great deal of motion imaging is based on images of people, this can be a useful technique. This technology could show great promise, for example, in face-to-face videoconferencing or low bit rate videophones.

Implementing an encoder to take advantage of all of the preceding tools is not a simple task. Recognizing the different types of objects inside a real image is complicated, and not always possible. As development work continues, these functions will no doubt improve. Even without these tools, the improvements in the video-coding aspect of MPEG–4, called Advanced Video Coding or MPEG–4 AVC, are able to create images with the same visual quality as MPEG–2 systems using half the number of bits. Table 4-6 lists some of the key advantages and disadvantages of the MPEG–4 technology.

**TABLE 4-6**

Advantages and Disadvantages of MPEG–4

*Advantages*

- *Large Toolset:* The large range of new video-coding techniques makes MPEG–4 very flexible for new applications. Particularly for computer-generated video and graphic (synthetic) objects, MPEG–4 provides a very efficient way to capture the essential information and transport it using extremely low bit rate signals.
- *Lower Bandwidth:* The advances that have been introduced in the Advanced Video Coding (AVC) system will make it possible to transmit high-quality natural signals in half the bandwidth of MPEG–2 signals. This technology will certainly improve the performance of Internet video and will also support deployment of more channels of video on a DSL or satellite circuit.
- *HD Support:* MPEG–4 AVC may also make it possible for high definition signals to be encoded at bit rates below 10 Mbps, opening up a much bigger range of technologies for transporting HD video signals.
- *Dual Use:* MPEG–4 AVC and H.264 are two different names for the same standard. By joining these two different fields together (video telecommunication and entertainment video) using identical technology, customers will benefit, and deployment will be speeded up. In particular, development of very low bit rate encoders and decoders for wireless applications should be accelerated.
- *User Control:* Because the MPEG–4 decoder can form a composite image from many different sources (such as cameras, computer-generated graphics, or text files), viewers can be given control over which parts of the image they want displayed and where they want those images to appear.
- *Stream Scalability:* A key technology in MPEG–4 is the ability to separate highly detailed portions of an image from less detailed portions. This allows an encoder to create multiple streams, one with low resolution to run on low-speed networks and multiple "helper" streams that add detail to an image. Users with low-speed networks can simply view the basic stream, and those with higher speed network connections can watch an image that is enhanced with the extra information contained in one or more helper streams. Scalability can also improve the robustness of a system, so that when the network becomes congested and the helper streams can't make it through, viewers can still enjoy an uninterrupted, albeit lower quality, video image.

*Disadvantages*

- *Immaturity:* Software-only MPEG–4 decoders have already reached the market for desktop video applications. Buyers need to be careful when purchasing these products, because many of the first-generation products may not implement all of the features that could be used by a video encoder.
- *Highly Complex:* MPEG–4 has a huge range of application profiles and performance points, significantly more than the number available for MPEG–2. This means that a wide range of devices will be able to claim they are MPEG–4 compliant without implementing some of the features that a user may desire. For buyers of MPEG–4 equipment, it will be necessary to ensure that the devices and technologies that are being purchased are capable of supporting the features required by the video application. It will likely take several design iterations to smooth out all the rough edges, a process that may take several years.

**TABLE 4-6** *(Continued)*

- *Low Integration:* As of this writing, specialized semiconductors that are specifically designed for MPEG–4 encoder and decoder applications have not reached the market. Naturally, this situation is expected to change over time, but complete system rollout may take several years to complete. This may limit the range of applications for MPEG–4 technology for a number of years into the future.
- *Installed Base:* Literally hundreds of millions of devices in consumers' and broadcasters' possession today implement MPEG–2 technology, as well as hundreds of satellite and other television broadcast channels. Migrating this installed base of technology to MPEG–4 will require a significant amount of expense and some headaches during the transition period. This changeover may not begin for a while unless there are compelling business reasons to switch to MPEG–4. However, many new installations, with little or no installed base, may move to adopt MPEG–4 from the beginning.
- *Processing Power:* Decoders are more complex for MPEG–4 than for MPEG–2. According to the MPEG–4 Industry Forum (www.m4if.org), an MPEG–4 decoder will be 2.5 to 4 times as complex as an MPEG–2 decoder for similar applications. This means more complicated (and therefore more expensive) hardware devices and greater demand on processor resources for software decoders. Before the decision is made to use MPEG–4 in a video delivery system, it is important to test any user devices (desktop PCs, laptops, etc.) that will be used to decode the video signal. Users may need to avoid using some of the advanced features of MPEG–4 and stick to the simpler profiles.

Overall, MPEG–4 is an exciting new collection of technologies that promises to greatly increase the amount of video information that can be squeezed into a given amount of network bandwidth. Through MPEG–4 AVC, much more efficient video coding is possible, and the variety of object types available makes integration with computer-generated graphics simple and extremely bandwidth efficient. Because of MPEG–4's complexity and its relative newness, much development work needs to be done to reach the level of sophistication and maturity presently enjoyed by MPEG–2 technology. As time progresses, more products will be available that employ MPEG–4 technology, and widespread adoption will follow soon.

## MPEG Audio Compression

Just like video compression, MPEG has a variety of audio compression options. There are three layers of MPEG audio (conveniently called Layers I, II, and III) and a newer audio compression standard called Advanced Audio Coding (AAC). In this section, we'll take a short look at each one of these. Note that all of these audio compression methods will work with any type of MPEG video compression, except that MPEG–1 streams do not handle AAC audio.

Before we get into the differences between these options, let's look at their similarities. All of the MPEG audio encoders are lossy, which means that they will lose some of the information contained in the source audio signal. Furthermore, they are all perceptual encoders, which means that compression is done based on what the human hearing system can and cannot detect (more on that in a moment). Also, all of the MPEG encoders use digital audio signals with any of three audio sampling rates: 32 kHz, 44.1 kHz, and 48 kHz. In addition, each of the decoders (except AAC) must work properly with streams that have been encoded for lower layers; that is, a Layer III decoder must accept a Layer I or II stream, and a Layer II decoder must accept a Layer I stream.

In audio, perceptual coding can provide a significant amount of compression. The human ear is actually more sensitive to small distortions introduced by compression than the human eye, so care must be taken to use a good compression system. However, because the human ear is not perfect, some information can be discarded from the audio signal with little or no penalty. For example, the ear cannot hear signals that last for less than a millisecond (msec). A loud signal will also mask (or cover up) a quieter signal that immediately precedes it or follows it. There are limits to the range of frequencies that the ear can hear. Furthermore, as mentioned earlier in this chapter, a loud signal at one pitch will mask quieter sounds at other pitches that are close by, and much quieter sounds at pitches that are not as close by (this is also why you can't hear the noise from an audio tape except during quiet periods). All of these limits to human hearing were taken into account when the MPEG techniques for compressing audio were designed.

All of the MPEG coding methods divide the incoming audio signal into 32 discrete audible frequency bands (sub-bands), and the different bands are processed separately. The concept of frequency bands is similar to the concept of different octaves in music, with one big exception.

In MPEG, the frequency bands are allocated linearly by frequency, which means that each band covers the same amount of spectrum. For example, if we were to divide 20,000 Hz of bandwidth into 32 linear bands, each band would cover a range of 20,000/32 = 625 Hz. In music, each octave is twice the width of the one below it, so the frequencies of the keys on a piano are closer together at the low pitch (left side) of the piano keyboard than they are at the higher pitches (right side). From a perceptual standpoint, this means that the MPEG bands are too wide at the low frequencies, and too narrow at the higher frequencies.[2]

MPEG audio Layer I is the simplest compression system. It uses 384 input samples for each compression run, which corresponds to 8 milliseconds of audio material using 48 kHz sampling. Each band is processed separately, and then the results are combined to form a single, constant bit rate output. Layer I can achieve a compression ratio of 4:1, which means that a 1.4 Mbps CD-quality audio signal can be compressed to fit into a 384 kbps stream with no noticeable loss of quality. Compression beyond this to 192 or 128 kbps does result in noticeable loss of quality.

MPEG audio Layer II uses more samples for each compression run, 1152 to be exact. This corresponds to 24 msec of audio at 48 kHz sampling. This allows frequencies to be resolved more accurately. Layer II also eliminates some of the redundancy in coding that is present in Layer I, thereby achieving better compression of up to 8:1. This means that CD-quality audio can be achieved with a stream rate of 192 kbps.

MPEG audio Layer III uses the same number of samples as Layer II, but it uses them more efficiently. It adds the step of compressing each frequency band using a modified version of the Discrete Cosine Transform that we discuss in Appendix A. Layer III has an audio mode called joint stereo, which capitalizes on the strong similarities between the signals that make up the left and right channels of a stereo program. It also uses variable-length coding to more efficiently pack the compressed audio coefficients into the output stream. As a result, Layer III

---

2. This situation occurs because the perception of differences in sound changes with the frequency. For example, a 200 Hz audio tone will be perceived as greatly different from a 100 Hz tone (a whole octave of difference for music lovers), but a 15,200 Hz tone will sound only slightly different from a 15,100 Hz tone.

encoders can pack CD-quality audio into streams as small as 128 kbps, achieving compression ratios as high as 12:1. Note that audio files compressed using MPEG Layer III often carry the file extension "MP3" and are popular in many music download and file-swapping systems.

MPEG Advanced Audio Coding (AAC) is available only with MPEG–2 or MPEG–4 video streams. It supports up to 48 audio channels including 5.1 audio, and it includes lots of tools that can be used by a sophisticated encoder to create high-performance audio streams. One option is a lossless compression mode, for applications that don't require the absolute highest levels of compression but do require high fidelity. In 2004, a new form of AAC was released, called aacPlus or HE AAC (for High Efficiency), with some advances in sound quality at higher sound frequencies. For MPEG–4, the stream can include various audio objects, similar to MPEG–4 video. These objects can be either natural or synthetic audio. The audio decoder is responsible for assembling all of the audio objects and producing a final combined output.

Overall, MPEG audio is flexible and does not require near the magnitude of processor involvement and MPEG video. As the layer number goes up, the complexity of both the encoder and the decoder go up, but so does the compression ratio. Software-only Layer III decoders can run smoothly in a wide variety of personal computers, including desktop and laptop systems. AAC decoders are not as common, possibly due to the complexity involved. When choosing an audio-encoding method, remember that the overall transport bandwidth must be high enough to carry the video signal, the audio signal, and some overhead to make the streams operate correctly. Audio-encoding methods with higher compression ratios will allow more bandwidth to be allocated to video signals.

## MPEG Video Comparison

With so many different flavors of MPEG available, many readers will be asking the question: "Which version of MPEG should I use for my application?" Of course, the only truly accurate answer is "It depends," but that isn't very satisfying. So, at the risk of starting some heated arguments (particularly among fervent believers in the various technologies), here is a list of general guidelines that readers might follow. (**Note:** These guidelines are solely the opinion of the author and should not be interpreted as hard-and-fast rules. Furthermore, as technology evolves, some of the following statements will become less accurate, particularly those about MPEG–4, which is still a relatively new technology as of this writing). With all that in mind, here is a comparison:

MPEG–1 is a stable, mature technology that requires less processing in both the encoder and the decoder than either of the other two technologies. It is designed to work only on non-interlaced video, so some of its applications are limited. For stream rates under 1.5 Mbps, some users have found MPEG–1 to provide a more pleasing image than MPEG–2 at the same bit rate, due in part to the lower overhead and simpler structure of MPEG–1 streams. One application in which MPEG–1 really shines is streaming video to large numbers of desktops. Because of MPEG–1's simplicity, most existing desktop systems can run software-only decoders, avoiding the cost, complexity, and expense of upgrading a large number of user desktops.

MPEG–2 is also a stable, mature technology that has widespread use in the video entertainment field. It is currently used for most professional video applications, including broadcast, satellite, cable TV, DVD, and HD video. Hundreds of millions of devices installed around the world are capable of receiving and decoding MPEG–2 video in a wide variety of flavors. MPEG–2 is commonly used in contribution, distribution, and delivery networks. The advantages of MPEG–2's superior video and audio quality are not readily apparent at stream rates below 2.5 Mbps and are judged to be inferior to MPEG–1 streams at rates below 1.5 Mbps. Accordingly, MPEG–2 is not typically used for desktop streaming unless high-bandwidth networks are used and hardware MPEG–2 decoders are installed in each user system.

MPEG–4, a much more recent standard, offers a huge range of operating profiles and levels for a wide variety of applications. MPEG–4 has not yet penetrated deeply into the video entertainment business, partly due to the large installed base of MPEG–2 equipment and comparative rarity of MPEG–4 equipment. Furthermore, prior to the very recent introduction of the MPEG–4 Advanced Video Coding (AVC) standard, MPEG–4 did not offer truly dramatic performance improvements over MPEG–2 for compressing live natural video sequences, including most types of news, entertainment, and sports broadcasts. MPEG–4 has a number of advantages for synthetic (computer-generated) video and has already deeply penetrated IP video streaming applications. (Apple's QuickTime has fully migrated to MPEG–4.) Most desktop PCs can already decode MPEG–4 video using software that is freely available on the Internet in the form of media players. MPEG–4's scalability also allows one video source to feed multiple users at varying quality levels, allowing each to get the best possible video quality that his or her network will support.

MPEG–4 AVC is newer still and has the potential to replace MPEG–2 in the long run. The reason is that MPEG–4 AVC can achieve quality levels that compare favorably to MPEG–2 at half the bit rate. Of course, there is a cost to this, in terms of the greater processing power needed to encode and decode AVC signals. In addition, because AVC is so new, the technology has not had a chance to pass through the learning and optimization process that MPEG–2 has undergone since 1996. As this process unfolds, expect to see multi-channel DSL networks and HD video on DVDs, both as benefits of AVC technology.

Table 4-7 summarizes the main differences between the various flavors of MPEG.

## OTHER COMPRESSION TECHNOLOGIES

Certainly, MPEG video compression technologies are very important to video networking. However, a number of other video compression technologies are used for video transport over IP networks. Fortunately, many of them use the same underlying technologies as MPEG, so our discussion can be much simpler. In the following sections, we'll look at some of these other technologies and where they are used.

## H.261 and H.263

H.261 and H.263 are international standards that are used extensively in videoconferencing, published by the International Telecommunication Union's Telecommunications Standardization Sector (ITU-T) for video compression. One of the most popular standards for

**TABLE 4-7**

MPEG Video Compression Comparison

|  | MPEG–1 | MPEG–2 | MPEG–4 | MPEG–4 Advanced Video Codec (AVC) |
|---|---|---|---|---|
| Standard Finalized | 1992 | 1996 | 2000 | 2003 |
| Supports Interlacing | No | Yes | Yes | Yes |
| Object Based | No | No | Yes | Yes |
| Decoder Complexity | Low | High | High | Very High |
| Decoder Chipsets | MPEG–2 decoder will handle MPEG–1 | Many | Limited | Soon |
| Encoder Chipsets | Few | Many | Mostly implemented on DSP chipsets or non-real-time in software | Soon |
| Common Stream Rates | 500–1500 kbps | 2.5–50 Mbps | 10 kbps–10 Mbps | 1–4 Mbps (Standard Def) 4–10 Mbps (High Def) |
| Profiles and Levels | Few | 12 | Many | Many |
| Audio Formats | MPEG Layer I, II, III | Adds Advanced Audio Codec (AAC) | Adds Audio Objects and Synthetic Audio | Same as MPEG–4 |
| Stream Scalability | No | Yes, but only at higher profiles (not used much) | Yes | Yes |

videoconferencing on IP networks, H.323 uses the H.261 and H.263 video compression standards. Other videoconferencing formats, such as H.320 (for ISDN networks) and H.324 (for standard dial-up telephone lines, including some wireless ones), also use H.261 and H.263.[3]

H.261 compression was designed for operation on digital telephone lines that operated in multiples of 64 kbps (one DS0 or one voice

---

3. Because of this shared use of H.261 and H.263, providing a gateway to interconnect between IP, ISDN, and dial-up videoconferencing systems is fairly simple. See Chapter 10 for more information.

connection) up to a maximum of 2048 kbps, which corresponds to the rate of an E1 line in Europe (see Chapter 1). These interfaces are collectively known by the label "p × 64" (read as "p times sixty-four") where "p" can range from 1 to 30. In North America, when "p" equals 24, the system bandwidth will be equivalent to a T1 signal. There is nothing in the compression algorithm that forces it to operate in multiples of 64 kbps, so this kind of compression is available for use on other networks, including IP networks.

The basic video resolution for H.261 is based on the Common Intermediate Format (CIF), which is not directly compatible with NTSC or PAL video framing. CIF operates at 29.97 frames per second and has a picture size of 352 pixels wide by 288 lines high. Note that these figures are half of the corresponding figures for the active picture area of a PAL signal (704 × 576). This means that CIF has half the horizontal and half the vertical resolution of a PAL signal, or one-quarter the number of pixels. The other important resolution for H.261 is QCIF, which has one-quarter the resolution of CIF, or 176x144 pixels. In H.323, any device that supports video communication must support H.261 QCIF mode. CIF mode can also be supported, but QCIF is required.

H.261 uses motion prediction and DCT coding just like MPEG. However, H.261 uses only I frames and P frames, not B frames. It uses 4:2:0 color space, so the resolution of the color signals is cut in half in both the horizontal and the vertical directions. This works out to 88 pixels horizontally and 72 lines vertically in QCIF mode. Considering these advantages, it is easy to see how H.261 is able to send video images over relatively low-speed telephone lines.

H.263 is an improved version of H.261, with a number of enhancements. They are similar in scope and application, and many devices that handle H.263 video will handle H.261 video as well (although the two compression systems are not interoperable). H.263 supports finer granularity of motion estimation, so the predicted frames can be more accurate, and thus less data needs to be sent for P frames. It has more picture-encoding options and uses a more efficient algorithm for variable-length coding of the DCT coefficients. H.263 also supports PB frames, which are a very efficient way to code information similar to an MPEG P frame coupled with a B frame, except that it does not work as well in scenes with heavy motion.

Because H.263 was designed to work at very low bit rates, it introduces a new frame resolution, called sub-QCIF. This provides 128 pixels horizontally and 96 lines vertically, which is a bit bigger than a postage stamp on a modern computer monitor. It also supports two larger modes: 4CIF (704 × 576) and 16CIF (1408×1152). Any H.323 device that uses H.263 must support QCIF resolution. Also, any device that supports H.263 CIF or higher must also support the H.261 CIF format. All of these rules help promote interoperability, so even if they appear to be somewhat confusing, they are very beneficial to the videoconferencing community overall.

H.263 version 2 provides other capabilities, including support for any number of lines between 4 and 1152 that is divisible by 4, and any number of pixels per line from 4 to 2048 that is divisible by 4. This version can be useful for specialized cameras and for displays that can show multiple images. It also supports some new encoding methods, including scalable streams (see the discussion in the MPEG section earlier in the chapter).

## H.262, H.264, and Standards Cross-Reference

Curious readers might be wondering why the previous section skipped over ITU recommendation number H.262. We did this for a very good reason: We already discussed this standard when we discussed MPEG–2! Similarly, H.264 is the same as MPEG–4's AVC. Table 4-8 helps show these relationships. Note that this table is intended to be a simple guide, not an authoritative reference that covers the multiple revisions that these documents have undergone.

## Motion JPEG

The Joint Photographic Experts Group developed the JPEG format for compressing digital still photographs, and it was a popular format at one time for files on video servers. JPEG is a lossy, perceptual encoder, based on the DCT algorithm. Newer versions offer lossless coding as well. When used for video signals, the format is called Motion JPEG. Each frame of the video is encoded as a separate

**TABLE 4-8**

Compression Standards Cross-Reference

| Common of Name Application | International Telecommunication Union (ITU) | International Organization for Standardization (ISO) |
|---|---|---|
| P × 64 Video ISDN Videoconferencing | H.261 | N/A |
| MPEG–1 Video and Audio Coding | N/A | 11172 |
| MPEG–2 Video Coding Only | H.262 | 13818–2 |
| MPEG–2 Advanced Audio Coding | N/A | 13818–7 |
| MPEG–2 Systems, normal audio, and other aspects | N/A | 13818–1, –3 to –6, –8 to –11 |
| Low Bit Rate Video IP, Dial-up Videoconferencing | H.263 | N/A |
| MPEG–4 (except AVC) Audio and Visual Objects | N/A | 14496 |
| MPEG–4 Advanced Video Coding | H.264 | 14496–10 |

picture, which makes the resulting stream very suitable for editing. It also makes the video stream bit rate higher than it would be with other technologies such as MPEG–2.

Two main video applications have been implemented using Motion JPEG:

- A number of video editing systems employ Motion JPEG as an intermediate format, because of the relative simplicity of editing these video streams. However, this format has become less popular in recent years, as more efficient coding methods have been introduced.
- At least one relatively successful video transport system was released that used Motion JPEG video over standard telco DS3 (45 Mbps) lines. These systems carried one video per DS3 and could be switched using standard telco equipment. A number of these systems were deployed for distance learning in the USA. With the coming of low-cost MPEG video encoders that could easily put three or more video signals into the same amount of bandwidth, these systems have become less popular. However, a meaningful installed base of this equipment still exists in a number of school systems.

## Windows Media and Other Streaming Formats

A number of proprietary video and audio encoder/decoder (codec) systems are on the market, and many of them are suitable for use in video transport over IP networks. Because they are proprietary, the exact details of their operation are normally not provided for general publication. In addition, the different codec manufacturers are currently engaged in heated competition, so product cycles are short and performance and other specifications can change rapidly. Let's look at three of the largest codec suppliers for the video streaming market:

Windows Media Player has a long development history from Microsoft. As of this writing, the latest version of the video codec is called Windows Media 9, also known as WM9. With this version, Microsoft has taken two unusual steps. First, Microsoft has pledged to freeze the video decoder design for a number of years, to provide an incentive for semiconductor and other hardware device manufacturers to spend the time and resources necessary to incorporate WM9 into a variety of low-cost products.[4] Second, Microsoft has released the applicable specifications for the video decoder to a standards body (the Society of Motion Picture and Television Engineers, or SMPTE) to begin the process of making the video decoder portion of WM9 a public standard. (In the SMPTE process, WM9 has been renamed VC-1.) If this effort is successful, any company that wishes to design a VC-1 decoder will be able to do so, provided that it obtains a license to use any of the patented intellectual property in the specification that belongs to Microsoft or other parties. (This patent licensing arrangement is very similar to the ones that are in place for MPEG–2, MPEG–4, and a host of other standard technologies.)

Microsoft intends to address a broad cross-section of the video compression market with WM9 technology. The company has already released a number of implementations of its technology that range from low bit rate streaming for handheld devices all the way up to

---

4. Newer versions of the Windows Media Player, server and other technologies are already entering the market as Windows Media 10 and above; however, these newer versions are supposed to use the same video decoding algorithm as WM9.

digital projection of first-run theatrical motion pictures. In addition to the video-encoding technology, WM9 covers other aspects of the complete package, including audio coding, stream formats, and Digital Rights management (also known as copy protection). Both real-time and non–real-time WM9 codecs have been released, although there are certainly more in development as of this writing. In addition, the company is being very aggressive in pricing licenses in order to make WM9 attractively priced relative to other technologies, such as MPEG–4.

Some readers may wonder about the differences between WM9 and MPEG–4 AVC. Both codecs offer significant advances in coding efficiency (i.e., fewer bits for a given picture quality) as compared to MPEG–2. To date, there hasn't been any compelling evidence to say that one is clearly better than the other for any large group of applications. Also, it is important to note that while efforts are under way to make VC-1 an international standard, the work is not yet complete. MPEG–4 AVC is already an international standard (although that doesn't mean that the technology is free—a license fee must still be paid to use MPEG–4 as well as VC-1 technology). Interestingly, many vendors of encoders and decoders are designing their hardware to support both technologies, through the use of general-purpose digital signal processing (DSP) hardware and downloadable firmware.

Real Networks is another major supplier of proprietary codec technology. Most of Real's products are targeted at the video streaming market, but more developments are sure to come. As with Microsoft's products, a number of third-party tools (from suppliers such a Adobe, Pinnacle Systems, etc.) can be used to create compressed video streams in both real-time and off-line production environments. A huge amount of content is available for streaming on the web in Real's SureStream format, which is designed to automatically adapt to suit the wide range of different network connection speeds used around the globe.

Apple Computer supplies QuickTime technology, which has migrated toward using standards-compliant technology, such as MPEG–4. Apple was one of the pioneers of video streaming and still has a significant amount of development activity under way for new technology.

One distinguishing feature of all three of the preceding proprietary codec suppliers is their willingness to provide a free software client (or "player") for receiving their compressed video streams. Literally hundreds of millions of personal computer users have downloaded and installed these players onto their desktop and laptop computers. In addition, most of these companies also supply a free encoder with limited functionality. More sophisticated encoders are generally available for a price; these versions often contain advanced features that can make the job of creating content files easier, as well as using more efficient compression algorithms.

So far, we have discussed mainly software-based proprietary codecs, but hardware-based ones are also available. These units tend to be designed for closed system applications, such as security cameras. Many of these codecs have been designed to efficiently handle specific types of video, such as security applications in which there is very little motion in the image for long periods of time. Since product cost is a big concern in many of these applications, designers will often use subsets of standard compression systems or completely proprietary algorithms that can be implemented inexpensively. As a result, most of these codecs will work only with other products from the same manufacturer.

There are no easy answers when deciding whether or not to use proprietary codecs. All three of the main software-based codec suppliers mentioned in this section have a long and distinguished track record of innovation and customer service. The same can be said for many hardware-based codec suppliers. Nevertheless, any users of a proprietary codec run the risk that their supplier will, for one reason or another, stop providing products. Prudent users will assess this risk and make sure to have a contingency plan in place in case this happens. Table 4-9 gives several other advantages and disadvantages of proprietary codecs.

## DV, DVCAM, and DVCPRO

The popular camera and videotape formats DV, DVCAM, and DVCPRO are intended for use in a video production environment. As such, they need to meet two requirements: The resulting video should

**TABLE 4-9**

Advantages and Disadvantages of Proprietary Codecs

*Advantages*

- *Innovation:* As compression technology advances, innovations can be incorporated into proprietary codecs very rapidly. Industry standards tend to have a slower rate of change, because of the need to achieve agreement between many different parties.
- *Pricing:* Many proprietary software codec suppliers offer basic versions of their players (decoders) free and have very low cost encoder options.
- *Backward Compatibility:* Proprietary codec suppliers have a strong incentive to ensure that new versions of their codecs work with previous versions and have typically done a good job in this area. This may not be as true with designs based on standards, unless backward compatibility is explicitly defined in the specification.

*Disadvantages*

- *Portability:* Because a single vendor controls when and how proprietary codecs are implemented, versions for alternative platforms may be late to arrive or never produced. This can limit users' choices, particularly in the selection of operating systems.
- *Change Control:* Major codec suppliers determine when new features are released to market and frequently encourage end users to upgrade to the latest version. This can make it difficult for large organizations to ensure that all users have the same version and to ensure that the codec software doesn't interfere with other applications.
- *Platform Requirements:* As codecs become more powerful, the minimum requirements for other system components (operating systems, processor speeds, etc.) can also increase. This can force users to deploy system upgrades in order to use the latest versions of some software codecs.
- *Archival Storage:* As with any rapidly evolving technology, long-term storage of encoded video files is useful only as long as suitable decoder software is available. In the case of proprietary codecs, the supplier controls software availability over the long term.

be easy to edit, and the image quality should be very high. Accordingly, these digital video signals operate at relatively high bit rates. Since the primary application is recording onto digital videotape, high-speed data is normally used. Methods have also been developed for sending these signals by means of IP networks, so looking at them may be worthwhile.

The base level of these formats is a 25 Mbps compressed video signal. This represents about a 5:1 compression of the raw video signal. This bit rate is set deliberately high, to satisfy the needs of professional video producers. Video compression is performed using the DCT algorithm, just like MPEG. In this case, each frame of video is coded separately, using I frames only. When only I frames are used, subsequent editing is very simple, because cuts and edits can be made before or after any frame in the image, since each frame is independent of the others. (Contrast this with P frames and B frames, which both use data from other frames to be decoded properly.) Other formats exist in this family, including DVCPRO operating at 50 and 100 Mbps. A high-definition version of the DVCAM signal also exists, called HDCAM. It operates at roughly 150 Mbps and is transported using the SDTI format (SMPTE 305M) that runs at 270 Mbps.

The Internet Engineering Task Force (IETF) has published RFC 3189, which defines a way to put DV-encoded video into RTP packets. (We'll discuss packing video into packets in more detail in Chapter 6.) It is unclear whether this standard has been widely adopted (or ever will be); however, it might be useful for networks used among editing systems. Given the high bit rates involved in this format, it is unlikely that this format will receive widespread use in general-purpose video networking applications.

## Wavelets

Wavelets are a very useful compression system for encoding still pictures. A number of devices have come on the market that use wavelets for video compression, although there is a lack of widely used standards. MPEG–4 supports the use of wavelets for encoding still pictures, which are called sprites in the standard. A number of video surveillance cameras also use wavelet video.

Wavelets perform a similar function to the DCT (Discrete Cosine Transform; see Appendix A) but use a different mathematical operation. Essentially, the function of both DCT and wavelets is to reduce the number of bits that are needed to represent a video image that is pleasing to the human eye. Both wavelets and DCT have supporters and detractors in the standards bodies, and both have advantages and drawbacks. Video system users should base their selection of a compression system on the overall suitability of a compression product for their application, and not get overly concerned about which particular mathematical compression technique is employed.

One advantage of wavelet encoding is that the process has built-in scalability. Remember that scalable streams are very desirable for broadcasting to a diverse group of viewers over networks that have a wide range of different user interface speeds. Low-speed users receive just one low-resolution stream, whereas users with higher speed interfaces can also receive "helper" streams that enhance the video signal. Wavelets naturally support this function due to the underlying mathematics of the algorithm. Wavelets are not as strong in dealing with motion compensation, so they have not yet penetrated nearly as many applications as the DCT compression algorithms.

## Dolby AC-3 Audio

Dolby AC-3 audio coding is also commonly known as Dolby Digital. It offers a high-quality audio experience with good compression characteristics and has been approved for use in both DVDs and in digital television broadcasts in the USA.

Dolby AC-3 uses a modified DCT algorithm to perform some compression functions. It also offers a sophisticated perceptual model of the human hearing systems, so extensive compression can be performed without any noticeable difference to the human ear. Dolby Digital also offers support for surround sound, including the popular 5.1 audio format (see Chapter 3).

Dolby AC-3 audio is included in some versions of MPEG–4 and is used on a number of satellite television systems.

## VBI COMPRESSION ISSUES

The Vertical Blanking Interval (VBI) is part of every standard video signal. For many programs that are broadcast, the VBI contains auxiliary data signals that provide special data services. Examples include closed captioning, electronic program guide data, teletext, and V-chip program ratings. These signals were discussed in more detail in Chapter 3.

As we have discussed in detail, MPEG and other video compression systems focus on eliminating redundant and unnecessary information from the incoming video signal. For normal analog video, the horizontal lines that make up the VBI fit both descriptions. The VBI is redundant, because it is in every video frame, and it is unnecessary, because the location of the active video pixels on every line is already part of the MPEG (or other) data stream.

However, when the VBI contains data, the situation changes. In this case, the encoder needs to handle the data and send it to the decoder. There are at least two ways of doing this. First, normal video compression techniques (you guessed it—DCT) are capable of accepting extra lines of video from the VBI and compressing them along with the other image data. This method works for low-speed data but may not be appropriate for higher speed data, where the patterns encoded in the VBI are very detailed. Second, the data in the VBI can be extracted and sent as a separate data stream embedded inside the compressed video stream. This method has the benefit of being very efficient, because the data rates of the embedded signals are very low (closed captioning runs at 420 bits per second, or 60 7-bit characters per second). However, this has the drawback of forcing the video compression devices to understand and interpret the format of the incoming VBI data, and to have a means of generating this data and reinserting it after the video has been decompressed. Note that this is not a simple process, due in part to the lack of standardization of VBI signals between countries or manufacturers. Users that depend on VBI signals need to ensure that compression devices properly handle all necessary signal types.

## COMPARING COMPRESSION TECHNOLOGIES

Users who deploy video transport systems often need to select equipment for compressing video and audio signals. Because of the wide variety of applications, it would be very difficult to describe one product that can fit all (or even most) needs. Plus, video compression technology is constantly evolving, and comparisons made at any one point in time can quickly go out of date. Instead of attempting to make comparisons of the various technologies, in the following sections we will discuss how the comparisons can be made and which aspects of compression are important to various applications.

## Video Quality

For many users, video quality is the most important criterion for selecting a video compression system. The level of quality required for a system to support medical diagnoses is far different from that needed for simple chats between co-workers in a videoconference. However, some guidelines listed in Table 4-10 can be used when making these comparisons.

**TABLE 4-10**

Video Quality Comparison Guidelines

- Use several video sequences that are similar to the scenes that will be used in the real application. For example, videoconferencing systems should not be evaluated using live sports footage, because sports footage may show weaknesses in the video compression system that would never be encountered in the real application. A number of standard video test sequences are available from SMPTE and other sources.
- Use high-quality video sources and displays for the evaluation. Digital sources are preferred for testing if the encoder and decoder have digital inputs; however, make sure to test the analog inputs and outputs as well if they will be used in the actual application. Low-quality sources can introduce artifacts that can have a major impact on compression systems. If live sources are used, make sure that high-quality cameras and lights are used as well.
- Examine the impact of transmission errors on the system. See what happens when bit error or packet loss rates climb. Since proper network error handling will have a big impact on end user satisfaction with the system, examine the impact of jitter (see Chapter 7) and changing the size of the video input buffer on the video decoder.
- Be sure to watch the video stream for several minutes, particularly when scene changes happen. Short test sequences don't always have the ability to check the buffer management in the receiver, and scene changes will stress the whole compression system by introducing lots of changes between adjacent frames, which in turn will create a peak in the compressed data rate. Errors, such as the appearance of squares in the image, sudden freezes of the image, or short losses of part or all of the video image, indicate that the system is not correctly handling challenging video.
- Test each system for audio/video delay matching. It is not uncommon to have synchronization problems appear after several minutes of playing. Because of the relative complexity of video compression/decompression as compared to audio compression/decompression, it is more common to see audio signals get ahead of video signals. This delay can be very disconcerting to a viewer.
- Test a range of different compression configurations, such as different GOP lengths and patterns and different stream rates. Even though the application may be fixed at first, many times equipment is re-deployed as networks evolve. Top-quality compression systems will work well at both high and low bit rates.

**TABLE 4-10** (*Continued*)

- Verify that the entire system works end-to-end with a full complement of video signals. Since many transport systems multiplex video signals together, it is important to test the system under a full load, to make sure that all necessary components are operating and that buffers are adequately sized. Pay particular attention to the useful maximum bit rate for each component in the system, to ensure that one device will not limit the performance of the entire system.
- Check how different manufacturers define the video bit rate. Some base their specifications on the total bit stream; others simply refer to the rate of just the raw compressed video stream. Check to see how these rates are controlled and configured by the system installer.
- Try to do head-to-head comparisons, where both systems are showing the same video and being displayed in the same manner, preferably on the same display (displays can be hard to match completely). Look for differences, particularly video image errors, which will most likely happen at different times on the two systems, even with identical input signals.
- Choose the most stressful system setup end-to-end. This typically includes the lowest bit rate that will be used and the most complex image and network path.
- If possible, use multiple observers to score the video performance. Since most encoding methods are perceptual, flaws that might not be noticed by one person might be very objectionable to other viewers. Remember, most compression algorithms were developed using panels of human observers as the ultimate test.

## Audio Quality

Unfortunately in the video transport business, most users end up focused on video quality and neglect audio quality. Worse yet, many audio evaluations are done with unsuitable source material and poor-quality speakers. Studies have shown that people perceive video quality to increase when audio quality is increased. The message is clear here: Make sure that audio performance is comparable to the level of video performance. Table 4-11 lists a few rules for evaluating audio compression systems.

## System Delay

End-to-end delay in a video transport system is normally significant only when two-way communication is taking place. Applications such as videoconferencing and distance learning fall into this category. For most other applications, the delay of a compression system does not add measurably to the tolerable amount of end-to-end delay in the system. For example, if the nationwide broadcast of a football

**TABLE 4-11**
Audio Quality Comparison Rules

- Use audio signals that match the application as closely as possible. What might be suitable for carrying normal conversations may not work well for a musical performance.
- Use high-quality audio sources and speakers for the evaluation. Use both digital and analog audio signal inputs and outputs if they are available. Low-quality sources can introduce artifacts that can have a major impact on compression systems. If live sources are used, make sure that high-quality microphones are used as well.
- Use a similar setup for all systems, including the sampling rates and bit rates, to allow a fair comparison.
- Evaluate the system performance at both high and low incoming sound levels. Make sure that loud sounds don't become distorted and that quiet sections of the program are not accompanied by audio noise.

match was delayed for several seconds, the delay would not have any appreciable effect on the entertainment value of the program.

The easiest way to measure delay is to have a camera and a display that are located in the same room. With the camera connected to the encoder and the display connected to the decoder, connect the encoder to the decoder using a network that closely models the actual network that will be installed in the system. Then, determine whether it is possible to notice the amount of delay through the system (clapping and hand waving are common activities). If the delay cannot be noticed, then the system is quite suitable for any application. If the delay is noticeable but lasts less than half a second, then use on an interactive system is possible, although there may be some discomfort with the users. If the delay is longer than half a second, then uses for interactivity should be limited.

Note that many systems can be configured to trade off bandwidth and quality for delay. In particular, MPEG systems can be configured for low delays by using very short GOP lengths, such as IP or I frame only. This reduces the delay in both the encoder and the decoder, but at a price: The amount of compression is reduced, and either the network bandwidth must be increased, or the quality level will go down. It is not uncommon for different applications to require different system configurations, so a certain amount of trial and error is reasonable.

When delay is being tested, it is also a good idea to check lip synchronization. This is very important for user satisfaction. If the video and audio portions of the program drift out of synchronization, viewer satisfaction drops rapidly. To properly test this, a known good source (such as a camera and a live subject) is required. Note that some DVD players will have trouble with video and audio synchronization, and may not be suitable sources for this type of test. In addition, audio/video synchronization should be tested over a significant period of time with uninterrupted source material. In this manner, low amounts of drift have a chance to accumulate and show up as a real difference in the displayed image and sound. Note that some equipment can introduce different delays in the audio and video paths; this can be expensive to correct with external pieces of equipment.

## Compression Efficiency

Even though we'd like to think that it doesn't matter, compression efficiency is important to evaluate when testing a video compression system. More efficient encoders can have wide-ranging impacts on a system. These impacts can include reduced use of network bandwidth, higher quality signals on fixed-bandwidth systems, and less consumption of storage resources, such as hard disks and removable media.

One way to test compression efficiency is to take a fixed video segment and record the compressed video file on a hard disk. The more efficient the encoder, the smaller the file. However, it is important to make sure that the quality levels delivered by both encoders are equivalent, or the test can lose meaning. Since video compression is based on human perception, the best way to compare quality is to have human observers compare the two resulting signals under controlled viewing circumstances and score the results. Use digital video sources whenever possible, and make sure that the video signals appear to be similar quality before compression. Only if both encoders deliver the same video quality level will the comparison be valid.

## APPLICATIONS

Video compression is an essential part of all video production systems today. Whether light, lossless compression is being used for a video camera's output, or heavy compression is used for creating streaming media, compression is everywhere. Table 4-12 lists a number of applications that would not be feasible without high-performance video compression.

## TECHNOLOGY LICENSING ISSUES

As we have seen in this chapter, a huge number of clever technologies have been applied to the art and science of video compression. Even though much of this technology is governed by international standards, not all of this technology is in the public domain. In fact, many of the key technologies used in MPEG and other compression systems were developed by individuals and corporations who still retain

**TABLE 4-12**

Video Compression Applications

---

- DVDs use compression to hold Hollywood movies. A standard DVD holds 4.7 Gigabytes of data, which would be enough to hold only 2½ minutes of uncompressed 270 Mbps video signal. With compression, the same DVD can easily hold 2 hours' worth of video and audio content.
- Digital satellite systems rely on high-performance compression to deliver hundreds of channels of programming. Without compression, the number of channels delivered would drop by a factor of six or more, and the high quality offered by digital technology would disappear.
- High definition television (HDTV) requires an immense amount of bandwidth in its uncompressed form, roughly 1500 Mbps. With compression, that signal can be reduced to less than 19 Mbps. This compression allows an HD signal to be broadcast in the same amount of radio spectrum as a traditional analog television broadcast.
- Streaming video depends heavily on video compression, simply because the amount of bandwidth that is available to most users would choke on uncompressed video content. Even DSL and cable modem users would not be able to handle the bit rates generated by an uncompressed video image that occupied a window as small as a large postage stamp on a user display.
- Consumer digital cameras, both still and video, use compression of various types, including JPEG, DV, and others.
- Portable audio players and file-sharing systems normally use compressed audio files, in formats such as MP3 and MP4/AAC.

---

ownership of their technology in the form of patents and other legally protected rights. For example, the patent portfolio for MPEG–2 technologies includes 630 patents from around the world.

Fortunately, the owners of these technologies banded together to set up an organization known as the MPEG LA (the LA originally stood for Licensing Administrator, but now LA is the official name). MPEG LA is responsible for establishing and collecting the license fees on the technology and for distributing the collected funds to the patent owners. This central clearinghouse provides big benefits to the users of this technology, because one simple payment to MPEG LA satisfies the patent obligations for the covered technology. Contrast this with the headaches and complexities that would be involved in negotiating separate license agreements with the 20+ companies that have patents included in the MPEG–2 technology pool.

The license fees are assessed on a per-item basis and are officially described on www.mpegla.com. For example, the fee listed on the website for an MPEG–2 decoding device (such as a DVD player, a set top box, or a computer with a DVD player, whether hardware or software) produced after 2002 is US $2.50. Other fees are assessed for MPEG–2 encoders, MPEG multiplexers, and other devices. Fees are also assessed for recorded media, such as DVDs, but the fees are relatively low ($0.03 for a single-layer DVD disc, although there are a number of different ways of calculating the fee).

For MPEG–4, there are similar fee arrangements for devices. In addition there are fees based on the number of streams that are created and on the number of subscribers that are served in cable and satellite television systems. Plus, there are fees for individual titles that are sold to viewers on a DVD or via pay-per-view, such as a Video-on-Demand system. These fees have created some controversy in the industry, because they include charges for the device itself (like MPEG–2) and also charges for viewing content using the device.

Where does this leave the owner of a video networking system? First, it is important to understand that fees for devices are normally collected from the device manufacturers, so end users of equipment generally don't need to worry about technology fees. Second, publishers of media, such as DVDs, are also responsible for paying the fees required for those items. Third, most of the MPEG–4 license fees that are payable on a per-stream or a per-subscriber basis are targeted at companies that are charging users to view the videos. When these videos are delivered to employees within a company or are distributed free of charge for education purposes, the intent is not to charge on a per-item basis. However, this arrangement may be subject to revision, so users of MPEG–4 would be well served by investigating the necessary license arrangements in detail before launching a large-scale system.

**Disclaimer:** Neither the author of this book nor the publisher claim any expertise in licensing law or in the terms of the MPEG LA license agreement. Readers should consult with MPEG LA and any other licensing bodies to confirm all details of the required licenses prior to installing a video network that relies on this technology.

## REVIEW AND CHECKLIST UPDATE

In this chapter, we covered the basics of video and audio compression. We looked at the benefits and drawbacks of compression. We spent some time discussing MPEG, because it is the most widely used technology for compression today. We covered a few other types of compression that are used in videoconferencing and other applications. We talked about the ways in which compression technology and devices can be compared. We also took a brief tour of some applications and concluded with a look at the technology licensing issues.

## Chapter 4 Checklist Update

❏ Decide if compression will be used on video and/or audio content. If compression isn't going to be used, will all the networks that will be used have adequate bandwidth to handle the digital video content?

❏ Examine the devices that will be responsible for transmitting and receiving the video/audio content. Will they have adequate performance to encode and/or decode the video in addition to other required tasks?

❏ If desktop PCs will be used, will hardware encoders or decoders need to be added, or will software encoders and decoders be adequate?

❏ If stand-alone hardware devices are to be used (such as set top boxes), how will the users select programming and control other functions?

❏ Will the system connect to other video networks and devices? If so, what standards will be used to permit interoperability?

❏ When selecting a codec technology, make sure that both content sources and destinations can be equipped with compatible technology. Even when the chosen technology is based on published standards, it is important to make sure that each supplier has implemented a compatible set of features. Users of feature-rich technologies such as MPEG–4 need to be particularly careful in this area, because two suppliers can correctly assert that their products are both MPEG–4 compliant without being able to work together if the suppliers have implemented different portions of the standards.

❏ For MPEG systems, a fair amount of configuration of the units may be required. Make sure both encoder and decoder are configured to identical values for all parameters. Users must select a GOP length and pattern, a target video and audio bandwidth, a video resolution, a network interface bit rate, audio format, etc. Longer GOPs and those that include B frames mean better video quality at lower bit rates, but they introduce delay in the transport path. Lower video resolution also reduces bit rate but can result in smaller or blurrier images on the display.

❏ Make sure to evaluate compression systems in all critical areas, including
  ❏ Video Quality
  ❏ Audio Quality
  ❏ System Delay and Audio/Video (lip) Synchronization
  ❏ Compression Efficiency

❏ Make sure to use high-quality source material, displays, and speakers for evaluations. Make sure to use multiple people to evaluate the systems and score the results; different individuals will have different perceptions of compression artifacts.

❏ Make sure that the encoder and decoder correctly handle any required data contained in the VBI.

❑ Ensure that equipment and software vendors have paid the appropriate licensing fees for any technology products that are being purchased and that the proper fees are paid to all content rights holders.

❑ For applications in which viewers will be charged for video and audio content, determine whether royalties need to be paid on a per-stream or per-user basis for the compression technologies used, such as MPEG–4.

❑ If new networks are to be constructed, make sure that they can handle the full number of streams with each one operating at the maximum allowed bit rate.

# 5

# IP NETWORKING BASICS

A basic understanding of the principles of Internet Protocol (IP) networking will make our discussions of video transport much easier to understand and to put into context. Video can be tricky to send over an IP network, and it is not at all unusual for an IP network to require special grooming or reconfiguration in order to handle video traffic. In this chapter, along with an overview of IP, we will discuss some technologies that can make the job of setting up a video network more complicated. In addition, we will look at Ethernet technology, which is the most commonly used network technology for IP transport.

Readers with significant networking experience may choose to skip reading this chapter, but please understand that we will cover terminology used in the remainder of this book. By the end of this chapter, readers should understand how both IP and Ethernet fit into the bewildering array of networking technologies and be familiar with some of the terminology that is associated with IP networking.

## HOW IP FITS IN

IP (Internet Protocol) provides a very useful mechanism to enable communications between computers. IP provides a uniform addressing scheme so that computers on one network can communicate with computers on a distant network. IP also provides a set of functions that make it easy for different types of applications (such as e-mail, web browsing, or video streaming) to work in parallel on a single computer. Plus, IP allows different types of computers (mainframes, PCs, Macs, Linux machines, etc.) to communicate with each other.

IP is very flexible because it is not tied to a specific physical communication method. IP links have been successfully established over a wide variety of different physical links. One very popular technology for IP transport is Ethernet (also commonly known as 10BaseT or IEEE 802.3, although these are not strict synonyms). We'll talk a little bit more about Ethernet later in this chapter. Many other technologies can support IP, including dial-up modems, wireless links (such as Wi-Fi), and SONET and ATM telecom links (see Chapter 1). IP will even work across connections where several network technologies are combined, such as a wireless home access link that connects to a CATV system offering cable modem services, which in turn sends customer data to the Internet by means of a fiber optic backbone (which is the network setup currently employed by the author). This adaptability is one of the things that make IP so widespread.

### A Simple Analogy

A very simple, limited analogy may be appropriate here. In some respects, an IP address is like a telephone number. If you know someone's telephone number, there is a pretty good chance that you can pick up your phone and call him or her. It doesn't matter what country the person is in, as long as you dial correctly (and add the country code if needed). It doesn't matter what kind of technology that person is using—mobile phone, cordless phone, fixed rotary, or tone-dialed phone. Several different network voice technologies may be used to complete the circuit, including copper cable, fiber optics, microwave links, satellite links, and other wireless technologies. Even so, the call can still go through. For data networks, an IP address provides the same function: a mechanism to uniquely identify different computers, and to allow them to contact each other and exchange data over a huge variety of different network technologies.

Stretching the analogy a bit further, just knowing someone's telephone number does not mean that you are going to be able to communicate with him or her. A call might be placed when there is nobody to answer the phone, or the phone is engaged in another call and not available. The call might go through just fine, but if both speakers don't use a common language, then communication won't occur. The same is true with IP networking—simply knowing another computer's IP address doesn't mean that it will be possible for two applications running on different machines to communicate with each other.

Of course, it is important to remember that IP networking and telephony are two very different technologies. Telephony is "connection-oriented," meaning that a specific circuit must be established between the sender and the receiver of information before any communication takes place (such as a voice conversation or a fax transmission), and that all the information will flow over this same route. IP, on the other hand, is "connectionless," meaning that the information (such as data, voice, or video) is broken up into subunits prior to transmission and that each subunit is free to take any available path from the sender to the receiver. We'll talk more about these subunits of data, also known as packets or datagrams, shortly.

## The Internet vs. internets

"Internet" is a term that is probably at least vaguely familiar to anyone who has read a newspaper in the past few years. (After all, without the Internet, we would not have had all those crazy dot-com television commercials and the Internet Bubble on stock markets.) Simply put, the Internet consists of a large number of interconnected networks, which provide communications between a huge number of users around the world. There is only one Internet in general use today, although a group of researchers have put together a newer high-speed network called "Internet 2." Once you have access to the Internet, you have access to a wide variety of applications, including web browsing, e-mail, file transfer, and a variety of video services.

However, it's important to understand that many companies also run their own private "internets," commonly called "intranets." These private networks often provide many of the services of the Internet, but in a closed environment (or one that has carefully protected links to the public Internet). Private internets are often constructed using private communications links, such as leased telecom circuits, ATM links, etc. Or, they can be constructed by using Virtual Private Network (VPN) connections that use the Internet to provide secure, private communication.

Both the Internet and internets commonly use the IP protocol to allow communication across a wide variety of technologies and architectures. IP addresses of individual devices can be used on an internet, on the public Internet, or on both. Also note that internets are, in many instances, more suitable for video transport than the Internet, simply because the behavior of the network can be more easily controlled.

## Limitations of IP

IP doesn't do everything. IP depends on other software and hardware, and other software in turn depends on IP. Figure 5-1 illustrates how IP fits in between the actual job of data transport performed by

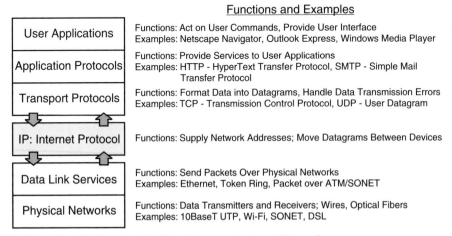

**FIGURE 5-1**  How IP Fits into the Data Communications Hierarchy

physical networks, and the software applications that use IP to communicate with applications running on other servers.

IP is not a user application or an application protocol. However, many user applications employ IP to accomplish their tasks, such as sending e-mail, playing a video, or browsing the web. These applications use application protocols such as the HyperText Transfer Protocol (HTTP) or Simple Mail Transfer Protocol (SMTP). These protocols provide services to applications. For example, one of the services provided by HTTP is a uniform method for giving the location of resources on the Internet, which goes by the acronym "URL." Many other protocols use IP, and we will discuss them throughout this book.

IP by itself is not even a reliable means of communications; it does not provide a mechanism to re-send data that might be lost or corrupted in transmission. Other protocols that employ IP are responsible for that (see the discussion of TCP in Chapter 6). Using the telephone analogy again, IP can connect the telephone call, but it doesn't control what happens if, for example, the person being called isn't home, or if the call gets interrupted before the parties are finished talking. Those occurrences are the responsibility of the protocols that use IP for communication.

## IP BASICS

By understanding a few basic concepts of IP, we will be able to discuss how video traffic can successfully be sent over an IP network. In the following sections we'll talk first about one of the most common features of IP: the IP address. Then, we'll cover the basic building block of any IP communication, the IP Datagram, and how this relates to the concept of an IP Packet. We'll also take a quick look at a couple of new technologies that affect how IP addresses are used in practice and how these practices affect video transport.

## IP Addresses

One aspect of IP that is easy to recognize is the special format that is used to give an IP address. This format is called "dotted decimal" and consists of a series of four numbers separated by periods (or "dots").

For example, 129.35.76.177 is the IP address for www.elsevier.com. Most folks who have had to configure their own home network or laptop connection have probably seen information in this form. A dotted decimal number represents a 32-bit number, which is broken up into four 8-bit numbers.[1]

Of course, being human, we have a hard time remembering and typing all of those digits correctly (even when writing a book). So, to make life easy, the Domain Name System (DNS) was invented. DNS provides a translation service for web browsers and other software applications that takes easy-to-remember domain names (such as "elsevier.com") and translates them into IP addresses (such as 129.35.76.177).

## IP Datagrams and Packets

Basically, IP works as a delivery service for "datagrams." They can also (somewhat confusingly) be called "IP packets." A datagram is a single message unit that can be sent over IP, with very specific format and content rules. Since there are many excellent references available that talk about the structure of an IP datagram, we'll just summarize the key header elements that an IP datagram needs to have in Table 5-1 and illustrate them in Figure 5-2.

The terms "datagram" and "packet" are used somewhat interchangeably in IP. A datagram is a single, logical block of data that is being sent over IP, augmented by a complete IP header. An IP packet is a generic term that applies both to a complete datagram and to the pieces of a datagram that has been fragmented. In most cases each datagram will be sent as a single packet, so fragmentation won't be needed.

A long datagram will be fragmented into smaller packets if the datagram is too long for a given network. For example, it is perfectly legal in IP to have a datagram that is, say, 3200 bytes long. However, if we need to send this datagram across an Ethernet network, we have to modify the datagram, because the Maximum Transmission Unit (MTU) of a

---

1.   IP version 4, which is what is used in the Internet today, uses 32-bit addresses. IP version 6 has a different addressing scheme, with 128 bits for each IP address. We will limit our discussions in the rest of the book to IP version 4, also known as IPv4.

**TABLE 5-1**

Key Elements of an IP Datagram

- *Destination Address:* The IP address indicating where the datagram is being sent
- *Source Address:* The IP address indicating where the datagram came from
- *Total Length:* A count, in bytes, of the length of the entire datagram, including the header
- *Header Checksum:* A basic error-checking mechanism for the header information in a datagram. Any datagram with an error in its header will be destroyed.
- *Type of Service:* A group of bits that can be used to indicate the relative importance of one datagram as compared to another. They will be discussed in Chapter 7 in more detail, but note that most Internet Service Providers (ISPs) and the public Internet do not routinely allow one user's datagrams to claim to be more important than another user's.
- *Time-to-Live:* A counter that is decremented each time a datagram is forwarded in an IP network. When this value reaches zero, the datagram is destroyed. This mechanism prevents packets from endlessly looping around in a network.
- *Fragmentation Control:* These bits and bytes are used when a datagram needs to be broken up into smaller pieces to travel across a specific network segment.
- Other items include the Header Length field, protocol identifier, version identifier, and options that are part of the specifications for IP but would require more detail to describe than we need for the purposes of this book.

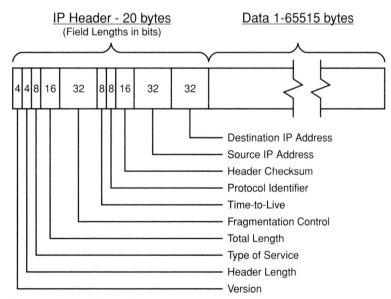

**FIGURE 5-2**   IP Datagram Format

standard Ethernet link is 1500 bytes, as defined in the RFC 894 (Request for Comments, one of the many standards for the Internet as defined by the Internet Engineering Task Force). What we do is fragment the datagram into three packets, two long and one short, as shown in Figure 5-3. Once a datagram is fragmented, it remains that way until the final destination is reached. At the final destination, the packets are reassembled back into the original datagram, which can then be processed by the higher-level protocols or user applications. Note that if one of the datagram fragments is corrupted or lost along the way, then the entire datagram will be destroyed by IP.

The process of sending a packet from one computer to another may involve transit through many different IP network links. At each step along the way, the IP packet must be processed. This processing involves the following procedures:

- The header of the IP packet must first have its header checksum verified. If the checksum is incorrect, then the packet is destroyed.
- The header is then examined to determine where the packet is going, by looking at the destination IP address. Based on this IP address, the network equipment (typically an IP router; see the description later in this chapter) determines what to do with the packet, such as send it out on another network or transfer the packet to a local area network connected to the equipment.
- The Time-to-Live counter is decremented, a new checksum is calculated, and both are inserted into the packet header in place of their former values. If the Time-to-Live counter reaches zero, then the packet is destroyed.

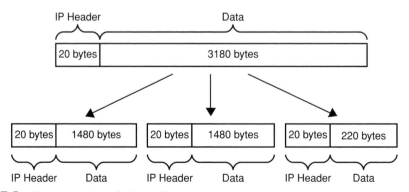

**FIGURE 5-3**  Fragmentation of a Long Datagram

We'll go into this in a little more detail when we talk about routers and switches later in this chapter.

## DHCP and NAT

Just over 4 billion unique IP addresses are available, meaning that there aren't always enough to go around. If this is surprising, take a moment to think about the number of IP addresses that a person might use, including a work PC, a home PC, a networked printer, a file server, a mobile device, etc., and then consider the billions of people who will have access to the Internet. To solve this problem, two technologies have been invented. The first, called Dynamic Host Configuration Protocol (DHCP) assigns a temporary IP address to each computer. The second, called Network Address Translation (NAT) allows multiple computers to share a single IP address.

DHCP is a required function in many corporate networks and with many Internet Service Providers (ISPs). The concept of DHCP is that an IP address is needed only when a computer wants to access the Internet or a company internet. If the computer is offline or powered down, then an IP address is not needed. DHCP is also of benefit for mobile workers, who might carry a laptop with them when they move from one location to another in a company and need to have a suitable IP address assigned in each location. Normally, DHCP works when a computer is first powered up (booting). First, the computer must find the DHCP server on the local network. It does this by broadcasting a request to all the local devices. When the DHCP server receives the request, it selects an available IP address and sends it (along with other setup data) back to the requesting computer. In many cases, the DHCP server also specifies a time duration for the use of the IP address, known as the "Lease" time. The computer then proceeds with the rest of the boot process and continues to use that IP address for as long as the Lease is valid, typically 1–3 days. A big advantage of the DHCP process for corporate and ISP network administrators is that they don't need to configure each user's PC with a fixed IP address.

NAT operates by translating addresses between two different address spaces. A NAT device can be used to separate a stub network from the main Internet. This is a common function of so-called "cable routers" and "DSL routers" that are installed by consumers who have broadband Internet connections. A common configuration is shown in Figure 5-4, which will serve as the basis for our explanation. To the Internet, the NAT device looks like a single (albeit very busy) device, with a single IP address. Inside the network stub, the NAT device looks like a connection to the Internet. Inside the stub network, all the devices are given an address from a special pool of private IP addresses. When a device in the stub wants to connect to a server located outside the stub network, the NAT device accepts the packet and replaces the private IP address with its own public IP address. At the same time, it records what it did in a table. When a response comes back from the external server, the NAT device accepts the packet and finds the entry in its table where the original private IP address was recorded. Then, the NAT device modifies the packet to send it out on the stub network to the original device.

For video transport, both DHCP and NAT can pose some challenges. In many cases, video encoders and servers are configured to be sources of data (sources of video data to be precise). In order for a user's computer to access that data, it needs to know the IP address of the data source. Both DHCP and NAT can interfere with this. If, for example, a video server was to be configured through DHCP, its IP address could change each time the server was rebooted, and it would be difficult, if not impossible, for clients to locate the server. In the case of a server that was on a private network stub behind a NAT device,

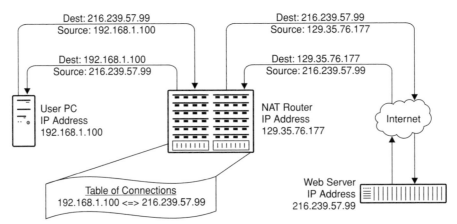

**FIGURE 5-4**  Example of a NAT Device in Operation

the IP address of the server would be hidden from the Internet at large, and the external client would again not be able to find the server. (Note that this might be desirable for companies that do not wish to have their video content made available to external users.) As a general rule, video devices that are supplying content to other clients need to have a fixed IP address that is not behind a NAT device and is accessible to any of the clients who wish to receive the video data.

## ETHERNET AND IP

Ethernet and IP are not synonymous, but they are closely linked in many people's minds. This has happened because Ethernet is one of the most widely used physical networking systems for IP traffic. In the following sections we'll spend some time talking about how Ethernet addressing works and how IP and Ethernet interoperate. Then, we'll spend a little bit of time discussing some of the hardware that is common in Ethernet networks and how the operation of this hardware can impact video transport.

### Classic Ethernet

Ethernet was invented in the 1970s as a means to interconnect workstations on a local area network (LAN). Originally, Ethernet used a shared medium (set of wires) for communications so that each workstation would send and receive data on the same interface. On this type of network, it is essential to prevent multiple workstations from trying to transmit data at the same time. Before transmitting, each workstation is supposed to check for the presence of a data carrier signal, which would indicate that another workstation was already transmitting data. If no carrier was present, then the workstation could begin transmitting its own data. In the event that two stations both happened to start talking at the same time, each was equipped with a mechanism to determine if such a "collision" had occurred. When a collision was detected, each station would then immediately stop transmitting, wait a random amount of time, and then listen and try transmitting again.

This system, known as Carrier Sense Multiple Access with Collision Detection (CSMA/CD) served as the foundation for Ethernet networks for many years and is still used today. However, as technology has advanced, and hardware prices have plummeted, a new architecture has emerged. In this system, a dedicated cable connects to each Ethernet port on each workstation. The most common kind of cable used today is CAT5 (which stands for CATegory 5 Unshielded Twisted Pair). The "5" means that it has been certified to rigorous specifications that ensure that the cable is capable of handling data transmission speeds up to 100 Mbps.[2] At the other end of the cable, a direct connection is made to an Ethernet hub, a switch, or a router. Each of these devices will be described in later sections of this chapter.

## Ethernet Addressing

Ethernet equipment uses Media Access Control (MAC) addresses for each piece of equipment. Readers who have done home networking projects may recognize MAC addresses because they use numbers 0–9 and the letters A–F for their addresses, which are then separated into six fields of two characters each. For example, a MAC address on an Ethernet card inside a PC might be 00:01:02:6A:F3:81. These numbers are assigned to each piece of equipment, and the first six digits can be used to identify the manufacturer of the hardware. MAC addresses are uniquely assigned to each piece of hardware by the manufacturer and do not change.[3]

The difference between MAC addresses and IP addresses can be illustrated with a simple analogy. When an automobile is manufactured, it is assigned a serial number that is unchanging and stays with that car permanently. This is similar to a MAC address for a piece of hardware. When an owner goes to register the auto, he or she receives a license plate (a.k.a. number plate or marker tag). The number of the license plate is controlled by the rules of the local jurisdiction, such as a state in the USA, a province in Canada, or a country in Europe. During its lifetime, one auto may have several different license plate numbers, as

---

2.  CAT6 cable is certified for operation up to 1000 Mbps (also known as Gigabit Ethernet).
3.  Some newer pieces of equipment, including many small routers made for sharing home broadband connections, have the ability to "clone" a MAC address of a different device. This allows a user to set up the router to match the configuration stored at the service provider.

it changes owners or if the owner registers the car in another jurisdiction. Similarly, one piece of physical hardware may have different IP addresses assigned at different times in its life, as the hardware moves from network to network. Stretching the analogy a bit further, an auto's serial number is somewhat private information, of interest only to the owner of the car and the agency that issues the license plates. In contrast, the number of the license plate is public information, and emblazoned on the auto for all to see. Similarly, a MAC address is important only to the local Ethernet connection, commonly on a private network. The IP address is public and is used by other computers all over the Internet to communicate with a particular machine.

## Ethernet Hubs

Ethernet hubs are simple devices that provide electrical termination of CAT5 cables. They also provide retransmission of any Ethernet data that arrives from any device connected to the hub out to all of the other devices connected to the hub. An Ethernet hub provides three main functions in a network:

- First, it acts as a repeater, taking an incoming signal, amplifying it, and sending it out onto all of the other ports on the hub.
- Second, the hub isolates the ports electrically so that you can add and remove connections without having to disable the rest of the network.
- Third, the hub can act as a splitter/combiner, allowing two devices to share a connection to a third device.

Hubs don't do anything to prevent collisions from occurring; they simply receive and retransmit signals. So, when multiple devices are connected to a hub, each one must follow the rules of CSMA/CD and make sure that they don't overwhelm the network.

## Ethernet Bridges

An Ethernet bridge can be used to connect different networks together. These networks can use the same technology, or they can use different technologies. The main function of a bridge is to take packets from one network and reformat them to send out on another network. In order to do this, the bridge has to keep track of the devices that are present on each of the networks. Whenever a packet comes in, the bridge looks at the destination address to determine if the packet needs to be sent out over a different interface. If it does, the bridge reformats the packet and sends it out using the correct protocol for the new network.

One of the other functions provided by a bridge is to isolate Ethernet network segments into different collision domains. This allows devices on one side of the bridge to send and receive packets without having to wait for devices on the other side of the bridge to stop transmitting. Segmenting an Ethernet network improves its performance, since the chances of collisions are reduced, and therefore the network can handle more traffic from each device.

## Ethernet Switches

An Ethernet switch takes the concept of segmentation to its logical conclusion: A switch provides a separate logical and physical network on every one of its connections, or ports. This makes each port a separate collision domain. Since devices need only to avoid transmitting data while other devices in the same collision domain are transmitting, a switch can greatly improve network throughput. Figure 5-5 illustrates a possible switch configuration. Note that devices A and B share a common port (through the use of a hub) and therefore must avoid data collisions. Device C is on a dedicated port, so it does not need to worry about collisions.

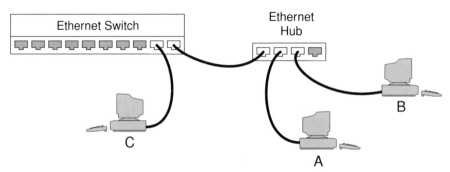

**FIGURE 5-5**   Ethernet Switch Setup Example

Common practice is to put a single device on each connection of an Ethernet switch. This practice provides three benefits:

- Each device can transmit and receive data without worrying about collisions with other devices, so data transmission speeds can increase.
- A switch will send out packets only on a port that is destined for a device that is connected to that port. This improves network security and reliability because it prevents a user's machine connected to one port of a switch from spying on or interfering with packets that are destined for a machine connected to another port on the switch.
- Certain devices can operate in full-duplex mode, which means that they can transmit and receive data at the same time. This is of particular benefit for video streaming applications, because the large amounts of bandwidth commonly used for video transmission can overwhelm a half-duplex connection (where only one direction of transmission is permitted at a time).

Switches play an increasingly important role between bridges on one hand and routers on the other. (We'll discuss the differences with routers after we have introduced them in the following section.) Most definitions of bridges describe them as a two-port device, capable of providing a connection between two different networks. In contrast, a switch can have anywhere from a handful of ports up to a hundred or more ports. In addition, switches tend to have most of their ports configured as a single type of interface (say, 10/100BaseT Ethernet) and have a few (or even no) ports of a different type (say Gigabit Ethernet).

## Routers

Routers[4] provide a crucial function for IP networks by examining the headers and addresses of IP packets and then transmitting them onward toward their destinations. Routers come in a wide variety of configurations, from small access routers that provide a connection to

---

4. Many people in the video industry are familiar with video routers, which we discussed in Chapter 3. Although IP routers and video routers provide similar functions (switchable connections between signal sources and destinations), they are completely different types of equipment, and will not work interchangeably.

an internet for a small group of users, through a range of enterprise routers that may handle the networking needs of an entire company, and on to core routers that provide IP connectivity at the heart of the Internet.

Routers are the workhorses of IP networks, and are the subject of many excellent books of explanations and documentation. Without going into much detail, the basic functions of a router include

- Accepting IP packets from devices and forwarding them to the recipient devices.
- Forwarding packets to another router when the recipient device is not local to the router.
- Maintaining "routing tables" for different destination networks so that an incoming packet can be forwarded along a path toward a destination IP address.
- Bridging between different network technologies, such as Ethernet LANs and ATM telecom circuits, so that IP traffic can flow over a variety of network types.
- Monitoring the status of connected networks, to determine if they are vacant, busy, or disabled, and routing packets to avoid congested networks when possible.
- Queuing packets of different priority levels, so that high-priority packets have precedence over low-priority packets. (**Note:** This feature is typically enabled only on private networks. Many public networks pay little or no attention to packet priority flags.)
- Informing other connected routers of network configurations and changes to available resources and network connections.
- Performing many other administrative and security-related functions that are too numerous to discuss here.

Routers differ from switches in that routers process the IP address of data packets, whereas switches process the MAC address. This simple concept has some important implications, because MAC addresses are important only in the local segments of an Ethernet network, whereas IP addresses have global meaning throughout the Internet. This means that switches can limit their focus to devices that are connected locally, whereas routers may need to know how to forward packets toward destinations that may be on the other side of the world. As a result, routers tend to have many more decisions to make before they can properly process a packet, and they require much more complex software. Accordingly, routers tend to be more expensive to purchase and operate than switches with similar amounts of bandwidth and port capacity.

## Ethernet Interfaces

Unshielded Twisted Pair (UTP) cabling is the most common physical interface used today for Ethernet cabling, also known as Category 5 or 6 UTP. The category indicates the rules that were followed for constructing the cables: Category 6 supports higher data transmission speeds than Category 5. Each cable contains four pairs of wires (a total of eight wires in all). Each pair of wires is twisted in a very precise pattern, and the pairs are not shielded from each other (hence the name UTP). Other forms of Ethernet wiring, including coaxial cable and fiber, are widely used, but we won't discuss them here.

Ethernet interfaces that use UTP cabling are a strict physical star. That is, each end device (such as a PC, a printer, or a server) must have a direct, uninterrupted connection to a port on a network device. This network device can be a hub, a bridge, a switch, or a router. The network device accepts the signals from the end device and then retransmits the data to the other end devices. In the case of a hub, this retransmission is done without any processing; any incoming signal is retransmitted out to every other port of the hub. With bridges, switches, and routers, processing is done on each incoming Ethernet data frame to send it out only on the proper destination ports.

Common UTP interfaces include

- 10BaseT, which operates at a nominal bit rate of 10 Mbps.
- 100BaseT, which operates at a nominal bit rate of 100 Mbps.
- 1000BaseT, also known as Gigabit Ethernet, which operates at a nominal bit rate of 1000 Mbps.

Note that all of the preceding speeds are described as "nominal." This is a reflection of reality because, due to overhead, required dead time, and turn-around time, actual sustained throughput will be much less,

depending on the application. For system implementers, it is important to realize that it isn't possible to send a 10 Mbps MPEG video
stream over a 10BaseT link.

## Wireless Ethernet Interfaces

Wireless Ethernet standards, such as 802.11a, 802.11b, and 802.11g,
offer unprecedented flexibility for users to move devices from one
location to another within a network's coverage area. Low-cost wireless access devices are available for desktop PCs, laptops, and for
connecting to (and sharing) high-speed network connections, such as
DSL and cable modems.

Video users need to be very careful about using wireless links for
high-quality, streaming video connections. The speed and quality of
a wireless link depends on a number of factors, including the distance between the wireless transmitter and receiver, the configuration of antennas, and any local sources of signal interference or
attenuation. If the local environment changes (say, a laptop is
moved, or a metal door is closed), the error rate on the wireless link
can change, and change rapidly. If the packet loss rate increases significantly, 802.11 links are designed to drop down to a lower operating speed, which helps lower the error rate. If the error rate goes
down, the transmission speed can be increased. For example, in a
standard 802.11b system, the bit rate can change to a different rate
between 11 Mbps and 1 Mbps at any time without warning, depending on the quality of the radio channel between the two endpoints.
When designing a video transport system, we need to look at the
bandwidth required by the video signal and compare it to the speed
of the link that will be transporting it. If the link speed is not adequate to carry the video signal, the receiving device won't be able to
produce a watchable image.

As we will discuss in the following chapter, streaming video often
uses protocols (such as UDP) that do not retransmit corrupted packets. In high packet error rate environments, video signals can
become corrupted. This can be at least partially overcome through
the use of an error-correcting code that allows a signal receiver to
correct some of the errors introduced into a data stream. However,

this added function could add complexity and delay into the video stream processing at both ends of the circuit. So, it is important to try to design networks to have the lowest feasible packet error rate possible.

## REVIEW AND CHECKLIST UPDATE

In this chapter, we covered the basics of IP transport. We looked at how IP fits into the overall world of data communications. We covered issues regarding IP addressing, including NAT and DHCP. We then spent some time discussing Ethernet, because it is the most popular technology for IP transport in the local area network (LAN) environment. We also talked about some of the devices that are involved in Ethernet transport, including hubs, bridges, switches, and routers. We also glanced at some of the issues surrounding video on wireless Ethernet.

## Chapter 5 Checklist Update

❏ What is the IP addressing scheme—private network or Internet compliant?
❏ For video sources, will NAT be used? If so, how will clients link to source?
❏ For video sources, DHCP may not be suitable.
❏ What types of networks will be used between the video source and video client? Will packet size limits cause fragmentation of IP datagrams?
❏ Will the Ethernet network have shared segments, or will each device have a dedicated switch port? Dedicated is preferred for high-bandwidth video.
❏ Will the Ethernet connections be half or full duplex? Full duplex is better for video, if available.
❏ Ensure that the network bandwidth is greater than the combined video/audio data rate and that there is enough bandwidth for other devices using the same network.
❏ Will wireless Ethernet links be used? If so, is the bandwidth sufficient, and will error correction be needed?

# 6

# FROM VIDEO INTO PACKETS

Now that we have looked at video, video compression, and the basics of IP, we are ready to look at the process of creating IP packets out of a digital video stream. This chapter will begin by covering the process of chopping up the video stream so that it will fit into IP packets, known as encapsulation. Then, we will discuss the ways that MPEG formats data for transport. We'll examine the different protocols that run on top of IP to control the flow of packets, and we'll look at a few techniques that are used to make video transport more reliable.

By the end of this chapter, readers should have a good understanding of the different forms of MPEG video streams and have developed a solid foundation in the UDP, TCP, and RTP transport protocols. Readers should also gain some insight into the trade-offs that happen in the encapsulation and stream formation process.

# ENCAPSULATION

Encapsulation is the process of taking a data stream, formatting it into packets, and adding the headers and other data required to comply with a specific protocol. In our case, we will be doing IP encapsulation, so we must take data and break it up into packets that will comply with the IP protocol that we discussed in Chapter 5. As we shall see, this is not simply a matter of taking a well-established formula and applying it. Rather, the process of encapsulation can be tuned to meet the performance requirements of different applications and networks.

Any data that is to flow over an IP network needs to be encapsulated into IP datagrams, commonly called IP packets. This is true whether the data is a pre-recorded file or a live digital video stream. Also, a variety of data needs to be inserted into each packet header, including both the source and the destination IP addresses, the Time-to-Live of the packet, the packet's priority indication, and the protocol that was used to format the data contained in the packet (such as TCP or UDP, which are explained later in this chapter). Software tools to perform encapsulation are included in a wide variety of devices, including desktop PCs and file servers. Packet encapsulation is done in real time, just before the packets are sent out over the network because much of the data going into the packet headers changes for each user (such as the destination IP address).

## Packet Size

Performance of IP video signals will be impacted by the choices that are made for the video packet size. Of course, the length of the packets must meet the minimum and maximum sizes that are specified in the specifications for IP. However, within those constraints, there are advantages and disadvantages to using long packets, just as there are advantages and drawbacks to using short packets. There is no simple recipe for choosing a packet length, but here are some of the advantages of choosing long packets, followed by the advantages of choosing short packets:

### Long Packet Benefits

- *Less Overhead:* Long packets and short packets both require the same number of header bytes to comply with IP. However, a longer packet will have less header information as a *percentage* of the overall packet size, since the packet data is longer. Therefore, less packet header overhead will be generated for a stream using long packets as compared to shorter packets. In other words, the total amount of network bandwidth necessary to transport a given video stream will be lower when long packets are used than when short packets are used.
- *Reduced Packet Processing Load:* Each time a packet is processed by an IP router, the packet header must be examined, a lookup must be performed in the router's forwarding table, the Time-to-Live counter must be decremented, and so on. The router must do this work for every packet, whether the packet is large or small. With larger packets, the amount of work that the router must do is reduced, which can result in the network operating more smoothly. Although newer generations of routers have more processing power to handle packet processing, this benefit may not be completely eliminated in a network with a mix of equipment.[1]
- *Greater Network Loading:* In Ethernet and other network technologies, short gaps must be present between each data packet sent by a transmitter. With longer packets, fewer gaps are required, meaning that more of the link's bandwidth can be used for user data.

### Short Packet Benefits

- *Lost Packets Are Less Harmful:* In the event that a packet suffers a bit error in the header, the packet will be discarded (and hence appear to be "lost" to the recipient). When short packets are used, each lost packet contains less of the overall video data. With some video streams (and some of the error-correcting coding mechanisms that we will discuss in Chapter 7), the video playback device may be

---

1. One of the best ways to test a router's performance is to send it large streams of minimum size packets, which will exercise the header processing mechanism as much as possible.

able to recover from data loss or at least mask it from the viewer. As packet lengths go up, each lost packet means more lost data, which in turn makes it harder to recover from lost packets or other network impairments.

- *Reduced Latency:* When a video stream is sent out over IP, each packet cannot be sent until it is full of data. With very low bit rate signals (such as a web camera with a very low frame rate), the amount of time that it takes to fill up a long packet can add to the latency of the overall transmission system. Also, some error-correction techniques process multiple packets in one batch; both the sender and the receiver must accumulate the correct number of packets before the calculations can be made, thereby increasing total system latency. Although this is not normally an issue for video signals, it can definitely affect live streaming signals used for voice over IP applications. This is why voice signals typically use a short packet length.

- *Less Need for Fragmentation:* The transmission path that will be used to send the packets can also affect packet length. For example, IP packets to be sent over Ethernet need to be less than 1500 bytes long. If longer packets are used, then the IP routers that transmit these packets over Ethernet links will split the packets up into smaller chunks using the fragmentation process that we discussed in Chapter 5. Fragmentation can create significant overhead for routers and other devices along a network and should be avoided. The best policy is to be sure to use a packet size that is less than the maximum packet size allowed by any hop of the network between the video source and the video destination.

Clearly, the decision about optimum packet length is affected by a number of parameters, which vary from network to network, and indeed from connection to connection. Typically, video signals tend to use the longest possible packet sizes that won't result in fragmentation on the network. Fine-tuning the packet sizes can help make a network run better. A major mistake in setting these values will generally not prevent the video from flowing, but it can create extra work for devices all along the path of a connection. Unfortunately, some IP devices won't even let a user configure a desired packet length. The best thing for a user to do is to start with a packet length that is reasonable given the network conditions and, if performance is below expectations, to test different packet length values as needed.

## MPEG STREAM TYPES

Even though MPEG is not the only kind of video that can be transported over an IP network, it is useful to look at the different stream types that have been constructed for MPEG. As you will see, each stream type has a specific purpose, and not all stream types are applicable to all situations.

Study of the MPEG stream types is useful, because the topics we will discuss in this chapter are all international standards and they are available in the public domain (for a small fee). Other video compression systems may be proprietary to a particular company, but they still need to solve the same problems that MPEG streams were designed to solve. In addition, because many MPEG applications involve the simultaneous delivery of multiple programs from different sources (e.g., DTH satellite systems), some very complex stream types have been developed for MPEG. So, understanding MPEG stream types will allow us to understand other video streaming protocols.

Before we begin our discussion of the different stream types, here is a brief overview of the different roles that each type plays. We'll go into more detail about each type in the following sections.

- *Elementary streams* are the raw outputs from MPEG video and audio encoders, and they are the standardized input for MPEG decoders. These streams contain only one type of content, so at least two elementary streams are required to produce an output that has both sound and an image. Elementary streams contain the raw content that the other types of MPEG streams are built from.
- *Packetized elementary streams* are easier-to-handle versions of elementary streams and contain timing information that allows video and audio streams to be synchronized. A packetized elementary stream can also be made up exclusively of data such as closed captioning information. Packetized elementary streams are normally used to create program streams or transport streams, but they can also be used directly in applications like digital video recorders.

- *Program streams* combine several types of packetized elementary streams (video, audio, and possibly data) to support production and recording tasks, and they are used on DVDs. All of the packetized elementary streams in a program stream must be based on a common clock source so that synchronization can be maintained between the constituent video and audio signals.
- *Transport streams* are another way of combining several packetized elementary streams into a single entity that can be transported across a network. Transport stream packets are fixed length, and the streams carry clock information that is needed for real-time signals. Transport streams can carry packetized elementary streams that were created from different clock sources, so they can be used for applications with multiple content sources such as DTH satellite, video over DSL, and video over IP streaming.

## Elementary Stream

The elementary stream is the most basic format for MPEG-encoded information. It is essentially the raw output of a video or an audio encoder. It contains the raw data output of a single encoder, such as DCT coefficients for video streams. Note that video elementary streams are separate and distinct from audio elementary streams. In fact, they are often created by separate chips within an MPEG-encoding device.

Elementary streams have an internal structure that is used by the decoder to determine how the data should be decoded. For example, the video frame type (I, P, or B; see Chapter 4) is indicated. The relative position of each data block on the video screen is indicated. Other information needed by the video decoder is also included, such as whether the video is interlaced or not, the aspect ratio of the video image, the frame rate of the video image, and other useful data. In audio elementary streams, the required data is much simpler and includes key information for the decoder such as the sampling rate of the original digital audio stream and the type of audio compression used.

Elementary streams are continuous by nature: An MPEG encoder will continue to create either a video or an audio elementary stream as long as it is activated. This is natural for video systems but not natural for IP data networks. IP networks need to have data broken up into logical chunks or packets. So, the next step is to "packetize" these streams.

## Packetized Elementary Streams

A packetized elementary stream (PES) is simply an elementary stream that has been broken up into easy-to-handle chunks, or "packets." We must use the word "packets" here carefully—although this is the name of this part of the MPEG standard, it should not be confused with the packets that we have been discussing related to IP. In fact, the PES packets are at least a couple of layers of abstraction removed from the IP packets that will end up being sent over an IP network. Nevertheless, we will call these chunks of an elementary stream "packets" so that we can be compatible with other industry documents on this topic.

Each packet of a PES will have a header, which includes a code number that indicates the source of the elementary stream. This will become important later, when we combine video and audio data from different sources, so that we can figure out which video and audio signals belong together. Also included in at least some of the PES headers are time stamps. Note that PES packets are variable length and can be a hundred kilobytes or more.

For video signals, two different kinds of time stamps can be used, presentation time stamps (PTS) and decode time stamps (DTS). The PTS of a frame indicates the time at which it should be presented, or displayed to the viewer as a video signal. The DTS of a frame indicates the time at which it should be decoded by the MPEG decoder.

To understand the difference between a PTS and a DTS, we need to think back to our discussion of I, B, and P frames from Chapter 4. Remember that I frames are intra-coded, meaning that the frame is coded without reference to any other frames in the video sequence. P frames are predicted, which means that they can be calculated based on the differences from a previous I frame or P frame. B frames are bi-directionally coded, which means that they can be calculated based on the differences from a previous or a subsequent I frame or P frame.

Let's look at an example of a GOP (Group of Pictures, from Chapter 4, Figure 4-6) of $IB_1B_2P$. In this example, frame I would be presented first, so it would have the earliest presentation time stamp (PTS) of these four frames. The first B frame, $B_1$, would be presented second, followed by the second B frame, $B_2$. They would have PTS values that were each one frame later than the frame before them. (Note that each frame does not need a PTS; if one is not present, then the decoder calculates the appropriate PTS.) Finally, frame P would be presented last, with a PTS that was three frames later than the original I frame. See Figure 6-1 for an illustration of how this would work.

Using the same example, let's look at the decode time stamps (DTS). In this case, frame I would again be first, so its decode time would be the earliest. However, the decoder needs frame P next, because without out the decoded data from the P frame, it is impossible to properly decode either of the two B frames. In other words, since a B frame is calculated "between" two reference frames, the decoder needs to know both the before and the after reference frame. So, in this example, the DTS of frame P would be set to be one frame later than frame I. Frame $B_1$ would have a DTS one frame later than frame P, and frame $B_2$ would have a DTS yet another frame later. Figure 6-1 shows how the DTS values would be calculated.

All this is important to understand for video over IP, because there is a trade-off between the total delay through a video link and the amount of bandwidth that it uses. Specifically, P frames use less data than I frames (half as much is a good estimate), and B frames use less data than P frames (half as much again would be another good estimate).

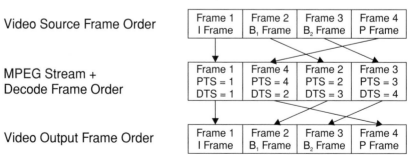

**FIGURE 6-1** Presentation and Decode Time Stamps

So, streams with lots of B frames use less bandwidth than streams with fewer B frames. Unfortunately, this comes at a cost of greater delay. In order to calculate the B frame values, the encoder needs to have already looked at the two reference frames (either I frames or P frames) that the B frame will be based on. For this to happen in live video, the encoder needs to wait until the video signal for the later P or I frames to arrive. On NTSC systems, this added wait will be 33 milliseconds per B frame; on PAL/SECAM systems this delay will be 40 milliseconds per B frame. Longer runs of B frames mean longer delays, so using more B frames to reduce the data bandwidth can increase the end-to-end delay of the system.

## Program Streams

A program stream carries a single program. It is made up of one or more packetized elementary streams and can have added data and control information. All of the elementary streams in a single program use a common time-base, which allows the audio and video portions of the program to provide lip-sync. Program streams are commonly used in DVD and other error-free[2] environments, such as tape or hard-disk recorders. Program streams can be variable bit rate and typically use large packets.

In MPEG, a program is a combination of video, audio, and related data (such as closed captioning) that make up a complete audiovisual experience. Typically, one video stream is combined with one or more audio streams and possibly some data streams. The first audio stream typically carries the main stereo sound track for the video; others can include surround sound, alternate language sound tracks, and commentaries. Data can include captioning information, information about the program stream (title, length, owner, content descriptions, etc.), and anything else the content owner wants to provide. Control information is another important type of data, and it can include

---

2.  The term "error free" needs to be used very carefully. In reality, no physical systems can truly be error free. When we use the term here, error free simply means that any errors that are detected can easily be recovered by re-reading the recording media. If the error is persistent (such as a damaged disk or tape), then the recording is faulty and should be replaced.

information needed by recording or playback devices. Encryption systems can also require data to be included with the program stream; we will be exploring this topic in greater depth in Chapter 11.

Note that multiple video streams can be included in a single program stream (up to 16 videos and 32 audios in some applications), but the requirement still remains that all of the information in a single program stream must have a common time-base. This generally means that raw video that was filmed using different cameras at different locations cannot be combined into a single program. However, if these videos have been given a common time-base through the use of a video editing system, then they can be included in a single program stream. One example of a program stream with multiple videos would be a sports video that offered multiple camera angles of the same action.

## Transport Streams

Transport streams are similar to program streams—they offer a way to combine video, audio, and related data into a logical grouping. Unlike program streams, transport streams are specifically designed to be transported across communication links that are not error free. Many applications fall into this category, including satellite, terrestrial broadcast, and all types of wired and fiber optic links.

Transport streams use fixed-length packets of 188 bytes each and are intended to work well in constant bit rate transport links, such as those normally provided by telecommunications providers. Each packet contains data from only a single elementary stream, so each packet is either video, audio, data, or control information, but not a mixture. Forward Error Correction (FEC) codes can also be added to transport stream packets through the use of standardized codes such as Reed-Solomon (RS), which is named after the authors of an early, influential paper on this topic. In a transport stream, commonly used forms of Reed-Solomon coding add either 16 or 20 bytes to the 188-byte packet, bringing the total packet length up to 204 or 208 bytes. Packets of 204 bytes are commonly used in applications relating to the Digital Video Broadcasting (DVB) consortium series of specifications, which have widespread use in Europe and a number of DTH satellite systems. Packets of 208 bytes are used in Advanced Television Systems Committee (ATSC) applications, which are used in terrestrial digital television broadcast applications in the USA (sometimes called DTV or HDTV). The primary benefit of adding Reed-Solomon coding to the transport stream packets is to give the receiver the ability to recover from transmission errors. A 16-byte RS code can correct for up to 8 byte errors in the transport stream packet; a 20-byte RS code can correct for up to 10 byte errors.[3]

It is important to recognize that the length of a transport stream packet is not the same as the length of an IP packet that carries a transport stream. Quite the contrary—IP packets will normally contain multiple transport stream packets. IP packets containing 7 transport stream packets are popular, because 7 is the highest integer number of transport stream packets that can fit into an IP packet and still be carried across an Ethernet network without fragmentation. (The maximum size payload for an IP packet sent over an Ethernet frame is 1500 bytes, as we discussed in Chapter 5.)

Another technique for handling errors in transport streams is the use of interleaving. In this process, transport stream packets have their order shuffled so as to make sure that no two adjacent packets are in the same IP packet. This can be very handy in case one of the IP packets is lost in transmission; the MPEG decoder is better at concealing the loss of several isolated transport stream packets than it is at trying to conceal the loss of a group of adjacent packets. The big benefit of interleaving is that it helps conceal errors without adding more bits (such as RS codes) to the video stream. The main drawback is that the shuffling introduces extra delay into the system, which could be a problem for some applications.

An important concept in dealing with transport stream packets is the concept of the Packet IDentifier, or PID. The PID uniquely identifies which elementary stream is contained in each packet. For example, the packets for a video signal within a transport stream might have a

---

3.  FEC codes don't provide much (or any) benefit for systems that use guaranteed delivery protocols, such as TCP, because packet errors will cause packets to be retransmitted until they arrive error-free.

PID of 42, and the primary stereo audio signal that is associated with that same video might be carried in packets with a PID of 38. A second audio (with an alternate language track) for that same video could be carried with a PID of 85. Of course, there will be a lot more video packets than audio packets, because of the higher bandwidth requirements of the video signal.

To keep track of all the PIDs, MPEG defines a series of tables that are sent as control data in the program stream. PID 0 is used to send the program association table (PAT), which gives a list of all the different programs contained in the transport stream. Each entry in the PAT points to a program map table (PMT), of which there is one for each program. (Remember that a program is a set of video, audio, and data that is from a common timing source. One program would typically represent one entertainment stream, complete with a video signal and audio signal, and possibly closed captions or other information.) Inside the program map table is a list of all the PIDs for that program, of whatever type. When a viewer chooses a particular program to watch, the PAT and the PMT are consulted to find the correct video streams to send to the video decoder chip, and the correct audio stream(s) to send to the audio decoder chip(s), as shown in Figure 6-2.

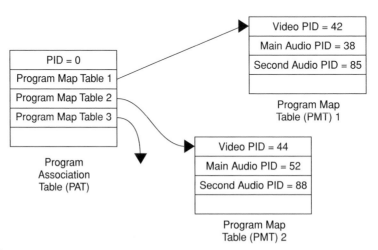

**FIGURE 6-2**  Program Table Usage in a Transport Stream

## Program Clock References

A program clock reference (PCR) is a 33-bit number that must be inserted periodically into every transport stream to allow an MPEG decoder to synchronize with the 27 MHz clock used by the encoder when the MPEG compression was done. Synchronization must be maintained to make sure that the decoder doesn't run out of data to decode (buffer underflow) and that it doesn't receive more data than it can handle (buffer overflow). It is the responsibility of the MPEG encoder to keep a running estimate of the amount of room left in the decoder's buffer, and both ends of the network need to be synchronized to the same clock in order for this to work.

A 33-bit counter that is linked to the encoder's 27 MHz clock represents the PCR. Periodically, the encoder copies the value of this counter and places it into a transport stream packet. At the decoder, these counter values are extracted and used to create a copy of the encoder's clock in order to achieve synchronization. The accuracy of the decoder's clock depends on a smooth, steady flow of data from the encoder to the decoder. Any changes in the amount of time it takes the packets to travel through the network (known as delay variation of packet jitter) need to be minimized or eliminated when possible. Nevertheless, some variation will occur, so it is important for the decoder to be designed to tolerate minor variations in the end-to-end delay.

## Stream Multiplexing and DVB-ASI

Very often, it is desirable to combine several transport streams together for transport across a network. Of course, this can be done by converting each stream to IP packets and sending them over an IP network. The Digital Video Broadcasting (DVB) Project developed another method to carry multiple transport streams over links that would normally handle an SDI signal (this is a 270 Mbps serial stream; see Chapter 3). This method, called DVB-ASI (Asynchronous Serial Interface), allows multiple transport streams to be combined on a single link, even if they are operating at different bit rates.

Essentially, a DVB-ASI stream consists of a 270 Mbps basic channel, with varying amounts of payload added in. The payload consists of one or more MPEG transport streams, each of which can be constant or variable bit rate. The total combined bit rate of the payload cannot exceed about 200 Mbps, but this is still lots of room for a large quantity of MPEG streams that might average between 4 and 8 Mbps each.

DVB-ASI is important because it is a common interface for a whole range of video compression and processing gear, as well as a number of video servers. For example, it is very common to see the input port on equipment that is used to create satellite signals configured for a DVB-ASI input. Many MPEG encoders have DVB-ASI outputs, and some decoders have DVB-ASI inputs. Also, DVB-ASI is easy to transport around a studio facility using equipment purchased for SDI transport.[4] Finally, a number of companies offer video transport services that operate at 270 Mbps across towns and across countries; most of these services can also be used for DVB-ASI.

## TRANSPORT PROTOCOLS

Transport protocols are used to control the transmission of data packets in conjunction with IP. We will discuss three major protocols that are commonly used in transporting real-time video:

- *UDP* or User Datagram Protocol: This is one of the simplest and earliest of the IP protocols. UDP is often used for video and other data that is very time-sensitive.
- *TCP* or Transmission Control Protocol: This is a well-established Internet protocol that is widely used for data transport. The vast majority of the devices that connect to the Internet are capable of supporting TCP over IP (or simply TCP/IP).
- *RTP* or Real-time Transport Protocol (or Real Time Protocol, if you prefer): This protocol has been specifically developed to support real-time data transport, such as video streaming.

In the networking hierarchy, all three protocols are considered to operate above the IP protocol, because they rely on IP's datagram transport

---

4. There is one practical difference between SDI and DVB-ASI signals. SDI signals are polarity insensitive, so if the signal gets inverted during transport (a surprisingly common occurrence), there is no problem. In contrast, DVB-ASI signals are polarity sensitive, so care must be taken to avoid inverting the signal during transport.

services to actually move data to another computer (host). These protocols also provide service to other functions inside each host (such as user applications) and so are considered to sit "below" those functions in the networking protocol hierarchy. Figure 6-3 shows how UDP, TCP, and RTP fit into the networking hierarchy. Note that RTP actually uses some of the functions of UDP; it operates on top of UDP.

## Ports

A common feature of UDP and TCP is that they use logical ports for data communications.[5] A basic set of ports that support well-known services such as e-mail or web browsing is defined and numbered by the Internet Assigned Number Authority (IANA).

Before we get too deep into this topic, let's explore a quick analogy. One way to think of a port is that it operates like a telephone extension inside a medium-sized company. All the employees at the company share the same basic telephone number, but each employee (or group of employees) can be given a specific extension. Each time people place

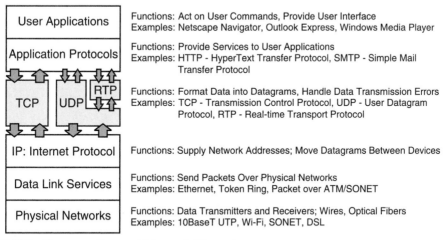

**FIGURE 6-3**  Transport Protocol Network Hierarchy

---

5.  Be careful not to confuse the concept of logical ports used by protocols with the reality of physical ports on devices, such as a 10BaseT "port" on an Ethernet switch. Ports are used to control how datagrams are passed from the IP layer and to make sure they end up in the proper application program.

a call to this company, they must dial the telephone number to reach the main switchboard and then tell the operator (or some annoying recorded voice system) which extension they want to reach. Similarly, when a remote device wishes to access a specific application in another device, it must send data to the correct IP address and then indicate to UDP or TCP which port the data is intended for.

By standardizing the numbering of ports for well-known services, the IANA has done a tremendous service. For example, a web server that is supporting a HyperText Transfer Protocol (HTTP) application always listens for remote devices to request connections on port 80. This makes it easy for a remote user with a standard browser to begin an HTTP session simply by knowing the IP address of the server, and send the proper packet to port 80 to begin an HTTP session. Wouldn't it be nice if company telephone systems worked in the same way, by always having the accounting department, say, on extension 80? Just think how much easier it would be for people calling that company to talk to accounting—they would just need to request extension 80, and they would always be connected to the right department!

## Sockets

A socket is a related concept to a port. A socket is formed by the combination of an IP address and a port number. For example, a socket could be formed with an IP address of 23.132.176.43 and a port number of 80. The name of this socket would be written as 23.132.176.43:80, and read as "port 80 on 23.132.176.43." Different transport protocols use sockets in different ways; we will discuss these differences in each of the following sections.

## UDP

User Datagram Protocol (UDP) is a connectionless transport mechanism that can support high-speed information flows such as digital video. It can support many other types of data transport and is frequently used when the overhead of setting up a connection (as is done by TCP) is not needed. For example, UDP is often used for broadcasting messages from one device to all the other devices on a network segment (say, a print server alerting all the users that the printer is out of paper).

UDP is a connectionless protocol, which means that there is no mechanism to set up or control a connection between a sending host and a receiving host. The UDP sender simply formats datagrams with the correct destination socket (IP address and port number) and passes them to IP for transport. Of course, this also means that there is no coordination between a UDP data transmitter and a UDP data receiver to ensure that the data is transferred completely and correctly from the sender to the receiver.

On the face of it, this lack of coordination would seem to make UDP unsuitable for video data transfer, since missing video data can interfere with the receiver's ability to display a correct sequence of complete images. However, it is important to remember that each image in an NTSC video stream is displayed for only 33 milliseconds (40 msec for PAL video). If part of the data for an image is missing, the ideal receiver would need to

1. Recognize that the data was missing.
2. Send a message back to the sender to tell it which data needed to be retransmitted.
3. Receive and process the retransmitted data.
4. Make sure that all this happened before the image was due to be displayed.

Since completing all of these steps within a 33 msec window can be hard, it may be wise not to even try retransmitting the missing data. Now some astute readers will be thinking that more time could be gained to correct these errors if we transmitted the data before it was needed to form the image, and we let it sit in a buffer for a short while. If errors or missing data was detected, then the corrected data could be retransmitted while the good data simply sat in the buffer. This scheme will definitely work; however, it has one drawback: The time that the video data sits in the buffer will add to the overall end-to-end delay of the video signal. Added delay can make users less happy, particularly if the users are trying to carry on a two-way videoconference.

Many video stream formats include a mechanism for detecting and correcting errors. For example, MPEG transport streams can include bytes for Reed-Solomon forward error correction, which we will discuss in more detail in another section of this book. When these bytes are included, the MPEG decoder can correct for bit errors and can sometimes re-create lost packets. In UDP, the originating device can control how rapidly data from a stream flows across the network. In other protocols (such as in TCP, as we shall see shortly) the network can drastically affect how data transfer works. When these capabilities are available, UDP is a logical choice for the transport protocol, since it does not add unneeded overhead to streams that already have built-in error correction functions.

Table 6-1 lists advantages and disadvantages of using the User Datagram Protocol.

Overall, UDP is a simple, low-overhead transport protocol that can be very useful for video traffic. UDP has a long history, and most IP-capable devices will support UDP. When video streams include their own error protection, when transmission paths are well-controlled or lightly used, and particularly when end-to-end delay must be minimized, UDP can be a good choice for video transport.

## TCP

Transmission Control Protocol (TCP) is a connection-oriented protocol that provides highly reliable data communications services. TCP is easily the most widely used protocol on the Internet and many internets.

When we say TCP is "connection oriented," we mean that TCP requires that a connection be set up between the data sender and the data receiver before any data transmission can take place. Either the sender or the receiver of the data can initiate a connection, but acknowledgment messages must be sent between both ends of the circuit before it is ready for use. A standard handshake sequence has been defined for TCP that handles essentially all of the different things that can and do go wrong in this process; however, it is beyond the scope of this book.

**TABLE 6-1**

Advantages and Disadvantages of UDP

*Advantages*

- *Very Low Overhead:* Packet headers for UDP are among the smallest of all the protocols that use IP. This helps keep the amount of non-video data in the overall data stream to a minimum.
- *Simple Port Addressing Scheme:* This scheme allows any data arriving at a particular socket to be forwarded directly to the application attached to that socket. It also removes the need for the transport protocol (in this case UDP) to keep track of multiple, different connections to a single port.
- *Very Fast Setup Time and Low Delays:* In UDP, the sending host does not need to communicate with the receiving host to set up a connection prior to starting data transmission (as would be the case in TCP). This allows the sending host to begin transmission without having to wait for setup requests to propagate to the receiving host and for an acknowledgment to propagate back through the network. Plus, UDP does not buffer data to wait for acknowledgments, so one big source of system delay is eliminated.
- *Flexible Architecture:* Because UDP does not require two-way communication, it can operate on one-way networks (such as satellite broadcasts). In addition, UDP can be used in multicasting applications where one source feeds multiple destinations (see Chapter 9 for more information on multicasting).
- *Wide Availability:* UDP is available on the vast majority of equipment used in IP networking.

*Disadvantages*

- *Unreliable Transport:* In UDP, there is no built-in mechanism to automatically retransmit data that has become corrupted or gone missing. It then becomes the responsibility of the data receiver to deal with whatever data is actually received and to make up for any lost packets.
- *Firewall Blocking:* Some firewall administrators configure their systems to block UDP traffic. This is done because it is possible for a hacker to inject malicious data packets into a UDP stream.
- *No Built-in Communication "Back-Channel" between the Receiver and the Sender:* This means that the sender does not have an automatic way to get feedback from the receiver. This would enable functions like automatic retransmission of lost packets or changing to a different video encoding rate or transmission speed when the receiver is on a congested link.
- *No Automatic Rate Control Function:* It is the responsibility of the sending application to make sure that the outbound data stream does not exceed the capacity of the transport link. Other protocols will automatically speed up or slow down data transmission, and can follow speed changes in the link, although this would not be desirable if the speed drops below the minimum rate that the video stream needs.

One of the essential features of TCP is its ability to handle transmission errors, particularly lost packets. TCP counts and keeps track of each byte of data that flows across a connection, using a field in the header of each packet called the Sequence Identifier. In each packet, the Sequence Identifier indicates the sequence number of the first byte of that packet. If a packet is lost or arrives out of order, the Sequence

Identifier in the next packet to arrive will not match the count that the receiver has made of all the previously received bytes. Through a fairly elaborate system of control flags and a field in the TCP header called the Acknowledgment Identifier, the receiver in a TCP circuit tells the sender that some data is missing and needs to be retransmitted. This is how TCP ensures that the receiver gets every byte that the sender wanted to transmit. This system is great for transmitting files that cannot withstand corruption, such as e-mails or executable program code.

Another feature of TCP is the ability to control the flow of data across a connection. This feature operates by using some of the same control flags that are used to identify lost packets and through the use of a data buffer in the receiver. The receiver tells the sender how big a buffer it is using, and the sender must not send more data than will fit into the buffer. More data can be sent only after the receiver acknowledges that it has processed at least some of the data in its buffer, and there is room for more. Flow control comes into play because the sender can recognize how quickly the receiver can accept and process data, whether this is due to the speed of the network connection or because the receiver is busy doing other things. Whenever the sender determines that the receiver's buffer is full, it will delay transmission of new data until the receiver acknowledges that it has processed the data that has already been sent. Note that in some instances this will mean that the sender has to retransmit some data that might have been lost along the way. When the receiver quickly acknowledges the receipt of new data, the sender can gradually increase the flow of data.

Unfortunately, some of these very mechanisms that make TCP valuable for data transmission can interfere with video transport. Remember, the data for a video signal not only needs to arrive intact, but it also needs to arrive on time. So, a mechanism that retransmits lost packets can be harmful in two ways:

- If a packet is retransmitted but arrives too late for display, it can tie up the receiver while the packet is examined and then discarded.
- When packets are retransmitted, they can occupy network bandwidth that is needed to send new data.

Also, the flow control mechanism that is built into TCP can interfere with video transport. If packets are lost before they are delivered to the receiver, TCP can go into a mode where the transmission speed is automatically reduced. This is a sensible policy, except when a real-time video signal needs to be sent. Reducing the transmit speed to less than the minimum needed for the video stream can prevent enough data from getting through to form any video image at all. With lost packets on a real-time video stream, the better policy is to ignore the losses and keep sending the data as fast as necessary to keep up with the video (and audio) content.

TCP uses ports and sockets differently from UDP. In TCP, each connection is set up as a socket pair—that is, an IP address and port number at each end of the connection. TCP requires that each pair be unique; that is, a connection must use a socket pair that is not being used by any other connection on the same host. It is permissible for one of the two sockets to be duplicated. So, for example, it is possible for two or more different connections to be made to 192.163.84.67:80, as long the other socket in each connection is unique. This is what allows a single web server to handle multiple clients simultaneously; as long as each client uses a unique socket number on its end of the connection, TCP will keep the connections separate. This is different from UDP, which combines all the data going to a single port.

Table 6-2 lists advantages and disadvantages of using the Transmission Control Protocol.

## RTP

The Real-time Transport Protocol (or Real Time Protocol, if you prefer) is intended for real-time multimedia applications, such as voice and video over the Internet. RTP was specifically designed to carry signals where time is of the essence. For example, in many real-time signals, if the packet delivery rate falls below a critical threshold, it becomes impossible to form a useful output signal at the receiver. For these signals, packet loss can be tolerated better than late delivery. RTP was created for these kinds of signals—to provide a set of functions that are useful for real-time video and audio transport over the Internet.

One example of a non-video real-time signal that is well suited to RTP is a voice conversation. As most early users of cellular or GSM telephones can attest, an occasional noise artifact (such as an audible

**TABLE 6-2**

Advantages and Disadvantages of TCP

*Advantages*

- *Automatic Data Retransmission:* TCP has built-in, automatic mechanisms to ensure that every byte of data that is transmitted by the sender makes it all the way to the receiver. If data is lost or corrupted along the way, TCP will retransmit the data.
- *Data Byte Sequence Numbers:* These numbers allow the receiving data application to determine whether data is missing or if packets arrived in a different order than they were sent.
- *Multiple Connections to a Single Port:* TCP keeps track of messages based on socket pairs so that multiple simultaneous connections can be made from a single port on one host to several other machines. This allows multiple clients to access a server through a single common port. This feature helps remove the burden on an application designer to implement this function when multiple connections must be managed.
- *Universal Availability:* Any device used in IP networking will support TCP.

*Disadvantages*

- *Connection Setup Required:* The connection setup process must be completed before communications can flow. In networks with long end-to-end delays, the back-and-forth handshake process can take a relatively long time. This also makes rapid broadcast alert messages impractical on TCP, because of the need to establish connections with each of the destination devices.
- *Flow Control Can Harm Video:* TCP's automatic flow control mechanism will slow down data transmission speeds when transmission errors occur. If this rate falls below the minimum rate needed by a video signal, then the video signal receiver will cease to operate properly.
- *Retransmission Not Useful:* If packets are retransmitted, they may arrive too late to be useful. This can interfere with other traffic that would have arrived in a timely fashion.
- *No Multicasting:* Multicasting is not supported, meaning that a separate dedicated connection needs to be established by the sender for each receiver. For signals that are being distributed to multiple locations, the network loads generated can be heavy. In addition, unidirectional networks cannot be used, because TCP requires handshaking.
- *Delay Reduces Throughput:* On networks with long end-to-end delays, TCP can dramatically reduce network throughput, because of the time spent waiting for acknowledgment packets.

"click") is not enough to grossly interfere with an ongoing conversation. In contrast, if a mobile phone were designed to stop transmission and rebroadcast the voice data packets each time an error occurred, then the system would become constantly interrupted and virtually useless. Video is similar: A short, transient disruption is better than a "perfect" signal that is continuously stopped and re-started to allow missing bits to be rebroadcast. RTP is built on this same philosophy: Occasional data errors or lost packets are not automatically retransmitted. Similarly, RTP does not try to control the bit rate used by the sending application; it does not have the automatic rate reduction functions that are built into TCP to handle congested networks.

RTP is used in a variety of applications, including the popular H.323 videoconferencing standard (which we will discuss in Chapter 10). One of the nice features of RTP is that it supports multi-party conferencing by allowing different parties in the conference to keep track of the participants as they join and leave. RTP can also support the transport of a single stream to multiple endpoints (called multicasting, which we will discuss in Chapter 9).

RTP also provides a time-stamping function that allows multiple streams from the same source to be synchronized. Each form of payload (video, audio, voice) has a specific way of being mapped into RTP. Each payload type is carried in separately by RTP, which allows a receiver to, for example, receive only the audio portion of a video-conference call. (This can be very useful for a conference participant who has access only via a slow dial-up data link.) Each source inserts time stamps into the outgoing packet headers, which can be processed by the receiver to recover the stream's clock signal that is required to correctly play audio and video clips.

RTP is not strictly a transport protocol, like UDP or TCP, as illustrated in Figure 6-3. In fact, RTP is designed to use UDP as a packet transport mechanism. That is, RTP adds a header to each packet, which is then passed to UDP for further processing (and another header). RTP can also work with other transport technologies (such as ATM), but these uses are not widespread.

RTCP, or the RTP Control Protocol (a somewhat confused acronym), is used alongside RTP. Whenever an RTP connection is made, an RTCP connection also needs to be made. This connection is made using a second neighboring UDP port; if the RTP connection uses port 1380, then the RTCP connection uses port 1381.

RTCP provides the following functions:

- Allow synchronization between different media types, such as video and audio. The RTCP carries time-stamp information that is used by the receiver to align the clocks in each different RTP stream so that video and audio signals can achieve lip sync, for example.

- Provide reception-quality status reports to the senders. This comprises data sent from each receiver giving a lot of valuable statistics about how the sender's data is being received, including the number of packets that were lost, the percentage of packets that were lost, the amount of jitter in the packet arrival time, and an exact time when the last packet was received. This latter information can be used by the sender to determine the amount of transmission delay that is present in the network.
- Provide identification of the senders in the RTP session so that new receivers can join and figure out which streams they need to obtain in order to participate fully. For example, if a three-way RTP session is connected to three different conference rooms, a desktop user would need to know the addresses of the other two rooms in order to hear everything that was being said.
- Provide identification of the other participants in the RTP session. Since each receiver is required to periodically identify itself using RTCP, each participant (sender or receiver) can determine which receivers are present. This is not really a security mechanism; for that purpose, some form of encryption or other access control mechanism should be used.

Each receiver is also required to maintain a count of the number of other receivers that are present in the session. This count is used to calculate how often each receiver should send out a report. As more receivers join a session, each one needs to send status reports less often, so as not to overwhelm the network or the other receivers. The guideline used for calculating this is that the RTCP traffic should be no more than 5% of the RTP stream that it is associated with.

Overall, RTP adds a lot of functionality on top of UDP, without adding a lot of the unwanted functions of TCP. For example, RTP does not automatically throttle down transmission bandwidth if packet loss occurs. Instead, RTP provides information to the sending application to let it know that congestion is happening. The application can then determine what it wants to do to compensate for the congestion. The application could, for example, lower the video encoding bit rate (sacrificing some quality), or it could simply ignore the report if, say, only a few of the receivers were affected by the congestion. RTP also supports multicasting, which can be a much more efficient way to transport video over a network, as we will see in Chapter 9.

Table 6-3 lists advantages and disadvantages of using the Real-time Transport Protocol.

## CASE STUDY: UNCOMPRESSED VIDEO OVER IP

Most of the video signals that are transported over IP networks have been compressed using MPEG or some other technology. However,

**TABLE 6-3**

Advantages and Disadvantages of RTP

*Advantages*

- *Many Standard Formats:* Built-in support for many different types of audio and video stream types allows applications to easily share MPEG video and many different types of audio using well-defined formats.
- *Packet Sequence Numbers:* These numbers allow the receiving data application to determine whether packets are missing, alerting the receiving application that error correction or masking needs to be performed. These numbers also allow packets that arrive in a different order than they were sent to be put back into the proper order.
- *Multicasting Support:* RTP streams can be distributed using multicasting, so that a single video source can feed several (or several hundred) destinations simultaneously.
- *Embedded Sync Data:* Synchronization between multiple stream types allows multimedia signals (video, audio, etc.) to be transmitted separately and realigned to a common time-base at the receiver.
- *Multiple Stream Speeds:* Receiving devices can choose to decode only portions of the overall program, so devices with low speed network connections could choose to only decode the audio portion of a program, for instance.

*Disadvantages*

- *Firewall Issues:* Some firewalls may block RTP traffic, because UDP packets are routinely blocked in many installations.
- *No Priorities:* There is no mechanism built into RTP that ensures the timely transport of packets (such as priority queuing). Other tools and techniques may need to be used on networks with heavy traffic loads to ensure that the RTP packets flow smoothly.
- *Limited Deployment:* Not all network devices support RTP, so care must be taken to ensure that the network is properly configured before using this protocol.

compression is not a requirement for successful IP transport. In this case study, we will discuss the MD6000 product from Media Links, Inc., of Shelton, Connecticut, that allows uncompressed digital video signals to be transported over IP networks.

Let's begin by reviewing what "uncompressed digital video" means, and why it would be desirable to transport these signals over an IP network. When digital video is in an uncompressed form, it means that all of the data in the original signal is present; none of it has been removed by processing. For standard resolution signals, this is normally referred to as "SDI" or "270 Mbit" video, and for HD signals, it is normally referred to as "HD-SDI" or "1.5 Gbit" video.

Uncompressed video is easier to work with in production applications for a number of reasons. First, because a complete set of data is present for each frame of video, editing is very simple; a video sequence can start and stop at any frame. Second, many compression systems introduce into the video signal path a delay that must be precisely duplicated in the audio signal path, or else audio/video synchronization problems will arise. Third, uncompressed signals can simplify production operations by eliminating expensive compression and decompression equipment and simplifying the connections between system components.

Of course, there is a major drawback to working with uncompressed video: System networking and storage resources can be heavily taxed. An uncompressed SDI signal will occupy over 2 Gigabytes of storage for every minute of video, and HD-SDI will take up close to 12 Gigabytes per minute. For networking, only high-speed network interfaces can be used, such as Gigabit Ethernet for SD signals or 2.488 Gbps SONET/SDH links for HD-SDI signals. The latter network interface is the main one used on the MD6000 product.

IP encapsulation is used in this application for a number of reasons. First, when the uncompressed video data is broken into packets, Reed-Solomon codes can be added to allow most errors that occur in the IP network to be corrected without affecting the video signal. Second, the IP packets can receive a time stamp at the origin that allows the destination device to accurately re-create the timing of the original signal. Third, use of IP standards allows other types of data to share the same transmission network as the video signal.

One other benefit of IP encapsulation in this application is the use of IP packet sequence numbering to support automatic protection switching. For this to work, the connection between the signal source and destination must have two different paths: a main path and a standby path. In the event of a failure of the main path, the destination device automatically switches to use the backup path. One complication is that in the real world, it is impossible to make two different network paths have the same exact propagation delay. This forces the destination device to compensate for the difference in packet arrival times by delaying one signal to match the other. IP encapsulation aids this process because each outbound packet can be given a sequence number, which the destination device can use to realign the incoming streams. Once the main and the standby signal are aligned, a failure of the main channel can be immediately recovered by a switch to the backup channel with no loss of video data.

This technology is currently deployed in Japan and is being used to make connections between broadcasters in different cities. It has also been used for broadcasting several major sporting events, including the 2002 FIFA World Cup soccer tournament in Japan and the 2004 Olympic games.

## REVIEW AND CHECKLIST UPDATE

In this chapter, we looked at how IP packets are created from compressed video streams. We began by discussing the tradeoffs of using long or short packets. Then, we looked at the different types of MPEG streams in order to gain an understanding of the role of each stream. We glanced at the popular DVB-ASI signal format, which is used throughout the video industry for carrying MPEG transport streams. We followed this with a detailed discussion of two transport protocols that can be used (with varying degrees of success) to transport video streams: TCP and UDP. We concluded with a look at RTP, which is a valuable method for handling real-time audio and video signals.

## Chapter 6 Checklist Update

❑ Determine if long or short packets are going to be used for video transport, keeping in mind the pros and cons of each approach.

❑ Make sure that the selected packet length will not be so long as to cause fragmentation over the data networks that will be used.

❑ When choosing a stream format, keep in mind that transport streams have several functions that are specifically designed to operate in difficult environments, such as RS error correction, and a robust mechanism for handling the required clocks.

❑ Elementary streams should not, as a general rule, be used for video transport.

❑ If multiplexed DVB-ASI signals with multiple transport streams are used, make sure that the receivers are configured to process the correct stream, based on the PAT, PMT, and PID values.

❑ If non-MPEG streams are to be used, make sure that a mechanism exists to identify which audio and video content belongs to a given program, and that there is a way to synchronize the streams after they have been transported across a network.

❑ Use Reed-Solomon forward error correction and packet interleaving to make video streams less sensitive to transmission errors. When doing so, keep in mind the extra bandwidth required for the FEC data, and be careful not to allow packets to become so large that they cause fragmentation.

❑ If possible, choose RTP instead of TCP or plain UDP. TCP has some built-in behaviors that are great for data transfer but are not well suited for real-time video transport. UDP alone lacks some of the nice features of RTP for real-time streams. RTP with UDP is well suited for video transport, provided the network devices support RTP.

❑ Keep in mind that RTP streams, which ride inside UDP packets, may be blocked by some firewalls. This should not be a problem for users with private networks (either physical or VPNs) but may be an issue if the streams are to be sent over the Internet.

# 7

# PACKET TRANSPORT

Once you have gone through the effort to put video, audio, and data into IP packets, chances are that you are going to want to move the packets from one network to another. One of the great strengths of IP networking is the huge variety of different technologies that have been successfully used to move packets over long and short distances. We begin this chapter with a discussion of some of the major technologies that are used to transport packets. We will then discuss several factors that need to be considered when evaluating transport technologies. A discussion of some of the impairments that can occur on networks follows next. The chapter concludes with a discussion of the Internet as a transport medium, and a brief look at service levels. By the end of this chapter, the reader should have a good appreciation of the wide variety of options that are available for IP packet transport and understand some of the network conditions that can affect video signal transport.

# TRANSPORT METHODS

In many cases, end users have little or no control over how their IP traffic is transported between their locations. Packets are handed to a network provider at one location and delivered back at another. In between, there may be multiple different networks, belonging to multiple different service providers. In other cases, users with private networks can decide which technologies they will use for video packet transport. In either case, the following sections will help users to understand a few of the more popular methods that are available and to understand some of the differences between the various choices.

One of the most popular network technologies for IP packet transport in local areas is Ethernet. It is the common interface between a huge variety of different networks. Unfortunately, Ethernet itself is not intended for long-distance transport; standard applications have a distance limit of 2 km from end to end. Fortunately, designers have been busy designing a whole range of network equipment that uses other technologies to transport IP packets over long distances and provide Ethernet interfaces at both ends. Since we spent a fair amount of time discussing Ethernet in Chapter 5, we won't repeat that discussion here. Instead, we will discuss some of the other technologies that are used for packet transport.

## Packet Over SONET/SDH

SONET, which stands for Synchronous Optical NETwork, and SDH, which stands for Synchronous Digital Hierarchy, are popular transport systems used by telecom carriers around the world. A significant majority of the world's long-distance telecommunications capacity uses either SONET or SDH technology, so it is important to understand how this technology works. Since we covered the SONET/SDH bit rates and hierarchy in Chapter 1, we won't spend more time on that here. Instead, we will focus on how SONET/SDH can be used for packet transport.

One innovation that has become popular is Packet over SONET/SDH (PoS) technology, which efficiently places IP packets into SONET/SDH payload envelopes for transport. Since all connections in SONET are logically point-to-point (even if they operate over a ring topology network), PoS is based on Point-to-Point Protocol (PPP). PPP offers basic framing for variable length packets and some error detection capability. PoS is primarily used between routers that have been equipped with internal SONET/SDH interfaces.

One of the biggest advantages for users of SONET/SDH transport is also one of the biggest dangers for video transport applications: the support of redundant networks. Much effort has been spent to make SONET/SDH networks continue operating even if a key component of the network fails, such as when an optical fiber is cut. To do this, SONET/SDH networks are commonly constructed in counter-rotating rings, where data can be sent either clockwise, or counterclockwise, or both ways around a ring. In the event of a failure anywhere around a ring, data can be automatically switched to flow in the opposite direction at the points near the failure. This process, called an Automatic Protection Switch (APS) event, is great for voice and data, because the restoration times are very quick. For the network, the total end-to-end recovery time must be less than 50 milliseconds, and is typically much less than that. With an interruption this short, all that a voice user might hear is an audible "click." Data users might lose some bytes during an APS event, but most times the data will either be retransmitted or recalculated using checksums.

Let's ponder the impact of a 50-millisecond APS event interruption for a live video stream. One frame of video lasts either 33 milliseconds (in NTSC) or 40 milliseconds (in PAL and SECAM; see Chapter 3 for more video information). Losing a frame can be very hard on a video display. Often, the display will lose synchronization and may need to take a short while to regain it. To a viewer, this interruption would be comparable to one caused by changing channels on a television—not horrible, but definitely noticeable. So, for high-quality video transmission, it is important to avoid APS events.

SONET/SDH network users need to know that an APS event could be caused by simple degradations in addition to complete failures. For example, if the bit error rate goes above a preset threshold, then an APS event can occur. Also, it is not uncommon for carriers to, without warning users in advance, force an APS event on a network when new equipment is being installed, or major repairs are being made. By making the active traffic flow in only one direction, they can perform maintenance on facilities used only in the other direction. Some carriers will tell users before these switchovers happen, but that works only for planned events. So, users should not be surprised if their SONET and SDH networks become unusable for 50 milliseconds every now and then.

Even though SONET and SDH are the current state of the art for long-haul fiber optic equipment, users need to understand that degradations can and will occur. These degradations can occur from simple bit errors (which any equipment may exhibit, not just fiber optic) to outages lasting up to 50 milliseconds at a time (or more, if the APS fails to work properly). By understanding this and by being prepared for the consequences, end users will be able to set their expectations and select or configure their video equipment appropriately.

## Cable and DSL

Many local service providers currently offer residential and business subscribers high-speed Internet connections based on cable modem and Digital Subscriber Line (DSL) technologies. These systems use specially designed protocols to deliver IP packets from the customer to the service provider. We won't go into a detailed discussion of these data formats, because most, if not all, of these services provide an Ethernet connection to the end user.

A key factor to keep in mind about DSL and cable modem services is that many are asymmetrical, which means that the data flows faster in one direction than the other. This design was based on observations of end users, who can type a few letters on a keyboard or click their mouse and thereby trigger a whole torrent of data to flow to them from the Internet. A common version of asymmetrical DSL service sold to consumers in the USA provides 128 kbps from the user to the provider (upstream) and 768 kbps from the provider to the user (downstream). Video users need to keep this in mind when deciding where to locate video sources—for many forms of video, 128 kbps simply won't be enough to support delivering video content from an end user location.

One major source of confusion when discussing cable modem and DSL is the concept of shared versus dedicated mediums. A shared medium means that multiple users share the same physical connection between the service provider and the end users. A dedicated medium means that only one user has access to the physical connection to his or her service provider. A classic example of a dedicated medium is a standard telephone line (or local loop), which can be used for normal telephone service, DSL, or both. Examples of shared media include cable TV connections and wireless connections. Figure 7-1 shows user access networks with shared (cable modem) and dedicated (DSL) access mediums.

From a user perspective, speed and security might appear to be two areas where shared and dedicated access networks differ. In reality, the differences depend more on the particular way in which a service provider has implemented its network than in the underlying technology.

For example, in the area of cable modem security, it is true that data going to or coming from a subscriber will travel over the same coaxial cable that is connected to a subscriber's neighbors, and data could potentially be accessible from another customer's cable modem. To counteract this, DOCSIS (Data-Over-Cable Service Interface Specification) compliant modems have (since 1999 when they were first introduced) provided encryption between the customer's modem and the service provider's head end. This prevents a neighbor's PC from being able to interpret the data without possession of the encryption key, which is stored inside each user's cable modem.

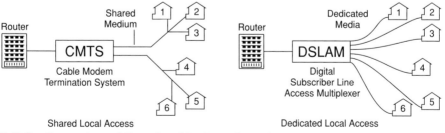

**FIGURE 7-1**  Comparison of Shared and Dedicated Local Access

A second common area of misunderstanding is the perception that DSL offers dedicated bandwidth access to the Internet, whereas a cable modem offers only shared access. In reality, both cable modem and DSL service providers will typically combine traffic from multiple users into a single high-speed Internet connection, unless specific arrangements have been made with the end user (normally only for business customers paying high monthly fees). The connection speeds that are available to each user depend much more on the internal capacity and configuration of the service provider's network than on the mechanism used to make the connection to the customer. This point is important for video users to understand—even though they might see great results when doing a speed test on their connection to their local service provider, the actual speed that can be sustained all the way through the Internet to the video source may be dramatically different.

When it's all said and done, users of cable modem and DSL services will see little or no difference as a result of the access technology chosen. There can be bottlenecks with either technology that can arise close to or far away from any user. Differences between service providers will exist, but this is due to the manner in which the providers have engineered their internal networks. When shopping for service, it is more important to look at the provider's reputation and quality of customer support than to look at which access technology is being deployed. As far as video is concerned, neither cable modem nor DSL service has any clear advantage over the other, and neither one may have the performance necessary for high-quality video transport.

## Optical Networks

As discussed previously, virtually all long-distance terrestrial networks today use fiber optic transport. In most cases, the user is not aware of the physical network; the services are provided as IP packet transport over the Internet, SONET/SDH transport, or a variety of other protocols.

A significant number of end users have the need or the desire to construct their own fiber optic networks. This decision can be driven by

any number of needs, including cost control, high-bandwidth requirements, special signal needs, fiber availability, or others. Generally, the
biggest barriers to construction of a private optical network are obtaining the necessary construction permits and rights-of-way, and the cost
of construction, which can easily range from $20,000 to $500,000 or
more per kilometer. "Dark" fibers, which allow customers to attach
their own optical networking equipment, can also be leased from
some local municipalities or service providers.

Private optical networks can offer users the ultimate in control over
their networks, but this freedom comes with responsibilities.
Providing a redundant or backup link in case of a network failure is
essential, since studies have shown that fiber cuts cause up to 70% of
all fiber optic network failures. Users also need to understand that,
like any other technology, fiber optics are not perfect—their error
rates are not zero.

Many video customers use fiber optic equipment that is specifically
tailored for transporting video signals in their native format (such as
SDI or DVB-ASI). They may also install a separate IP transport network that can be used for data transport. This approach makes sense
for large users of video networking, such as a television broadcaster.
Separate video networks may also be used for security cameras and
other special purposes.

For large users, or those with special needs, dedicated, private fiber
optic networks can offer premium quality transport for any kind of
signal. Once the initial costs have been recovered for purchasing and
installing the equipment and the fiber cables, these networks offer
high reliability and low recurring costs. Video users should always
consider using private fiber networks if they are available.

## IP Over ATM

While using Asynchronous Transfer Mode (ATM) networks to transport IP video may seem like a waste, this is actually a fairly common
situation within a carrier's network and inside some private networks. For carriers, ATM is a convenient tool to manage a customer's
use of the network, since the exact amount of bandwidth given to a

customer can be dedicated and limited with most ATM devices. Also, because ATM is connection oriented, the exact path from source to destination can be managed, minimum bandwidth guaranteed, and data from different users can be kept separate. As in many IP networks, end users might not have any idea that their IP packets are flowing over a carrier's ATM network.

Users of IP over ATM services need to understand that a significant amount of bandwidth can be used by the overhead when using these protocols in combination. The overhead comes from the fact that IP adds headers to raw video to form video packets and that ATM uses 5 bytes out of every 53 for its own framing structure and overhead. So, with a DS3 telephone circuit operating at 44.736 Megabits per second (Mbps) running ATM, the bandwidth available for IP traffic drops to less than 40 Mbps, without even counting the IP and MPEG overhead.

What does all this overhead buy for the user? Well, for starters, users or carriers can carve up the ATM bandwidth into dedicated "virtual circuits" for each application. This can mean that a video signal gets a fixed amount of bandwidth that doesn't have to be shared with other applications, such as e-mail. These circuits can be essentially any size; they don't need to conform to the standard rates of the SONET/SDH hierarchy. Also, ATM's structure makes it easy for a carrier to ensure that data from one customer doesn't end up at another customer. ATM also supports multicasting, which involves sending video from one source to multiple destinations (and will be discussed in Chapter 9). ATM's sophisticated bandwidth management tools can set up a dedicated circuit from a video source to a destination so that the video signal won't suffer interruptions or delays caused by data traffic competing for bandwidth. For occasional-use networks, some ATM service providers offer management tools that allow circuit bandwidth to increase and decrease on a pre-scheduled or dynamic basis.

When an IP over ATM system is properly configured, and the bandwidth limits are observed, the solution can be very satisfactory. Because ATM networks are used in some private organizations and a number of carriers, end users should not be surprised if their IP video traffic is transported over ATM.

## MPLS/GMPLS

Multi-Protocol Label Switching (MPLS) and its more all-encompassing form Generalized MPLS (GMPLS) were developed to improve the management of IP network resources, simplify the functions of high-speed routers, and support multiple priority levels for data traffic. MPLS works on IP, ATM, and Frame Relay networks. GMPLS extends the function of MPLS to other network technologies, including time, fiber, and wavelength multiplexing and switching. MPLS has been successfully implemented on a number of networks. GMPLS is (as of this writing) actively undergoing standardization efforts and being incorporated into advanced products.

The basic concept of MPLS is label switching, which uses simple labels on packets, cells, or frames to send data along pre-established paths, known as Label Switched Paths (LSPs). MPLS is connection oriented, which means that a path from the sender to the receiver is established prior to data transmission, similar to ATM and TCP. LSPs run from one edge of the MPLS network to the other, and can be configured using a variety of different software protocols that are used by routers. This task is not easy; a significant amount of effort has gone into creating the software that distributes the labels to all of the routers along a given LSP. Once the labels have been distributed to all the network elements, MPLS networks are very fast, because each router along the LSP needs to look only at the label, rather than processing the entire packet.

Each LSP is a unidirectional flow of data from a source to a destination. For applications requiring bi-directional data flows (such as voice calls and most data applications), two LSPs must be constructed—one in each direction of communication. Note, however, that the protocols that are used to set up LSPs (such as LDP—the Label Distribution Protocol) require bi-directional communications between the routers that will carry the LSPs.

A big advantage of LSPs is that they are connected before data begins to flow, and can be used to reserve bandwidth from one end of a network to another. This function is very useful for video streams, because a properly constructed LSP can ensure that all of the packets of a video stream arrive at the destination on time and in the right order. Although this is similar to the functions provided by TCP, MPLS achieves this result without the constant back-and-forth communications required by TCP. MPLS makes the job of the video decoder easier by smoothing out the packet delivery, and it potentially supports the delivery of higher quality video.

As currently specified (as of this writing), MPLS networks do not offer multicast services, which allow a sender to deliver one stream to the network and have the network copy and deliver the stream to multiple receivers. Work is under way to extend the MPLS specification in this area, primarily because multicasting offers many benefits to users of video and audio streaming. We'll talk more about multicasting in Chapter 9.

MPLS functions are not normally available throughout the public Internet. Instead, MPLS is normally implemented on private networks that have the ability to configure their routers to offer MPLS services. Some carriers also offer MPLS services for interconnecting customer locations with virtual private networks. GMPLS functions, due to the later creation of the standards and the relatively more complex implementations, are not currently available on a widespread basis.

## RPR

Resilient Packet Ring (RPR) is a newly developed protocol that provides packet transport using counter-rotating rings over existing SONET/SDH and Ethernet networks. RPR accomplishes this by providing a different Media Access Control (MAC) function than the one traditionally used by Ethernet, while still being able to use most existing Ethernet and SONET/SDH hardware (cables, interface chips, etc.). RPR is not a physical network technology; it can be successfully implemented on SONET rings or a collection of point-to-point Ethernet connections that are arranged to form a ring. RPR is packet based, but it can support connection-oriented protocols such as MPLS.

RPR technology has been developed to offer some of the benefits of ring architectures to pure IP transport systems. Ring benefits include:

- Rapid, automatic recovery from most network failures.
- Simplified network architecture—a single, high-bandwidth connection that extends from node to node, instead of a collection of point-to-point connections between different nodes.
- Simple reconfiguration to adapt to changing bandwidth needs, which reduces or eliminates the need to construct new networks when demand shifts from one node to another.
- Ability to use both main and protection networks to carry live traffic; when failures occur, low-priority traffic is removed from the system until repairs are completed.

One of RPR's big benefits is that it supports statistical multiplexing of packets at each node in the network. This means that the overall bandwidth of the network is used more efficiently. Efficiency is gained because all of the packets can share a single, large-bandwidth connection between nodes on the network, instead of being wastefully divided among a collection of low-bandwidth point-to-point connections that each take up part of the network bandwidth.

Video signals can benefit from RPR technology because of two main factors. First is the ability of RPR to provide dedicated bandwidth to applications, which ensures that a guaranteed amount of bandwidth is provided through the network. This is very beneficial to real-time video and voice data, which operate better in fixed-delay, lossless transport networks. Second is the availability of multicasting services, which is very useful for video streams going to multiple destinations simultaneously (see Chapter 9 on multicasting).

The Institute of Electrical and Electronics Engineers (IEEE) released the RPR standards as 802.17 in June 2004. A number of networking and test equipment vendors have begun to deliver RPR-compliant equipment. It is expected that carriers who provide metropolitan and wide area network services will be the primary target market for RPR technologies; large end users with private wide area networks may also deploy RPR.

## Wireless

Wireless Ethernet provides essentially all the same functions as normal Ethernet, without the need for wires to connect the data sender and receiver. Instead, high-frequency radio waves are used to carry the signals, similar to cordless telephones and other RF-based devices. Interest in Wireless LANs (WLANs) is high and has spurred a whole range of manufacturers to produce equipment. To get an appreciation for the excitement this technology has created, simply do a web search of some of the popular terms that have been developed for this technology, including "Wi-Fi" (a registered mark of the Wi-Fi Alliance) and "802.11." The number of hits will be staggering.

Wireless Ethernet can offer significant benefits to LAN users. By removing the need to have physical wires connected to each source or destination for data, wireless Ethernet provides users with much greater flexibility to change location at their whim. Wireless access points (also known as "hotspots") are available in a number of public venues, including restaurants and airports. Companies can save considerably on expenses for reconnecting cables to employees each time they move offices and provide them with desktop-quality data services as they move around the facility. See Figure 7-2 for an illustration of a typical wireless network. Note the variety of different devices that can be used to provide access, including laptops with built-in wireless modems, internal PCMCIA modems, and external USB modems, as well as hand-held devices and wireless webcams.

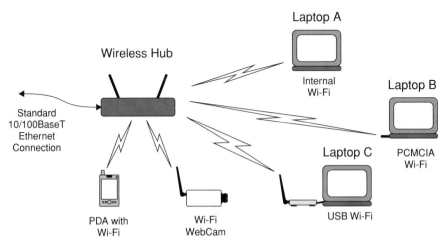

**FIGURE 7-2**  Typical Wireless Ethernet Network

There are three principal forms of wireless Ethernet: 802.11a,802.11b, and 802.11g. Let's discuss them in the order of their release:

- 802.11, originally released in 1997, operated at speeds of either 1 or 2 Mbps in the unlicensed 2.4 GHz microwave radio band. It has been effectively superseded by the other standards.
- 802.11b, released in 1999, became popular because it still worked in the same 2.4 GHz frequency band as 802.11 but offered transmission speeds up to 11 Mbps. Note that this is the raw bit rate; with overhead and other factors, the effective maximum throughput is on the order of 5 Mbps.
- 802.11a, also released in 1999 took longer to become popular, both because it operated in a different frequency band (5 GHz) and because it offered high speeds: 54 Mbps at the top end, although the effective rate is in the vicinity of 25 Mbps (both of these factors made 802.11a more expensive initially). Also note that approval for use of the 5 GHz band was not available in Europe when the standard was originally released.
- 802.11g, approved in 2003; products based on this standard actually appeared on the market before final approval. This system offers raw transmission bandwidth up to 54 Mbps (actual throughput is much closer to 25 Mbps) and operates in the 2.5 GHz band. Note that 802.11g is backward compatible with 802.11b.

Unfortunately, wireless Ethernet is not an ideal medium for high-quality video traffic, because interference is difficult to control. Interference on a wireless system can cause bit errors and packet loss, both of which are bad for video and data signals. Video can be made to work, but it is more challenging than on a standard wired or fiber optic network. To understand why, we first need to look at the bands where 802.11 operates: the 2.5 GHz band and the 5 GHz band. These are both unlicensed bands in the USA, which means that users don't need to get a license from the FCC to transmit data (the 2.5 GHz band is also unlicensed in Europe). This is both good news and bad—good because it eliminates paperwork and avoids payments of fees, but bad because users cannot be sure that other users won't be using the same frequencies. (This contrasts with broadcast television stations, which do need a license but are protected by regulations from interfering signals.) Small variations in the local environment, caused by, say, people walking around, can also cause significant changes in system performance.

Because of the difficult environment that they were intended to operate in, the 802.11 standards have been designed to work with significant levels of bit errors and packet loss. When bit errors occur or packets are lost, the wireless receiver notifies the wireless transmitter. The transmitter can choose from two automatic mechanisms that are used to cope: Either the bit rate is reduced, or lost packets are retransmitted, or a combination of the two.

Unfortunately, video, which can be more severely impacted by delays than by occasional bit errors, can potentially be harmed when either of these mechanisms is used. If the bit rate of the wireless link is dropped below the rate of the video stream, then the video signal will essentially become useless. Similarly, if the wireless system retransmits packets, then chances are that they will arrive too late and clog up the data channels and the buffer of the video receiver. Neither situation is particularly good for video.

Overall, use of wireless Ethernet technology should be considered carefully for video and audio streams. Since the amount of bandwidth available over the link can change rapidly in response to subtle variations in the RF environment, video users need to approach the use of these networks with caution. Clearly, this area will be the subject of a significant amount of work in standards and product development over the coming years, so it would be reasonable to expect that this issue may become less important as wireless technology advances.

## TRANSPORT CONSIDERATIONS

When video is being transported over an IP network, users need to consider a number of factors. These factors can significantly affect the end users' viewing experience, so they should be taken into account when planning a network. The topics described in the following sections are not listed in any significant order, so most readers should review all of them.

### Multiplexing

Often in a video distribution system, it is necessary to combine video streams from different sources. This procedure requires a multiplexer, which needs to process the video signals as they are combined. The output of a multiplexer can be a single data signal (for example, a Gigabit Ethernet signal) or multiple signals, each of which contains multiple video streams. Multiplexing can be done for a number of reasons:

- One large stream can be easier to transport and administer than several smaller streams.
- When variable rate streams are combined, the peaks in one stream can correspond to valleys in another, allowing the overall system bandwidth to be used more efficiently.
- Some transmission channels, including satellite and telecom links, have fixed amounts of bandwidth per channel. When these systems are used, it makes good economic sense to combine as many streams as possible to completely fill up the channel.

Of course, multiplexing is not a free lunch. Adding a multiplexer, either as a stand-alone box or as part of another piece of equipment, can add cost to the transmit side of a network. Typically, a minor cost is also added on the receive side of the network, because many video receivers and decoders have built-in demultiplexers. (**Note:** Not all integrated demultiplexers are capable of working with all multiplexers, so a bit of caution is in order.) Many low-cost decoder devices were developed to work in multi-channel applications, like consumer set top boxes. (Keep in mind, however, that just a small amount of cost added to each receiver can add a lot of cost to a network with many viewers.) Multiplexing can also add a small amount of delay to the video signals. Plus, if the video signals are coming from different locations, they will typically need to be transported to a common location where the multiplexer is installed.

Two forms of multiplexing are commonly used today: time division multiplexing and statistical multiplexing. See Figure 7-3 for a comparison.

- *Time division multiplexing* provides a fixed amount of bandwidth to each incoming (tributary) stream. Operation is simple: Packets from each incoming stream are placed into timeslots in the combined stream. Each timeslot is a fixed portion of the total stream bandwidth. In many systems, several timeslots can be combined to accommodate large tributaries. In some systems, this allocation

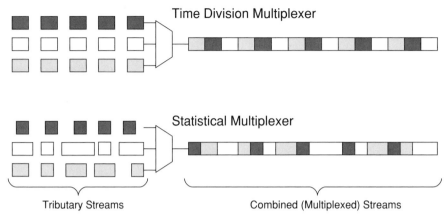

**FIGURE 7-3**  Comparison of Time Division Multiplexing and Statistical Multiplexing

can be changed to accommodate streams that require more or less bandwidth, although the allocation cannot typically be changed very rapidly, or while the system is in use.

- *Statistical multiplexing* provides bandwidth to incoming channels in response to their instantaneous rate; higher speed tributaries are given a larger amount of the overall network capacity. Many systems can be configured with a maximum and a minimum bit rate for each tributary stream. In most systems, a rate limit is also imposed on the combined stream.

Time division multiplexing has the advantage of being fairly simple and generally has very low overhead. It is also used extensively in modern telecommunications, including SONET/SDH networks. For fixed-rate tributary streams, it can be quite efficient. However, when the tributaries are variable rate, overall efficiency drops, because each timeslot needs to be given enough bandwidth to handle the peak rate of the tributary, or else data loss can occur. Time division multiplexing also has the benefits of providing constant end-to-end delay through a network (which is good for video) and being easy to switch (more on switching later in this section).

Statistical multiplexing works well when the tributaries have data rate peaks that occur at different times, as is common in compressed video where different amounts of data are created for the different MPEG frame types (I, P, and B). Video streams typically have variable data rates, with peaks occurring when rapid movement is present in a video scene, and lower data rates occurring when there is little action or movement. A statistical multiplexer takes advantage of the fact that the peaks and valleys in the data stream generally occur at different times for different content. When these signals are combined, as shown in Figure 7-4, the peak data rate of the combined data stream is less than the sum of the peaks of the individual streams, so the network bandwidth is used more efficiently.[1]

Another key function of a video multiplexer is the correction of the presentation time stamp (PTS) and program clock reference (PCR) values contained in the MPEG streams. As we discussed in Chapter 6, these values are inserted into the MPEG stream by the MPEG encoder and are based on a 27 MHz clock that is present in the encoder. At the decoder, a copy of that clock is reconstructed from the data contained in the PCR and used to control the timing of the video decoding. When MPEG signals are sent through a multiplexer (statistical or other), these values need to be recalculated and reinserted into each video stream. The reason is that the multiplexer, while it is doing its job, may need to slightly delay a packet from one stream while a packet from another stream is being transmitted. This has the effect of requiring the video decoder to use a larger buffer to smooth out the

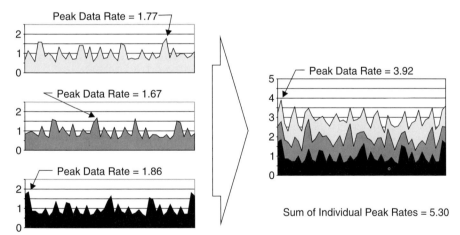

**FIGURE 7-4**   Effect of Multiplexing Data Streams

1.   Some statistical multiplexers take this process a step further by actually controlling the amount of data produced by the tributary MPEG encoders. For this scheme to work, the multiplexer needs to be tightly coupled with (and generally co-located with) the MPEG encoders.

delay variations. The multiplexer therefore has the responsibility to make sure that the PCR and PTS values are properly recalculated on all the streams that are being processed by the multiplexer.

Statistical multiplexing has the drawback that it is generally more complicated than time division and that it can require more overhead to supply the information needed to demultiplex the stream at the receiving side. Note that Ethernet networks are inherently statistically multiplexed, because nodes that send packets more often are automatically given more bandwidth under the CSMA/CD mechanism. (See Chapter 5 for more information on CSMA/CD.)

*Switching* is used whenever video signals from one data stream need to be transferred into another data stream, such as when satellite signals are switched into a terrestrial network. When data is traveling on a time division multiplex link, switching is very simple. The switch just needs to copy all the data from a timeslot within an input signal to a timeslot of the same bit rate on an output signal. With statistically multiplexed links, the case is quite different: The switch needs to look at the entire contents of the input signal to find all of the necessary packets. (Note that they may arrive sporadically or in bursts.) Then, the switch needs to transmit these packets while making sure that the output link has enough capacity and making sure that the newly added packets don't collide with other packets that are being sent on the same output link. Buffers can be used to handle this task, but they can have other effects on the video stream, as we will discuss later.

When you are deciding whether to use multiplexing, you should analyze three cost factors:

1. The cost of adding the multiplexer at the signals' origin.
2. The cost (if any) of adding a demultiplexer to all of the signal destinations.
3. The network cost savings generated by transporting one multiplexed signal in place of multiple individual signals.

Time division multiplexing is simple, but not as bandwidth efficient as statistical multiplexing for signals like video that have large bit rate peaks and valleys. Statistical multiplexing is more bandwidth efficient for video signals but can be more costly to implement than time division multiplexing. In general, multiplexing should be considered whenever multiple video signals need to be delivered to the same set of destinations or when network costs are high.

## CALCULATING NETWORK BANDWIDTH

Calculating the amount of actual bandwidth consumed by an MPEG stream is very important. It is also somewhat tricky. Let's look at how one manufacturer (HaiVision Systems of Montreal, Quebec) does this for one MPEG–2 product (the hai500 series Multi-stream encoder/decoder/multiplexer).

As in most MPEG devices, the hai500 user is given control over the rate of the raw MPEG stream. For this device (which is pretty typical), the video bit rate can be set anywhere from 800 kbps to 15 Mbps, in steps of 100 kbps. The user can also set the audio stream rates over a range from 32 kbps to 448 kbps. For the purposes of our example, we will use a video bandwidth of 2.5 Mbps and audio bandwidth of 256 kbps.

Since we are going to be transporting these raw streams over a network, the first thing we want to do is convert the raw MPEG streams (also known as elementary streams; see Chapter 6) into a transport stream (TS). For audio, this will add about 20% to the raw bandwidth and 7% to the raw video bandwidth. So, our original audio stream is now a 307 kbp TS, and our video TS now occupies 2.675 Mbps. We also need to add 45 kbps to these streams to provide room for the PCR (program clock reference; see Chapter 6). Figure 7-5 illustrates this example.

The next step is to calculate the IP and Ethernet overhead. Since the Hai500 uses RTP over UDP, we must allow for a 12-byte RTP header and an 8-byte UDP header. Then, we must add a 20-byte IP header and a 26-byte Ethernet header, bringing the total of all the headers to 66 bytes. We can accommodate anywhere from two to seven MPEG–2 TS packets (which are always 188 bytes long) in each Ethernet frame. For our example, let's use seven TS packets (or 1316 bytes) per Ethernet frame, because this gives us the highest ratio of data to headers. With 66 bytes of header for 1316 bytes of data, we have an overhead of approximately 5%. So, our total bandwidth for both the audio and video streams (with a little rounding thrown in because you can't have a partial packet) come out to 3.18 Mbps. This calculates to 15.4% overhead on the original raw streams (2.5 Mbps plus 256 kbps). In terms of packets, this equates to roughly 288 packets per second.

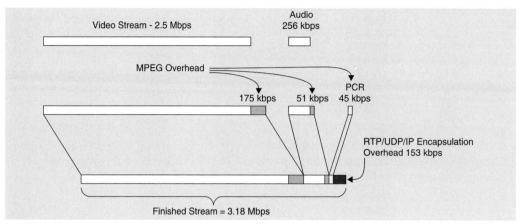

**FIGURE 7-5** Sample Total Bandwidth Calculation for an MPEG 2 Stream

## Traffic Shaping

Video traffic shaping consists of various techniques that are used to make video traffic easier to handle on a network. Shaping can consist of a variety of technologies, but often the overall goal is to make a stream less prone to sudden peaks in bit rate. Traffic is considered to be well shaped if the peaks are relatively small (or non-existent) in comparison to the average bit rate. Figure 7-6 shows the difference between a poorly shaped and a well-shaped stream.

Networks generally operate more efficiently with streams that are well shaped. Since most networks have a constant basic bit rate (e.g., Ethernet runs at 10 Mbps, a SONET OC3 or SDH/STM-1 runs at 155.52

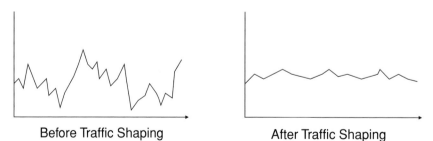

Before Traffic Shaping                    After Traffic Shaping

**FIGURE 7-6**  Comparison of a Stream Before and After Traffic Shaping

Mbps), more total data can be carried if all the streams are well shaped. For example, if a group of video streams has an average bit rate of 20 Mbps and a peak data rate of 50 Mbps, then an OC3 or STM-1 could carry only three of these signals. If, on the other hand, a group of video streams had an average bit rate of 20 Mbps and a peak bit rate of 30 Mbps, then the OC3/STM-1 link could carry five of these signals. In the first case, the SONET/SDH link would be 40% utilized on average (3 streams at 20 Mbps in a 150 Mbps pipe), whereas in the second case, the SONET/SDH link would be 66% utilized (5 streams at 20 Mbps in a 150 Mbps pipe).

Video elementary streams are prone to having a lot of peaks. For example, in MPEG–2 video streams, an I frame requires much more data than a B frame, even though they both represent the same amount of time in the video signal (33 milliseconds for NTSC, 40 milliseconds for PAL/SECAM). So, if the MPEG–2 encoder transmits data exactly as it was created, the bit stream would have a peak whenever an I frame was being created. Also, since MPEG and other video compression systems rely on the fact that video signals are relatively similar from one frame to the next, each time the video scene changes (say, from an indoor scene to an outdoor one, or from program to commercial), the amount of data that needs to be sent also jumps.

One version of traffic shaping operates using the "leaky bucket" approach, which is a good analogy. Think of a bucket with a small hole in the bottom. The hole is where the useful data comes out. Now think about data sources, such as an MPEG–2 encoder. Each time the encoder has some data ready, an amount of water is put into the bucket. If it is an I frame or a scene change, then a lot of water is put in. If it is a B frame, then a small amount of water is added. As long as the hole is big enough to handle the average rate of the data inflow, then the bucket will never overflow, and the output stream will be constant. If the data comes too fast, then the bucket will eventually overflow, causing MPEG picture data to be lost. So, the temptation is to use a large bucket. But, as the bucket size goes up, there is a penalty for this smoothing: The data has to sit in the bucket waiting to leak out. This causes delay in the transmitted video signal, which can be bad for applications that require low delay.

Overall, traffic shaping is a good thing for video networking. In fact, many newer MPEG encoders have a built-in traffic shaping capability. Shaping increases the number of channels that can be carried on a data link. It also makes the streams more predictable so that equipment in the network will not have to work as hard to accommodate dramatic changes in bit rates. However, traffic shaping needs to be used carefully, because it can create additional delay in the network.

## Buffering: Pros and Cons

A buffer is basically a collection of memory that is used to temporarily store information prior to taking some action. Possible actions can range from transmitting data on a network, to performing scrambling, to waiting for the data necessary to re-create an image. Buffers are used throughout video processing and can have a major impact on video network performance.

In MPEG, certain buffers are required. They are used on the encoding and decoding side to support motion estimation, which compares successive frames to see what has moved from one frame to the next (see Chapter 4). Buffers are also used to support the frame reordering function that allows B frames to work. An important function of an MPEG encoder is making sure that these buffers that are present in every MPEG decoder are never filled beyond its capacity.

Error correction also requires use of buffers. Typically, a whole packet needs to be processed to add Forward Error Correction (FEC) coding. Also, packet interleaving uses buffers with room for multiple packets. (Both of these topics are discussed in Chapter 6.) For low-quality networks, larger buffers are needed to support these functions, because of the increased amount of data that needs to be transmitted.

Buffering is normally also needed in a network receiver. Buffers are needed to smooth out variations in data arrival times that are caused by statistical multiplexing and switching. Other buffers are needed to perform the FEC calculations and to de-interleave the incoming packets. Depending on the network, these buffers can be very small or quite large.

For one-way broadcast video, the total amount of end-to-end delay can be fairly large (as much as 5 to 10 seconds) without having any impact on the viewer. In fact, it is very common for live shows with "Viewer Call-In" to use a device called a profanity delay to inject several seconds of delay into the outgoing signal. If a caller uses inappropriate language, then the studio staff has time during the delay to remove the offensive language before it is broadcast. We are free to conclude that, for pre-recorded shows and even sports programs, broadcast delays amounting to handfuls of seconds are not an issue, and special effort is not needed to reduce the delay.

In contrast, interactive or two-way video is very sensitive to delay. As delay is increased, it becomes difficult for normal conversation to occur, because it is hard for speakers to know when the other person is beginning to talk. Table 7-1 shows what the International Telecommunications Union (ITU) specifies in Recommendation G.114 for one-way delay of a link used for a two-way conference.

Large buffers in the receiver can make up for a lot of network transmission problems. If packets are temporarily misrouted, they can be reinserted in their proper position in the bit stream after they are received. If the packet arrival rate is jumpy instead of smooth, a receive buffer can be used to smooth them. The receive buffer is also the ideal place to perform any needed error correction or to de-interlace the packets.

Large receive buffers are almost universally used in IP streaming media applications. In fact, these buffers can hold 10 to 20 seconds'

**TABLE 7-1**

One-Way Delay Recommendations (Based on ITU G.114)

| Delay | User Impact |
| --- | --- |
| 0–140 milliseconds | Minor or unnoticeable impairment to normal conversation; acceptable to most users. |
| 140–400 milliseconds | Possible to notice impairment; acceptable for use; however, some user applications may be impaired. |
| Over 400 milliseconds | Not acceptable for general use; should be avoided in network planning; may be used in exceptional circumstances. |

worth of video and audio information. To keep viewers entertained while the buffers are filling, many Internet video player applications will show a user the status of the receive buffer—either through some kind of graphic (such as a bar graph) or by means of a text status message (such as "Buffering: 87%"). The main purpose of the buffer is to ensure that adequate data is ready for the video decoder when it is needed, even if the incoming stream is disrupted momentarily, or even for a few seconds. If the buffer ever does become empty, then the video will stop, and most player applications will display a message to the user indicating that the buffer is being replenished. Unfortunately, for real-time applications, such as videoconferencing, the use of a large buffer won't work, because of the amount of delay added to the signal by the buffer.

Overall, the benefits and drawbacks of buffers are summed up in Table 7-2.

**TABLE 7-2**

Buffer Advantages and Disadvantages

*Buffer Advantages*

- Large buffers can make up for a large number of network impairments, such as uneven packet arrival rate and packets arriving in the wrong order.
- Buffers are mandatory for MPEG compression, since successive frames of video need to be compared as part of the compression process. If B frames are used, then additional buffering is needed to put the video frames back in the correct order for presentation to the viewer.
- Buffers can be an ideal place to perform functions such as traffic shaping, forward error correction, and packet interleaving.

*Buffer Disadvantages*

- Buffers add delay to the end-to-end video delay. Large buffers can make the delay unacceptable for applications in which interactivity is involved, such as videoconferencing. One-way delay in a two-way conversation should be kept below 150 milliseconds; one-way delays over 400 milliseconds should be avoided.
- Even for non–real-time video, the delay that a user experiences while the buffer is filling up can become annoying if it is excessive (just ask anyone trying to watch a movie preview over a dial-up link).
- Buffers can add cost and complexity to both the video encoder and the decoder. While this is typically not an issue for rack-mount servers and desktop PCs, as more hand-held devices are configured to work with video, the additional memory and power consumption of large buffers needs to be considered.

## Firewalls

A firewall is used to control the flow of information between two networks. In many cases, firewalls are used between user computers and the Internet, to keep unauthorized users from gaining access to private information or network resources. While it may be true that a firewall would not be needed if each user PC and server in a network used proper security policies, it is generally more convenient for a system administrator to manage the security policies for a whole group of users on a single device such as a firewall.

Firewalls vary greatly in their level of sophistication and in their methods for providing security. Most firewalls provide at least a packet filtering function, which examines each packet passing through the firewall on a packet-by-packet basis. More sophisticated firewalls provide stateful inspection, which not only examines the contents of each packet, but also tracks the connection status of each of the TCP or UDP ports that are used by the packet.

Packet filtering involves looking at the source and destination IP addresses of each packet, as well as the source and destination TCP and UDP ports in each packet. This inspection is generally direction sensitive, where internal users are allowed to perform one set of functions, and external users are allowed to perform another. For example, consider TCP port 80, which is used by HyperText Transfer Protocol (HTTP) on the World Wide Web (www). Anytime a user types "http://www.xxx.com" on his or her web browser, a packet is sent to port 80 on the "xxx" server (see Figure 7-7). This packet will also include a port number on the user's PC for the reply from the website to come back to, in our example 2560. Once a connection is established, every packet between the user and the server will contain the user's IP address and user's port number (2560) as well as the server's IP address and port number (80).

Let's assume that the user does not have an HTTP server in his network that he wants to make available on the Internet. Then, it is very easy to exclude external HTTP users; all the firewall needs to do is block any incoming packets that are addressed to port 80. This can prevent tragedy if, for example, one of the PCs in the user's network was set up to be an HTTP server by a careless or uninformed user.

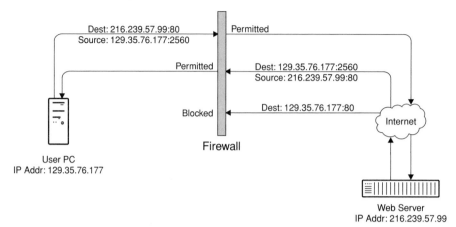

**FIGURE 7-7**   Web Browsing Firewall Example

The firewall can also make sure that any HTTP servers that are for internal use only (such as an employee directory) cannot be accessed from the Internet. The firewall can also be configured to block other well-known TCP and UDP ports, such as e-mail portals.

Firewalls can interfere with video traffic in two main ways. First, the firewall can block outside users from being able to access a video source or server. Since many video servers will not send video data to a user until requested to do so, it can be impossible for a user to make a request if all the well-known ports (such as 80) are blocked by the firewall. Placing the video server outside the firewall, at an Internet hosting service, for example, can solve this problem. Alternatively, a special sub-network can be created that is only partially protected by the firewall, commonly called a DMZ (after the military term "Demilitarized Zone").

The second way in which firewalls can interfere with video traffic is by blocking all UDP traffic, which is a very common setup. UDP traffic is harder to police than TCP traffic, because it is possible for an intruder to insert unauthorized packets into a UDP stream. (Remember—TCP packets use sequence numbers for bytes, which are not present in UDP packets.) Unfortunately, UDP has a number of benefits for streaming video, so many video sources use the UDP protocol. So, if UDP is to be used for streaming, any firewalls that are along the path from source to destination must be checked for proper configuration. We will discuss some other stream format alternatives in Chapter 8 when we talk about streaming protocols.

Overall, video system implementers need to be aware of the constraints that firewalls impose on video services. Firewalls create a quandary for network administrators, who must balance the need for users to have access to services versus the need for administrators to ensure network security. Careful planning can avoid making a firewall a barrier to IP video transport success.

## NETWORK IMPAIRMENTS

Many things can happen between a video source and a video viewer. Of course, there are gross network failures (such as the northeastern USA blackout of 2003), but there are also subtle failures. In the following sections, we are going to look at some of these more subtle failures, also known as impairments. While they may not be as dramatic as a power failure that affects 50 million people, these impairments can mean the difference between success and failure on a video network.

### Packet Loss

A packet is declared "lost" when it does not arrive at its intended destination. This can be caused by any number of circumstances, such as network failures. It can also be caused by subtle errors, such as a single bit error inside a packet. It can also be caused by faulty network configuration, which sends packets to the wrong destination. In any case, packets will occasionally get lost in transmission on essentially all IP networks.

IP packets include a checksum in each header. This checksum is used to test whether the header has become corrupted in transmission. Each time a packet is received, the checksum is recalculated. If the result of the calculation does not match the incoming checksum, then the header has been corrupted, and the packet will be destroyed.

To get a feel for how often this can happen, let's think about some ways to measure an error rate on a network. We could, for example, ask our network to deliver packets from one end to the other with a Six Sigma success rate. Six Sigma means 3.4 parts per million, or 99.9997% defect free, or one packet error out of every 294,000 packets, on average. Using the example given earlier in this chapter for a 2.756 Mbps combined audio and video stream, we came up with 288 packets per second. At a Six Sigma packet loss rate, this would mean that a packet would be lost every 1021 seconds, or about once every 17 minutes. Since we don't know what data would be contained in that packet, it could cause anything from some minor loss of data in one video frame to a complete screen freeze for a fraction of a second, or an audio noise spike or audio dropout.

Another way to calculate error rates on networks is to look at the Bit Error Ratio (BER). A BER is the number of bit errors divided by the total number of bits transmitted. Many types of fiber optic telecom systems specify their BER performance as 1 bit out of every billion in error, or an error rate of $1 \times 10^{-9}$. Going back to our example, each packet is 1382 bytes long (66 header and 1316 data), which is 11,056 bits. At 288 packets per second, we have just over 3.18 Mbps (million bits per second). We would see a billion bits every 314 seconds, or about every 5¼ minutes. Again, since we don't know where the error would be, we can't really know if the error would affect a small part of one video frame, or a group of video frames, or one of the audio channels.

Packets can also get lost when networks become saturated with traffic. In fact, IP routers have built-in mechanisms to discard packets when more arrive than can be sent over a network segment. As traffic builds up, and the router's buffers fill up, more and more packets are discarded. This is all done with good intentions; by discarding packets, the router is trying to trigger a mechanism in TCP devices that makes them automatically slow down their transmission speed when packets are lost along the way. Unfortunately, video encoders typically cannot adapt easily to bit rates below the rate they have been configured to use, so lost packets means lost video data. Compounding this problem, many video streams use the UDP protocol, which does not have a built-in rate reduction mechanism.

Clearly, packet errors are part of life on an IP network. Even when these errors are reduced to fairly low intensity, they can still cause errors in the displayed video pictures. When you are configuring a network, it is very important to make sure that there is enough bandwidth to carry the video from end to end in order to minimize packet loss due to congestion. It's also important to monitor packet loss rates on transmission links to ensure that the loss rates don't become worse over time, which could indicate a problem in the network.

## Packet Reordering

Packet reordering occurs in a network when the packets arrive in a different order than how they were sent. For many types of data, such as e-mail or file transfer, this is not a problem, since the data is not normally used until all the packets have arrived. However, for video data streams, out-of-order packets can cause problems.

Streaming video data, particularly MPEG video packets, has a very precisely defined structure and sequence. This structure is necessary to allow the decoder to correctly determine where each pixel needs to be placed in the image. The timing of this data is important as well. If some of the data for an image is not available when it is time to display that image, then the image can have missing portions or might not be displayable at all. When packets arrive out of order, they must be put back in the right sequence for the video decoder to operate.

Packets can get out of order in a network for a variety of reasons. One possible cause was discussed earlier in this chapter—automatic retransmission in a wireless link. When there are multiple paths from the source to the destination, packets can (under certain circumstances) take different paths and take different times to arrive.[2] Also, as networks become congested, packets may get delayed while waiting for their turn to be sent.

---

2. Routers are designed to forward packets in a repeatable manner based on a set of rules. Typically, all packets from the one source to a single destination will take the same path. However, video packet receivers need to be able to handle any exceptions.

Packets that arrive out of order can easily be put back into order through the use of a buffer. However, this can add delay to the signal (see our discussion earlier in this chapter on buffers). Plus, if the buffer isn't large enough, a severely delayed packet will have to be treated as a lost packet.

Hence, when you are evaluating a network for video traffic, make sure to examine the packet reordering performance. If reordering happens frequently, the network may not be a good choice for video.

## Delay

Delay is going to happen in any network, whether from a desktop to a server or around the globe. There are two main sources of delay on an IP network: propagation delay and switching delay. We'll examine these two separately, although combined impact must be considered when looking at the end-to-end delay of a network.

Propagation delay is the amount of time it takes for information to travel from one location to another. As any physics student knows, the speed of light is an absolute limit on how fast information can travel (although a lot of us are ready for someone really clever to come up with a solution to this "problem"). This limit does affect modern communications networks, since we can easily send information at the speed of light using radio waves or optical fibers. (Although the light is slowed down somewhat in a fiber, it still goes pretty darn fast.) Table 7-3

**TABLE 7-3**

Propagation Delays

| Some Examples of Propagation Delay | Approximate Delay |
| --- | --- |
| One foot of optical fiber | 1.5 nanoseconds |
| One meter of optical fiber | 5 nanoseconds |
| 1000 kilometers of optical fiber | 5 milliseconds |
| 1000 miles of optical fiber | 8 milliseconds |
| Halfway around the world (12,000 miles or 20,000 km) of fiber | 100 milliseconds |
| Earth to Geosynchronous Satellite and back | 240 milliseconds |

gives a few examples of the propagation delays that could be encountered in real networks. (Note that a millisecond is equal to 1,000,000 nanoseconds.)

Switching delay occurs at any point in the network where a signal needs to be switched or routed. Switching can occur when moving from one network to another, or within a network any time that a router is used to process packets. Delays inside a router are not easy to calculate or predict, because the delay depends on so many different things. Delay for any packet can be affected by many things, including the total number of packets that a router is processing, by the presence of other packets with higher priorities, by congestion or failures of some of the links leaving the router, or simply by the processing time of the router itself. Routers use mechanisms called "queues" to handle packets; they are very similar to the cashier lines at a large supermarket. Packets get placed in different queues depending on their priority, their size, the time of day, the phase of the moon (well, not really). The amount of time that it takes a packet to travel through a router is affected by the queue that it is placed in, and whether there are other packets in the queue in front of it. Just like in a supermarket, the user has essentially no control over the other packets in the same queue, so delays can climb if a number of large packets are in line to be sent first. As a general rule, the lower the number of routers in the path, the lower the delay in the path.

## Jitter

**Note:** This section gets a bit technical and can be safely skipped by the casual reader. For those of you who want to know about the seamy underside of an IP network, read on!

Jitter is a measurement of variation in the arrival time of data packets. To get an understanding of this, think about how a well-behaved video source would send data out into a network: nice, even-sized packets at a regular rate. Another way of saying this is that the time between packets is always the same. Ideally, if the packets arrived at the receiver in this same way, with exactly the same time between each packet, the network would be perfectly jitter free. However, that's not how the world really works. In reality, receivers must be built to tolerate jitter, and networks should be designed not to create a lot of jitter if they are to be successfully used to transport video streams.

Let's look at an example of jitter where the sender is transmitting 500 packets per second, or one every 2000 microseconds. (This corresponds to an MPEG video rate between 3 and 4 Megabits per second, which would give a fairly high quality picture.) Ideally, with zero jitter, the packets would arrive at the receiver at the same timing, i.e., one every 2000 microseconds. Jitter happens when the packets arrive with different timing—say 20 microseconds early or 50 microseconds late.

For normal data, such as e-mail or a file download, jitter doesn't have much of an impact. However, for real-time data such as video, audio, and voice signals, timing is very important. MPEG video streams include a clock reference (called the program clock) that allows the MPEG decoder to match its clock precisely to the one used by the MPEG encoder.

If jitter becomes excessive, it can interfere with the recovery of the clock that is included in MPEG and other video streams. Since it is critical that the receiver's clock matches that of the sender, the sender periodically includes a snapshot of the 27 MHz program clock that was used to encode the video picture (see Chapter 6 for more details). In the receiver, these snapshots are used to synchronize a local clock. Any jitter that is present makes synchronization harder to achieve, because the jitter adds inaccuracy to the time stamps.

In the receiver, buffers can be used to reduce the jitter, by smoothing out the packet timing, and by giving late packets more time to arrive. Of course, this comes at a cost—adding a buffer increases the amount of end-to-end delay in the network. Also, the start-up time (measured from when a user requests a video until when the video actually starts playing) will increase when a buffer is used to remove jitter.

Overall, in any packet video network, some form of buffering will be needed at the receiver to accommodate jitter. The best systems on the market today use adaptive buffering—making the buffer small (and the delay short) when network conditions are good (i.e., low jitter and low packet loss). Buffer size is correspondingly increased if network conditions are poor or become worse. With any video stream, clean, uncongested networks, with minimal packet loss and low jitter are the best choice for transport.

## INTERNET TRANSPORT

At first glance, the public Internet appears to be an attractive method for video transport. It has incredible bandwidth, reaches all corners of the globe, and has little cost to the user beyond the costs of access. Unfortunately, the Internet is far from an ideal network for video traffic. Table 7-4 lists some of the key features of an ideal video network, and discusses how the public Internet measures up on each feature.

**TABLE 7-4**

Key Features of a Video Network

| Feature | How the Public Internet Measures Up |
| --- | --- |
| High Bandwidth | The public Internet certainly has a large amount of bandwidth; however, there are also a large number of users. No single user can count on having a large amount of bandwidth available at any given time for a video application. |
| Low Jitter | Jitter is difficult to control in private networks and almost impossible to control in the public Internet. Because there is no universal mechanism to ensure that packets from a video stream all follow the same route, some jitter and packet reordering are inevitable. |
| Low Delay | Network delay depends on two things: the time it takes a signal to physically travel over a link and the time it takes to process packets at each step of their journey. In the public Internet, users do not have control over how their packets are routed. This means that the delay can be long or short, depending on the route used and the congestion level of the networks used. |
| Priority Control | The public Internet provides essentially no priority control, because the Internet connects all users equally. There is no reliable mechanism to reserve bandwidth for a specific user or to make specific packets for one user take priority over other traffic on the public Internet. |
| Lossless Transmission | Overall, the public Internet is extremely robust; communications can take place even if major portions of the network are not operational. However, packet loss is a fact of life on the Internet: Some carriers promise only 99% or 99.5% packet delivery, meaning that losses of 0.5% or 1% of a user's packets are not unusual. |

With care, and the proper equipment, the Internet can be used to transport high-quality, high-bandwidth video. For example, a network has been constructed to operate over the public Internet between Moscow, Russia, and New York City in the USA. Table 7-5 gives the performance levels measured between these two cities during the video transmission.

Based on the values in Table 7-5, it might appear the reliable video transmission isn't possible. However, in this situation, the customer chose to use a pair of devices from Path 1 Network Technologies of San Diego, California. These devices (CX1000) take a standard video stream, add a user-selectable amount of Forward Error Correction (FEC; see Chapter 6), and also interleave the packets. In this case, the units were set to apply 40% FEC, which means that 4 FEC packets are sent for every 10 actual data packets. (This is a large amount of FEC, needed primarily to compensate for the high number of lost packets.) Also note that the end-to-end delay in this example is near the upper limit of what would be desirable for interactive video, but it is acceptable in this case because this is a one-way video broadcast from Moscow to New York.

## QUALITY OF SERVICE

Quality of Service (QoS) is a term that is often used to describe the overall suitability of a network for a particular use. A number of factors can

**TABLE 7-5**

Moscow to New York Network Performance

| Network Feature | Results |
| --- | --- |
| End-to-End Delay | 120 msec |
| Maximum Jitter | 25 msec |
| Raw Video Rate | 5 Mbps |
| Packet Transmission Rate | 1350 per second |
| Packet Loss Rate | ~1000 per hour |
| Packet Reorder Rate | ~10,000 per hour |

affect network QoS, including delay, delay variation (jitter), bandwidth, packet loss rates, and network availability. We discussed all but the last of these factors earlier in this chapter, so let's first get an understanding of network availability. Then, we'll look at classes of service, which are a means of giving different types of data different QoS links. Finally, we'll take a brief look at some of the items that are commonly found in Service Level Agreements (SLAs) for network services.

## Network Availability

Network availability is a measure of what portion of the time a network is available for use by a customer. Carriers will typically guarantee a minimum level of network availability for each month (or other service period).

A network is said to be "Unavailable" whenever it cannot be used for customer traffic, either due to a complete loss of connectivity or an excessively high error rate. For example, a complete loss of connectivity would occur when a network is physically disabled due to, say, a cut fiber optic cable or a loss of power at a critical equipment location. The high error rate threshold for many telecom networks is set to trigger when performance degrades to the point where at least one bit is in error out of every thousand bits transmitted. This high an error rate (also known as an error rate of $10^{-3}$) can result in an error in every packet. Also, there may be a minimum amount of time that a network must remain unavailable before the counter starts. In many instances, a network link is not deemed to be unavailable by networking equipment until a severe error condition has lasted for 10 seconds or more. From a carrier billing and service guarantee perspective, the criteria can be very different. A carrier might not consider a link to be unavailable until it is out of service for 5 minutes or more, based on the carrier's Service Level Agreement.

Typically, network availability is measured as a percentage of the amount of time that the network was available (or not unavailable) out of the total measurement time. For example, a provider that promises 99.99% network availability would guarantee that the service does not become unavailable for more than 52 minutes per year.

## Classes of Service

Classes of service are used to give different types of data different levels of access to network resources. Network administrators can assign different classes of service to different types of data, allowing each class to experience a different service quality. For example, messages that are needed to control or maintain the network are given a very high QoS, because if these packets get blocked, the entire network can become unstable or fail completely. Similarly, data packets containing e-mail can be assigned a low class of service, because a short delay in transmission usually does not affect the value of e-mail messages. In between are classes of service used by real-time applications, such as database queries, voice over IP calls, and video and audio streaming.

Within the data networking community, a number of different opinions about the class of service should be assigned to video traffic. This occurs as a natural result of different opinions of the value of video traffic. On one hand, video could be viewed as a mission-critical function for a broadcaster sending programming to a remote broadcast location. On the other hand, a college network administrator could view video as a nuisance when hundreds of students try to watch the latest music video online. Also, priority conflicts can arise when a single network is used for both voice over IP and video over IP. So, it is important to assess the value of video to an organization before the correct class of service can be assigned.

As we have discussed in this chapter, in order for video to display properly for a user, the video data needs to arrive in a smooth, continuous stream. One way to accomplish this on a crowded network is to assign a high-performance class of service to video traffic. In effect, this instructs a router or other network device to give priority to these packets. Let's take a short look at how priorities are handled; refer to Figure 7-8.

In Figure 7-8, three different priority queues are shown; we'll call one high priority, one medium priority, and one low priority. These queues operate just like a line at a market for a cashier—new packets enter the rear of the queue and wait until they reach the head of the queue before they are transmitted. In this case, all of the queues are competing for a single output resource, so we have to assign operating rules.

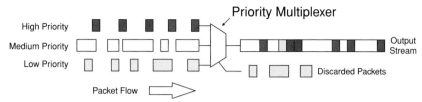

**FIGURE 7-8**  Example Using Three Priority Queues

Let's set up a simple set of sample rules and see how they affect the behavior of the system.

1. Each time the output resource becomes available, a packet is chosen from one of the three queues. If no packet is available in any queue, then a null packet is sent.
2. If a packet is available in the high-priority queue, then it is sent immediately.
3. If no packet is available in the high-priority queue, and a packet is available in one of, but not both of, the medium- and the low-priority queues, then that packet is sent.
4. If no packet is available in the high-priority queue, and packets are available in both the medium- and low-priority queues, then packets are sent in a ratio of three medium-priority packets to one low-priority packet.

Using this example, we can see why it would not be prudent to send large video or other frequently occurring packets using the high-priority queue: It would be very difficult for other packets to get through. Sending video as low priority would also be unsuitable to the video users; their packets would be delayed while other packets were processed. Medium priority could be a choice for video, provided that most non-video traffic was made low priority.

Low-priority packets can get delayed, or sent by a different route, or, worst case for an extremely congested network, get deleted because they were not deliverable. Deletion will occur if a packet waits too long in a queue and its Time-to-Live counter expires, or if the router uses "random early discard" to keep queues from overflowing. A great deal of intense science and mathematics is involved in queuing theory, so we won't spend any more time on it.

The total amount of traffic that can be handled by a network faces a firm upper limit. Assigning different classes of service to different types of data can make sure that important traffic gets through the network, potentially at the expense of other traffic. Because of this, classes of service are generally only usable on private networks. Consider the dilemma if classes of service were available to everyone on the public Internet. What would keep everyone from assigning his or her own traffic to be the highest possible class of service?

Overall, classes of service can be useful tools to help ensure that video traffic flows smoothly across a network. However, they are not a panacea, since high-priority video service can affect the performance of other data, and because their use is basically limited to private networks. Used with discretion, and with suitable policies of use, classes of service can help ensure a pleasant experience for video users.

## Service Level Agreements

Service Level Agreements (SLAs) are contracts between carriers and users that specify the quality of services that a carrier will deliver. These contracts are legally binding and can sometimes be modified for large users. SLAs can cover a wide range of network features and functions and can cover any type of service, from plain voice to sophisticated private network and hosting services.

An SLA should not be confused with a tariff. A tariff is a document that specifies prices for specific telecommunications services that must be filed by a licensed common telecommunications carrier in the USA with a regulator (the Federal Communications Commission or a state Public Services Commission). Services covered by tariffs must be offered to all customers on a non-discriminatory basis. While tariffs sometimes include a description of the level of service that will be provided by the carrier, they are typically not as detailed and generally offer fewer specifics than SLAs.

SLAs sometimes include a unique feature: automatic compensation when the promised service level is not reached. Typically, these remedies take the form of automatic credit to the customer's bill for each instance of a problem that has occurred in a specific time period.

Table 7-6 provides a description of some items that can appear in SLAs.

For video services, packet delivery or loss ratios are crucial. As loss ratios approach 1%, video becomes very difficult to deliver smoothly, unless very robust FEC is used. Network delay may also be a consideration, but it usually comes into play only for interactive video. On the other hand, delay variation (jitter) will affect all video and should be tightly controlled. Network availability is important to all services, including video.

**TABLE 7-6**

Service Level Agreement Items

| SLA Items | Description |
| --- | --- |
| Availability (%) | The proportion of the time that the service is available for use, i.e., not out-of-service. Typical SLA values are 99% and greater. |
| Packet Delivery Ratio (%) | The proportion of packets that are delivered to the destination out of the total number of packets sent. Note that this may be measured as a monthly average and be based on sample data, not on a count of every packet sent. Typical SLA values are 99% or greater. |
| Packet Loss Ratio (%) | The converse of Packet Delivery Ratio; i.e., the number of packets lost out of the total number sent. Typical SLA values should be 1% or lower. |
| Network Delay (msec) | This number specifies the average amount of time that it takes data packets to flow across the network. Notice that this specification may be just between points inside the provider's network; it may not include the time needed for customer data to enter or leave the network. Also note that this measurement may be based on samples and not every packet, and may be averaged over a week or a month. |
| Delay Variation (msec) | Although it would be nice, a limit on delay variation is probably not in most current carrier SLAs. This factor is only really important for streaming applications, such as video and voice over IP. As more end users deploy streaming, expect to see this enter into new SLAs. |
| Service Response Time (hours) | This is the maximum amount of time from when a network problem is reported to the provider until when the provider has to be ready to begin correcting the problem. This may vary depending on time of day (e.g., longer times at night and on weekends) and may include travel time from the provider's site to the customer's location. |
| Time to Repair (hours) | This is the maximum (or sometimes average) amount of time that it will take the provider to correct a service problem. Note that customers may need to wait through both the service response time and then the time to repair before their service is restored. |

# REVIEW AND CHECKLIST UPDATE

In this chapter, we focused on moving packets from one location to another. We covered network transport technologies such as SONET/SDH, cable and DSL, ATM, MPLS, RPR, and wireless Ethernet. We looked at an example illustrating how to calculate network bandwidth. We discussed a number of aspects of transport, including multiplexing, traffic shaping, buffering, and firewalls, and how these technologies impact video transport. We then examined how network impairments can affect video traffic, including packet loss, packet reordering, delay, and jitter. We focused on how the public Internet can (or cannot) be used to transport video, in light of its standard behavior. And, we wrapped up with a discussion of how Quality of Service can impact video traffic and looked at some of the factors involved in a Service Level Agreement.

## Chapter 7 Checklist Update

❏ Verify that the wide area network capacity and technology are suitable for the video traffic that is to be transported.

❏ Set up the video endpoint devices to handle impairments to the video stream. Consider the impact of packet loss, packet reordering, and jitter.

❏ Calculate the total bandwidth needed for the video signals, including any associated audio signals, ancillary data, MPEG overhead, and IP and Ethernet encapsulation overhead. Make sure the network can handle the peak bit rate expected.

❏ Make sure network delay is suitable for the application. For interactive video, one-way delay should be below 150 msec, and normally must be below 400 msec. For one-way applications, delay is not a significant factor.

❏ Consider using multiplexing to reduce the cost of bandwidth when multiple video signals are being transported.

❏ Ensure that network firewalls are configured correctly. In particular, make sure the necessary TCP or UDP ports are unblocked. Also, check whether UDP traffic is allowed to flow when RTP over UDP streams will be used.

❑ Decide whether the public Internet will be used. If so, ensure that video sources and destinations are configured to handle lost packets and large delay variation.

❑ If private networks will be used, determine whether different classes of service will be employed for video. Create policy for video QoS; make sure adequate bandwidth is available for non-video communications.

❑ Examine carrier SLAs. Will networks provide a suitable level of service for video?

# 8

# VIDEO STREAMING AND MEDIA PLAYERS

Video streaming is the process of delivering video content to a viewing device for immediate display. Streaming is often the first application that springs to mind when people think about transporting video over a network. As discussed in this book, many other types of applications are possible with video over IP. Nevertheless, streaming is an important application for video over IP networks, and it makes sense for us to cover it in some detail.

Many users will have encountered video streaming while surfing the web, particularly if they sought out video content. Popular video sites include CNN.com for news stories; sonypictures.com, warnerbros.com, and Disney.com for trailers of upcoming movies; and mtv.com or music.yahoo.com for music videos. In addition, a number of sites offer actual television programming over the Internet, including researchchannel.com (a lovely 1200 kbps signal) and Bloomberg television (at http://www.bloomberg.com/streams/video/

LiveBTV200.asxx). All of these sites provide users with full-motion and synchronized audio that can be played on a normal PC equipped with a suitable-speed Internet connection and the software necessary to receive, decode, and display the video streams.

In this chapter, we will be limiting the discussion to one-way delivery of video content over a general-purpose data network. Two-way (or more) videoconferencing will be handled in Chapter 10. Video delivery over special-purpose video networks will be discussed in Chapter 13 on IP video to the home. We'll begin with a discussion of some of the key concepts related to streaming, including some of the basic technology. Then, we'll look at some of the applications of this technology. We'll conclude with a look at some of the most popular streaming formats.

## BASIC CONCEPTS

"Video streaming" is a generic term that covers a couple of different technologies. The most common ones are

- *True streaming,* where the video signal arrives in real time and is displayed to the viewer immediately. With true streaming, a 2-minute video takes 2 minutes to deliver to the viewer—not more, and not less.
- *Download and play,* where a file that contains the compressed video/audio data is downloaded onto the user's device before playback begins. With download and play, a 2-minute video could take 10 seconds to download on a fast network, or 10 minutes to download on a slow network.
- *Progressive download and play,* which is a hybrid of the two preceding technologies that tries to capture the benefits of both. For this technique, the video program is broken up into small files, each of which is downloaded to the user's device during playback. With progressive download and play, a 2-minute video might be broken up into 20 files, each 6 seconds long, that would be successively downloaded to the viewer's device before each file is scheduled to play.

In the following sections, we'll investigate these technologies in more depth and take a brief look at how these three techniques differ.

A simplistic analogy might be useful here. Consider two of the options that are available for supply of fuel used for home heating. One alternative is natural gas, which is piped by means of a distribution network that runs into each customer's home. Another alternative is fuel oil, which is delivered on a periodic basis to each customer's home. A true streaming system is somewhat like the natural gas system—the fuel (content) is delivered at exactly the rate in which it is consumed, and no storage is present inside the consumer's home. A download and play system is like the fuel oil delivery system since each user must own and operate a large tank (disk drive) in which the fuel (content) is loaded periodically by a fuel supplier. If the natural gas supply becomes inadequate, the rate of gas delivery to each consumer can slow down, possibly causing difficulty in heating some customers' homes. With the fuel oil tank, once the delivery has taken place, customers have control over that fuel oil and can use it however they wish.

## True Streaming

True streaming really harkens back to the origins of television—and the way that broadcast, satellite, and CATV work today. In these systems, the video is displayed as soon as it reaches the viewer's television; there is no way of storing the video signal. This immediacy has many benefits, not the least of which is the ability to show live content. This also helps make the viewing device less expensive, since image storage is not needed.

True streaming over an IP network starts by taking a digital video signal and breaking it up into IP packets. The video signal can be uncompressed, but generally when we are discussing streaming, the video content has been compressed using some form of MPEG or one of the proprietary video encoding formats (such as RealVideo or Windows Media). These packets are then "streamed" out over the network, which means that the packets are sent at a data rate that matches the rate of the video. In other words, a video program that lasts 10 minutes, 6 seconds will take 10 minutes, 6 seconds to stream. Special software, called "player software," accepts the incoming packets and creates an image on the viewing device.

For streaming to work properly, video content needs to arrive at the display right when it is needed. This is not as simple as it sounds, because many factors can affect the timely delivery of the video packet data. Servers running specialized software (and often containing specialized hardware) are used to send video content in a smooth, constant speed stream over a network. The network needs to be capable of delivering the stream to the viewer intact without losing or changing the timing of the packets. The player software needs to accept the incoming packets and deal with any imperfections in the data flow that was caused by the network. Typically, this requires a small amount of buffering in the player device.

Streaming has been used successfully on a number of different network technologies, from low-speed, dial-up connections to broadband access networks.

Table 8-1 shows some of the advantages and disadvantages of streaming.

## Download and Play

Download and play takes a video content file and transfers a copy to a viewing device, where it can then be decoded and shown to the viewer. This technology is very similar to the process used by websites, where user browsers are constantly requesting web pages from a server. In fact, download and play uses the same protocols as normal web surfing: HTTP and FTP over standard TCP.

Whether web pages or video clips are being requested, operation of a download and play network is fairly simple: Each time content is requested, it is sent to the requesting device. If the content is a 2 Kilobyte web page, then the download can occur fairly rapidly, and the page will quickly appear on the user's browser, even if a slow network connection is used. If, however, the content is a five-minute video clip, the time to download the clip to the player software can be quite long, even on a fast network connection.

Video and audio content can be hosted on standard web servers when download and play is used. Although the files can be very large, the protocols and procedures needed to send the content to a viewer are the same for download and play content as for simple

**TABLE 8-1**

Advantages and Disadvantages of Video Streaming

*Advantages*

- Content is delivered to the viewer when it is needed and is not stored inside the viewer's device. While this will not deter the determined hacker, it can make it easier for a content provider to control how a user handles copyrighted or other valuable content.
- True streaming can be used for widespread viewing of live content, particularly in hard real-time applications. In particular, if the network is multicast enabled (see Chapter 9), then true streaming is the preferred technology, since one stream can be replicated inside the network and delivered to all viewers simultaneously.
- Video streaming can be set up to allow users to begin watching video and audio content at any point in the stream and can allow users to jump ahead or back in the stream (like switching chapters while playing a DVD). This technique will work only if the server that is delivering the stream supports this capability and the content is pre-recorded. This function is frequently implemented through the use of the Real Time Streaming Protocol (RTSP), discussed later in this chapter.
- For applications where viewers will be changing frequently between content streams (as in multi-channel television delivery to the home), true streaming is normally used. This approach eliminates the delays that would occur if the playback device had to wait for content to be downloaded before playback could begin each time the viewer changed television channels.

*Disadvantages*

- The quality of the network between the streaming source and the destination can have a major impact on the quality of the video signal that is delivered to the user. Any interruptions or congestion that occurs in this network can severely degrade the video image.
- Firewalls and Network Address Translation (NAT; see Chapter 5) can interfere with video streaming. Many firewalls are configured to prevent RTP and UDP traffic from passing, so streaming data can't get through. NAT's IP address substitution function can make it hard to set up a streaming sessions and can make UDP ports difficult to assign.
- Lost video packets are not re-transmitted in true streaming, so the playback device should be designed to handle any lost packets in a graceful manner.

pages of HTML text. However, just like any web server, system performance may need to be tuned to handle high volumes of requests for large blocks of content. This is no different than what would be required of a server designed to handle a number of large documents or images.

One big advantage of download and play technology is that it can work over any speed network connection. The reason is that there is no requirement for the packets containing the video data to arrive at any specific time, since all of the content is delivered before playback begins.

Table 8-2 shows some of the advantages and disadvantages of download and play.

## Progressive Download

Progressive download is a variation on download and play. It is used to simulate streaming for applications in which streaming won't work properly, such as when true streaming behavior is blocked by a firewall. Progressive download takes the video content file and breaks it up into smaller segments, each one of which can be sent in turn to the player software. As soon as a segment is completely downloaded, the player can begin to process it and display it, while the

**TABLE 8-2**

Advantages and Disadvantages of Download and Play

*Advantages*

- Firewalls and NAT routers are less of a nuisance for download and play files, because normal HTTP and FTP transfers over TCP are used for delivering the content to subscribers. Since these protocols need to be supported for normal web browsing, they can be used in the download and play process with little fear that they will be blocked by firewalls and other network security devices.
- Download and play servers for video can use normal FTP or HTTP software, because content files are treated just like any other web content. This can create savings for a content supplier by removing the need to purchase, install, and support special video streaming software on content servers.
- Network errors that cause bit errors or lost packets while the video file is being downloaded are automatically corrected by TCP, helping to make the job of the playback device much simpler.

*Disadvantages*

- As each file is being downloaded, even slight network delays or degradations can trigger TCP's flow control mechanism. This can cause the video source to drop immediately to a slower file-sending rate. If this happens, the video playback can be delayed significantly while awaiting the video file to be transferred.
- Video and audio content must generally be completely downloaded from start to finish, without allowing random access for viewers.
- Enough storage (either memory or disk space) must be available on the playback device to store the video file before it is played.
- Because of their large size, video files can be difficult to work with, both on the content server and in the network. If a major problem occurs during file transfer, the whole download process may need to be repeated from the beginning.

next segment is downloaded. As long as each new segment arrives before its designated time to play, the playback device will be able to create a smooth, unbroken video image.

Download and play was very prevalent in the early days of multimedia on the web, and used to be pretty much the only way for audio and video content to be distributed. (The main standard on RTP wasn't published until January, 1996.) Progressive download evolved from basic download and play as the server and viewer software became more sophisticated.

Anyone who has tried to watch a trailer for a movie on-line has probably experienced progressive download. A typical user scenario would be for a user to click a link on a website to request a video clip. Then, a new window would pop up containing the controls for the video, such as pause, play, and volume controls. This new window would display a message saying something along the lines of "Connecting to Media" or "Buffering" and a percentage of completion that could last for several minutes. Once the first segment was completely downloaded, playback would begin. If the next file was ready when the first segment finished playing back, then playback could continue uninterrupted. If, however, the next segment was not ready, then the video viewing window would go blank or begin to display the "Buffering" message once again.

Progressive download can best be thought of as a compromise between streaming and download and play that takes some of the benefits of each. Table 8-3 summarizes the advantages and disadvantages of using this technology.

## STREAMING SYSTEM ARCHITECTURE

When implemented on an IP (or any other technology) network, streaming requires a fair amount of infrastructure. One of the key pieces is the streaming server, which has the responsibility to deliver the video just when it is needed. Another key piece is the viewer software that actually receives the incoming video signal from the IP network and generates an image on the user's display. The final pieces

**TABLE 8-3**

Advantages and Disadvantages of Progressive Download

*Advantages*

- Progressive download provides a quicker start for playback than a full download and play (which can be quite a long process for a high-quality two-minute movie preview).
- Progressive download avoids the headaches brought on by RTP for traversing firewalls and handling NAT routers, because it uses HTTP and TCP/IP, which are passed by most firewalls.
- The entire video file eventually arrives on the viewer's PC and is stored (temporarily) on disk. Once the file arrives, some viewers (such as QuickTime) allow the user to move around inside the content, much like operating a VCR's fast forward and rewind buttons.

*Disadvantages*

- Content has to be specially segmented into progressive download format, and not all media players support it.
- Managing the multiple files that make up a single element of content on the server and during playback can add cost and complexity to both the server and the playback software.
- Progressive download works best on networks where the available bandwidth is well in excess of the speed of the stream. That way, each segment can be downloaded well in advance of the time when it needs to playback.
- As the available network bandwidth degrades, it becomes much more likely that the next file in a progressive download won't be completely stored in the viewing device when it is needed, and then the stream will temporarily halt.

in this puzzle are the content preparation station and the transport network between the server and the viewing device. Figure 8-1 shows how these key functions work together. In the following sections, we'll examine each of these pieces in more detail.

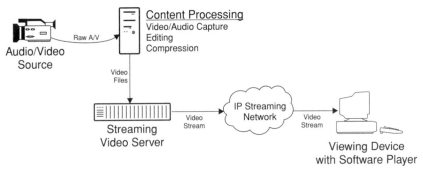

**FIGURE 8-1** Architecture of a Typical Streaming System

## Content Preparation

Raw video content, such as a live image generated by a camera or video that has been recorded to a tape, is generally not well suited for streaming applications. Normally, the content needs to be processed to make it ready for streaming. Processing can include format conversion, video compression, labeling and indexing, and publishing for streaming.

Capturing and preparing content for viewing can be a simple or a highly complex process, depending on the goals of the users and their budget for time and money. For some users, taking a home video camera and placing a compressed video image on their personal website is adequate. For others, professional production, with carefully edited images and graphics designed for web viewing, is required. Setting aside these artistic considerations, a certain amount of processing needs to be done to prepare video content for streaming. Table 8-4 shows some of the main functions that are performed during content preparation.

Content can come from a variety of different sources: video cameras, pre-recorded tapes and DVDs, downloaded video clips, and others. In many editing systems, the content is all converted into a common format before processing takes place. A number of formats can be used; one that is commonly used is a 32-bit RGB format, where each pixel of each frame has 8 bits of data for each of the three primary colors red, green, and blue.[1] This format is very easy to work with and produces very high-quality results, but has the drawback of requiring a large amount of disk space (Megabytes for each second of video). When the video arrives in a compressed format (such as on a DVD), it must be decompressed into this common format.

When the video comes from an analog format, such as from a camera or videotape, a video capture device is used to convert the video into the correct digital format. This device can be a stand-alone device or a card that is inserted into a computer workstation. Some video cam-

---

1.  The remaining 8 bits can be used for various purposes. One popular use is to store an indication of the transparency of the pixel, commonly called the "alpha channel."

**TABLE 8-4**

Streaming Content Preparation Functions

- *Capture:* This is the process of gathering video content and placing it into the preparation system in a common format.
- *Editing:* This is the process of organizing the content into the form that viewers will see, complete with synchronized audio, music, overlaid text, and other visual and audio effects.
- *Pre-processing:* This is the process of conditioning the edited video prior to compression, and can include color correction, noise removal, image resizing, and other processing needed to get the best results possible from compression.
- *Compression:* This is the process of converting the video and audio streams into the formats that will actually be streamed out to viewers. If different steam rates, video resolutions, or types of player software are to be supported, then the compression process is normally repeated for each combination.
- *Labeling and Indexing:* This is the process of making the content accessible to viewers, by providing descriptions of the content and organizing it so that viewers can locate the form of the content that is most suitable to their needs.
- *Publishing:* This is the process of transferring the content to the streaming server and creating the web pages and other materials that will contain links to the media streams.

eras and camcorders are also capable of delivering digital video content directly into a workstation using an advanced digital interface named IEEE 1394 and also known as FireWire. Many newer PCs, laptops, and all recent-vintage Macintosh computers come equipped with IEEE 1394 ports.

Many times, content preparation is done off-line, which allows enough time for a sophisticated compression algorithm to operate. A skilled operator can adjust compression parameters during the process so that different settings can be used for rapid action sequences versus detailed scenery shots with little movement. Live production is also feasible, although less production can typically be done on a live feed, simply due to time and processing power constraints.

## Streaming Server

The streaming server is responsible for distributing media streams to the viewers. It takes media content that has been stored internally and creates stream for each viewer request. These streams can be either unicast or multicast, and can be controlled by a variety of mechanisms. We'll discuss unicast in this section, since it is by far the most prevalent form of streaming. We'll discuss multicast in more detail in Chapter 9.

Content storage and retrieval is one of the main functions of a streaming server. When content is prepared, it is normally produced in a variety of compression ratios so that users with different network connection speeds can select the video rate that they require. For example, on many websites the user is given a choice between playback speeds that are suitable for a dial-up connection (56 kbps, sometimes called "low speed"), a medium-speed connection (100 kbps, sometimes called "ISDN" speed), and a high-speed connection (300 kbps, sometimes called "broadband" or "ADSL/cable modem" speed). Each of these different playback speeds requires a different version of the content file to be created during the compression process. This means that one piece of content may be contained in three different files inside the server—one for each of the playback speed choices.

This situation can be further complicated by the fact that a server may support several different, incompatible types of players. For example, content that was created for the RealPlayer can't be played using a Windows Media Player. Since most content providers want to reach as wide an audience as possible, they will normally encode the video to be compatible with two or three of the most popular player software packages.

Tallying this all up, a streaming server can end up with a multitude of different copies of each piece of content. For example, if the server needs to handle three different connection speed options (dial-up, medium, and high) and three different media player formats (Real, Windows Media, and QuickTime), then a total of nine different video file formats would need to be stored on the server.

A significant processing job of the streaming server is to create packets for each outbound stream. As we have discussed, each IP packet must have a source and a destination IP address. In order for the video packets to reach the correct destination, the server must create headers for these packets with the correct IP destination address. If the server is sending out standard RTP packets, the video and audio streams must be sent as separate packet streams, each to a different port on the receiving device (see Chapter 6 concerning ports and RTP).

Another responsibility of the server is to encrypt the packets in the outgoing stream, if required by the content owner. Since most modern encryption uses public key cryptography (see Chapter 11), each stream will need to be encrypted with a unique key for each user. Accordingly, encryption needs to be done on each stream while it is being sent out of the streaming server.

Since streaming is done on a real-time basis, the server must also create well-behaved streams, meaning that the pace of the packets should be regular and should not rapidly speed up or slow down. The rate of the packets also has to be controlled such that the player device receives only as many packets as needed to render the video and audio correctly. Too fast a pace, and the player would be required to store the extra packets before playback, creating havoc with the playback if the buffer overflowed. Conversely, if the pace drops too low, the player would be starved for data and would have to freeze or interrupt the user display to compensate while waiting for new data to arrive. Although software players normally include small buffers to smooth out the inevitable variations in packet arrivals caused by IP networks, the goal of a streaming server is to deliver a 5-minute, 10-second stream in 5 minutes and 10 seconds.

Sometimes, streaming servers are given the responsibility to change the rate of the stream being sent to a viewer based on changing network conditions. For example, a stream could start out at 300 kbps and then drop to 100 kbps if the network became congested. This function is accomplished through having the player software send commands or status reports back to the streaming server. As network congestion increases, the number of lost or severely delayed packets as detected by the player will also increase. The player then informs the server, which will select a file that contains a version of the content that was recorded at a lower speed. The real trick is to get this to happen smoothly so that the user doesn't notice the switchover, other than a small drop in video or audio quality. This process, also know as "scaling" a stream, is a feature of many advanced streaming systems.

One of the big benefits of streaming technology is that it allows a user to have "random access" to a variety of media streams. This means that the user is permitted to jump ahead or back within a piece of content. In order to implement this function, close cooperation is required between the streaming server and the player software. The player software must accept user commands and transmit them to the server. The server must be capable of accepting those commands and then changing the outbound stream appropriately. This can be fairly tricky to implement, because the size of the jump needs to be designed such that the user can know how far forward or how far back the jump will be.

Streaming servers supplying a number of simultaneous viewers also require high-speed storage and network connections. A 2 GHz Pentium server could easily source enough simultaneous video streams to overwhelm a 1.5 Mbps T1 line several times over, and put a serious dent in a 10BaseT Ethernet link. For large servers handling broadband streams, use of Gigabit Ethernet network interfaces is becoming common. Also, in order to support hundreds or thousands of users, the video content can be copied to multiple servers at different physical locations around the Internet.

## IP Streaming Network

Although it would be great if any IP network could be used for streaming, in reality, a streaming system will function better if some of the key network performance variables are controlled. Table 8-5 gives a list of some of the network parameters that can affect streaming performance. (See Chapter 7 for more discussion of these parameters.)

## Player Software

Player software is responsible for accepting the incoming stream and converting it into an image that can be shown on the viewer's display. A number of functions need to be performed in this software, and the performance of this software can have a major influence on how satisfied the user is with the streaming system overall.

**TABLE 8-5**

IP Network Parameters That Affect Streaming

- *Packet Loss Ratio:* If too many packets are lost, then streaming video performance will suffer. (An occasional packet lost every now and then can generally be hidden.) Packet loss ratios should be kept below one out of every thousand, if possible.
- *Packet Delay Variation:* Because streaming is a real-time activity, if a packet arrives too late, it can't be used in the playback. Conversely, if packets arrive too early, they need to be stored, which can overload the incoming signal buffer and cause errors. Ideally, if the delay variation can be kept below 50 milliseconds, the player can accommodate the variation.
- *End-to-End Delay:* This parameter is not terribly important, unless the link is being used for a two-way conversation. In this latter case, total one-way delay should be kept below 400 milliseconds (see Chapter 10 for more on videoconferencing).

Before streaming can begin, the user must select the content. This can be a complex process, because maintaining an accurate, up-to-date list of the available content can be a daunting task. As we will see in Chapter 13, services provide this data for commercial broadcast networks, but for most private streaming applications, the content supplier must maintain this list. Typically, the list is presented to the user inside a web page that is hosted on the streaming server, and the user simply clicks on the appropriate hot link to begin content playback.

If the streaming server has encrypted the content, the player software needs to decrypt the incoming packets. This is a fairly simple process once the key is known. The keys can be obtained by communicating with the server or by connecting to a third-party authentication service.

The player software is responsible for managing a buffer that receives the incoming packets. This buffer is necessary to absorb any timing variations in the incoming packets and to place packets that arrive out of order back into the correct order. Buffer underflows (too little data) and overflows (too much data) can severely impact the video image, so the buffers need to be sized appropriately for the application. On the downside, large buffers can take awhile to fill when a new stream is starting, or if the user decides to select a new stream. Overall, careful buffer design is a key factor in player success.

Since some streaming protocols, such as RTP, separate the audio and the video signals into two different streams, the player software is responsible for resynchronizing the incoming streams. This is accomplished by looking at the time-stamp data contained in each stream and comparing it to the time-stamp data contained in the associated RTCP overhead packets.

One of the most intensive jobs of the player software is to decompress the incoming signal and create an image for display. The amount of processing required varies depending on the size of the image and on the compression method. Older compression systems (such as MPEG–1) tend to be easier to decode than newer systems (such as MPEG–4) and therefore place less of a burden on the decoding device. Smaller images, with fewer pixels to process, are also easier to decode. Stand-alone devices, such as set top boxes, usually have hardware-based decoders and are generally restricted to a limited range of compression methods (primarily in the MPEG family).

Most recent-vintage personal computers are also capable of running player software. This category includes desktop and laptop machines, as well as Windows-, Macintosh-, and Linux-based systems. Some hand-held devices also are capable of running player software. Determining whether a particular machine is capable of decoding a particular video stream is somewhat tricky; performance depends on the processor speed, the amount of memory (of all types—cache, RAM, and on the video card), and the number of other tasks that the processor is performing. Generally, disk drive capacity is not a big factor, since the buffers required for video processing are generally held in memory rather than disk. (This make sense, when you consider that a moderate-quality stream that runs at 1 Mbps requires only 2 Megabytes of memory to hold 16 seconds of compressed video.) For high-quality, full-screen video decoding, a number of hardware decoder cards can also be added to a personal computer to boost performance.

## STREAMING APPLICATIONS

Video streaming is an ideal way to accomplish narrowcasting—the process of broadcasting to a specialized audience. There are literally hundreds of applications on the Internet today, and thousands more that are hosted in private corporate settings. Some applications require live streaming; others can use previously recorded content very effectively. Let's take a brief look at some of the ways in which streaming video is being used today.

## Entertainment

Video over the Internet really got a jump-start in the late 1990s with the availability of Hollywood movie previews on websites. No longer constrained to showing their wares on expensive television commercials or as "coming attractions" in theaters, movie studios began to reach out to the online community. At first, much of this content was set up for download and play, because very few home users had access to broadband connections that were suitable for high-quality streaming. One of the classics was the *Star Wars Episode 1* trailer at a hefty 10.4 Megabytes; it was released in March 1999, and downloaded 3.5 million times in its first five days of availability, according to a press release at the time.[2] (A good source of movie information and trailers can be found at www.imdb.com, the Internet Movie Database.)

By the end of 2003, 20% of US homes subscribed to a broadband service (cable modem, DSL, wireless, or similar). As a result, more and more content is available in streaming form. Today, a user can log onto a number of different websites and look at movie trailers, music videos, animated shorts, and a huge amount of adult content. A substantial amount of free material is available, and a good deal more requires payment of subscription fees.

## Corporate Video

Corporate video consists of content that is intended to improve the performance of an organization. We'll use the term "corporate" loosely here, because we want this term to apply to all types of public and private organizations, including government agencies, not-for-profit organizations, and true private corporations.

---

2. A copy of this release was available at http://www.starwars.com/episode-i/news/1999/03/news 19990316b.html on April 8, 2004.

Corporate video tends to focus on two areas: employee education and information sharing. Education can cover a wide range of topics, including training for new employees, instruction on new work procedures and equipment, job enrichment training, and personal skills development, to name a few. Corporate executives use information sharing to make employees aware of corporate or organizational performance, to improve communication with employees, and to deal with unusual challenges or opportunities. Sometimes the corporation produces this content strictly for internal consumption; other times content is acquired from outside parties.

Live streaming is normally used for time-critical corporate video applications, such as company news distribution or executive speeches. Before streaming video became feasible, some companies had gone to the expense of renting satellite time and deploying portable satellite receivers for special events. Permanent satellite systems have become popular with retail chains that have a large number of fixed locations with heavy needs for live video transmission, but this tends to be the exception rather than the rule. Today, high-quality streaming has made it possible to use corporate IP networks for this same function.

Many other forms of content are well suited to storage and subsequent on-demand streaming playback. For example, recorded training video material is very effective, because it allows students to watch at their own pace; they can review material or skip ahead without the possibility of disturbing other students. Material can also be stored and played back at different times to meet the schedules of employees who work on different shifts or in different time zones, or those who may have missed the original presentation. With a centralized streaming server, content can be managed in a controlled environment, and outdated versions of content can easily be purged. Plus (particularly for content that is owned by third parties), a centralized server can be a good control point to keep track of the number of times that each piece of content is viewed, which can affect the royalties paid. Contrast this with a download and play environment, where content gets dispatched to users around the network, thereby making accurate usage accounting difficult.

## Investor Relations

One result of the wave of corporate scandals in the USA that began in 2001 was an increased focus on treating all investors equally. Toward that end, many companies decided to give both large and small investors the ability to participate in major corporate events. An increasingly popular way of accomplishing this is by using streaming video to transmit live meetings over the Internet. The content can also be recorded and played back on demand for users who were not able to watch the original live broadcast, or for those who wish to review what had transpired.

During live corporate video coverage, it is not unusual for several hundred simultaneous users to be connected. Multicasting (see Chapter 9) can be used to reach viewers located on network segments that are properly equipped. Typically, this applies only to private networks, where multicasting can be enabled on the IP networking equipment. For users who are not connected to a suitable network, simulated multicasting can be used. With this technique, special servers are used to take a single incoming stream and produce multiple outgoing streams. This technology is particularly useful for investor relations uses, because it can scale up as more viewers connect by adding new server capacity as it is needed.

## Internet Radio and TV

A number of free and subscription services have appeared on the Internet to provide both audio and video content. There are literally thousands of Internet radio stations, due in part to the relatively low cost of equipment and the low bandwidth required. Internet television stations are much less common, but they are becoming more feasible as the number of users with broadband connections increases.

Video and audio streaming sites have been developed for a number of purposes, including corporate branding (free sites), advertising supported (also free), and subscription (monthly or other periodic payment system). A huge variety of content is available, including newscasts, music, adult programming, and entertainment. Because this material is organized similar to a traditional radio or television broadcast, users are restricted to viewing the content in the order that it is presented. It is not a content-on-demand service, where each user can watch any content he or she chooses in any order.

Much of this content is pre-recorded, so download and play technology is perfectly adequate. However, this can be somewhat disruptive to the flow of the broadcast, because each file must be downloaded before play can begin. (This technology is much more disruptive for video files than audio files, simply because video files are much larger and take much longer to download.) Progressive download greatly alleviates this problem, because playback of each new file of content can begin as soon as the first segment of it is downloaded to the PC. Of course, for live broadcasts, only streaming will do.

## TECHNOLOGIES FOR STREAMING

As streaming software vendors continue to innovate, the quality of streamed video continues to go up even as bit rates drop. Today's compression algorithms are 20–30% more bandwidth efficient than those introduced two years ago. Progress continues, as more powerful compression systems allow even more sophisticated techniques to be used on the encoder, and more powerful PCs are available to users for running player software. In addition, research continues on new algorithms that can make lower bit rate pictures even more appealing to the human eye.

In the following sections, we will discuss a number of different technologies that are used for video streaming. We'll begin with a discussion of the Real Time Streaming Protocol, or RTSP, which is used to set up and control streaming sessions. Then, we'll take a quick look at the Synchronized Multimedia Integration Language, or SMIL (pronounced "smile"), that can be used to integrate video, audio, text, and still images into a web-based presentation. We'll then look at the three most popular streaming formats: Apple's QuickTime, Microsoft's Windows Media Player, and RealNetworks' RealPlayer.

## RTSP

The Real Time Streaming Protocol (RTSP) provides a means for users to control video, audio, and multimedia sessions. RTSP does not actually provide for the transport of video signals; it allows these signals to be controlled by a user. Like a dispatcher for a delivery service, RTSP does not go out and actually deliver packages; it controls when and how packages are delivered by other protocols such as RTP.

A good way to think about RTSP is that it is like HTTP for real-time files. A command like "rtsp://content.com/mymovie.rm" begins playback of the video file named "mymovie" on the server named "content." As you can see, this is very similar to the command that would fetch the page named "webpage" from the same site: "http://content.com/webpage.htm." In the first case, the actual video would be transported by RTP over UDP. In the second case, the web page would be transported by TCP.

An analogy might be useful here. Consider, for a moment, a VCR (normal consumer-grade videocassette recorder) with an infrared (wireless) remote control, as shown in Figure 8-2. A user enters a command by pressing buttons on the remote control, which in turn sends the command to the player. It is useful to think of the VCR as taking the role of the video server, ready to play out content upon command. The video server plays out content using RTP, because that protocol is needed to make sure that the video signals make it across an IP network. Think of the remote control as playing the role of the user's software interface. This could be implemented as a browser displaying web pages that include SMIL functions, as we will discuss in the following section. Then, the infrared link between the remote control and the VCR plays the role of RTSP—a standard way for commands to be sent from user interfaces to streaming servers. The real beauty of RTSP is that it provides a standard interface so that differ-

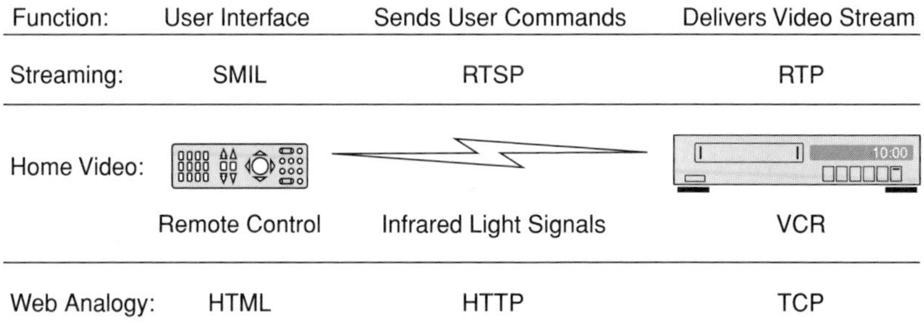

| Function: | User Interface | Sends User Commands | Delivers Video Stream |
|---|---|---|---|
| Streaming: | SMIL | RTSP | RTP |
| Home Video: | Remote Control | Infrared Light Signals | VCR |
| Web Analogy: | HTML | HTTP | TCP |

**FIGURE 8-2**  Relationship between RTP, RTSP, and SMIL

ent browsers can easily work with a variety of servers. Going back to our analogy, this would be the situation if all remote controls worked with all VCRs (wouldn't that be nice?). Of course, RTSP isn't implemented in every streaming product, at least not yet.

RTSP is specifically intended for use with time-oriented content, including streaming audio and video. It has the ability to move around inside content based on time stamps contained in the video, allowing a user to, say, skip ahead exactly 10 seconds in a video clip while maintaining audio synchronization. Contrast this with HTTP, which doesn't have this rich set of features for managing timed content and is further hampered by its reliance on TCP, which, as we discussed in Chapter 6, is not well suited for delivering streaming media. RTSP is also designed to work in multicast environments, which, as we will see in Chapter 9, is very useful for video and audio delivery to a number of clients.

RTSP uses Uniform Resource Locators (URLs) to identify content on servers, just like HTTP. When a server receives an RTSP command, it will begin to play the stream to a specific destination, which is generally to the client that sent the RTSP command. RTSP requests can go from a client to a server, or from a server to a client. Both the server and the client must keep track of the current status of the stream so that both will know when playback has begun. Table 8-6 lists some of the functions that RTSP can support.

## SMIL

The Synchronized Multimedia Integration Language (SMIL) was developed to allow the design of websites that combined many different types of media, including audio, video, text, and still images.

**TABLE 8-6**

Some RTSP Functions

- Set up a stream for playing and begin client-to-server communications.
- Begin playing a stream or several related streams.
- Play a segment of a stream, beginning at a specific point in the stream.
- Record a stream that is coming from another source.
- Pause a stream during playback, without tearing down a connection.
- Tear down a stream and cease communications with the client.

With SMIL, the web page author can control the timing of when objects appear or play, and can make the behavior of objects depend on the behavior of other objects.

A good way to think about SMIL is that it is like HTML for multimedia. SMIL scripts can be written and embedded into standard web pages to cause actions or reactions to user inputs. For example, a SMIL script could be written as a portal into a library of multimedia content. SMIL could allow the viewer to select several pieces of content, play them back in any order, and provide a smooth video transition (such as a dissolve or a wipe) between each piece.

One example of a SMIL application would be a web-based presentation complete with graphics/animation/video that had a synchronized sound track playing along with each slide. (Think of a web-based PowerPoint presentation complete with narration.) Another nice feature of SMIL is the ability to play different types of media in parallel—such as a video stream with accompanying audio. User controls can be provided to allow the content to be stopped, fast-forwarded, or rewound. Table 8-7 provides a list of some of the capabilities of SMIL.

A number of commonly used software packages include support for SMIL, including Microsoft's Internet Explorer (version 5.5 and 6.0) and RealNetworks' RealOne platform. SMIL is a standard created by the World Wide Web Consortium, also known as the W3C. In 2003, work began on a new common standard for timed text, which supports captions, subtitles, karaoke, and other applications where text displays are timed to coincide with other media.

**TABLE 8-7**

Some SMIL Capabilities

- Simple animation, such as moving objects around the screen or changing background colors of a web page.
- Content control, such as starting, stopping, or rewinding.
- Layout, such as positioning player windows on a web page.
- Timing and synchronization, such as cuing an audio track to play when a graphic is displayed, or highlighting a graphic when it is being discussed during narration.
- Video transitions, such as fades and wipes.

## COMMERCIAL PLAYERS

A number of companies have developed video and audio player software that operates on personal computer platforms. In the following sections, we will discuss three major products: those supplied by RealNetworks, by Microsoft, and by Apple Computer.

All of the major players will play content that has been encoded using standards such as MPEG and MP3, along with a variety of other proprietary and non-proprietary formats. In these sections, we will discuss the three most popular players and see how their technology works. Most of the other software player packages that are available will have capabilities that are more or less similar to these three packages; unfortunately we don't have enough space in this book to discuss all of the other player offerings.

## RealNetworks

RealNetworks has long been a major innovator in multimedia players and servers. The company has developed a number of innovative compression techniques and has had its software deployed worldwide. RealNetworks offers a number of streaming-related products, including

- *RealPlayer,* a version of player software for content encoded in RealAudio and RealVideo formats. A second version, caller RealOne Player, also has an integrated media browser and a provision for managing premium (paid subscription) content.
- *Helix Servers,* which come in a variety of models to handle streaming functions for servers ranging from small, private streaming sites to large, professional sites that provide massive amounts of public content.
- *RealProducer* and *Helix Producer,* which take video and audio content and convert it into RealAudio and RealVideo formats for storage and playback to streaming clients. Note that these file formats support encryption so that files can be protected when they are stored and while they are being transported over the Internet.

RealNetworks was one of the important early contributors to SMIL technology, and their RealPlayer technology provides a high level of support for the latest SMIL version 2.0. RTP and RTSP are also important technologies that have been used by RealNetworks for controlling and delivering video and audio streams. The RealPlayer also supports a variety of other media file formats, including many types of video and audio MPEG files, including MP3 audio files and MPEG–4 video files.

In January 2004, RealNetworks released version 10 of its popular RealVideo and RealAudio encoder and decoder. These formats employ advanced encoding techniques that compare favorably to other compression schemes such as MPEG–4 and Microsoft's Windows Media 9, at least according to test results provided by RealNetworks.[3] Several different file formats and extensions are commonly used for RealNetworks content, as follows:[4]

- *RealAudio clip (.ra):* A clip that contains content audio encoded using the RealAudio format.
- *Real Media clip (.rm):* A clip that contains audio and video content that has been encoded using the RealVideo encoder. This type of clip can contain multiple streams, including both audio and video.
- *RealVideo metafile (.ram or .rpm):* The file that connects a web page to one or more RealVideo or RealAudio clips. The metafile contains the address of one or more clips located on a server.

To understand how a metafile works, it is good to understand what happens in order to make media clips play inside a browser. First, the browser will display a page that contains a hotlink to a metafile. When a user clicks on this link, the web server delivers the metafile to the browser. The browser looks at this metafile and determines that it needs to run a plug-in (i.e., the RealPlayer) to process the metafile. The browser then loads and starts the plug-in running, and then passes data from the metafile to the plug-in. The plug-in analyzes the metafile data to determine where the actual media files are located. Then, the plug-in makes a request to each of the servers

---

3. "RealVideo 10 Technical Overview" Version 1.0 by Neelesh Gokhale, RealNetworks 2003.
4. Adapted from "Overview of RealVideo" located at http://service.real.com/help/videoccg/overview.html on April 12, 2004.

listed in the metafile to start the appropriate streams flowing to the user. When the streams arrive, the plug-in takes the incoming streams and converts them into images and sounds that can be displayed to the user.

RealVideo 10 uses motion compensation and a variety of patented techniques for delivering compressed video streams with high quality at low bit rates. Two-pass encoding is used, which means that the video is encoded once, then evaluated, and then encoded again for the final output. The benefit of a two-pass system is that the results of the first pass can be used to control how the second pass is performed. If, for example, the scene being encoded has a lot of motion, then the second pass encoder can be set to accommodate the motion. Drawbacks of two-pass encoders are that they require more processing power than a single-pass encoder, and they increase end-to-end delay, although this is not an issue for content that is being stored on a server for later playback.

The RealOne Player interacts with a Helix server using SureStream technology, which automatically switches between different stream versions based on network performance. The goal is to send the highest speed (and therefore quality) stream to the user as possible for a given amount of network performance. Multiple streams are encoded at different resolutions (number of pixels), frame rates, and quality levels to balance the rate of the stream against the user experience of the video. As the stream rate decreases (which broadens the potential audience for a stream), the number of pixels, the frame rate, and the image quality can all be decreased to allow video to go through even low-speed connections.

The fact that RealNetworks compression algorithms are private delivers both benefits and drawbacks to users. One benefit is the rapid pace of innovation for these products. While standards bodies serve an extremely critical function for the network as a whole, the due process rules can extend approval times for new compression methods into periods lasting several years. RealNetworks can develop and deploy new encoder/decoder technology more rapidly because standards bodies are not involved. This also drives another benefit, in that one company is responsible for both encoder (producer) and decoder (player) functions, so compatibility is assured.

RealNetworks' proprietary stance has some drawbacks. Because the algorithms the company deploys are not accessible to third parties, users are restricted to using software tools supplied by Real-Networks. Users who have operating systems that are less popular than those supplied by Microsoft and Apple can have trouble using these products. Also, since one company has to bear all of the development costs, the resources available for innovation might be smaller than what would be available if multiple firms were all developing products. Finally, users who have large libraries of content to be encoded may have some concerns about relying on a single company for all future support.

Third-party editing and encoding software, available from a number of sources, is capable of creating RealVideo and RealAudio compressed files. Many of these packages are compatible with other streaming formats that we will discuss in this chapter. One benefit of some of these third-party packages is that they make it possible to create video files in several stream formats simultaneously. This capability can greatly simplify the amount of effort required to created streaming content in many different permutations of stream rate and player software type. Many of these packages combine content capture, editing, streaming file generation, and other useful video tasks into a single, versatile package. (**Note:** It is not at all unusual for these packages to be quite expensive, particularly for those that handle multiple users and have a rich feature set. On the other hand, it is good to note that RealNetworks offers free copies of limited-capability versions of its Producer software.)

## Microsoft

Microsoft developed Windows Media Player to allow video and audio files to be played on PCs running Microsoft operating systems. Movie Maker is a free utility that allows users to capture video from camcorders and other devices and create finished movies that can be viewed with Windows Media Player. In addition, Microsoft has developed a number of file formats that are specifically designed to support streaming.

Several different file formats are commonly used for Windows Media content, including:

- *Windows Advanced Systems Format File (.asf):* A file format that is designed specifically for transport and storage of content that is intended for streaming applications.
- *Windows Media Audio File (.wma):* A file that contains audio signals encoded using the Windows Media Audio compression system and is in the ASF file format.
- *Windows Media Video File (.wmv):* A file that contains video and audio signals encoded using the Windows Media Video and Windows Media Audio compression system and is in the ASF file format.

Let's take a closer look at the ASF file format. Microsoft developed ASF and controls its destiny, due in part to patents on the fundamental stream format. ASF files can contain video, audio, text, web pages, and other types of data. Both live and pre-recorded streaming signals are supported. ASF can support image streams, which are still images that are intended to be presented at a specific time during play. ASF provides support for industry standard time stamps and allows streams to be played beginning at times other than the start of the media file. Non-Microsoft encoders and decoders are supported inside ASF files; however, their data is treated as pure data, and not supported by some of the nifty features that allow skipping forward and back in a stream—this task needs to be handled by specific user applications.

Microsoft has begun working to have Windows Media 9 video compression adopted as a standard by the Society of Motion Picture and Television Engineers (SMPTE), who have renamed the compression technique "VC-1." As of this writing, efforts are under way inside an ad hoc group in the Technology Committee on Television Video Compression to make this into a reality. Once (if?) this happens, VC-1 will join MPEG, JPEG, H.263, and other standards as open standards for video compression. As with other standards, including MPEG, license fees for the intellectual property (such as patented algorithms) included in the standard must be paid to the owners of that property. However, standardization means that the license for the essential patents for VC-1 must be provided in a manner that provides fair and reasonable access to all users of the technology, on a non-discriminatory basis.

In addition to seeking standardization, Microsoft is actively soliciting hardware developers to create designs that support Windows Media

9 at the chipset level. Presumably, this is to allow the creation of low-cost WM9 players for embedded or cost-sensitive applications, such as set top boxes. Developers of hardware-based encoders are also active so that real-time encoding can be performed on live video content. Attention is also being paid to portable device manufacturers, who would be able to install WM9 video and audio decoder functions in hand-held devices once the costs are reduced sufficiently.

## Apple

Apple Computer has been very active in developing a number of industry standards for streaming media and has made significant contributions of intellectual property into streaming standards. Many of these innovations center around QuickTime, which is Apple's name for its media streaming system. Apple also provides free movie editing software (iMovie) as part of some software releases and sells a highly respected professional tool for editing movies called Final Cut Pro. Apple has also actively embraced international standards, including MPEG–4.

QuickTime was originally created to support video clips that were stored on CDs and played back on personal computers. It has become a widely used format, with hundreds of millions of copies downloaded for both Windows and Macintosh PCs. Some of the best uses of QuickTime combine video, audio, animation, and still images into a virtually seamless presentation to the viewer. A huge number of computer games and multimedia titles have been produced using QuickTime tools.

As in the other technologies described previously, several different pieces of technology are used together to support QuickTime streaming. There are components for content preparation, streaming server management, and various versions of player software. Like some of the other systems, content can be prepared and streamed on the same physical device, although system performance needs to be watched carefully to ensure that users will have their streams delivered smoothly.

For content owners and creators, Apple's use of standards can be a big positive. The QuickTime file format is the foundation for the MPEG–4 file format. The latest versions of QuickTime also use MPEG–4 compression technology. Apple provides players that work on both Windows and Macintosh PCs, and other companies produce player software for other operating systems. A version has even been designed for some Linux installations.

## Selecting a Streaming Format

All three of the streaming solutions discussed in this chapter (Real, Windows Media, and QuickTime) are capable of delivering high-quality video and audio streams to the desktop. Because the market is competitive, these different formats are constantly being updated and upgraded to deliver more pleasing visual and audio results with fewer and fewer bits.

When you are selecting a streaming format to be used for content preparation, the most important consideration is to choose one that the target audience will have available. This does not necessarily mean the player that came with the operating system for the PC; all the three leading players have versions that work on both Windows and Macintosh PCs. The players are not interchangeable; so a RealVideo stream needs to be played using a Real Networks player, a Windows Media 9 stream needs to be played with a WM9 player, etc.

Another important consideration is the version of the player that viewers will be using. If the video stream is created using the latest version of an encoder, but the viewer's player has not been upgraded, the video stream might not play. (This is true for some upgrades, but not all.) Of course, this can be remedied by having a user download and install a new version of the player. But this may not please dial-up network users, who could face the daunting prospect of downloading a 5 to 10 Megabyte file containing a player software update.

Many third-party content-processing solutions will produce output in multiple formats and at multiple stream speeds. These tools, including offerings from Adobe, Discreet, and Pinnacle (and others), allow the creation of a group of output files from a single source stream. They allow one tool to be used to produce content for, say, QuickTime and RealVideo at the same time, or all three different formats (plus many others, such as MPEG). When you consider the number of different stream rates that might be required, it is easy to see a dozen or more different output files being created, each with a different combination of stream rate and player format. Many websites will list several combinations of stream format and bit rate, allowing users to select one that is compatible with their installed viewer software and network connection speed.

## REVIEW AND CHECKLIST UPDATE

In this chapter, we investigated streaming. We began with the basic concepts, including a look at how streaming differs from download and play and progressive download. We analyzed the different parts of a modern streaming system, including content preparation, streaming servers, networks, and player software. We discussed a number of applications of streaming, including entertainment, corporate video, investor relations, and Internet radio and TV. Then, we took a more detailed look at two key streaming technologies: RTSP and SMIL. We followed this with a look at the three main vendors of streaming technology—RealNetworks, Microsoft, and Apple—and wrapped up with some thoughts about how to make a choice between the streaming formats.

### Chapter 8 Checklist Update

❑ Determine the number of users who will want to view the content and determine the maximum number of simultaneous viewers permitted.

❑ Determine if public, private, or virtual private networks will be used (or some combination thereof). If video content is going to be delivered to the general public, then ensure that there is a mechanism for viewers to get the necessary viewer software and load it onto their personal computers.

❑ Select a video streaming format—download and play, progressive download, or true streaming—based on the application and the capabilities of the viewer devices.

❑ For live content, true streaming is used.

❑ Determine the requirements for a content preparation system. Will this system be used frequently or occasionally? All three major streaming format vendors offer free or very low cost software encoders for their own format.

❑ Capacity requirements can vary greatly for streaming servers, depending on the amount of content, the number of simultaneous viewers, and the speed of each created stream.

❑ Evaluate and select authoring tools to create the necessary compressed data files.

❑ If third-party content is to be used, ensure that reliable copy protection/encryption software is available for file creation, storage, and playback.

# 9

# MULTICASTING

Multicasting is the process of simultaneously sending a single video signal to multiple users. All viewers get the same signal at the same time, just as in traditional television broadcasting. Virtually all commercial video broadcasting operates using the concept of multicasting—including cable TV, satellite TV, and over-the-air TV broadcasting. However, when IP networks are used, multicasting is the exception rather than the rule. In this chapter, we'll look at how multicasting works and then look at a few applications. We'll also investigate the technology of IP multicasting and get an understanding of the impact that multicasting has on a data network.

## BASIC CONCEPTS

If you want to understand multicasting, it is helpful to compare it to the process of unicasting. In unicasting, each video stream is sent to exactly one recipient. If multiple recipients want the same video, the source must create a separate unicast stream for each recipient.

These streams then flow all the way from the source to each destination over the IP network.

In multicasting, a single video stream is sent simultaneously to multiple users. Through the use of special protocols, the network is directed to make copies of the video stream for every recipient. This process of copying occurs inside the network, rather than at the video source. Copies are made at each point in the network only where they are needed. Figure 9-1 shows the difference in the way data flows under unicasting and multicasting.

Note that IP networks also support a function called broadcasting, wherein a single packet is sent to every device on the local network. Each device that receives a broadcast packet must process the packet in case there is a message for the device. Broadcast packets should not be used for streaming media, since even a small stream could flood every device on the local network with packets that aren't of interest to the device. Plus, broadcast packets are usually not propagated by routers from one local network to another, making them undesirable for streaming applications. In true IP multicasting, the packets are sent only to the devices that specifically request to receive them, by "joining" the multicast.

To compare unicasting and multicasting, let's use an analogy. Take a moment and think about how a printed memorandum might be circulated to every employee inside a large corporation. One way

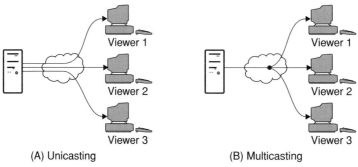

(A) Unicasting                    (B) Multicasting

**FIGURE 9-1**   IP Unicasting vs. Multicasting

that this could happen is that the originator could take the memo and make a copy for each employee. Each copy would get individually addressed and then sent via intra-company mail. For a large corporation, taking these steps would be a significant amount of work for the originator and would put a lot of mail through the system. If a number of employees were located in a remote location, then enough copies of the memo would need to be delivered to that location for every employee. This is similar to the way unicasting works.

A different way to send the same memo would be analogous to multicasting. In this case, the originator would send one copy of the memo to a special person at each company location. This person would, in turn, be responsible for making copies of the memo for every employee in that location. These copies could then be addressed and delivered to each employee locally.

There are several benefits to the company that uses multicasting for memos:

- The burden on the sender is greatly reduced. When the memo is unicast, the sender has to make a copy of the memo for every employee and then apply individual addresses. When the memo is multicast, the sender needs to send only one copy of the memo to the special person in each company location.
- The amount of mail that is sent between locations is greatly reduced. In unicasting, a copy of the memo has to be delivered for every employee in every location. In multicasting, only one copy of the memo has to be delivered to each location.
- In unicasting, the sender has to know the address of each recipient. In a large corporation, the names and addresses of employees can change on a weekly or even daily basis. Tracking all of these addresses can be a huge burden. In contrast, when multicasting is used, the sender needs to know only the special addresses for the designated person in each location.

Of course, there is a cost for all of these benefits. The bulk of the cost falls upon the special people at each location who are responsible for copying the memos and redistributing them. These people also need to recognize which messages need to be redistributed, which might be in the form of a special address or a note attached to the memo. This copying function is very similar to the functions performed by routers in an IP multicast network, as we shall see.

## Unicasting

When we talk about unicasting in an IP network, we are talking about the traditional way that packets are sent from a source to a single destination. The source formats each packet with the destination IP address, and the packet travels across the network with only minor modifications along the way (such as updating the Time To Live counter, see Chapter 3). When the same data needs to be sent to multiple destinations, the source prepares separate packets for each destination.

Each user who wants to view a video must make a request to the video source. The source needs to know the destination IP address of each user and must create packets addressed to each user. As the number of simultaneous viewers increases, the load on the source increases, since it must continuously create individual packets for each viewer. This can require a significant amount of processing power, and also requires a network connection that is big enough to carry all the outbound packets. For example, if a video source were equipped to send 20 different users a video stream of 2.5 Megabits per second (Mbps), it would need to have a network connection of at least 50 Mbps. Some companies sell specialized video servers that are specifically designed to handle this type of load.

An important benefit of unicasting is that each viewer can get a custom-tailored video stream. This allows the video source to offer specialized features such as pause, rewind, and fast-forward video. This is normally practical only with pre-recorded content but can be a popular feature with users.

Table 9-1 summarizes some of the major advantages and disadvantages of unicasting as compared to multicasting.

**TABLE 9-1**

Advantages and Disadvantages of Unicasting

*Advantages*

- Network equipment does not need to be equipped for multicasting. This means that unicasting will work on standard IP networks, including the public Internet.
- Each user has an independent video stream. This allows the video source to offer each user "VCR"-like controls, such as pause, fast-forward, and rewind. Users can typically start watching the video from the beginning whenever they want, instead of waiting for regularly scheduled broadcasts.
- The source can determine precisely which unicast destinations are allowed to receive the data stream and keep records of each recipient.

*Disadvantages*

- The video source must have enough processing capacity and network bandwidth to create a stream for each user. When the source's bandwidth is fully consumed, no more users can be added.
- There must be enough network bandwidth between the source and each viewer's device for an entire copy of the video stream for each viewer. If 50 people located in the same building all want to watch a video at the same time, then the network connection to that building must be at least 50 times greater than the bandwidth consumed by one copy of the video stream.
- The video source must know and manage the correct IP address of every active viewer's device.

## Multicasting

For any video over IP delivery system to work, packets containing the video content must be delivered in a continuous stream to each viewer. In unicasting, as we discussed in the preceding section, the burden of creating these packets falls on the video source. It must create a stream of packets for each destination device and send them into the network for delivery.

In multicasting, the burden of creating streams for each user shifts from the video source to the network. Inside the network, specialized protocols allow the network to recognize packets that are being multicast and send them to multiple destinations. This is accomplished by giving the multicast packets special addresses that are reserved for multicasting. There is also a special protocol for users that allows them to inform the network that they wish to join the multicast. (We will discuss these special protocols in more detail later in this chapter.)

Many existing network devices (such as routers) have the capability of performing multicasting, but this capability is not enabled in many networks. Why not? Well, multicasting can place a tremendous burden on the processing resources of the equipment. Let's say, for example, that a router has users on 12 different ports that want to watch the same multicast stream. These ports could be connected directly to end users or could be connected to another router farther down the network. Multicasting requires the router to make 12 copies of each packet and send one copy out on each port that is requesting the video feed. In addition, the router must be able to listen for and to process requests for adding new ports to the multicast, and to drop ports that are no longer requesting the multicast. These functions are typically handled in the router's control software, so the processor burden can be significant.

Keep in mind that multicasts operate in one direction only, just like an over-the-air broadcast. There is no built-in mechanism to collect data from each of the endpoints and send it back to the source (other than some network performance statistics like counts of lost packets). This means that any interactivity between the endpoints and the video source must be handled by some other mechanism.

Table 9-2 summarizes some of the major advantages and disadvantages of multicasting as compared to unicasting.

## Joining and Leaving a Multicast

One advantage of multicasting is that it gives users the ability to control when they join and leave a multicast. This control is accomplished inside the network; the multicast source does not need to take any special actions when a user is added or removed from the multicast. In contrast, the router nearest the user is heavily involved in this process. In a moment, we'll look at how this works.

Before we begin talking about how users join and leave a multicast, let's talk about why they need to do so. In a multicast, all users receive the same video stream at the same time. That is, when users want to watch a multicast program, they must join in at whatever

**TABLE 9-2**

Advantages and Disadvantages of Multicasting

---

*Advantages*

- The amount of network bandwidth required by the output of the video source and the band-width used between locations can be greatly reduced using multicasting. Only one copy of a video stream needs to be sent to a building with multiple users, because multicast-enabled routers inside the building have the responsibility to make copies of the stream for users in the building.
- Video sources can be much simpler. Since the multicast network takes care of making multiple copies of the video stream, the source needs to be capable of transmitting only a single copy of the stream.
- Video distribution systems can be implemented at fairly low cost in an existing private network with software-based media players. Contrast this with the expense of building a cabled video distribution system to every desktop in a large building.
- Higher quality video can often be used for multicasting, since the load on the network for a single multicast stream is much less than that of multiple unicast streams.

*Disadvantages*

- All viewers of a single multicast get the same video at the same time. Individual users cannot pause, rewind, or fast-forward the content.
- The network equipment must be multicast enabled along the entire route from the source to every multicast destination, which is normally possible only in private networks. This can require reconfiguration or possibly hardware/software upgrades for some legacy equipment.
- The network equipment must be capable of recognizing when a user wants to receive a copy of the stream and must make copies of packets as necessary to get them to the user. This can become a significant burden on routers.
- Controlling who has and does not have access to specific video content can be complicated on a multicast network.
- When hybrid public/private networks are used, system installation can be complicated.
- Some firewalls and NAT devices can block protocols used in multicasting.

---

point the program happens to be in. This is exactly analogous to broadcast television, through which users can watch only what is coming from the broadcaster's antenna at any given time. Similarly, if a multicast program is already flowing through a network, users have the option of joining or leaving that multicast, but they cannot start or stop it. In many implementations, multicast programs are sent in a continuous loop so that users who miss the beginning of a program can just keep watching to see what they missed.[1]

---

1.  Some video providers offer several simultaneous multicasts of the same video content at stag-gered start times. This technique is used for Near Video on Demand and will be discussed in more detail in Chapter 13.

Multicast sources are responsible for periodically announcing the availability of their data stream to the network user community. (This is accomplished by means of SAP packets, which we will discuss later in this chapter.) Users who are interested in receiving a multicast must listen for these announcements, which contain details on how the multicast is configured. Once the user receives the details, the user can then make a request to join the multicast.

When a router receives a request from a user to join a multicast, it must do several things. First, the router must determine whether it is already processing the multicast for another user. If it is, then the router simply needs to make a copy of the multicast stream and send it to the requesting user. If it is not, the router must request the stream from a device that is closer to the multicast source. As soon as it begins to receive the stream, the router can send the stream to the user. Note that in this scenario, requests are made from router to router; this technique can be repeated as many times as necessary to find a complete route from the user's location to the multicast source.

The key point to observe in this process is that each router must know whether or not it is already receiving the multicast stream before it requests a copy form elsewhere in the network. If it is already receiving the stream, it must make a copy for the new user. Only if it is not receiving the stream is it allowed to request it from another router closer to the source. This is the beauty of multicasting—only one copy of the multicast stream needs to be sent to each router on the network, and then only to the routers that have users (or other downstream routers) that are actually using the stream. This means that the bandwidth between routers is used very efficiently: A router that may be a gateway to a complex network hosting hundreds of users needs to receive only one copy of the multicast stream. Compare this to what would happen in a unicast environment: A gateway router supporting hundreds of users would need to have enough capacity to handle a full video stream for each user who wanted to watch.

So far we have talked only about joining a multicast, but the process of leaving is also very important to maintain overall system efficiency. When users want to leave a multicast, they must inform their local router that they want to do so. The router in turn must stop sending the stream to the users so that the users' bandwidth can be freed up for other uses. Likewise, when a router no longer has any users (or other routers) that are requesting the stream, it must inform the network to stop sending it the stream. This process is important; without the ability for users to leave a multicast and have the network connections torn down, a multicast-enabled network could easily become choked with streams that nobody is watching.

In the preceding discussion, we talked about a user taking actions to join and leave multicast streams. In reality, the user himself or herself doesn't need to send arcane commands into the network. Instead, the device that he or she is using must recognize user's inputs (such as a mouse click or the press of a button on a remote control) and send the appropriate commands. Similarly, these end devices are responsible for gathering the program announcements (SAPs) and providing a list of the available multicast programs for the user to select. Design of this software, sometimes called interactive program guides or media players, can be very important to the overall success of the multicasting system.

## APPLICATIONS

Multicasting is uniquely suited to transmitting live video to many viewers simultaneously. Because only one stream is created by the source, all the viewers receive the video data at the same time. Unless a user decides to store the video data on his or her local PC for later playback, all the viewers will see the same video at the same time. Let's look at some of the applications for this technology.

### Live Events

For many corporations and other organizations, delivering a message to many people simultaneously can have some big benefits. Whether the news is good or bad, the value of having every participant get the same message at the same time can be very high. If some kind of audience participation is allowed (such as questions for the speaker), then the broadcast has to be live and with a minimal amount of delay.

In the past, organizations have gone to great expense to broadcast speeches or other messages to a widely dispersed audience. Temporary satellite links have often been used, which involves dispatching satellite receivers to each location that is to view the video. The output of these receivers is then sent to display devices (video projectors, television sets) that are located in areas where employees can gather to watch them. Typically, these types of transmissions have to be planned well in advance to handle the complicated logistics. Equipment needs to be rented and shipped to each location, and technicians need to be dispatched to set up the equipment and make sure it operates correctly during the event. Clearly, this type of broadcast can be justified only for very valuable content. Figure 9-2A shows a typical temporary satellite broadcast.

If an IP multicast is used instead, the situation changes dramatically. Now, users with desktop PCs can watch the video from the comfort of their own office. Any of a number of low-cost, stand-alone IP video decoders can be used to receive and decode the video for display on video projectors or television for employees without PCs. Although the setup time required to enable and test multicasting across an organization's network is not trivial, once the basic hardware and software components required for multicasting have been installed, they can be left in place. Prior to each major multicasting event, network technicians should verify that the networks connecting to each location have enough bandwidth for the video stream; however, if multicasting is used, only one copy of the stream needs to be sent to each location. Figure 9-2B shows an example of multicasting for use in a live broadcast.

## Continuous Information

Another application for multicasting is to send information that is continuously changing. Live pricing data for shares and bonds is very popular, but applications also exist for weather and automobile traffic data. In these environments, live broadcasts are required, since old data are of little value.

Unfortunately, because the public Internet is not multicast enabled, these applications are limited to private networks. However, that has

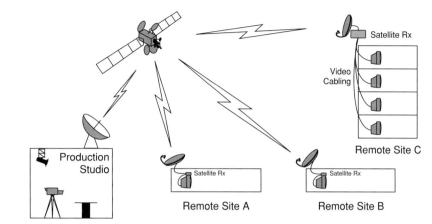

**FIGURE 9-2A**  Live Broadcast Using Temporary Satellite

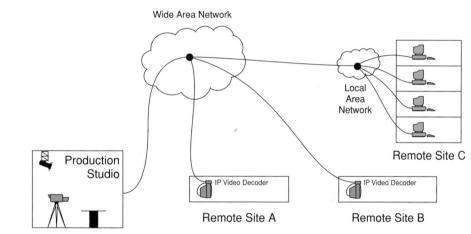

**FIGURE 9-2B**  Live Broadcast Using IP Multicast

not stopped their deployment. IP multicasting is used by a number of brokerage firms not only to transmit share data, but also to transmit live news feeds from a variety of sources that can affect share prices. A number of installations of highway traffic monitoring systems use IP video transport; multicasting has been used where a number of viewing locations need to get simultaneous feeds. Similarly, weather or any other continuously changing data can be efficiently transmitted to a number of viewers on a multicast network.

## Entertainment

The market for multicast entertainment is currently limited by the lack of support for multicasting on the public Internet; if this situation were to change, the market could explode. Nevertheless, there have been successful trials of live video multicasting on an experimental basis so far. As the number of digital cinema projectors and venues grows, this activity is only likely to increase.

One place where IP multicasting for entertainment is likely to be deployed is in the delivery of video services to the home over Digital Subscriber Line (DSL) or other bandwidth-limited networks. Because a DSL line will support only a single video stream (or possibly a handful as technology advances), it is not possible to simultaneously send every viewer the dozens or hundreds of channels that consumers have come to expect from their entertainment suppliers. Instead, as a viewer changes from one program to another, the network is reconfigured to deliver different video streams over the DSL line. One method of controlling this process is to use the multicasting protocols that are already well established for IP networks. Each time a consumer clicks a channel change button on his or her remote control, the consumer's set top box sends two commands to the central office equipment: one command to leave the existing video multicast and another one to join the desired new video multicast. We will talk more about IP video to the home applications in Chapter 13.

## Continuous Presence Conferencing

Continuous presence conferencing is a high-end form of videoconferencing in which the participants in each conference location can hear (and see) all the other locations during the entire conference. It is also known as telepresence or virtual meeting. Continuous presence is often used for creating the illusion that all the participants are in the same room, which is important both for executives in demanding meetings and for schoolchildren who could become distracted by video switching.

One requirement for a continuous presence videoconference is having enough displays in each room to show the video images coming from all the other rooms. This can be accomplished, for example, in a four-location conference by having three displays (and one camera) in each location. IP multicasting is an ideal mechanism to support this architecture. Video (and related audio/data signals) can be encoded and placed into IP packets as a stream originating at each location. Then, the network is used to multicast the packets to all three destinations. At each destination, a device is used to receive each stream from the network and generate the video/audio/data signals for display. Since video encoders are generally more expensive than decoders, the cost is not exorbitant. Also, the need for a central unit to control the video switching is eliminated. One drawback to this type of system is the need to have enough incoming bandwidth at each location to handle a full video stream from each other location; as the number of sites per conference goes up, the equipment and bandwidth costs can also climb rapidly.

## Case Study: Multicast Security System

One ingenious application of video over IP multicasting that was developed by Teracue AG ( formerly inPhase Fernseh-Studiotechnik) of Odelzhausen, Germany has been deployed by the City of Mannheim in Germany. In this application, a number of video cameras were set up in public spaces to allow live monitoring of public activities. The system has produced a number of benefits, which include providing records of reported crimes that can be used in prosecutions and an overall drop in crime in the areas under surveillance due to the watchful eye of the video camera.

In this system, multicasting was a key enabling technology. It allowed two different viewing stations to observe the video simultaneously— one located in the police headquarters and one located in the local fire station. Multicasting also allowed a server system to be set up to record the video signals on hard disk for later reference if needed. Let's look at this system, illustrated in Figure 9-3, in some detail.

Each camera location is equipped with a stand-alone video encoder. The encoder takes the live video signal from the camera, compresses it using MPEG technology, and formats the video data into IP packets. These IP packets are fed to a multicast address over the local access loop. This local access loop that is connected to each camera

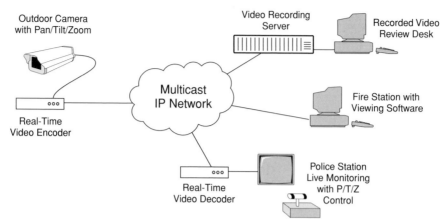

**FIGURE 9-3**   A Multicast-Enabled Security Network

location has only enough bandwidth for one copy of the video stream, so multicasting technology is used inside the IP network to allow the video from the camera to flow to multiple destinations. Three destinations are shown in Figure 9-3: the video recording location, the fire department viewing location, and the video control location at police headquarters. The fire department viewing location has a PC equipped with viewing software that supports live event viewing as well as viewing of previously captured and stored video.

The video recording location is equipped with servers that take all the incoming MPEG video streams and record them onto hard disk for possible later viewing. Special software is used to file the video content so that it can be rapidly retrieved, based on the time that the video was recorded for each camera. All of the recorded video is connected to a master timeline so that views from different angles can be cross-referenced and compared for gathering evidence. Also, the video from different camera locations can be cross-referenced, to allow movements of key subjects to be tracked both before and after a reported incident.

The video control location has multiple monitors and MPEG decoders, although only one is shown. This location is also equipped with camera control devices that allow a user to aim the camera in different directions and to zoom in on interesting action. The control devices operate using the same IP network as the video signals.

Commands from the user are converted into IP packets, which are sent to the camera locations. At each camera location, the video encoder device receives the IP packets and then sends data signals to the camera controls.

It is important to remember that there is only one signal that comes out of each video camera, so every viewer of that camera will see the same image. Although it is possible to have more than one control station for the video cameras, it is good practice to ensure that each camera is controlled from only one station, or else chaos can ensue. The recording station can capture only one signal for each camera, so any decisions that have been made about aiming or zooming a camera are part of the permanent video record and can't be undone in later processing.

User stations were also set up to review the recorded video. One of the key performance objectives was to make sure that the video could be viewed immediately after it was recorded, to allow a police officer to double-check an event that had just occurred, to gather additional information. The recorded video can also be reviewed if a report is made about an incident that occurred during the most recent week. Local regulations dictate that video files cannot be stored more than seven days unless they have been made part of an incident report. When the video is reviewed, more accurate information could be provided about an incident, such as the make and license plate of a car or the exact time of an incident.

The multicast-enabled IP network provided a number of benefits to the City of Mannheim, including

- One network is used for all video and data transport, eliminating the need to install separate links for video and data signals.
- Low-cost data circuits can be used each camera location, because only one copy of the video stream needs to flow from the camera. For most applications, a high-speed DSL link can be used, which is relatively inexpensive to lease from the local telecom service provider.
- This same network also supports video playback from the servers, allowing users to analyze video and prepare reports without tying up the live viewing stations.

- Multicasting allows the video to be observed in several locations simultaneously, while also being recorded on a video server.
- The video server provides secure reliable video storage. The system also supports a rapid rewind function, allowing users to quickly look back at video that was recorded as little as a few seconds or as much as a few days before.

Overall, the City of Mannheim system has benefited from installing an all-digital video networking solution. Although the initial cost was somewhat higher than competing technologies (based on analog video transport and tape-based recording), the long-term savings in operation cost and the higher quality of the resulting video have more than compensated for the cost.

## Simulated Multicasting: Content Delivery Networks

Simulated multicasting occurs when the result of multicasting is achieved without using actual multicasting technology. In other words, a stream is sent to multiple recipients simultaneously, but the protocols discussed previously are not used (Join, Leave, et al.). Instead, specialized servers are used to receive a broadcast stream and then re-transmit it to a number of users on a unicast basis.

The term "content delivery network" (a.k.a. CDN) is very broad. When you stop and think about it, what is the use of any kind of network if it can't deliver content in some form? But we digress. In the current vernacular, a content delivery network is generally taken to mean a system of servers distributed around the edges of the Internet that assist companies in delivering content to end users.

One common example of an application for a CDN is to deliver static web pages to viewers for popular websites. For example, consider the case of a large automobile manufacturer who created a website with a great deal of lush photography, possibly some video clips, and links from popular magazine and television advertisements. The manufacturer needs to determine the best way to provide this rich content to potential customers. One way the manufacturer could do this would be to build a large server (or cluster of servers) in a central location and serve up web pages upon request from users all over the world.

Another way to accomplish the same result would be to hire a firm that provides content delivery services. This firm would make copies of the manufacturer's content (a process called "mirroring") in a number of servers scattered around the world with fast connections to large groups of users. When a user tries to access a page of content, one of the local servers handles the request and sends the user the correct information. This process can greatly reduce the load on the central servers and can more easily handle sudden spikes in user demand (such as those that might be caused by the broadcast of a television commercial to a large viewing audience), because the load is geographically distributed around the Internet. A major challenge for this kind of system is to ensure that the content on the remote servers remains current.

Another application of a CDN is to provide simulated multicasts of video and audio streams to users. As we discussed previously, the Internet is not multicast enabled. If a single video stream is to be sent to a number of users simultaneously, a unicast stream must be set up to each user from a server. Each user will receive a unique stream of packets, targeted to a specific IP address. This type of broadcast is difficult to scale up, because the load on the server increases as each additional viewer is added. In large broadcast applications, with hundreds or thousands of viewers, the burden on a central server can be very heavy. A CDN can be used to provide what is called a "reflected multicast." Just as in the case of static web pages, where static web pages were mirrored in remote servers, in the case of live streams, the content is "reflected" by the remote servers. As shown in Figure 9-4, a central server is responsible for delivering a unicast copy of the video stream to each remote server. The remote servers then take that incoming stream and make copies of it for each viewer. Some interesting software is needed to establish the connections between the viewers and the remote servers, but once this happens, the streams can be sent continuously. As shown in the illustration, the content arrives from the central location, and then it is copied and sent out to each viewer by the CDN servers.

## MULTICASTING SYSTEM ARCHITECTURE

In the following sections, we are going to delve a little bit deeper into the technology of IP multicasting, as based on the

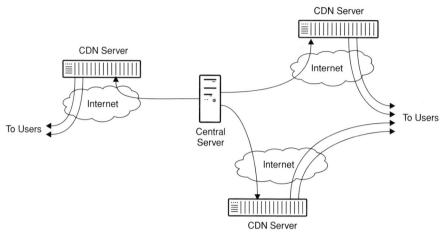

**FIGURE 9-4**   Content Delivery Network Servers Being Used for Reflected Multicast

Internet Group Management Protocol (IGMP). This protocol was first released in the 1980s and has undergone several revisions since then. The most widely used version is IGMP Version 2 (V2), which has been available for a number of years. A newer version, IGMP V3 is defined as a standard but is not yet widely deployed.

The purpose of IGMP is to give information to routers on a network about streams that are being multicast. Routers have a big job in a multicast environment: They are responsible for forwarding and replicating multicast streams to all the devices that are entitled to receive the streams. Forwarding is fairly straightforward; it involves taking packets from an input and sending them to the correct output. Replication takes this a step further, and is used when a single incoming stream of packets needs to be sent on more than one output. To replicate a packet, the router must make a copy of the packet for each destination and send each of them via the proper outbound port.

In the following section, we will discuss SAPs, which are used to inform user devices about available multicast programs. Then we will talk about the processes required for a user device to join and leave a multicast session.

## SAPs

Session Announcement Protocol (SAP) is used to periodically inform multicast-enabled receivers about programs (such as video or audio streams) that are currently being multicast on a network. In concept, SAP is similar to the TV guide service that is broadcast on many cable television systems. Each of the programs that is currently playing is listed, along with the channel number for that program. Similarly, SAP is used to send out information about each of the multicast streams that are available on a network, along with information that user devices need in order to connect to a multicast.[2]

Perhaps the most important part of a SAP message is the multicast address of the multicast stream. Once the user device has this address, it can send a request into the network to join that multicast. A single multicast source may generate multiple streams; each one of these can be announced via SAP. For example, a video encoder could provide two versions of a video stream (one for high-quality and one for low-bandwidth users) and three different audio streams (at varying bandwidths and quality levels). An end user equipped with a low-speed dial-up connection to the Internet might choose to receive only the low-bandwidth audio signal, whereas a cable modem user might want to receive high-quality video and surround-sound audio.

By default, SAP communications always take place on the multicast group address 224.2.127.254 on port 9875. Specialized software on the user device (frequently called a multimedia player) converts the information received from SAP into a list of choices that the user can select from. As soon as the user has made a selection, the multimedia player will send out commands to join the multicast.

---

2. Readers should be careful to distinguish SAP, the Internet protocol, from SAP, the manufacturer of enterprise management software, and from the video term "SAP," which stands for Secondary Audio Program. Although all three use the same initials, the second is an application that is designed to allow firms to manage many different aspects of their organization, including materials, finances, and personnel, and the third was a method originally developed to allow television programming to be broadcast with different language audio tracks. The protocol named SAP that we are talking about in this section is used for announcing multicast services, which is defined in IETF RFC 2974.

## Join/Leave

"Joining" and "leaving" a multicast are key concepts for multicasting. When a user device joins a multicast, the network must be reconfigured to deliver a copy of the required packets to the user's port. Similarly, when a user device leaves a multicast, the network must stop delivering those packets to the user, so as to make the network bandwidth available for other uses. In the following paragraphs, we will discuss some of the functions provided by IGMP.

Joining a multicast can be a fairly complex process. If the user device is the first one to request a particular multicast stream, then all the network devices that lie along the path between the multicast source and the user device must be configured to transport the stream. Consider the sample network shown in Figure 9-5. In this case, User Device 1 (UD1) is the first user to request the multicast being offered by the source. UD1 sends out a command to "join" the multicast being advertised by the source. R3, which is the closest router to UD1, determines that it is not currently receiving the multicast and requests it to be sent from R2. R2 in turn requests the multicast from R1. R1 then starts sending the multicast stream to R2, which then in turn sends the stream to R3. R3 then supplies the stream to UD1.

When UD2 requests the stream, the request is processed first by R5. Since it is not currently receiving the stream, it makes a request to R4. R4 then makes a request to R2. R2 then begins sending the stream to

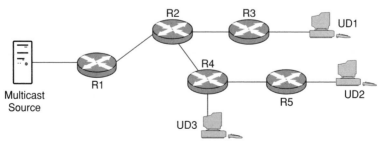

**FIGURE 9-5**  Multicast Join/Leave Network

R4, which in turn forwards the stream to R5. As soon as it begins receiving the stream, R5 can forward it to UD2.

When UD3 requests the multicast stream, it sends a request to R4. Since R4 is already processing the stream, it doesn't need to obtain the stream from another router. Instead, R4 can simply begin sending a copy of the stream to UD3.

Leaving a multicast can also be a fairly complex process. Let's look at what happens when UD1 decides to leave the multicast. This request is made by sending a "leave" report to R3. R3 can then stop forwarding the stream to UD1. R3 must then check to see whether any other devices connected to it (user devices or other routers) are still using that multicast stream. Once it determines that no other device is using the stream, it can then send a "leave" report to R2. When R2 receives the "leave," it can then stop sending the stream to R3. When R2 checks to see whether any other devices are using the stream, it determines that R4 still needs the stream, so it can take no further action.

As this example illustrates, the process of joining and leaving a multicast is fairly complex. This is the price that is paid to achieve network efficiency. Handling all of these IGMP transactions can create a significant processing load, so many routers do not have this function activated. Note that in each case in the preceding example no more than one copy of the multicast stream was sent between any pair of routers, no matter how many users downstream from the router were receiving the stream. For instance, only one copy of the stream was sent from R1 to R2, even though three separate user devices downstream from R2 were receiving the stream. If unicasting were used in this example instead, then three copies of the stream would have been sent from R1 to R2.

It is important to note that the "leave" process described here was first implemented in IGMP V2. In version 1, the routers would periodically send out a request to determine whether any devices were listening to the multicast. If no device responded, then the router could stop sending out the multicast. This system worked fine, except that the router could drop multicasts only after making a poll and waiting enough time to allow any device to respond. If the router polled too often, it ran the risk of tying up useful network bandwidth. Imagine the chaos that would result if this system used for the network was delivering Video on Demand over DSL: The connection going to each user's device could easily become choked with multicast streams that the user was no longer watching but that hadn't been disconnected yet. IGMP V2 greatly improves this situation by allowing devices to send a "leave" report as soon as they no longer want to be part of a multicast. This frees up the bandwidth for use by another application, possibly a multicast stream from another source (such as a different television channel).

## SYSTEM IMPACT

Multicasting can have a range of impacts on a data network. Because many networks are installed with multicasting disabled, it is important to understand what can happen when it is enabled. Let's look at the system impact from a few perspectives, including the impact on routers, servers, and network bandwidth.

### Router Reconfiguration

Because there are dozens of different networking equipment vendors and thousands of different models of routers, it is impossible to describe in detail how to reconfigure each device to handle multicasting. But, it is possible to discuss the impact that multicasting can have on a router.

First and foremost, multicasting can increase the workload of a router. Here is a list of some of the functions that a router must perform to support multicasting that are beyond the support needed for standard unicasting:

- Receive, duplicate, and forward SAP packets, which are sent to each device that may wish to receive a multicast. Even though SAP packets do not occur very frequently, they do need to be processed and forwarded to all the ports on the router that have devices that might want to receive the multicast.

- Process IGMP packets as required to determine when a device wants to join or leave a multicast. Note that this requires the router to figure out when a device it serves makes a request to join a multicast that the router is not yet handling, and so needs to obtain the multicast stream from another source. This also requires the router to determine when all the devices it serves have left a multicast and can thus stop receiving the multicast.
- Duplicate multicast packets as needed to supply them to any requesting devices. This can be a heavy load on a router, particularly if packet replication is done using software, as is the case on a number of older routers. This process takes cycles from the CPU that could otherwise be used for other functions, including handling IGMP messages. For a multicast video stream, a router might be required to duplicate several hundred packets per second.

Many times, system administrators are reluctant to enable multicasting on their networks precisely because of the impact that multicasting can have on the performance of their routers. It is not unusual for one or more key routers on a private network to require a hardware or software performance upgrade to handle multicasting. Depending on the network, this can be an expensive and time-consuming process. Therefore, users who are planning to deploy multicast services should consult with network managers.

## Server Usage

For servers, multicasting can mean a significant decrease in workload as compared to unicasting. In unicasting, a server must create a separate stream for each receiving device. For servers that serve numerous clients, this can be a huge processing burden. In many cases, multiple unicast servers need to be provisioned to share the workload of sending streams to hundreds of simultaneous viewers. Specialized servers from companies such as SeaChange or Ncube are designed to handle these loads, with the added benefit of being able to provide true Video on Demand services such as pause, rewind, and fast-forward.

Multicast servers, in contrast, have a relatively light burden. Because the network makes copies of the stream, only one stream needs to be provided by the source. This can be accomplished with a low-cost, low-performance server. Because all the viewers watch the same stream at the same time, the server does not need to handle Video on Demand commands from users. This does, however, limit the flexibility for users, who normally must join a video broadcast that is already in progress. To make this more palatable to viewers, program providers will frequently offer longer content in multiple streams with staggered start times, or transmit content in a continuous loop, or both. Although these options increase the burden on the server, they are still much more manageable than trying to support hundreds of simultaneous unicast streams.

## Bandwidth Considerations

With multicasting, only one copy of each stream needs to be sent between each pair of routers on the network. This can provide a tremendous savings in bandwidth usage as compared to unicasting. Let's look at a quick example.

Take a network with 100 users, of whom 16 want to view a single program. Let's say there are four routers in the network, all connected directly to each other (a "full mesh network," for those who like technical jargon). Let's say that the video source is connected to one of the routers (let's call it Router A), and the viewers are evenly distributed among all four routers (A, B, C, D). Here is how the bandwidth would break down.

In unicasting, the source would need to provide one copy of the video stream for each active user, for a total of 16 streams leaving the source and going into router A. Router A would then take all of these streams and forward them to their destinations. Four streams would be sent from A to its local viewers, and four streams would need to be sent to each of the other three routers. This is shown on the left in Figure 9-6A.

With multicasting, the source needs to provide only one copy of the stream to Router A. Router A would make seven copies of the stream

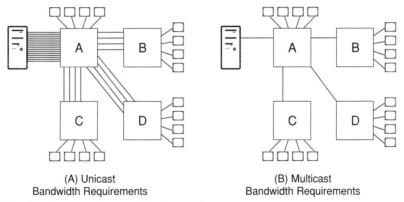

(A) Unicast
Bandwidth Requirements

(B) Multicast
Bandwidth Requirements

**FIGURE 9-6**  Multicasting Bandwidth Comparison

and send four to the local viewers. The other three streams would be sent to the other routers, one each to B, C, and D. Each of these three routers would in turn make four copies of the incoming stream and send one copy to each connected local user. This is shown on the right in Figure 9-6B.

The big difference in these two illustrations is the amount of bandwidth needed between the source and A, and the amount of bandwidth needed between A and the other routers. In the first case, the bandwidth required drops by a factor of 16, and in the latter cases the bandwidth drops by a factor of 4. This can be an important savings; if the stream occupied, say, 1 Mbps of bandwidth, with multicasting the source could use a 1.5 Mbps T1 telephone link to reach Router A; without multicasting a 45 Mbps DS3 link would be required. Similarly, lower usage of the valuable backbone connection between A and the other routers would allow a great deal of other traffic to flow.

## REVIEW AND CHECKLIST UPDATE

In this chapter, we looked at multicasting, which is a way to use an IP network to act like a radio or television broadcasting station. We began with a discussion of unicasting and how it differs from multicasting. We discussed unicasting and multicasting in more depth, including a look at the benefits and drawbacks of each technology. We then looked at some applications of multicasting, including live events, continuous information, entertainment, continuous presence conferencing, and a city security system that used multicasting to great benefit. In addition, we covered the technology of streaming, including the process of controlling the users who are joining and leaving the multicast. We finished by looking at the impact of multi-casting on a data network.

Overall, multicasting is a powerful technology and can be used to save a lot of network bandwidth and server load when it is deployed. The cost is mainly in the form of complexity (for managing joins and leaves, etc.) and in the extra processing power that is required from the network routers to do the packet replication. When (or if) the Internet becomes multicast enabled, then the possibilities for broad-casting content to many users simultaneously will create an amazing variety of content providers and choices for consumers.

## Chapter 9 Checklist Update

- ❏ Determine whether multicasting is possible. Are all viewers going to be satisfied with receiving the same video/audio at the same time?
- ❏ If a private network is used, will it be technically possible to enable multicasting on all of the network routers? If so, the router network layout should be reviewed to ensure that router performance will be adequate at each of the major nodes.
- ❏ If true multicasting isn't possible, it can be simulated using a unicast network or a CDN.
  - ❏ Make sure that the stream bandwidth is calculated correctly, and determine how much total bandwidth is needed by multiplying the number of viewers by the bandwidth of the stream. Make sure to add some spare capacity to handle peaks, extra viewers, etc.
  - ❏ Consider the use of a content delivery network provider for non-multicast applications that require very large numbers of viewers (thousands or more). Contract with a CDN provider to support reflected multicasts of the streamed content.
- ❏ For networks that won't allow multicasting, determine the maximum number of simultaneous users that will be connected at one time. Then, determine if more than one server will be required to create all of the required streams.

# 10

# VIDEOCONFERENCING OVER IP

Videoconferencing uses synchronized audio and video signals to permit two-way communication between distant locations. As any telephone user can attest, a lot of the communication that takes place between people is non-verbal, involving gestures and facial expressions that simply can't be seen when using a telephone. Videoconferencing attempts to address this shortfall by allowing users to both see and hear each other.

For many users, videoconferencing over IP networks is the ideal marriage of video technology and advanced networking. Many frequent business travelers have thought (at least on occasion) how nice it would be to replace some of their less important business trips with a videoconference. As high-performance networking becomes more widespread in the business world and more affordable for residential connections, the demand for videoconferencing services will continue to increase. This rapidly growing market is being driven both by company cost-saving efforts (reduce those travel budgets!) and by employee demand (do I have to leave my spouse and kids for another trip this month?). So, it should not surprise any practitioner of video over IP networking to receive at least an occasional request for an IP videoconference.

Videoconferencing became feasible in the early 1990s because international standards (H.320, among others) were approved and compliant equipment emerged from a variety of vendors. However, high costs of implementation limited the market penetration of this technology. Many end-user companies created specialized conference rooms equipped with cameras, microphones, video displays, and all of the other equipment needed to make videoconferencing feasible. H.320 systems use special digital telephone lines (ISDN), which can have substantial installation and usage charges. Because of the expense involved for the equipment and the telephone lines that were required, the number of rooms with equipment remained fairly small, and the costs per use were high.

New technology was developed and standardized in the mid-1990s to provide videoconferencing over IP networks. This new standard, called H.323, eliminated the need for special ISDN circuits from the telephone company. This also made practical the concept of desktop videoconferencing (DTVC) using either dedicated hardware or a properly augmented personal computer.

The goal of this chapter is to give readers an understanding of how videoconferencing works in general and how some specific technologies have been developed to support videoconferencing on IP networks. In this chapter, we will look at the basics of videoconferencing, such as connection setup and multipoint conferencing. We'll discuss the types of equipment that are normally used in videoconferencing, both at user locations and in the network. Then, we'll cover some applications of videoconferencing and examine the technologies that are used to make IP videoconferencing a reality. By the end of this chapter, readers should have a basic understanding of the technologies that are available for creating an IP videoconferencing network.

## BASIC CONCEPTS

In the following sections we will discuss a number of topics that are related to videoconferencing in general. Just like telephone calls, videoconferences can be set up in several different ways. A simple point-to-point connection can be made between two locations. A three or more party conversation can be supported by switching the video and audio signals in response to user action (through the use of a multipoint control unit). Or, a multi-party conversation can be supported with continuous presence, where each party can see and hear all of the other parties at the same time. Also, a variety of specialized processing equipment (such as echo cancellers) is used to support video conferencing. We will cover all these aspects of video-conferencing in the following sections.

## Session Setup

Before a videoconference can take place, a number of tasks need to be completed. This is really no different in principle than setting up a normal face-to-face meeting. Because a videoconference is inherently live and two-way (or more), special care must be taken to ensure that all of the parties are properly alerted and their equipment is properly configured before the conference can proceed. Sometimes this is done by means of a specialized communication protocol between the devices. Other times, a central reservation-and-control system is used to make all the connections. Here are some of the key tasks that need to be performed in order to establish a videoconference:

- The caller needs to find the addresses of parties that are to be called. Addresses are listed in public or private directories. Note that these are not the same as IP addresses, because IP addresses can change each time a device connects to a network (see the discussion of DHCP in Chapter 5). Also, some protocols support user mobility, allowing incoming calls to follow users as they move from one office or device to another.
- The calling and the called parties both need to be available for the call, and enough bandwidth needs to be available to handle the streams that will be generated. Most end devices support multiple different video speeds, allowing a variety of networks to be accommodated. Higher bandwidths generally mean higher signal quality, so different data rates are often negotiated for each call, depending on the network being used.

- When a call request is received, each involved piece of equipment must make sure that it is not otherwise occupied and that it can perform the requested functions. If so, an affirmative acknowledgment is sent. If not, then that device rejects the request.
- Many conferences also employ alternative means of communication such as document exchange or sharing a whiteboard for drawing. If these tools are to be used, then the conference setup process needs to establish connections to support these devices.
- Many videoconferencing systems gather usage and other data that can be used to send out bills to users or to manage system performance. Much of this data is gathered during the reservation and/or the connection processes.

Videoconferencing standards include reams of information about how the connection process takes place and how it works under a variety of network configurations. Call setup is very complex, but it is also very flexible. It would not be unfair to compare this process to the complexity of connecting a normal voice call, which requires literally millions of lines of software and constant upgrading inside telephone companies.

Common channel signaling is frequently used for videoconference setup. This type of signaling uses a separate, limited bandwidth communications path. A variety of different signals flow over this path, including conference requests, acknowledgments, and device commands, such as alerting (ringing) and connecting (that actually begins the user conversation). Note that common channel signaling frequently uses a specialized protocol just for conference setup and teardown. Also note that the signaling channel is used only for conference control, not for actually sending the audio and video streams that make up the videoconference.

Some IP videoconferencing systems don't use a handshaking protocol for conference setup, but instead rely on a centralized server to establish and track connections. Users make a connection by contacting this server to select the devices that will be in a conversation and then indicate when the conference is to take place. Some systems allow users to reserve conference equipment and network bandwidth in advance. Specialized software manufacturers have developed sophisticated systems for doing this. Some systems can also configure a variety of equipment in the videoconferencing room, as well as gateways that allow a conference to be established between one conferencing technology and another (such as between H.320 and H.323). This process is also known as bridging.

## Multipoint Conferencing

Multipoint conferencing is extremely popular in both audio and video communication. A conference is deemed to be "multipoint" whenever the number of participating locations (endpoints) is greater than two. Note that if multiple people are using a single endpoint, possibly with multiple cameras, this counts as only one party to a conference as long as only one outgoing video and one outgoing audio stream are created. As soon as a conference consists of more than two video and audio streams, it is considered to be multipoint.

In the audio world, multipoint conferencing is normally known by a name like "three-way calling" or "conference calling." It is rare indeed to find an employee of a major corporation or government agency that hasn't participated in (or been subjected to) a conference call. Special devices, called conference bridges, are used inside the telephone network to connect multipoint conversations. Each listener hears a combination of all the talkers on the line, with the exception of his or her own voice. A good conference bridge will amplify all the talkers on the conference to an equal level. The result is similar to what would be heard if all the talkers were in the same room.

In videoconferencing, this situation is not so simple. There is really no practical way to combine multiple video images in a single image that would make it appear that all the participants are sitting in the same room. So, for the purposes of multipoint conferences, there are two basic choices: MCU switching or continuous presence.

### MCU Switching

When the MCU switching method is used, each endpoint receives a single video stream that is switched as the conference progresses. A central device, called the multipoint control unit (MCU), performs the switching. Various different modes are used for switching the video; here are a few popular ones:

- *Chair or Lectern Control:* A single endpoint is designated as the chair of the conferences, and it controls what the other endpoints can see. This is particularly useful in distance learning environments. Procedures exist for changing which endpoint acts as the chair, so this can be a flexible but stable means to control a conference.
- *Follow the Speaker:* The MCU attempts to send video from the endpoint that is currently speaking to all of the other conference participants. Usually some delay is involved before a switch takes place, so latency can be built into the process to prevent a switch caused by a single short noise. This is one of the most popular forms of video switch control.
- *User Control:* Each endpoint can select any one of the other locations to watch. This places a burden on the end user and can be hard to keep up during a long conference. In the eyes of some users, this can be as annoying as watching someone change channels repeatedly on a television set.
- *User Controlled Broadcast:* A user can request the MCU to send his or her endpoint's video to all of the other endpoints in the conference. This might, for example, be used when one party is giving a presentation.

Figure 10-1 allows us to look at an example of a Follow the Speaker conference in action. The network consists of four endpoints, A through D, and a central MCU. Each endpoint sends a video into the MCU and receives a single video back from the MCU. When the conference

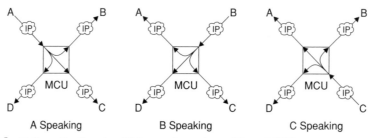

A Speaking          B Speaking          C Speaking

**FIGURE 10-1**  Follow-the-Speaker Videoconferencing with an MCU

begins, A is speaking. The MCU sends the video from endpoint A to endpoints B, C, and D. Endpoint A can receive video from any location, possibly the last one to join the conference. After a while, B begins speaking. The MCU switches to send the video coming from B to the endpoints A, C, and D. Endpoint B will continue to receive video from A, since it doesn't make sense to send B its own image. When C takes a turn speaking, the MCU reconfigures itself again; now A, B, and D will receive the picture from C, and C will continue to receive a picture from B. As this example shows, the conference really does "Follow the Speaker" as the conversation progresses.

### Continuous Presence

When the continuous presence method of multipoint conferencing is used, each site can see all of the other sites on a continuous basis. This method requires more network resources than with MCU switching. For example, in a four-way conference, each site needs to be able to receive three incoming video signals. This method may also appear to be more natural to users than with MCU switching, because the video disruptions caused by switching are avoided.

Setting up a continuous presence conference can be more complicated than when using MCU conferencing. When an MCU is used, each endpoint in the conference simply needs to be connected to the MCU, which handles the rest of the functions. In continuous presence, multiple copies of each signal must be created, and each copy must be sent to a different location. As we discussed in Chapter 9, one way of handling this function is multicasting, where the network is responsible for making all the necessary copies of the streams coming from each endpoint. If multicasting isn't available, then each video endpoint needs to create a separate unicast stream for each destination, thereby increasing the amount of bandwidth required to transmit from each endpoint.

Figure 10-2 shows an example of a four-way videoconference using the continuous presence method on a multicast-enabled network. The video signal from A is sent to B, C, and D. Similarly, the video from B is sent to A, C, and D, and so on. In each location, three video signals are displayed. Note that all of the different switching modes delivered by an MCU (Follow the Speaker, Lectern Control, etc.) are not needed

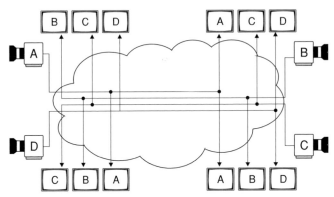

**FIGURE 10-2**   Continuous Presence Videoconference

in a continuous presence conference, because each endpoint can see all the other endpoints during the entire conference.

## Video and Audio Processing

By itself, videoconferencing requires relatively little equipment in a room. A simple setup with a camera, a microphone, a television with speakers, and an audio/video encoder/decoder (normally called a codec) is all that is truly required for a conference. In reality, many videoconference rooms are equipped with a much broader array of equipment. Table 10-1 gives a short list of some of the optional equipment that can be found in a modern videoconferencing room.

Let's take a closer look at the last two items in Table 10-1.

### Quad Split Converters

Quad split converters are used to combine multiple video images into a single, composite image, primarily for use in continuous presence conferences. There are two main reasons for doing this:

- A single, large video display may be easier to manage than four smaller video displays, particularly if the videoconferencing system is moved from one room to another.

## TABLE 10-1

Optional Equipment for Videoconference Rooms

- Document camera, for sending video images of documents to other conference participants.
- Camera selector, to allow different views to be sent, possibly depending on the number of people in the room.
- Room lighting control, to allow the lighting to be properly configured for the camera that is in use.
- Camera Pan, Tilt, and Zoom (PTZ) control, to allow the camera to point at specific locations in the room, such as different seats at a conference table. This function can also be connected to the audio system to allow the camera to point at whomever is speaking.
- Electronic whiteboard, which allows participants to send sketches to each other.
- Quad split converter, to display four video images on a single video display.
- Echo canceller, which is required to produce acceptable audio in many cases.

- When four video signals are combined into one, it is possible to configure a continuous presence system with just one video signal delivered to each site.

Figure 10-3a shows just such a videoconference network. Each location (A, B, C, and D) sends out a full-resolution video signal to a central location. At this location, all of the signals are sent into a quad split converter to be combined. The output of the converter, which is a normal video signal that contains images from all four input signals, is then sent to every location.[1]

It is important to keep in mind that the video signals in this type of network may be compressed. As shown in Figure 10-3b, each location is equipped with a video encoder and a video decoder. Also, the central location is equipped with four video decoders and a video encoder (to respectively send and receive the video signals to and from the quad split converter). This system will operate correctly, although the compression delay will be double that of a normal compressed system. To understand why, think about the path that each video takes. Before leaving the originating site, the video is com-

---

1. Note that it is also possible to place a quad split converter at each endpoint to take multiple video signals and show them on one display.

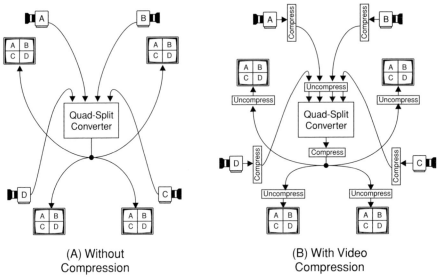

(A) Without
Compression

(B) With Video
Compression

**FIGURE 10-3**   Continuous Presence Videoconferencing Network Using Quad Split Converters

pressed before it travels to the central site. Then, it must be decompressed at the central site before it is fed into the quad split converter. At the output of the converter, the multi-image video is compressed before it is sent back to each site. Finally, the multi-image video is decompressed at each destination. So, from start to finish, each video signal has undergone two full compression/decompression cycles, which is double what would happen in a standard network. So, the trade-offs are clear: When continuous presence videoconferencing is implemented with a quad split converter and video compression, the amount of bandwidth needed to feed each site is reduced, but the end-to-end delay increases.

### Echo Cancellers

Echo cancellers process the audio signals to remove the echo signal caused by the round-trip delay of a network. They are required pieces of equipment in many videoconferencing networks. To understand the role of an echo canceller, let's trace the route of an audio signal during a videoconference (see Figure 10-4). First, a person in location 1 speaks into his or her microphone. This sound is converted into an audio signal, which travels to location 2, where loudspeakers send

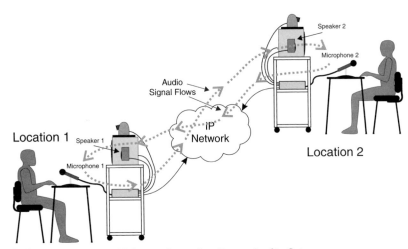

**FIGURE 10-4** Two-Location Videoconferencing Room Audio Setup

the sounds into the room. Because this is a two-way conference, the microphone in location 2 picks up any sounds inside the room and sends them back to speakers in location 1. If the speakers' volumes were set high enough, and the microphones were sensitive enough, the sound would continue to reverberate from room to room. Because this signal is delayed during each round trip, it can be very disconcerting to people while they are talking, becoming more noticeable as the delay increases.

An echo canceller is needed in location 2 to prevent sound that comes out of the speakers in that room from being sent back to location 1. Similarly, another echo canceller is needed at location 1 to prevent speaker sounds from being sent back to location 2. A variety of different technologies can be used for echo cancellation, but most devices need to process the incoming signal to each site, as well as the outbound signal created at each site.

ITU-T G.131 specifies that echo cancellers should be used if the one-way delay for a voice circuit exceeds 25 milliseconds. Since many video encoder/decoder pairs introduce at least this much delay, this limit is quickly exceeded. So, echo cancellers are a fact of life for most videoconference rooms and are incorporated into a number of commercial videoconferencing devices.

## TECHNOLOGIES

A variety of technologies are used to implement videoconferencing over IP networks. In the following sections, we will look at four key technologies.

The first two technologies, H.323 and Session Initiation Protocol (SIP), support the handshaking and connection setup functions required for a videoconference. H.323 has evolved from the first generation of international standards (H.320) to become widely used in many companies for specially equipped videoconferencing rooms. SIP has been promoted as a simplified method for setting up voice over IP calls, but it also includes the ability to set up video and other types of conferences.

The other two technologies, H.264 and T.120, are used to format the video and data signals that are sent between endpoints during a conference. H.264 is the next generation of video compression, which will be used both for videoconferencing and broadcast television. T.120 is a technology for data conferencing that is widely used on IP networks, either on a stand-alone basis or in conjunction with video and audio conferences. Each is described in more detail in the following sections.

## H.323 Multimedia Conferencing

H.323 is an international standard for packet-based multimedia communication, as defined by the International Telecommunications Union (ITU). It works on a variety of packet networking technologies, including both reliable (TCP-based) and unreliable (UDP-based) IP networks, as well as ATM networks. It is multimedia, because it supports video, audio, and data communication. H.323 does not stand alone as a standard; numerous other ITU specifications are used to support functions such as conference setup, video and audio compression, inter-network communications, etc.

Videoconferencing over IP, as implemented in H.323, is connection oriented. This means that a connection must be established between the parties in the conference before communication can take place. This is only logical, because each party's device needs to be configured to send and receive both video and audio in order for a conversation to occur. Also, because many videoconferences are used for business purposes, connection-oriented protocols help ensure that each packet is received from a single sender, not some malicious outsider. Finally, some types of networks (such as those using dial-up IP services) need to be activated prior to use in order to provide the bandwidth needed to support a videoconference; the connection process can initiate actual allocation of the bandwidth.

A number of devices can be included in an H.323 network to support various functions. The four main device types, illustrated in Figure 10-5, are described next:

- *Terminal:* This is the endpoint of an H.323 conferencing system. It typically resides in the videoconference room and connects directly to the camera, microphone, video display, and other room devices. It contains the circuitry needed to compress and decompress the video and audio signals, as well as the equipment needed to connect to the IP network.
- *Gateway:* Allows H.323 equipment to connect to other videoconferencing networks, such as the older H.320 systems. It performs translation of the protocols that are used for call setup and teardown and converts the voice and video signals back

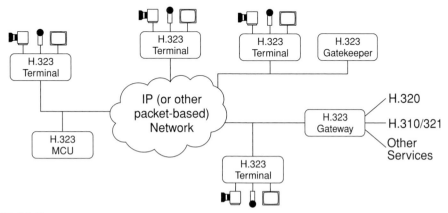

**FIGURE 10-5** Main Components of an H.323 System

and forth between the formats. A gateway is required for communication between H.323 and dissimilar networks, but is not used for communications between pure H.323 terminals.

- *Gatekeeper:* Although it is not a required function, a gatekeeper can provide valuable database services to an H.323 network. Gatekeepers can keep directories of terminals and help remote devices contact ones on a local network. They can help route connections and allocate bandwidth. They can also gather and report network usage and billing information.
- *Multipoint Control Units:* These units are used whenever three or more terminals are connected in a conference. They can either be installed at a central location (such as a telephone company central office), or they can be co-located with one of the conference endpoints.

Although they each perform a separate function on the network, these devices do not have to be physically separate. In fact, it is common for MCUs, gatekeepers, and gateways to share hardware resources and even reside in the same processing chassis.

Overall, H.323 is a highly integrated, sophisticated videoconferencing platform. It has many features and functions, and has been implemented by a number of vendors. It is a relatively mature standard, so equipment from different manufacturers will work together under most circumstances. On the downside, H.323's complexity makes software development expensive, and it is difficult to install on low-cost, low-power devices. Since it was designed for LAN or private networking applications, there are limitations on how easily it can scale up to large networks. Fortunately, groups are working to overcome these limitations and greatly expand the system's scalability.

## SIP Session Initiation Protocol

Session Initiation Protocol (SIP)[2] is a rapidly developing standard for multimedia communication over IP networks. It is being developed under the auspices of the Internet Engineering Task Force (IETF) and

---

2.  Note that this should not be confused with SAP, which we discussed in Chapter 9:

is capable of supporting many of the connection setup and teardown functions of H.323. Most of the current deployments of SIP are focused on voice communication (voice over IP, or VoIP), but the standard has capabilities that can be used to support video and other types of real-time streaming.

SIP is a signaling protocol (like portions of H.323) that is used for setting up sessions, but not for actual transport of multimedia data. Devices that wish to connect use SIP to communicate about how to address each other, how they are configured, and the types of streams that they want to send and receive. SIP provides a number of call control functions, such as ringing, answering, and disconnecting. SIP can also support changes in call status, such as a call that starts out as a voice call and changes to a videoconference. Actual transport of voice, video, and data is handled by other well-established protocols such as RTP (which we discussed in Chapter 8).

SIP has been designed from the ground up to be highly compatible with other protocols and services that are used on the public Internet. For example, SIP messages are text based, similar to HTTP messages. SIP is intended to work on a wide variety of devices and be easy to extend to new functions. The designers also sought to make the protocol fairly simple, so that the software required to implement SIP could be installed on inexpensive and portable devices.

When you boil it all down, what SIP does, and does well, is resolve the IP addresses and port numbers that devices need to use in order to communicate. Since the actual session data (such as voice or video signals) doesn't flow over SIP, it is quite common for this data to take a different path than the SIP commands. Figure 10-6 shows how data flows in a normal session being set up with SIP.

Servers are commonly used in SIP for a variety of functions. Figure 10-6 shows how a proxy server and a location server can be used in a typical call setup. Let's say the originating party (A) wants to communicate with the called party (B). Terminal A can communicate with the proxy server to send an invite message to terminal B; it is up to the proxy server to figure out the correct address for B by using the location server. Once the proxy knows the correct address for B, the invitation from A can be sent along to B. B can then respond to A's invite

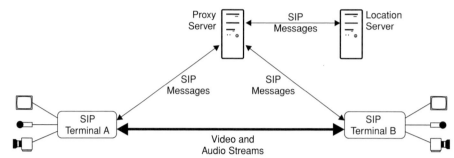

**FIGURE 10-6**  SIP Messages, Servers, Signaling, and Data Flows

by way of the proxy server. Once A has received a suitable response from B, the two terminals can bypass the proxy and communicate directly to set up multimedia connections and actually pass video and audio signals. One very useful function of the location server is called "redirection," which can be useful for instances when users have moved to a new location or want to have their calls forwarded to a different location, either temporarily or permanently. Either A or B can redirect incoming calls simply by sending the appropriate data to the location server. Other types of servers can be used to offer more advanced functions.

Inside SIP messages, a data format known as Session Description Protocol (SDP) is used by the endpoints to describe their capabilities and the types of streams that they are capable of supporting. SDP can specify things like the media type (audio, video, etc.), the encoding format (MPEG, wavelet, etc.), and the transport protocol to be used (RTP, etc.). Once both end devices agree on all the specifics, then communication can take place.

SIP does not offer some of the functions that more complex protocols (such as H.323) provide.[3] SIP does not offer multipoint conference control mechanisms (such as Follow the Speaker, described previously); instead, it provides a flexible set of functions (called primitives) that

_____

3.  This simplicity is one of the key features of SIP; it helps ensure portability to a variety of plat-forms and eases the task of implementation. New functions may be added in the future but likely won't be if they add undue complexity.

can be used to create advanced services. SIP also does not provide any capabilities to reserve end-to-end bandwidth for a given session. When multiple forms of media are used (such as those normally found on a videoconference), some mechanism outside SIP needs to be used to synchronize video and audio. SIP does provide a number of functions that can be used to help ensure the privacy and security of sessions.

Work is under way to extend SIP to offer two features not found in basic H.323: support for Instant Messaging and presence. Instant Messaging (IM) supports real-time, text-based communication between two or more users, and has become very popular for both desktop and mobile users. "Presence" involves informing users about the current status of other users that they are interested in. One popular use of presence is the "Buddy List" feature of some IM systems that lets users know whether other people that they want to communicate with are on-line or off-line. This concept is being extended to let users know if, for example, one of their buddies is available for a full videoconference or just for text-based messaging. SIMPLE, the SIP Instant Messaging Presence Leveraging Extensions working group of the IETF, is responsible for this work.

Overall, a great deal of development work is currently going into SIP. Companies are building all kinds of devices that use SIP, including low-cost IP telephones. The standard is being updated to support session setup for mobile devices, such as mobile telephones that can carry videoconferencing signals. As this work continues, SIP will become a more and more important tool for IP videoconferencing.

## Comparison of H.323 and SIP

When installing videoconferencing systems, users will have a variety of different choices for a system to use when making connections between participants. The three main choices are

- H.323-based conference equipment
- SIP-based conference equipment
- Proprietary conference equipment

Proprietary systems will typically be limited to single vendor solutions and may be hard to connect to equipment not owned by the user's organization. With respect to H.323 and SIP, there are benefits and drawbacks to each system. Table 10-2 attempts to highlight some of the major differences between the two systems.

**TABLE 10-2**

Differences between H.323 and SIP

| Comparison | H.323 | SIP |
|---|---|---|
| *Maturity* | Mature. Has been through several iterations since 1996 and covers many advanced features such as call waiting. | Basic functions becoming mature. A great deal of effort is currently going into the enhancement of SIP standards to include more features. |
| *Complexity* | High. Has a number of sophisticated features, requiring a great deal of software. | Variable. Can be implemented very simply without a rich feature set. More features require more development. |
| *Flexibility* | Medium. Supports a variety of different audio and video compression systems; however, all implementations must have audio capability. | High. Wide variety of different types of sessions can be initiated, and more are constantly being added. Similar procedures are used to initiate voice, data, video, and Instant Messaging sessions. |
| *Compatibility with Public Switched Telephone Network* | High. Was developed from the ground up to be compatible with public telephone networks as well as other videoconferencing standards based on ISDN and circuit-switched networks. | Not integral to the specification. Implementations can be made to be compatible with public networks, but this functionality is not an inherent part of the standard. |
| *Compatibility with Other Technologies* | High. Because the specification is very detailed, most systems will work together provided the standards are followed. Interoperation is common between units from different suppliers. | Variable. Less rigorous standards generally mean differences between products, but the inherent simplicity of SIP means that basic operations are simple and straightforward to implement by different suppliers. |
| *Installed Base* | Large. There are millions of H.323 installed systems around the world, and the base continues to expand. | Growing. Certainly fewer installations than H.323 (particularly for video), but growth rates are high, particularly in the area of voice telephony. |
| *Backward Compatibility* | Rigorous enforcement. Each new generation is specified to be compatible with previous versions. | Not assured. Features can be added or removed from newer implementations, and different versions are not required to be fully compatible by the standards. |

## H.264 Video Compression

As we discussed in Chapter 4, H.264 is another name for the MPEG–4 Advanced Video Coding (AVC) standard. H.264 is flexible enough to be used for both low bit rate videoconferencing systems as well as for the relatively higher bit rates normally used with entertainment video.

Several different types of video compression technology have been used over the years for videoconferencing. The first, H.120, was developed in the early 1980s to run on 1.544 or 2.048 Mbps telephone circuits. This was followed by H.261, which was developed in the late 1980s and was designed for "p × 64" telephone circuits, or those operating on digital data circuits that function on lines running at speeds that are multiples of 64 kbps. In the 1990s, H.263 was developed to allow even better compression efficiency, particularly at low bit rates. Over time, the H.263 standard has had a number of improvements incorporated.

It is important to understand that the choice of video compression technology for a videoconferencing system can be made separately from the choice of conference communication technology. In other words, H.264 video compression can be used with H.320 (for ISDN lines), H.323 (for various packet-switched networks), or with SIP (for IP networks). Similarly, H.263 video compression can be used in H.320, H.323, and SIP applications.

H.264 implementations for videoconferencing generally use the Baseline profile. This profile uses some of the key features of H.264, but not all of the more advanced ones. One unique feature that is well suited to videoconferencing applications is relaxation of the requirements in MPEG–1 and MPEG–2 that all the data for each slice of a video image arrive in order; some variability is allowed in H.264, helping to reduce the delay in the encoder and decoder. Baseline does not permit B frames, which can add significantly to round-trip delay due to reordering (see Chapter 4). Baseline profile also does not support interlaced video (as would be found in broadcast television signals), but it does work with progressive scanned images and the CIF image format, which are commonly found in videoconferencing applications.

H.264 will be an important growth area for videoconferencing, particularly because of the advances in coding efficiency that support higher quality images at lower bandwidths. Product development efforts should also benefit from the ability to share technology (software, custom chips, etc.) between the videoconferencing and broadcast television industries.

## T.120 Data Protocols for Multimedia Conferencing

T.120 is an international standard for data conferencing. It is specified by the ITU, and is used by H.323 and other software. One popular implementation of T.120 was Microsoft's NetMeeting product. Although T.120 is not strictly a videoconferencing protocol, it is commonly used in conjunction with these protocols and can provide many of the benefits of a videoconference to users who may not have access to true videoconferencing equipment. In addition, T.120 connections can normally be used on a much lower bandwidth link as compared to real-time video transport systems.

The basic function of T.120 is to support data conferencing, similar to voice and videoconferencing. This means that multiple users can all share the same data in real time. One popular use of T.120 is to allow multiple people to share a common virtual whiteboard, where they can draw pictures and have them show up on every other user's screen. When this function is combined with an audio conference, it can be quite useful for discussing information that lends itself well to illustration (engineering drawings, architecture, etc.). T.120 also supports file sharing, so multiple users can all look at a file, such as a document or a presentation.

One application for T.120 is a videoconference in which the video and audio signals are carried by normal video and audio circuits, and the presentation is transmitted over a T.120 circuit. The beauty of this arrangement is that viewers at both locations are able to see the presentation at full computer resolution. In the past, without T.120, viewers at one end might have been forced to watch the presentation through the videoconferencing circuit, with the conferencing camera pointed at a projection screen where the presentation was displayed. The resulting low-quality images can be very hard on the eyes and the concentration level of the involved parties (based on the personal experience of the author).

T.120 actually is a suite of protocols, called the T.120 series. Here is a list of the related standards and their titles:

- T.120: Data protocols for multimedia conferencing
- T.121: Generic application template
- T.122: Multipoint communication service—Service definition
- T.123: Network-specific data protocol stacks for multimedia conferencing
- T.124: Generic conference control
- T.125: Multipoint communication service protocol specification
- T.126: Multipoint still image and annotation protocol
- T.127: Multipoint binary file transfer protocol
- T.128: Multipoint application sharing

As you can see from the preceding list, a number of different functions can be accomplished with T.120. Let's take a quick look at some of the ways in which these technologies can be applied to users:

- *Application viewing:* Allows one user to run an application on his or her own PC and show the output (window) on other users' PCs. This is particularly useful for presentations being given by one participant.
- *Application sharing:* Allows one user running an application on his or her PC to permit other users to take control of the application. For example, a user running a word processing program on his or her PC could allow other users to edit the actual document. In this situation, only one user's PC needs to actually run the application; all of the other users can observe and control the application.
- *Whiteboarding:* Rather like a paint program for multiple users, this allows users to draw simple pictures on a shared screen. In some implementations, these pictures can be captured and copied to disk for later reference.
- *File transfer:* Much like sending attachments with e-mail, this function allows users to transfer files from one user PC to another.
- *Chat:* Permits users to exchange short text messages with each other. This function might not be used when a videoconference is in session or when only two users are connected, but it can be a

handy feature for large conferences, particularly when one user is doing most of the talking.

Security can be an issue for users who wish to conduct T.120 conferences over the public Internet. Because the set of supported functions is so powerful, malicious use of T.120's capabilities can be very damaging to a computer system. For example, a malicious user could plant viruses or worms on a user's PC with the file transfer capability. Or, if application sharing was running, a user might be able to gain control of a user's PC and modify or delete files, system settings, or other items.

Because of these security concerns, many companies do not permit T.120 sessions to pass through a company firewall. Other companies use a device called a "conference server" that handles all of the connections required for a T.120 conference; it can therefore authenticate users and perform other security functions. Still other companies allow only a subset of the T.120 functions, such as whiteboarding and application viewing for sessions that go outside the company's private network domain. Overall security—requiring data encryption, user authentication, and user passwords—is also widely used in T.120 applications.

## REVIEW AND CHECKLIST UPDATE

In this chapter, we discussed videoconferencing, which is one of the most common uses of video transport of IP networks. We began by looking at some of the common aspects of any type of videoconferencing, including the concept of session setup. We examined how a multipoint control unit (MCU) can be used to switch video and audio for conferences that involve more than two endpoints. Then we discussed continuous presence conferencing and how quad split converters can be used for this application. We covered echo cancellers, which are important for almost any type of videoconference. We closed the chapter with a discussion of some of the key technologies that are used in videoconferencing, including two different types of conference setup/control procedures (H.323 and SIP), a video compression system (H.264), and a standard that is widely used for data conferencing (T.120).

## Chapter 10 Checklist Update

❑ Videoconferencing involves live, two-way transport of video and audio signals, and is a very popular application for IP networks. It is also one of the most delay-sensitive applications for video technology.

❑ Ensure that each videoconference location is properly equipped with cameras, microphones, and echo cancellers.

❑ Multipoint conferencing (with more than two parties involved in the conference) can be implemented in two different ways: switched video and continuous presence.

    ❑ Consider using switched video for applications with limited network bandwidth and where a central video switch (MCU) can be installed.

    ❑ Consider using continuous presence for high-bandwidth networks and for applications where users may be distracted by video switching (such as schoolchildren).

❑ If multicasting is to be used for continuous presence conferencing, make sure that all segments of the network are capable of supporting multicasts.

❑ Consider using H.323-based videoconferencing systems, which currently have a very large installed base of compatible systems, if videoconferences will frequently be held with parties that are outside the user's network.

❑ Consider using SIP-based videoconferencing systems when multiple types of media need to be involved during a conference, and the videoconferencing system will be built from the ground up, due to the greater flexibility of SIP and less complicated set of specifications.

❑ Before purchasing new systems, determine whether the supplier has a migration strategy for H.264.

❑ Many remote meeting needs can be handled with audio and data conferencing alone.

❑ If T.120 data conferencing is to be used, make sure that appropriate security measures and restrictions are put in place.

# 11

# CONTENT OWNERSHIP AND SECURITY

Content is a generic term that we use to describe video and audio programming. Without content, a video network would have nothing to transport. In most cases, the companies and individuals who want to view content need to purchase the rights to do so from the companies and individuals who produce and own the content. Usually, these rights are limited in some way—to a specific number of broadcasts, over a defined period of time, to a certain number of views/downloads, or to any other limit that the content owners and users agree. These rights are usually spelled out in detail in a contract (a license) between the parties.

Enforcing these contracts is the responsibility of the content user or distributor (such as a satellite broadcaster, CATV/DSL broadband provider, or end-user corporation). The user is responsible for ensuring that unauthorized copies of the content are not made and that the rights defined in the contract are enforced. The penalties for not doing so can be severe—large financial penalties and often the loss of access to content in the future from that supplier. So, it is quite important for any content user or distributor to ensure that the content is stored securely and viewed only in a manner permitted by the content owner.

In this chapter, we are going to look at managing content, including where to get it and the responsibilities that come with it. Then, we'll discuss some ways to protect the content from unauthorized copying, or at least determine who made the copy. Finally, we'll take a short look at some commercial systems that are available for controlling viewer access to content. By the end of this chapter, readers should have a basic understanding of the rights and responsibilities of content owners and users, and have learned about some of the techniques that are used to protect those rights.

## ACQUIRING CONTENT

Acquiring content is easy in this day and age. A simple trip to a video store or any of a variety of retailers suffices to obtain a huge amount of high-quality pre-recorded content. Internet retailers, specialty on-line video suppliers, and video streaming websites can all be sources of content. A number of video production companies also can create customized footage of almost any topic imaginable.

Unfortunately, acquiring content and acquiring the rights to re-use content are two very different things. Most everyone has seen the warnings on pre-recorded DVDs and videotapes that read something like: "This material contained on this videotape is licensed exclusively for private home viewing. Any other commercial or non-commercial use, rerecording, rebroadcast or redistribution of this material is strictly prohibited." The owners of this content are sending a clear message: The owner of a DVD is allowed to view the content but not to use it for a commercial purpose. The definition of "commercial purpose" can be quite broad. For example, exhibitors at a trade show are not allowed to show movies or play music unless they have obtained a license to do so from the content owner. Similarly, owners of restaurants or other public businesses are not allowed to show videos or play music that they may have simply purchased on a CD; rather, these businesses need to obtain a license to play the content, since it is providing a commercial benefit to their business (i.e., improving the ambience of their building and making it more attractive to customers). A corporation is not allowed to receive an over-the-air radio or television broadcast and re-broadcast it to company employees in an office tower without a license. Owners of telephone systems aren't even allowed to entertain callers when they are placed on hold with recorded music unless it is properly licensed.

Fortunately, obtaining a license for many routine uses of music is fairly straightforward (although not necessarily inexpensive). For example, the American Society of Composers, Authors and Publishers (ASCAP) acts as a central clearinghouse for thousands of music and video suppliers in the USA. ASCAP offers over 100 different licenses for various types of establishments, ranging from television stations to hotels to circuses. Similar organizations exist throughout the world to provide licensing services in other countries.

Many sources also exist for non-entertainment video and audio. There are a number of distributors of corporate or classroom training videos, television news archives, and stock footage, such as city scenes. Some of the content is distributed royalty-free, so that once a license is purchased, the content can be broadcast and used to produce programming that can be put to many different uses. With a little research, it is often possible to purchase good-quality stock video content for many different purposes.

## Custom-Created Content

For many users, purchasing pre-produced audio and video content is not suitable. For these cases, contracting for custom-produced video or creating self-produced video is very popular. Production choices range from simple hand-held video camera pieces to fully scripted and professionally videotaped works. No matter what the method, a few key rules apply for any custom created video. These rules are listed in Table 11-1.

Custom-created video can be a powerful business tool when it is done correctly. With time, care, and a reasonable amount of money, great results can be achieved.

**TABLE 11-1**

Rules for Custom-Created Video

- Obtain a signed release from all people who appear in the video, whether they are paid or not. Make sure that all employees who appear have signed a release so that their images and/or performances can be used even in the event that the employee leaves the company.
- Ensure that all necessary rights for material have been secured. This includes music, script, shooting locations, and anything else that will be in the video that is intellectual property of another person or company. Your company or organization is ultimately responsible for the finished product; make sure that all subcontractors have followed the correct procedures and obtained any required permissions.
- Check that each license has sufficient permissions to allow the content to be fully utilized. For example, a training video might have been created that was originally intended only for in-house use by an organization, and the content rights were licensed accordingly. If, at a later time, the video is to be sold to a third party, new licenses may need to be obtained, possibly including the payment of royalties to the original creators or performers.
- Use high-quality cameras, media (film or videotape), lighting, and sound equipment. Small degradations in the original recording can dramatically affect the quality of the finished product, particularly if the video is to be highly compressed for, say, streaming.
- A well-written script is always a big plus. Even if the idea is to capture "candid" comments, many people have difficulty in acting natural in front of a camera. Give your performers a break and let them practice their lines.
- Use professionals whenever time and budget allow. This can include videographers, light and sound people, directors, performers, etc. Many talented people can be hired for reasonable prices, particularly outside major cities.
- One of the cheapest elements of the production process is the recording media, so use it liberally. Take extra shots and re-takes to provide plenty of material for editors to work with.
- Keep it simple. Complicated camera angles, special effects, and fancy sets aren't needed for effective communication. Instead, strive for simple, high-quality images that get the message across. Simple scenes are also easier to compress efficiently.
- Consider using a professional post-production service, to properly edit, time, and color-correct the video. A number of hardware and software tools can improve the overall "look and feel" of finished material and hide some minor defects; however, these tools can be expensive and hard to operate for the inexperienced user.

## RIGHTS MANAGEMENT

Rights management is the process of controlling the usage of and access to content. The rights that each licensee has are described in a license agreement for a particular piece of content that is negotiated between the content owner and the licensee. There are many different possible terms, ranging from the right to a single, immediate viewing (such as those offered by Video on Demand systems or movie theaters), all the way to the permanent, unlimited rights to the complete content. Typically, the rights for most content fall between these extremes, creating the need to manage the rights to view content.

Three basic tasks are required for effective content management. First and foremost, the content must be kept secure so that it does not fall into the wrong hands. Second, usage of the content must be controlled and measured in some way, such as number of viewers. Third, proper payments must be made to the content owner. We'll look at each of these in the following sections.

## Content Security

The need for content security must not be underestimated. Unauthorized copying of first-run movies can cause the loss of millions of dollars' worth of theater admission fees and DVD sales. Without security, it becomes difficult or impossible to restrict copying of content, thereby making proper accounting for royalty payments virtually impossible. Furthermore, content owners will be reluctant to provide their content to any application where security cannot be guaranteed.

The most common way to provide security is encryption, which will be discussed later in this chapter. Other methods include physical security (i.e., locked vaults to hold films when they aren't being shown) and copy prevention. Let's take a short look at these latter two methods.

Physical security can be very effective, although it depends on people to properly implement it. Since it is typically facilities based (i.e., at a movie theater), physical security can interfere with a goal of maximizing the number of viewers. Due to the expense and complexity of physical security, it is normally only worthwhile for high-value content.

Copy prevention is common in many pre-recorded video titles, such as Hollywood movies on videotape or DVDs. This is in addition to the encryption on DVDs, which we'll discuss shortly. The purpose of this copy prevention scheme is to make sure that a user doesn't take the analog video signal out of a videotape or DVD player and try to make a recording of it. This system, frequently called Macrovision after one of the leading technology suppliers, actively interferes with the video signals in a manner that affects recorders (videocassette, digital video recorders, etc.) but not televisions. Macrovision achieves this by distorting the video signal in the horizontal blanking interval, an area that the television really doesn't care about, but which distorts the operation of the circuits that handle the video during the recording process (the automatic gain circuits, for those of a more technical bent). Attempting to record a signal that is protected by Macrovision results in a recording that will have the video image slowly cycling from light to dark, and, in some cases, red and blue stripes cascading down the video display.

In order for Macrovision to work, every videotape and DVD player device needs to have a special chip to detect content that is to be protected, and to add the necessary distortions to the video output signal. A different type of circuit is installed in computer DVD drives, which also looks for the Macrovision signal. When it is present, the DVD drive will not allow the video content from the DVD to be copied to hard disk or another recorder.

One drawback of this system is that it protects video content all the time; there is no way to turn it off to make legitimate copies. (Although some content owners believe that there is no such thing as a legitimate copy.) Another drawback is the requirement for the chip to be in every playback device, which requires good enforcement of the technology licensing rules for player manufacturers that may be in other countries with different legal systems.

Many manufacturers of MPEG and other streaming equipment have successfully used their products to encode and transport video that feeds directly out of a DVD player. This has obvious benefits for demonstrations to potential customers but could result in a violation of the rights of the content owners. Users thinking of installing systems to transmit video from commercial tapes or DVDs should make sure that their video encoders and network adapters are not affected by any of the copy protection schemes, and, of course, that they have the rights to transmit the content.

## Digital Rights Management

Digital Rights Management (DRM) is a collective term for mechanisms that are used to control access to content through encryption or other means. DRM is virtually always a requirement for use of any recent digital motion picture or television content on a distribution system such as a DTH satellite system, a DSL network, a CATV system, or on a private network. Content owners are extremely reluctant to provide content to a distributor that doesn't have an effective DRM system because of the chance that a perfect digital copy of the content could be used to create copies for illegal resale. This control needs to prevent copying not only at the distributor facility, but also on any device that a user may use to play back the content, such as a set top box or a PC.

DRM policies can be very loose or very tight; the content owner determines the policies for this control. Once these policies have been determined, it is the responsibility of the DRM system to enforce these policies. Let's look at how a DRM system could work. Figure 11-1 provides a simple block diagram of a DRM system.

In a typical DRM system for a Video on Demand system, the content owner has two responsibilities. First, the content must be transferred to a secure server, where it can be accessed as needed based on viewer requests. Second, the rules for viewing must be defined. For example, viewers paying one price might be able to view the content once via

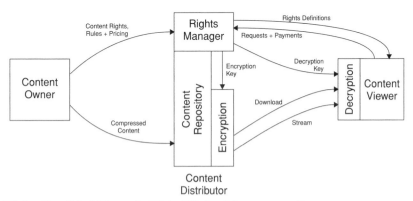

**FIGURE 11-1** Simplified View of a Digital Rights Management System

streaming only, whereas other viewers may be able to download the content and play it for several days. Of course, the rules stored in the rights manager system must be flexible, so they can be updated as viewers join and leave the system, or when content owners wish to add or remove content or change the rules for viewing their content. These rules are stored in the rights manager and are used whenever customer requests are made.

The rights manager system is responsible for enforcing the rules that the content owner has set up. It is also responsible for making sure that the viewers receive the content that they have paid for. Sometimes, the rights manager and the content server are separate machines; in other cases they are closely connected or resident on the same machine. The rights manager system swings into action whenever a viewer makes a request for content that the rights manager controls. The rights manager system is responsible for making sure that the viewer has paid for the content, either by means of a payment per viewing, a valid subscription plan, or referral by a third party that handled the payment. Note that rights management systems may still be required for free content, because the content owners want to protect the content from unauthorized duplication or re-use.

Once the rights manager system has determined that the viewer is authorized to view the content, the viewer needs to be provided with the proper digital key to unlock the content. The rights manager enforces the user rights policies by controlling access to these keys. This control can be quite literal: Many suppliers of encryption and key management systems require that their equipment be installed in a locked room with access permitted only to employees of the supplier. This high level of security is driven by the high potential value of both the content and the keys stored on the system to a thief. Keys can be provided to users in a number of ways, which will be discussed in the following sections on encryption.

Tracking the users is another issue. Typically, the rights manager system is responsible for tracking each time a user decides to view a piece of content and for reporting each viewing to the content owner for the purposes of paying royalties. This system has to be relatively foolproof to satisfy any contractual obligations with the content owners and to provide an audit trail so the payments can be verified. Each of the major commercial rights manager systems has a mechanism for doing this; failure of this mechanism can cause contract violations and some very upset content owners.

One other function required of a rights manager is creating the data used to prepare bills for customers. This is necessary in a system such as a cable television pay-per-view system, in which customers are billed at the end of each month for their usage. Failure is not an option here, because the revenue from the viewers will depend on this function working smoothly. In some cases, charges are billed directly to credit cards. In most cases, billing data from the rights manager needs to be fed into the distributor's billing system that prepares monthly bills for each subscriber.

# ENCRYPTION

Cryptography is the science of making messages unreadable to everyone except the intended recipient. Encryption is the first step—taking the raw video and audio and encoding it in a systematic way so as to become unreadable to anyone without the necessary key. Decryption is the reverse process—taking the key and the encrypted file and decoding it to produce an exact copy of the original signal. Proper management of the encryption keys is essential; the decoder needs exactly the same key for decryption that the encoder used for encryption. Overall, encryption can be a very complicated subject and can involve a great deal of arithmetic in different number bases (see, for example, Appendix B), which we won't go into here. Instead, we will focus on the practical aspects of encryption.

## Secret vs. Public Keys

In order for an encrypted message to be decoded, the correct key must be supplied to each intended recipient. In secret key applications, the sender and the receiver have some mechanism for communicating the key information between themselves, and preventing it from falling into the hands of a would-be content thief. Sometimes the postal sys-

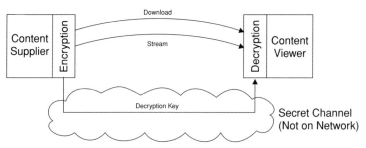

**FIGURE 11-2**   Secret Key Encryption System

tem or a fax machine is used for this purpose. The encryption process becomes worthless if the key is compromised. Figure 11-2 shows an information transfer taking place with a secret key.

Another problem with secret key cryptography is that it doesn't scale well. Sharing a single key between two people (or from one sender to many recipients) is fairly simple. However, consider the situation in which 10 parties wish to communicate securely. In this case, each user would need to manage 9 keys—one for communicating with every other person. All told, a total of 45 keys would need to be created and communicated secretly.

Public keys are quite different, although the need for secrecy is still present. Public keys are often used for encrypted e-mail or e-mail sender authentication. Public key cryptography is also used for secure Internet web browsing using Secure HyperText Transfer Protocol (HTTPS) and is commonly found on websites that deal with financial transactions or on-line shopping.[1]

In a public key system, each user is issued one or more pairs of public and private keys. The private key of each pair must be kept secret by its owner, whereas the public key is shared with anyone who wants to send encrypted messages to the owner. These two keys need to be related to each other by a mathematical formula that allows messages that are encoded with one key to be decoded only with the other key

---

1.   Many browsers indicate that secure communication is taking place by displaying a small icon of a padlock on the user display.

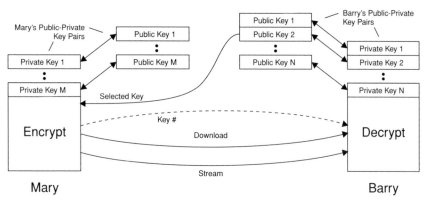

**FIGURE 11-3** A Public Key Encryption System

(don't worry—these relationships exist; see Appendix B). Let's look at how a public key encryption system would work in Figure 11-3.

In this example, Mary wishes to communicate with Barry. First, Mary must select one of Barry's public keys and use it to encrypt her message. In this case, she has selected Barry's public key number 2. Mary uses this key to encrypt her message (or video stream) and sends it to Barry. Any eavesdropper who picks up the encrypted message at this point would see nothing but gibberish. When Barry receives the message, he is able to decrypt it using his private key number 2. Barry must keep his private keys a secret, because anyone who obtained one of his private keys would be able to read any messages sent to Barry that was encrypted with the paired public key.

Once Barry receives the message, he might wish to communicate back to Mary. In order to do this in a secure manner, he would need to select one of Mary's public keys and use it to encrypt his message. This illustrates the rule: The sender uses the public key of the recipient for encrypting messages sent to that recipient. The private portion of the key is never known by anyone but the recipient, so that even if several parties were all communicating with Mary simultaneously using the same public key, none of them would be able to decrypt the messages from the other senders. Only the holder of the private key linked to that public key would be able to decrypt the messages.

Public keys can also be used to authenticate the sender of a message. Using the preceding example, Mary could encrypt a short data file using her private key and send it to Barry. Once he received the file, Barry could decrypt it using Mary's public key (this process works because of the mathematical relationship between the public and the private key). When Barry successfully decrypts the file, he knows that nobody else but Mary could have sent the file to him. Barry has now authenticated Mary as a sender.

## Watermarking

Watermarking is the process of inserting data into video or audio streams in order to track usage or prove ownership of the streams. It is similar in concept to some of the techniques that are used to protect currency and checks against forgery or counterfeiting. The basic idea is to insert identification without impairing the user's enjoyment of the content. Digital photographs can be watermarked to show copyright ownership and terms; these watermarks can be read by most of the major image-editing software packages. Video and audio content can also be watermarked with copyright data that can be read by some video recording and playback equipment to prevent unauthorized copying or distribution.

With digital content files, inserting a pattern into some of the less important bits in the file can be quite effective for watermarking purposes. For example, in a file with 16-bit audio samples, the least significant bit of any sample represents $1/65536^{th}$ of the total output signal. When these bits are subtly manipulated, a watermark pattern can be inserted in the file with essentially no impact on the sound of the resulting piece.

Watermarking can be done differently depending on the objectives of the creator of the watermark. A watermark can be specifically designed to be fragile so that any change to the file destroys the watermark, thereby proving the file was tampered with. Alternatively, a watermark can be designed to be robust so that even if the file was significantly altered, the watermark could still be discerned. This form is useful for tracking content that has been duplicated without permission; there are even web crawlers that spend their time looking at millions of web pages to see whether they have unauthorized content.

Watermarking helps in rights enforcement when a unique watermark is created for each individual user. Individual watermarks can serve as a deterrent to unauthorized use of the content, since any misappropriations can be traced back to the specific source of the leak. If users know that any misappropriated files can be traced back to them, that can be a powerful incentive NOT to illegally share files.

## Smart Cards

One of the most common ways of distributing keys used for secure video transport is the smart card. These cards are called "smart" because they incorporate a processor and memory that can be used by a variety of applications. Billions of smart cards are sold around the world each year for a variety of uses, including identification cards, pre-paid telephone cards (outside the USA), debit/credit cards, and a host of other applications. Typically, a smart card contains a processor that is capable of performing basic calculations and executing simple programs, and memory that can hold both variable and permanent data.

Smart cards must be connected to a reading device in order to operate. In some cases, this connection is made physically, using gold-plated contacts. Figure 11-4 shows two different types of smart cards and their associated contact areas. Some cards can also connect wirelessly

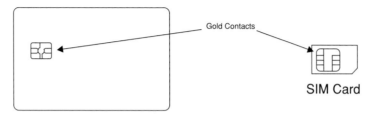

Consumer Smart Card

**FIGURE 11-4**   Two Common Types of Smart Cards

to special readers using short-distance radio signals, eliminating the need to physically insert the card into the device.

A key feature of many smart cards is their ability to securely store data. The cards can be programmed to store secret information, such as the private part of a public/private key pair. Any unauthorized attempts to read that data would result in the card becoming permanently damaged and the data destroyed. The smart card's internal processor can be used to decrypt data using this stored private key, and the results can be sent back out of the card without ever exposing the key to any external device.

For video applications, smart cards are one way to deliver video content descrambling/decryption keys to a user device. Each content stream (or television channel, if you prefer) has a unique descrambling key that is created when the content is prepared for broadcast. This key must be delivered to the viewer's device in order for it to be able to properly descramble the content. One way of doing this would be to simply send the key to the viewer's device; however, any other device that was connected to this communication path (think of a satellite link) would also receive this key and be able to decrypt the content. Instead, the descrambling keys are encrypted before they are sent to a viewing device.

When smart cards are used for delivering descrambling keys, each viewer device must be equipped with a smart card reader, either built in (as in many set top boxes, or STBs) or connected through an external port (such as a USB port on a personal computer). When an authorized viewer wants to watch scrambled content, the viewer's device needs to locate the correct descrambling key for the desired content. Instructions on how to find the appropriate decryption keys are contained in messages that are periodically sent by the server to authorized individual STBs or groups of STBs. The server then sends the encrypted descrambling key out over the communication path to the viewer's device. When it arrives, the encrypted key is fed into the smart card, and the smart card performs the decryption operation. The viewer device can then use the decrypted descrambling key to process the incoming signal and play the content for the viewer.

## ENCRYPTION SYSTEMS

There has been a great deal of work put into designing encryption algorithms, due to the many constraints that need to be respected to create a successful design. First and foremost is the need for security so that encrypted content and the keys needed to decrypt the content are not able to be discovered by a third party. Second, the system needs to be easy to use, or else users will not accept the system for regular use. Third, there needs to be an efficient mechanism for adding new users to the system and for assigning them keys that can be used for secure communication.

In the following sections, we will look at two commercial encryption systems. The first one is used to protect content (such as Hollywood movies) on DVDs and is used in basically every DVD player in existence. The second, called Pisys, is a commercial product offered for use in video delivery systems, such as CATV and satellite systems for residential viewers.

### DVD Encryption

One interesting encryption system is the one used to encrypt DVDs called the Content Scramble System (CSS). The information on each DVD title is encrypted using a unique 40-bit key. Any device that is going to play a DVD needs to have this key in order to descramble the content that is on the disk. Since other means of distributing the key were deemed unfeasible (can you imagine having to type a secret code into your DVD player each time you wanted to play a new disk?), encrypted copies of the key are also recorded on every disk. In fact, the disk key is encrypted with over 400 different player keys—one for each of the different manufacturers of DVD players (both hardware and software players). Each player type has an embedded key; the player simply needs to use its key to decode the master key for the disk in order to start the process needed to unlock the content.

CSS was defeated because one player manufacturer neglected to encrypt the player's key. Due to this lapse, certain people were able to design software to decrypt any DVD using this key. In addition, by using this key as a guide, they were able to discover over 100 other player keys. These discoveries spawned the development of a number of different software programs (called DeCSS) that are available today for (illegal) copying and playing of DVDs. This example illustrates the necessity to ensure that decryption keys are well secured for both the production and the playback steps of any video distribution system.

## Irdeto Pisys

The Irdeto Pisys system from Irdeto Access of Hoofddorp in The Netherlands is a good example of how a conditional access system is designed to work in a real-world environment. This technology has been successfully deployed by a number of satellite, CATV, terrestrial broadcast, and IP video network providers for both video contribution and distribution applications. Secure connections can be established for unicast (one source to one destination), multicast (one source to multiple, selected destinations), and broadcast (one source serving an undefined number of destinations) operations.

As is common in many conditional access systems, one security option supplied by Irdeto Access uses a hardware-based system for managing the decryption keys used by the viewers. This takes the form of smart cards that are issued to each viewer and a mechanism (card reader) at each viewing location that can access the data and processing functions stored inside the cards. A second security option from Irdeto Access is a specialized module of software code located in each viewing device that offers many of the same security capabilities as smart cards without requiring management of physical smart cards and associated reader hardware.

Pisys operates as a type of middleware—connecting a variety of equipment and software from multiple vendors. At the video source location, Pisys controls the hardware and software devices that encrypt or scramble content, and manages the keys that are required for this process. Content can be scrambled or encrypted "on the fly" (as it is being transmitted in real time), or it can be scrambled or encrypted ahead of time and stored on a server before it is sent to the viewer. Pisys also interacts with a variety of set top box devices that are responsible for descrambling or decrypting the content when it arrivers at the viewing location, and it distributes the keys to these devices using encrypted communications (triple DES or AES). Subscriber management and billing are handled by external software; this software manages a database containing subscriber contact information (address, account type, contact details, purchased services, etc.) and prepares and ships bills to customers. This software sends requests to Pisys to provision new services and change existing ones, as well as to send messages of any kind to individual subscribers over the broadcast network. The subscriber management software also allows Pisys to determine the associations between the subscribers and the smart cards that they possess, so that descrambling/decryption keys can be sent to the proper viewer devices.

Overall, Pisys and similar systems from other manufacturers provide a variety of valuable services, allowing encryption, decryption, and subscriber management systems to be simply and securely interconnected. Any company using satellites for video contribution or distribution should strongly consider employing a high-grade encryption system such as Pisys. Similarly, terrestrial broadcasters and video service providers using IP networks that need to securely deliver content can also benefit from this type of comprehensive solution.

## REVIEW AND CHECKLIST UPDATE

In this chapter, we discussed two very important aspects of content management: ownership and security. There are many sources for content, both pre-recorded and custom created. Whenever content is to be used by a business, it is essential to obtain all necessary rights in advance from the content owner. Failure to do so can be extremely expensive and damaging to future business opportunities.

Content owners may insist that their content be protected from copying or unauthorized viewing as a condition for granting rights to a distributor; failure to properly protect the content can be as damaging (or worse) to the content owner as failing to obtain the proper rights.

Content scrambling and encryption can also be used to protect the rights of content owners. These systems require a mechanism to scramble or encrypt the content prior to transmission, a means to descramble or decrypt the content at the viewer's location, and a way to securely transmit the necessary descrambling keys to the viewer's playback device. We reviewed several technologies for accomplishing this and looked at two examples illustrating how these technologies have been successfully implemented.

## Chapter 11 Checklist Update

❑ Make sure that all video and audio content that is to be transmitted on a network is licensed for use on that network. Failure to do so can expose network owners and users to potential claims for royalties, lawsuits, and loss of access to content in the future.

❑ Consider using copy prevention circuits within video playback devices such as videotape players, DVD players, and STBs to make recording of the video content impractical or of exceedingly poor quality. Make sure copy prevention is also implemented in DVD players inside laptop and desktop computers.

❑ When authorized to use pre-recorded content from videotapes or DVDs, make sure that copy protection schemes won't interfere with the video capture or encoding process.

❑ Encryption or scrambling is normally required when transmitting valuable content over public or private networks with multiple users.

❑ Consider using automated key distribution. The biggest challenge for encryption and scrambling systems is ensuring that the proper keys are distributed to users whenever they have acquired the rights to view a piece of content.

❑ Smart card systems, with card readers at each viewer location, are a popular means for securely distributing descrambling or decryption keys to viewers. Many STB manufacturers have incorporated smart card readers into their products, and readers are also available for personal computers.

# 12

# TRANSPORT SECURITY

As we discussed in the preceding chapter, a number of technologies can be used to protect content from being copied when public networks are being used. In this chapter, we are going to look at providing security for content through the use of secure transport technology. This is one of the best ways to provide security for high-value content, such as raw footage or first-run movies. Secure transport may also be a necessity for corporate video networks, particularly for those that carry videoconferences between senior executives.

We'll begin by discussing how IP packets can be transported over some popular private network technologies, including Frame Relay, ATM, and optical technologies. We'll follow this with a look at how private IP networks can be constructed on public IP network facilities, through the use of technologies called tunneling and IPSec. By the end of this chapter, readers should have a basic understanding of some of the ways that secure transport facilities can be used to provide content protection.

## PRIVATE NETWORKS

A network is considered to be private when a single person or organization controls all the content (voice, data, and video) flowing over the network. Sometimes, the circuits that make up the network are privately owned and operated; other times, the circuits are leased from a network provider. In most cases, the network is permanently connected so that data can flow without having to wait for a network connection to be set up.

Before the Internet arrived on the scene, pretty much the only way for companies to provide data communications between different locations in their business was to own and operate a private network. Dial-up connections could be used, but their use was mainly limited to services that needed to operate only occasionally and at low speeds. Many times, these data networks were devoted to providing remote locations (such as sales offices or manufacturing facilities) with access to central corporate computing resources, such as mainframes. Applications were typically limited to accounting, order entry, materials management, or other hard-number–oriented activities. Communications between employees were handled with printed memos and telephone calls, instead of e-mail and instant messaging. As a result, many private networks were low speed and poorly suited for video traffic.

Modern private networks are much snazzier, with high-speed connections more widely deployed, to support a variety of internal communications functions. Most private networks support applications such as e-mail, file sharing, and corporate web intranets. Other services, such as voice over IP and instant messaging are growing in popularity. As network speeds increase in order to support these applications, it also becomes feasible to transport video signals on private networks.

### Leased or Private Lines

Leased lines are telecommunication circuits that are provided by a carrier for exclusive use of a single customer on a long-term (monthly or yearly) basis. If the network facilities are owned by the user, they can be called private lines, although that term is also used for leased facilities. Historically, data speeds on these networks could be very low (such as 300 bits per second), but more modern circuits operate at speeds of 56 kbps and above. Popular speeds today include T1 (1.544 Mbps), E1 (2.048 Mbps), E3 (34 Mbps), DS3 (45 Mbps), and OC3/STM1 (155 Mbps).

Many private lines carry a mixture of services, including voice and data services. For example, it is not at all uncommon for a T1 private line, which has a capacity of 24 channels running at 64 kbps each, to have a dozen channels reserved for voice traffic and the other 768 kbps allocated for data traffic. At the customer location, the voice circuits might be connected to a telephone system and the data circuit connected to a local data router.

Leased lines are normally installed as point-to-point circuits that start and end at customer locations. These circuits are handled as totally private, dedicated data circuits; no data is added or removed by the carrier in transit, even if one end of the circuit is sending empty packets. In between, multiple carriers and carrier equipment locations may be involved; each is responsible for providing a full-bandwidth connection across its own network. In essence, the customer's data "tunnels" through the rest of the network, without interaction. Figure 12-1 shows an example of a private line T1 circuit. Note that the T1 signal is carried intact from Site A to Site B, without intermediate processing. Note that carriers will normally combine multiple T1s and other voice and data traffic through the process of multiplexing, and much higher

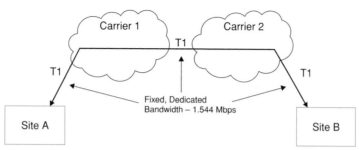

**FIGURE 12-1** Leased Line Example

data rates will normally be used to provide connectivity and transport between carrier locations.

Leased lines can offer a great deal of security for customer traffic. In order to get access to the data on a leased line, an outsider would need to obtain physical access to the data circuit, either in the local access network or inside the carrier's network. Aside from obvious legal violations, on a practical level this is a difficult task.

In small networks, with relative few connected locations, a few leased lines can provide good connectivity. However, as the number of network locations grows, the number of leased lines needed to interconnect all of the locations grows rapidly. To solve this problem, many times the networks are arranged in a hub-and-spoke configuration, with one location serving as the central hub, and the other locations connected via spokes that all originate at the hub. When a location on one spoke needs to communicate with another spoke, the data must transit through the hub before it is passed along. This architecture requires large-capacity connections near the network hub and can create a significant amount of load on the networking equipment located at the hub. Other possible network configurations include tree-and-branch networks and various types of rings.

Another drawback to leased lines is that they are inefficient for data flows that vary greatly over time. Because the capacity of a standard leased circuit is unable to change rapidly, a customer has two choices. One choice is to purchase a circuit that has enough capacity to handle the expected peak data load, which would leave the circuit operating below capacity most of the time. The other choice is to buy a circuit that can carry less than the peak amount of data, thereby creating congestion whenever peak loads occur. In either scenario, the data communication resources are used less optimally than would be the case if a variable rate service were used.

There are a number of mechanisms for sending IP packets over a standard telecom circuit, so we won't go into details here. One of the most common protocols is the Point-to-Point Protocol (PPP) because it is very simple and easy to implement. PPP doesn't have many of the advanced features of other packet transport protocols, so it isn't suitable for use on networks other than point-to-point leased lines or on access lines from a customer to a provider's packet network.

## Frame Relay

Many carriers offer a service called Frame Relay as an alternative to leased lines for packet-based traffic. Frame Relay is a data network protocol that was designed specifically to transport packets in frames, which are logical groups of bits complete with headers that can flow across a data channel. This service is typically less expensive than a leased line because the network is shared by other Frame Relay users (apart from the local access line from the customer to the carrier's network edge). This allows carriers to use their networks more efficiently, because idle times in one customer's data can be filled with other customers' data. Connections to Frame Relay networks are normally supplied by a local service provider, who sets up a data connection to each customer location. See Figure 12-2 for a simple example of a Frame Relay circuit.

At the customer site in a Frame Relay network circuit, a special device can be used to take IP packets and insert them into and remove them from the data frames. These devices, called Frame Relay Access Devices (FRADs), can be owned and managed by the carrier. Alternatively, this function can be incorporated into routers or other devices that belong to the customer.

Data from the FRAD is sent to a local carrier over standard telecom circuits, such as a T1 circuit. When the data arrives at the carrier, it is

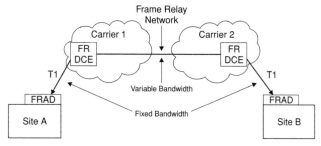

**FIGURE 12-2** Frame Relay Circuit Example

processed by a Frame Relay Data Communications Equipment (DCE) device. This device is responsible for receiving the data frames, multiplexing them with frames sent by other customers, and sending them into the carrier's data communications backbone. Note that the carrier is not required to keep the data in any specific format in the internal data network; Frame Relay data can be sent over IP, ATM, or any other type of network that the carrier chooses, provided that the data is kept private from any other customers.

Frame Relay connections are priced partly on the basis of the Committed Information Rate (CIR) and partly on the basis of the access link speed. The CIR is a data rate selected by the customer that the carrier promises will be available at all times to the customer, regardless of any other traffic on the network. The access link speed is fixed, and normally must be a specific interface speed in the telecom hierarchy (T1, DS3, etc.). Customers are allowed to send more data than their CIR rate; however, the network can delete any frames in excess of the CIR at any time. Higher level protocols (such as TCP) can correct for these lost frames, so customers usually choose to keep their CIR as low as possible (a CIR of zero is permitted by some carriers, meaning that all the customer's frames can be discarded if the network becomes congested; this would make sense only for data such as e-mail with little time sensitivity). For networks with heavy video usage, it might be necessary to pay for a CIR that is greater than the expected video signal rate to ensure that adequate network capacity is also available.

One nice feature of Frame Relay networks is the ability to combine data from multiple links coming from different sites into one high-speed link to another site. This is particularly useful for a corporation with multiple small satellite offices that all need to communicate with a central facility. In Frame Relay, each remote site can use a medium speed link (a T1, for example), and the central site can use a higher speed link (a DS3, for example). This is much more economical and efficient than using multiple leased lines between the remote sites and the central site. Figure 12-3a shows a leased line network layout, and Figure 12-3b shows the same network implemented using a Frame Relay network.

Frame Relay networks can also be configured to provide multicasting, so a single data stream from one site can be sent to multiple

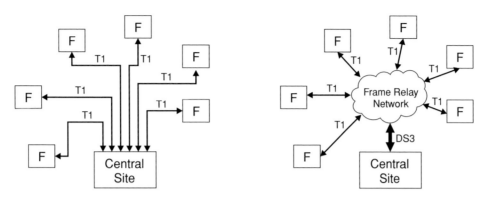

(A) Leased Line Network                    (B) Frame Relay Network

**FIGURE 12-3**   Comparison of Leased Line and Frame Relay Networks

other sites. As we discussed in Chapter 9, multicasting is very useful for video streaming networks. In Frame Relay, one site can be
designated as the main site, and can multicast data to all of the other
sites in the network. Communications back from these sites to the
main site would be on a one-to-one basis. Alternatively, every node
in the network can be designated as a multicasting site. Different
carriers implement different aspects of the Frame Relay standard,
so it is always wise to check with a carrier before installing a network to see whether multicasting or other configurations will be
supported.

## ATM

Asynchronous Transfer Mode (ATM) is a networking technology
based on the transport of fixed-length packets of data, called "cells"
in ATM standards. Developed in the 1980s, ATM became popular in
the 1990s for transport of many different types of services, including
video. Carriers still offer ATM services today, and many organizations use ATM circuits in their backbone core networks to provide private networks for voice and IP traffic.

ATM services are popular partly because of the ability to control how
data is routed within a network. All data in an ATM network flows
over a Virtual Circuit (VC), of which there are two types: Permanent

Virtual Circuits (PVCs), and Switched Virtual Circuits (SVCs). As their name imply, SVCs are switched connections that are set up between source and destination each time they are needed and then disconnected when the data transfer is complete. In contrast, PVCs are established upon command from the system manager, and they remain connected until commanded to disconnect, which could be a period lasting days, months, or even years. (Note that PVCs do not have to be fixed bandwidth; it is perfectly acceptable to have a PVC carry data only when necessary, and remain connected but carry essentially no data when not needed.)

A big advantage of ATM transport is that the PVCs and SVCs can be carefully managed, to ensure that data from one VC does not appear in a different VC. Even though the flows are mixed within the network, the ATM multiplexing equipment keeps the data isolated at the user connections. This provides a degree of security for customer data that is more difficult to implement on a IP-based network.

Another advantage of ATM over leased line service is the added flexibility in allocating bandwidth. Normally, for leased line service, bandwidth must be sold in fixed-size increments according to the telecom hierarchy—a T1, a DS3, an STM-1, etc. In contrast, ATM circuits can be configured in any size—such as 15 Mbps or 22 Mbps.[1] This gives users much more flexibility in configuring their networks.

Figure 12-4 shows a simple point-to-point ATM network that crosses between two different carriers. At each customer site, an ATM multiplexer is installed; this multiplexer takes voice, data, and other services such as video and converts them into ATM cells. (Note that in some networks, Frame Relay circuits are used to connect to local customers, and the carrier converts incoming traffic into ATM cells within their network.) Inside the carrier's network, an ATM switch is used to take the incoming cells and route them toward their selected destination. As mentioned previously, these destinations can either be configured manually by the network operator (a PVC) or dynamically upon

---

1. This discussion relates to the actual data-carrying capacity of the ATM circuit for local or long-distance service. The physical local access line from a customer's facility to the local telephone company office will normally be a standard rate for the telecom hierarchy—a T1, a DS3, an STM-1, etc.

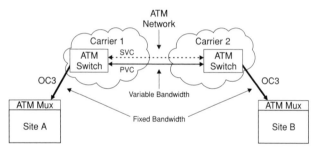

**FIGURE 12-4**  ATM Circuit Example

request by the user (an SVC). The switch is also responsible for managing any congestion that might occur on the network; congestion can be handled either by delaying specific cells (queuing) or dropping cells that cannot be transmitted over the congested network link.

It is also possible to reserve bandwidth for a particular VC from one end of an ATM network to another, thereby ensuring that time-critical data such as video is able to get through unimpeded. A VC that is set up to have a constant bit rate (CBR) will always have the same amount of data flowing through it; if the customer's data isn't flowing fast enough to fill it up, then empty cells will be sent to fill up the rest of the data pipe. Because the bandwidth that is set aside for a constant bit rate circuit is unavailable to other users of the ATM network, carriers normally charge higher rates for those services. A VC can also be set up to use a variable bit rate (VBR) so that the end-to-end data rate varies as the customer data rate increases or decreases. Prices for variable bit rate services are generally lower than constant ones; however, carriers need to enforce a priority system to allocate the network bandwidth when multiple variable bit rate services are all trying to increase their bit rate. The lowest class of service, called available bit rate (ABR), simply uses any bandwidth that is left over in the data pipe. This service, although it is typically the least expensive, is normally not well suited for video traffic, because it can quickly have its bit rate reduced to zero if other higher priority services such as VBR need the bandwidth.

IP packets are frequently transported over ATM circuits. Carriers like ATM because they can use a single networking technology to serve multiple needs of a customer. Voice traffic can be transmitted using constant bit rate services, and data traffic can be transmitted using variable and available bit rate services. Multiple customers can be served on a single communication link, because ATM has the built-in mechanisms to control the amount of bandwidth that each customer is allowed to use, and carriers can enforce these policies. Since most customers today have a changing mixture of voice and data services, carriers that use ATM can adapt to these changing needs without having to construct separate voice and data networks.

One drawback to ATM networks is the complexity of establishing and tearing down VCs, and also the overall management complexity of the ATM network. Because a VC must be established from end to end before data can flow over that VC, all of the intermediate equipment must be configured whenever a VC is established or modified. This can be a complex process and requires a great deal of software in the ATM network elements. Because of this complexity, service guarantees, and a variety of other factors, ATM services are more expensive than IP services operating at the same bandwidth from many carriers.

## Fiber Optic Networks

Fiber optic networks use tiny glass fibers along with sophisticated optical transmitters and receivers to send digital data over long distances. At the transmitter, digital data is converted into pulses of light, which are then fed into one end of the optical fiber. At the far end, the fiber is connected to a receiving device, which accepts the incoming pulses of light and converts them back into electrical signals. Networks can be easily designed to reach 100 km without any intermediate amplification of the signals; with amplification and signal regeneration, optical networks can reach across any ocean.

Many large users of video and data transport services would benefit by installing their own private fiber optic network. The biggest benefit is a long-run cost reduction, because the cost of buying equipment and fiber is a one-time charge as compared to a recurring monthly fee from a carrier. Another benefit is the flexibility of services (but not of location) because of the huge variety of fiber optic equipment

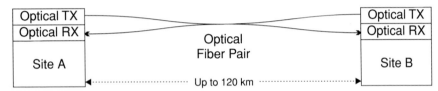

**FIGURE 12-5**   Optical Fiber Circuit Example

available to transport almost any type of signal. One more benefit is the privacy that can be achieved with fiber optics. Of course, there are downsides, including the need to hire or train staff to maintain the network. Also, geographic flexibility is essentially non-existent once the fiber is installed.

Figure 12-5 shows a simplified diagram of a typical fiber optic private network. At each site, an optical transmitter (TX) and an optical receiver (RX) are installed, along with the necessary electronics to send and receive data on the local data network. Typically, a pair of fibers is used, and one site's transmitter is connected to the other site's receiver. There are many variations on this theme, with different devices using different optical wavelengths (colors of light) on the same fiber, and with multiple fibers being combined into a cable serving one or multiple customers. None of this, however, changes the fact that a fiber needs to be connected from each transmitter to each receiver in an unbroken, continuous path.

Optical fiber networks are hard to beat for quality, speed, and security. Because the signals flowing inside an optical fiber are almost perfectly isolated from the outside world, interference from other signal sources is not an issue. Contrast this with microwave or other radio links that must contend with interference from any number of sources. This lack of interference on fiber translates into very low error rates for the desired signals. High speeds are also possible on optical fibers; rates of 10 billion bits per second are easy to achieve with modern optical devices, and more than a hundred sets of these devices can share a single optical fiber. Security is also high, since the only way to tap into the signals flowing down a fiber requires physical access to the fiber itself.

Of course, there are some difficulties for users who wish to use optical networking. In order for the network to function, the data sender and receiver need to be connected by a single continuous optical fiber. While this type of networking is relatively easy to establish in a suburban college campus, it can be very difficult to achieve in a modern metropolitan area, let alone across longer distances. The technology of installing the fiber is usually not an issue, but obtaining permission from all of the property owners along the fiber route can be incredibly difficult and time consuming. Since telephone companies are often reluctant to simply lease fiber, prospective users will need to lease fibers from other providers such as power or water utilities, or even from municipalities that have installed networks of fiber cables under streets and into many buildings.

Several techniques are used to send IP packets over optical fiber. Many routers can be equipped with fiber interfaces that send packets using optical Ethernet standards, which have been developed to use both short distance and longer distance optical technology. Longer distance links typically require the use of telecom-style interfaces, such as SONET/SDH technology. IP packets flowing over these networks can use specially developed protocols such as Packet over SONET/SDH (PoS). This service ends up behaving similarly to ATM service with a large PVC.

Some specialized video transport systems even use optical fiber available from a number of manufacturers, although many of them don't use IP technology. These devices can transport video inputs directly over fiber links to video outputs, allowing network setup and maintenance to be very simple.

## VIRTUAL PRIVATE NETWORKS

Virtual Private Networks (VPNs) offer many of the benefits of private networks but use the public Internet as a transport mechanism. This allows users to share a single Internet access link for both private data and for connections to the Internet. Similarly, by using the Internet for transport between locations, a VPN user avoids the expense of installing or leasing a circuit between locations, although local access link charges may still apply. Some service providers also offer VPN services over shared networks that aren't part of the Internet.

VPNs are all about security. Without security, the data traveling over a VPN is subject to all types of eavesdropping, or worse, malicious data alteration. Four key security functions need to be accomplished by a packet transport system that is to be used by a VPN[2]:

- *Authentication:* The receiving device needs to know and confirm that the data came from the device that the data claims to be coming from. This can be accomplished with digital signatures provided by a centralized authority.
- *Confidentiality:* The data that is carried in the VPN must not be understandable by other devices or users on the network, even if they are able to get copies of the packets. This can be accomplished through the use of a good encryption algorithm on all packet data.
- *Access Control:* Networks that are part of the VPN should be blocked from being accessed by users who are not part of the VPN. Also, all of the user networks that are connected to the VPN need to be properly isolated from third parties who might attempt to gain unauthorized access to the VPN. This can be accomplished through a good combination of authentication and confidentiality for all packets, as well as a good firewall.
- *Data Integrity:* Any data that passes through the VPN should be protected from tampering, and if the data is tampered with, it should be obvious to the receiving device. This can be accomplished though the use of a secure encryption system and an effective mechanism to ensure that extra packets are not inserted into the data stream.

## Tunneling

Tunneling involves sending data through a network without making it available to other users of that network. In order for this process to work, the data must be encrypted to prevent it from making sense to others. When a tunnel is in place between two locations, it is generally used for all of the data communication between these two

---

2. Adapted from Web ProForum Tutorial titled "Virtual Private Networks (VPNs)" from The International Engineering Consortium, http://www.iec.org.

endpoints, requiring many different kinds of packets to be encrypted. (Contrast this with the discussions in Chapter 11, where we focused just on encrypting video streams.) Tunneling is generally used over a public wide area network for communication between two local networks in different locations. Other forms of secure transport such as PPTP or L2TP are used when a single user connects to a remote network, which we won't discuss here.

Tunneling works by encrypting normal IP packets before they are transmitted over public IP networks such as the Internet. During this process, the entire packet is encrypted, including the header information. A second, non-encrypted header is then placed onto each packet so that they can be sent through the Internet. (If this second header wasn't added, then the packets would be impossible to route, because the routers wouldn't have access to the source and destination IP addresses inside the encrypted header.)

The operation of a tunneling system is shown in Figure 12-6. An IP tunnel is in use between Router A and Router B. Router A is responsible for taking packets from LAN A that are intended for LAN B and encrypting them before sending them into the Internet. Router A is also responsible for accepting packets that originated at Router B and decrypting them before placing the packets on LAN A. Router B fulfills the same functions for LAN B. Note that either or both routers can be configured to send all packets from their local LAN to the other LAN, or they can filter the packets and send only some through the IP tunnel.

## IPSec

Internet Protocol Security (IPSec) was developed to provide secure transport for IP packets over non-secure networks. It uses a variety of

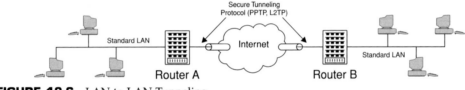

**FIGURE 12-6**  LAN to LAN Tunneling

tools to ensure the security for each of the packets, including encryption and authentication. IPSec is described in a number of Internet Engineering Task Force (IETF) RFCs, many of which were finalized in November 1998. Since then, IPSec has become one of the preferred methods for secure IP transport in use today.

One big advantage of IPSec is that it can be used to encrypt all packets at the IP level, so changes are not required to applications or higher-level protocols, such as TCP or UDP. There is also no special training required for users; the security functions are taken care of by the lower layers of the protocol stack that are not normally exposed to users.

Three main aspects of IPSec are covered in the IETF standards:

- *Internet Key Exchange (IKE):* This secure mechanism is used for exchanging keys between known entities, thereby allowing them to send encrypted messages to each other. There are several different ways to achieve this, but one of the most popular methods is to use digital certificates that are signed by a mutually trusted Certificate Authority, or CA (VeriSign is a common one). Once the two parties have verified each other's identities, they can use the Diffie-Hellman Key Exchange (see Appendix B) to create a private encryption key that is known only to them.
- *Authentication Header (AH):* This header is used to make sure that the packet senders are who they claim to be, and that the contents of the packet haven't changed in transmission. In order to do this, each packet must use a checksum that is generated from certain portions of the packet that don't change in transmission, and a secret key, known only to the sender and the receiver of the message. A software algorithm is applied to manipulate these values and produce a "Message Digest" or a "Hash" result, which is then appended to the message being sent. At the receiving end, the same calculation is performed, and a second result is calculated. If the two results match (both the one sent with the message and the one calculated by the receiver), then the packet is assumed to be authentically from the real sender.
- *Encapsulating Security Payload (ESP):* ESP takes the authentication header concept one step further and actually encrypts the contents of the packets so that outsiders cannot read the data inside each packet.

Before communication can take place between a receiver and a sender using IPSec, the two parties must agree to a Security Association (SA). The SA is established when a secure session is first set up, and includes all of the information that is needed by the receiving party to understand the transmitting party. Each SA is unidirectional and unicast, meaning that the SA is valid in one direction only, and only for a single recipient IP address. For a two-way IPSec connection, at least two SAs must be established—one in each direction.

One important aspect of an IPSec connection that must be specified by the SA is whether the connection will be made in transport mode or in tunnel mode. If the connection is between two gateway devices (such as firewalls or routers), then the connection must be tunnel mode, and every packet flowing between the source and the destination must pass over the IPSec link. In tunnel mode, a new (non-encrypted) IP header is applied to each packet after it is encrypted so that they can be handled in the network by routers that aren't able to decrypt the original packet. At the receiving end of the tunnel, the extra packet headers are removed, the packet is decrypted, and then it is sent to the correct destination. In contrast, transport mode can be used only between end devices on the network (such as user PCs or servers), and the original destination IP address remains visible on the packet. Only the contents of the IP packet are encrypted in transport mode. The choice of whether to use transport mode or tunnel mode really depends on whether the secure connection is between networks (such as from LAN to LAN) or between devices (such as one processor to another). Individual devices are also permitted to use tunnel mode, but gateway devices are not permitted to use transport mode.

Overall, a VPN is a very desirable method for implementing secure communication over a public network, such as the Internet. By using a VPN, users can avoid many of the headaches involved with setting up and maintaining a private network, and still receive many of the benefits. Of course, nothing is free, and charges from a local ISP may increase if significant local access bandwidth is added to support VPNs. Plus, the performance of the virtual network will be no better (in terms of error rates, etc.) than the actual network underneath it. The only real drawback to a VPN is that guaranteeing a large amount of bandwidth can be difficult, unless the network provider makes specific accommodations for the VPN.

# REVIEW AND CHECKLIST UPDATE

In this chapter, we investigated secure transport from two aspects. First, we looked at transport technologies that provided physical or other forms of data security, including leased lines, Frame Relay, ATM, and optical networks. Then, we examined two aspects of virtual private networks and saw how tunneling and IPSec could be used to transport confidential traffic securely over the Internet.

## Chapter 12 Checklist Update

❑ Transport security can be supplied with private networking technology such as ATM, Frame Relay, leased line, and optical networks.

❑ ATM, Frame Relay, and leased line services can be obtained from most public network providers (telephone companies). Local and long-distance segments may need to be purchased from different suppliers, which may need user supervision.

❑ Optical networks are typically built to customer specification and may require the end user to purchase and maintain the necessary optical equipment. Obtaining fiber and associated rights of way can be expensive and difficult.

❑ Virtual Private Networks need to be configured properly to protect video content. A secure encryption scheme such as IPSec needs to be implemented to prevent content from being copied by others sharing the same network.

❑ Private networking technology does not prevent authorized viewers from making unauthorized copies of content (such as copying video being streamed over a private network). To prevent this, some form of copy protection is needed, as discussed in Chapter 11.

# 13

# IPTV—IP VIDEO TO THE HOME

IPTV means television that is delivered over an IP network, primarily to home viewers. Any discussion of a video transport technology would not be complete without an analysis of the impact of that technology on video delivery to the home. In the case of video over IP, this discussion is particularly important because of the emergence of new technologies and market forces that are making IP technology more and more appealing for delivering video to consumer homes. Indeed, for new deployments, IP is becoming the technology of choice for more and more service providers.

In this chapter, we will start out by looking at three examples in which IP technology is used to deliver video to the home. We'll look at the reasons for using this technology. Then, we will examine some of the key technologies that support IPTV. We'll conclude with an example of a real deployment of IPTV technology.

## APPLICATIONS

Many readers of this book are aware of the rich variety of technologies that can be used for video delivery into the home. Several different technologies have already proven themselves to be reliable and economical means to deliver content, including terrestrial broadcast, cable television (CATV), and satellite direct-to-home (DTH) broadcast. These systems were originally built for the sole purpose of delivering content to the home. With IP networks, the situation is different, because most of these networks were originally built to deliver data to the home or business. With this in mind, let's look at three different types of services that IP networks are currently being used to deliver: entertainment to the home, narrowcasting to homes and businesses, and hotel/motel applications.

## Entertainment

A number of IP video networks have been installed to provide home video services, similar to those provided by traditional CATV and DTH satellite providers. In all these systems, individual households are supplied with a variety of broadcast television channels in exchange for a monthly subscription fee. These fees are used to pay for three basic costs of the service provider: the cost of the programming, the initial cost of installing the video delivery system, and the ongoing costs of performing maintenance on the delivery system and providing customer service.

Typically, entertainment systems provide service for a particular geographic area, such as a city, a town, or a neighborhood (or, in the case of satellite services, a country). In many cases a license or franchise from the local government is required to operate the system; this may require an annual fee to be paid to the government (called a franchise fee). Exclusive rights for a certain territory are sometimes given to the service provider in exchange for certain concessions, such as providing video services for governmental or educational use. However, just because a service provider has an exclusive franchise for an area, this does not mean that the provider is guaranteed to capture all of the television viewers in that area.

In any video delivery system, a number of potential subscribers will choose not to receive video programming and become actual subscribers. The ratio of actual subscribers to potential subscribers is called the "take rate" and can be influenced by a number of factors. These factors include the availability of competing video services (such as CATV and satellite), the take rates of those other services, the amount of local programming available, the intensity of the marketing program for the service, and many other factors.

Normally, a service provider does not install all of the equipment that is needed to service every single residence in a given area, because the take rate will begin at a low percentage. Instead, distribution equipment is added as needed to handle new subscribers as they sign up. However, a large amount of common equipment (for content gathering and system operation, as described later in this chapter) must normally be installed to equip an area for video delivery. Because of this, the system economic breakeven point might not be reached unless the take rate reaches 20–30%, or possibly even more. Overall, it is difficult to design a profitable business plan for a new video-only network unless one out of every five households (a 20% take rate) that can subscribe to the service actually does.

IP technology offers a way for these service providers to capture more than just video subscribers: the ability to offer "triple play" services. For example, many CATV companies are adding IP capabilities to their networks to provide voice over IP and data services. On a properly designed pure IP network, video services can be offered, data services such as Internet access can easily be supported, and voice services can be provided using voice over IP technology. With a triple-play network, a service provider can more easily achieve the take rate needed to reach economic breakeven.

## Narrowcasting

In narrowcasting, IP video signals are sent over an established data network to reach an audience for programming that might not appeal to a large audience. For example, for the past five years the PGA Tour has broadcast live IPTV golf coverage of every player on a single hole of the first two days of a tournament (the island 17th green of the Tournament Players Club at Sawgrass course used for The Player's Championship tournament, for those who must know). There are also major league baseball games available, television feeds from a number of different countries, and a great deal of pre-recorded content. A surprising amount of content is available by narrowcast; consumers need only go to the homepages of any of the major media player companies to see a smattering of what is available.

Narrowcast video streams are normally displayed only on a user's PC, but the same signal can be processed for display on a normal television as well, using a PC equipped with a video output card or a stand-alone set top box (STB). Narrowcasting content is provided free of charge (supported by advertising), on a pay-per-view basis, or on a subscription basis (such as Real Networks' SuperPass).

A typical narrowcasting system is set up using a centralized server for video content. Viewers obtain the video by connecting to the server through the Internet or other IP communications network. The streams can be served using a streaming protocol such as RTP or a download and play protocol such as HTTP. Because the Internet is not multicast enabled, the server needs to create a stream for each user. For unexpectedly popular live services, viewers can experience choppy or even frozen video if the servers don't have enough capacity to meet the surge in demand. To prevent these problems, an admission control method is needed to deny service to newcomers once system capacity has been reached.

## Hotel/Motel Video Services

IP video technology can also be applied to delivering in-room entertainment video to hotel guests. This technology can be used to provide all of the video services to each room, or just the premium movie channels offered by many hotels. Because the video display in a hotel room is normally a television set, an IP-enabled STB is required in each room to receive the incoming signals and convert them.

Typically, hotel systems are configured to use a video server in each building. The server outputs are connected to a data transport system that delivers the IP streams to each room in the hotel. This can be accomplished using existing telephone wiring if DSL technology is used. IP traffic can also be sent over coaxial cable normally used for distributing television signals in a hotel through the use of IP cable modem technology.

## BASIC CONCEPTS

Video delivery to the home has created a variety of new terminology and business models that need to be understood in order to make sense of the reams of articles and company literature that has been produced on this topic. In the following sections, we'll look at some of these new terms and how industry insiders are using them. Along the way, we'll also discuss some of the market forces that are pushing service providers to seek out and apply innovative new technologies, such as video over IP.

### Why Use IP for Video to the Home?

The hardware and software systems that deliver terrestrial broadcast, DTH satellite, and CATV services are the products of hundreds of thousands of hours of development and refinement, and provide services that are very popular with the home viewing audience. In the face of all this proven technology, the logical question becomes: Why introduce a new technology, such as IP video transport, for video delivery to the home?

The answer is not a single compelling reason, but instead a combination of factors that can influence this decision. Briefly, these factors are local loop technology, user control, convergence, and flexibility. Let's look at how IP technology can impact each of these factors.

Local telephone technology has been evolving rapidly over the past decade. With the emergence of Digital Subscriber Line (DSL) technology, service providers are now able to deliver hundreds or thousands of kilobits per second of data to each customer's home. This capacity far exceeds what was possible even a decade ago, when speeds were typically limited to a basic rate ISDN line operating at

144 kbps or a simple dial-up modem circuit operating at 56 kbps. With the new added capacity of DSL, the logical question for providers has become: What other services besides telephony can we provide to customers that they will be willing to pay for? The answer is, in many cases, "video services." To accomplish this, IP technology has often proven to be the best choice for providing new telephony and video over DSL circuits.[1] Data services are predominately delivered using IP already.

User control is another powerful trend in the video delivery business. By giving users the ability to choose what they want to watch at any time, service providers have been able to simultaneously increase user satisfaction and increase the fees that customers pay. For example, personal video recorders (PVRs, which have been popularized by suppliers such as TiVo) allow users to automatically record television broadcasts on a computer hard disk for later, on-demand playback (sometimes called "time shifting"). This service is not free: Users have to pay a significant sum to purchase the PVR device, and then many pay an additional monthly service fee to receive the electronic program guide that is necessary to operate their device. Another example of users' willingness to pay for increased control of their viewing is a service being offered by cable television companies in the USA called HBO On Demand; this service allows users to select programs from a list of shows and movies for viewing at any time, in exchange for a substantial monthly fee. This service has become popular with customers in those cable systems that offer it. Clearly, users are demanding, and willing to pay for, programming that they can control to meet their viewing habits. Video over IP is a good technology for providing this control capability.

Another big market driver is convergence. Unfortunately, the term "convergence" got rather a bad reputation during the "dot-com" bubble in the late 1990s. However, the concept is still with us today, and it is a powerful force in the video delivery business. By convergence, we mean the use of a single network to deliver multiple services to

---

1. Although many DSL circuits are ATM-based, many of them use IP technology for delivering services.

consumers. The term "triple play" has come to mean the simultaneous offering of voice, video, and data services. By voice, we mean traditional telephony, possibly implemented by use of voice over IP technology. By video, we mean entertainment programming delivered to the home. And by data, we mean access to the public Internet and all of the services that network carries. Of course, other services can be offered (such as mobile phones), but many providers have found that offering these three is a significant technical (and business) challenge, and that most consumers will be satisfied with service providers who offer a well-executed "triple play."

As the pace of technical innovation has picked up, so has the need for service providers to add flexibility to their service offerings. From a purely economic standpoint, providers that are installing new networks today need to feel confident that the technology will still be usable 10–20 years into the future. (Without that kind of life cycle, it is hard to justify the significant up-front capital costs of the network while still being able to offer services at prices that customers will pay). By making sure that their networks are flexible, service providers can adapt to changing market demands while minimizing the cost of adding these new services. IP networks have certainly proved to be one of the most flexible technologies ever created and should remain so because of the relentless march of technology in the computer industry.

Faced with the above market forces, many service providers have decided to take a hard look at using IP as their basic technology underlying a variety of other service offerings. Not all video providers will adopt IP technology, but many will give it serious consideration.

## Video on Demand

Video on Demand (VOD) has a great deal of appeal to many consumers. The luxury of being able to sit down in front of the television and select a program or a movie and begin watching immediately is very attractive to a number of consumers. From a service provider's standpoint, implementing VOD can be very expensive and hard to justify economically. Accordingly, several different flavors of VOD have been created:

- *True VOD* is designed to give viewers the same range of functionality as they would receive from renting and playing a videotape or a DVD in their home. The viewer simply needs to order the content using a simple on-screen menu, complete the required payment, and, within a short time, the show begins. During the show, if a user wants to pause, rewind, or fast-forward the video, the VOD system would accept these commands and perform the requested functions. In many cases, viewers are permitted to view that content only during a specified time interval, say 24 hours from the initial purchase. For this kind of service to work, the VOD system must be capable of delivering a separate video stream to each viewer who is using the VOD service. A specialized video storage and playback device called a "VOD server" is responsible for creating all of the individual video streams for each user; this server must also be able to respond to commands sent by the user. As users are added to a VOD system, additional server capacity and delivery network bandwidth needs to be installed to handle system growth.
- *Near Video on Demand (NVOD)* is a close approximation of the functions of VOD, with a much simpler delivery architecture. In this system, multiple copies of a movie (or other content) are broadcast with staggered starting times over a broadband infrastructure such as a cable television system. If, for example, a 2-hour movie were being offered, with a 5-minute interval between showings, a total of 24 copies of the movie would need to be playing at all times. When a viewer orders a movie, viewing begins as soon as the next movie showing starts. In this example, the viewer would need to wait a maximum of 4 minutes and 59 seconds for the next available copy of the movie. If the viewer wanted to pause, rewind, or fast-forward the move, this would always need to happen in 5-minute steps, because these actions would be simulated by switching to a different showing of the movie. While this system may sound a little clumsy, not to mention wasteful of bandwidth, it does remove the need for the service provider to install all of the infrastructure necessary to provide a separate video stream to each user (as is required for VOD). As an added bonus, NVOD is easy to scale, meaning that additional subscribers can be added to the system without any impact on the capacity of the video network. Indeed, it is possible to have tens or even

hundreds of thousands of subscribers all using NVOD and being supplied video by a single, relatively small video source.

- *Subscription Video on Demand (SVOD)* is a variation of VOD that replaces the fee for each piece of content that is viewed with a monthly subscription fee. Thus, it becomes an "all you can view" system instead of a "pay per view" system. This can be beneficial for viewers who watch a lot of content and for providers who replace a highly variable income stream that has high marketing costs with one that has steady revenue flow. Of course, if SVOD subscribers watch significantly more content than VOD customers, the service providers will need to increase the capacity of their video servers and delivery networks.

Let's look at the architecture of a typical VOD system that uses video over IP technology, as shown in Figure 13-1. There are four main components to a VOD system. First, the content must be prepared for storage and delivery by compressing it and (usually) encrypting it on a content preparation station. A VOD server is used to store the content and to create the streams that are sent to viewers. At each viewer's location is an STB (or properly equipped PC) that receives the content, decrypts it, and generates a signal to feed the viewer's display. The STB also provides a means for viewers to order VOD services from the fourth and final element of the system shown: the

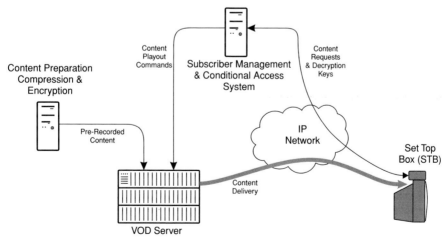

**FIGURE 13-1**  Typical VOD System Architecture

subscriber management and conditional access system. This device takes commands from viewers, sends appropriate commands to the VOD server, and delivers decryption keys to the STBs.

Content acquisition and storage are required for any type of Video on Demand service. This process involves gathering content from multiple sources and placing it onto the networks that will be used to deliver it to viewers. Sometimes, the content needs to be compressed or reformatted to be compatible with the delivery system. This process, which is sometimes known as "ingest," also needs to capture the rules for using the content, such as limits to viewing duration, permissions for downloading, etc. These rules are generally consistent within most categories of content; however, the content preparation system must be able to handle special rules that may apply only to a single content item.

The conditional access system is required to make sure that video content is delivered only to the appropriate viewers. This system needs to be linked with the subscriber management system and the order entry system. More details on conditional access can be found in Chapter 11.

At each subscriber's location, a format converter is required to convert the incoming signal format, such as DSL, into a standard local area networking format, such as Ethernet. Outputs from this device are fed to an IP-compatible set top box that is required to receive the incoming video streams and decode them for display on the viewer's television, and send the user channel selection commands upstream. For data services, typically a 10BaseT port is required on the incoming format converter. For voice services, standard 10BaseT ports can be used to support IP telephones, or a device can be used to convert standard telephony signals into IP telephony signals.

## Interactivity

Interactivity is like beauty, and very much in the eye of the beholder. Because of the many different meanings that can be assigned to this word, let's examine three different ways in which viewers can interact with their televisions. We'll begin with basic interactive functions, then look at "VCR-like" controls, and we'll end with content-oriented interactivity. Each of these terms will be defined in this section.

The most basic way that viewers interact with a television ("basic interactivity") is to turn it on and off and to select a programming channel to view. In a typical broadcast, DTH satellite, or CATV system, this is a very simple function to implement and can be completely controlled by equipment in the viewer's location, such as a TV tuner or a set top box. With the current generation of video over DSL, there is usually only enough network bandwidth to deliver one video signal for each viewer's television. This forces the channel switching function to move out of the viewer's location and into the provider's facility. The equipment required to implement this for a DSL system is a bit more complex than for a CATV system, as shown in Figure 13-2.

In this example, the viewer interacts with her digital STB. Whenever he or she wants to select a new channel, the viewer presses the appropriate command on his or her remote control. The STB takes this command and relays it to the Digital Subscriber Line Access Multiplexer (DSLAM). As soon as the DSLAM receives the command, it locates the new content and begins sending it to the viewer. This is a relatively simple process for broadcast channels where the DSLAM is already receiving the content. The switch inside the DSLAM is reconfigured to stop sending one video channel to the viewer and start sending another. Although this takes a little bit of time to accomplish, it does not take noticeably more time than switching channels on a digital satellite system.

The next higher level of interactivity, "VCR-like," occurs when viewers are given the same set of controls that they would have if they were operating their own personal video cassette recorder—that is, start, stop, pause, rewind, and fast-forward. Implementing these functions puts a much higher burden on the video delivery system,

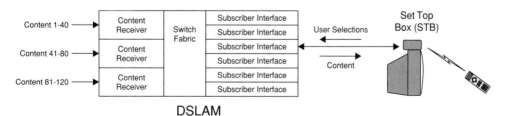

DSLAM

**FIGURE 13-2**   Example of a DSL Video Delivery System

because each viewer needs to be supplied with a video stream that is unique to him or her and completely under his or her control. There are a number of ways to achieve this functionality, as we discussed in the previous section on VOD. One thing that must be recognized is that the amount of bandwidth needed to serve multiple viewers for VOD increases as the number of viewers increases. That is, as more subscribers are added to a DSLAM, chances are more video bandwidth will be needed to feed the DSLAM.

"Content-oriented interactivity" occurs when users are given the ability to respond directly to the content itself. One example of this would be responding to an advertisement by requesting more information or possibly even placing an order for a product directly through a web interface on the television (a dream of many infomercial vendors). Another example would be influencing the outcome of a video program, such as voting for the winner of a talent contest during a live broadcast and then seeing the results of the voting during the broadcast. Note that for live content, the servers used for VOD do not come into play, because the content must be distributed from the source directly to viewers without being stored on servers. Instead, a mechanism must be provided to transmit the viewers' commands or choices back to the origin of the broadcast. In the case of pre-recorded content with different program branches that are selected by the viewer (similar to DVDs with alternate endings), the VOD server can simply treat each branch of the content as a separate piece of content that can be selected by the viewer, and the interactivity flows would terminate at the server.

The impact of these different levels of interactivity is shown in Figure 13-3. This diagram shows the data flows that occur in an IP video over DSL system under each of the preceding scenarios. For basic interactivity, the data flow starts at the user's remote control, passes through the set top box, and then moves to the DSLAM, where it terminates. For "VCR-like" user control, the data starts out the same way but ends up passing through the DSLAM to video servers that are located further upstream. With content interaction, the viewer responses are sent even further upstream, to the content provider. It is possible that all these different data flows will need to be accommodated in a single video delivery system, as individual subscribers may choose different levels of interactivity.

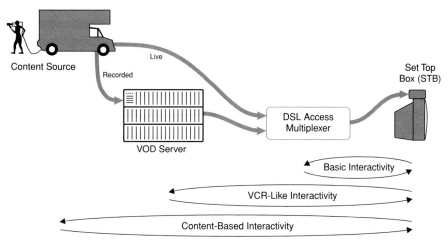

**FIGURE 13-3**  Interactivity Data Flows

Two notes on video servers: First, there are ongoing debates about whether large, centralized servers are better than small, distributed servers. Proponents of large servers point out the low cost of IP transport and the ease of maintenance and lower cost per stream of big servers. Proponents of smaller servers point out the low upfront costs of smaller servers and the greater survivability of the more widely dispersed set of servers. Second, servers are typically sized in terms of number of simultaneous streams that can be provided, rather than the amount of content storage that the servers can provide. A VOD server's performance is typically limited by the amount of processing power that is available to create all of the individual video streams, not by the amount of storage. We will discuss server technology in more detail later in this chapter.

## Operations Support Systems

Profitable delivery of video services to the home requires much more than a high-reliability hardware platform. A great deal of software is also required for managing a huge array of tasks, from informing customers about the programming that is available on the different broadcast channels to capturing the data needed to bill subscribers for the services they have purchased. Collectively, these software systems are known as Operations Support Systems (OSS), and they can take many forms. Table 13-1 lists many of the key functions that are provided by IPTV OSS systems.

OSS systems can be a major portion of the investment for an IPTV service provider, in terms of both time and money. Because of the wide variety of functions that can be provided, it is likely that software will need to be purchased from multiple vendors to implement the full range of functions selected by the provider. Integrating these systems can take months of time, much of which needs to be completed before large numbers of subscribers can be serviced. Furthermore, these expenses are essentially fixed costs whether the service attracts 1000 or 100,000 subscribers. As such, the costs of installing OSS systems

**TABLE 13-1**

Key OSS Functions for IPTV Systems

- An *electronic program guide* gives viewers a list of the available programming on each broadcast channel and also lists the content that is available for viewers to order for VOD services. This guide can be either a simple broadcast channel that scrolls through all the program choices every minute or so, or it can be interactive. Interactive program guides allow the user to navigate through the listings, possibly to look at programming that is scheduled in the future. One significant challenge for network operators is to gather and manage the descriptions and schedules for the programming on all of the different channels that they broadcast. As a result, outside companies (such as *TV Guide* in the USA) have taken on the role of supplying program guide data to video network operators.
- An *order entry* system is required when customers are permitted to purchase content (or other items and services) through the IPTV system. This system needs to be able to verify that the customer's account information is valid and that the order can be filled as requested. This system needs to connect to the subscriber billing system and may also need to connect to external services for credit card validation, etc. A secure (encrypted) link is required to customer homes when personal data is being collected. This system may also need to be connected to the interactive program guide if viewers can place orders directly using their STB.
- *On-line content access* (e-mail, web surfing) is provided by some IPTV systems, allowing viewers to use their television sets for functions that might otherwise require a PC.
- *Internet access,* in which a home PC is connected to the DSL system, is widely available. These connections need to be managed to ensure that adequate bandwidth is provided to each customer and that suitable connections are provided to the Internet in order to provide acceptable response times to users.
- A *subscriber management and billing system* maintains crucial data about each subscriber to a system, including contact and billing details, account status, and equipment identifiers. Many of the other OSS components will refer to this data to obtain information needed to authorize new services, deliver video streams, and so on. Customer service personnel will likely also be heavy users of this system as they support subscribers who move, upgrade, or downgrade their services; add or remove televisions; and require repair services.

need to be carefully considered in a service provider's business plan, recognizing that in the early stages of deployment, these costs can exceed the costs of the system hardware for low subscriber counts.

One other factor to keep in mind is the cost of maintaining the integrity of the data in the OSS databases. Clearly, it is essential to keep up with the continual changes that occur in programming schedules in order to have an effective electronic program guide. Similarly, maintaining an accurate subscriber database, as customers add or remove services, move apartments, break equipment, etc., is important to maintaining a high level of customer service. In addition, changes made by the service provider, such as adding new equipment or launching a special marketing program, need to be tracked in the OSS. Human input will be required for most of these modifications to the database, and the service provider will need to hire and pay staff to make these data entries. These database maintenance costs should not be overlooked when developing a business model for an IPTV system.

## IPTV DELIVERY NETWORKS

A wide variety of networks are used in delivering IPTV. There are the basic delivery mechanisms, such as DSL, Passive Optical Networks (PONs), and traditional cable TV lines. In addition, traditional high-speed data networks connecting offices and homes can be used for applications with widely dispersed viewers. We'll take a closer look at all of these network technologies in the following sections.

### Digital Subscriber Lines (DSL)

DSL technology was discussed in some detail in Chapter 1, so we won't repeat that discussion here. Instead, we'll look at how IPTV systems are implemented over DSL circuits.

Current generation DSL technologies, such as Asymmetric Digital Subscriber Line (ADSL), provide relatively limited amounts of bandwidth from the service provider to the consumer, and even more restricted links from the consumer back to the provider (hence the "Asymmetrical" element of the acronym ADSL). With current

MPEG–2 processing technology, it is difficult to produce good-quality standard definition video and audio streams with a combined bit rate less than 2.5 Mbps. To keep overall speeds reasonable, and to allow for other services (such as Internet access) on the ADSL link, it is normal to find only one, or at most two, video signals on a single ADSL circuit. High definition video, which requires at least 10–12 Mbps with MPEG–2 technology, is out of the question for ADSL deployment.

VDSL technology (Very high-speed Digital Subscriber Line) supports significantly more bandwidth on each subscriber line. Accordingly, more video channels can be transmitted to each VDSL subscriber, with three or four simultaneous videos possible. High definition video signals could also be transmitted (possibly multiple ones) if the VDSL speed permits. One drawback to VDSL is that the range of operational distances is less than that of ADSL, so subscribers need to be closer to the service provider facilities. Also note that the speed of DSL services varies with distance, so good planning for varying data rates is essential.

Each television set that receives IPTV signals over DSL requires an STB to decode the incoming video. (Although, televisions with an RJ-45 Ethernet connector and built-in MPEG decoder have already started to appear on the market.) These STBs can act as the residential gateway in the home and provide connections for other voice and data communications equipment. However, it is much more common for the residential gateway to be permanently installed in a central location in each home. IP traffic from this gateway is then routed to each STB located inside the subscriber's home. Connections on this gateway are also provided for the customer's telephone and PC in many systems.

Because of DSL speed limitations, each time a viewer changes channels on the DSL IPTV system, a command must be sent back to the service provider to command that a new video stream needs to be delivered. This can take the form of a multicast leave command followed by a join command, provided that the DSL Access Multiplexer supports IP multicasting. If it doesn't, then a unicast stream needs to be created by one of the servers or switches in the service provider's system. Also, when a user orders a true VOD service a stream needs to be delivered the entire distance from the server providing the content to the subscriber's STB.

## Passive Optical Networks (PONs)

Passive Optical Networks, or PONs, are all-optical networks with no active components between the service provider and the customer. PON technology is reaching price levels at which service providers can begin to think about deploying Fiber To The Home (FTTH, also known as Fiber To The Premises, or FTTP) as an economical alternative for new construction. As costs continue to drop, and if service providers can achieve good take rates, it will even make sense to replace aging copper local loops with FTTH systems. Since we talked about PON technology in Chapter 1, we won't repeat that information here. Instead, we'll look at how IPTV systems can be implemented over PON systems.

To begin with, it is important to realize that the G.983 technology that we discussed in Chapter 1 does not specify how video traffic is to be carried on a PON system. In particular, the system we discussed that used a separate wavelength for carrying an analog broadband signal (CATV-like) for broadcast video distribution to a cable-ready television in the home is not required. It is perfectly acceptable to use IPTV technology for distributing one or more video signals to a home using the data portion of a PON. When used in this manner, the IPTV system will look very much like the IPTV system we discussed for DSL: Individual channels will be requested by the viewer at each STB, and the service provider's IP network will deliver the requested video channels.

Another alternative is a hybrid system. In this system, broadcast channels are delivered by one wavelength of light in the PON system, and the VOD and other user-specific video channels are delivered using the data transport paths. This means that the analog broadband signal can be distributed to all viewers, and televisions that are not going to be used for IPTV services would not require an STB. A potential drawback to this system is the requirement for the STB to be able to handle both broadband video and IPTV, which may increase the complexity of the STB somewhat. The STB would need to determine if a requested channel was going to be present on the broadband broadcast signal or if a stream needed to be requested over the IPTV system. One advantage of this type of a hybrid system is that the IPTV equipment at the central location could be scaled back in capacity, since it is unlikely that all viewers would be watching the user-specific services provided by the IPTV system at the same time. Based on studies of US television viewing habits, no more than 5% of the total subscriber population views interactive or premium programming at any given time.

## IPTV Over Cable

Traditional cable television (CATV) networks have excelled in the delivery of hundreds of channels of video content simultaneously to thousands of users. Each user could select any one of the broadcast channels that was available, simply by tuning a television or STB to the correct channel. These systems were easy to scale; adding new customers simply required splitting and amplifying the signal to reach more households. Interactivity was extremely limited or not available at all, since all the content was sent in one direction only—to the viewer.

As new competition has entered the business of video delivery to the home, this business model has come under attack. On one hand, consumers are demanding more control of what they view and when they view it, and many also want a triple-play provider. On the other hand, competing service providers have introduced interactive television systems that fulfill many of these customer desires. Increasingly, CATV providers have begun to look at how to provide more advanced video delivery systems and ones that allow them to offer triple-play video, voice, and data services.

IP technology is a natural platform for converging these different services. Clearly, IP transport is a natural for data traffic, such as Internet access. For voice, IP telephony has made great technical strides and has already begun to establish a significant presence in the market. This leaves video services, which have traditionally been delivered to CATV consumers using broadband, broadcast technology, which does not lend itself to individual control by each viewer. To offer advanced services, CATV providers have developed a range of technologies that involve specially designed STBs and video servers that create digital video streams that are customized for each viewer. However, some industry suppliers have proposed an alternative solution: using IPTV over a standard CATV plant.

To make this operate, it is necessary to transmit IP data packets over the cable network. To do this, special digital modulation schemes with acronyms like QAM (Quadrature Amplitude Modulation), OFDM (Orthogonal Frequency Division Modulation), and VSB (Vestigial SideBand) are used. The specific meaning of these terms is not important, since they all describe complicated mathematical formulas that allow a large number of bits to be transmitted in a given frequency band. What is important is the capacity of the cable—on the order of 35–40 Mbps in place of every 6 MHz analog video channel. This is quite attractive; if an average digital video stream operates at 2.5 Mbps (including overhead), the system can carry 15 digital video channels (for a total of 37.5 Mbps) in place of a single analog video channel. Since CATV systems typically provide in excess of 100 analog video channels, use of digital technology would permit 1500 digital video channels to be transmitted. If IPTV was being used for each of those channels, then 1500 individual viewers could be supported. Since not all televisions are likely to be on simultaneously, this would be enough capacity to serve well in excess of 1000 homes, even if each home had more than one television.

## Shared Data Networks

In order to deliver IPTV services to widely dispersed viewers for narrowcasting and corporate video applications, it is not normally economical to construct special-purpose networks, such as DSL or CATV. Instead, it is common practice to share existing broadband IP networks to reach these viewers. These networks can take many forms, such as corporate networks or the public Internet, or as part of a standard ISP's offerings. To ensure success, several factors need to be considered, including bandwidth requirements from source to destination, multicasting capability of the network, and supported interactivity levels. Let's look at each of these factors in more detail.

Adequate bandwidth is a key requirement for any type of video delivery system. This bandwidth needs to be available over the entire path from the video source to each destination. The amount of bandwidth required at each point in the network depends on the number and size of the video streams that pass through that point. This calculation can be difficult, particularly for corporate networks where large clusters of potential viewers are interconnected by limited bandwidth backbone links. Public Internet connections can also be used but have unpredictable performance. For an IPTV system to work properly, each segment of the network must have enough capacity to handle the total bandwidth of all the simultaneous video streams passing over that segment.

Multicasting (as discussed in Chapter 9) is one way to reduce the amount of bandwidth needed to deliver IPTV services on a private network. If the network is multicast enabled, users who are viewing the identical content can share one video stream from the source to the point where the paths to the viewers diverge. For this to work, all of the users who share one stream will need to view the same content at the same time, thereby effectively preventing the use of VCR-like interactive playback controls.

Any use of VCR-like interactivity in IPTV systems implemented over shared networks needs to be planned very carefully. As we just discussed, it is not feasible in multicast configurations. Interactivity places two burdens on a network. First, a path must be provided for the interactive control signals to travel from the viewer back to the IPTV source. (This is not normally a problem for shared data networks but can be difficult for certain network topologies.) Second, the amount of two-way data transit delay between the video sources and the viewers needs to be controlled so that user commands (say to play, pause, or rewind) can be processed promptly. This can be an issue for Internet-based systems, as well as some other architectures.

Overall, it is quite feasible to implement IPTV services on a variety of different shared networks. A number of active implementations are in service today. The key to a successful IPTV deployment is ensuring that adequate capacity is available to service the peak number of simultaneous viewers, both in terms of video server capability and network capacity.

## TECHNOLOGIES FOR IPTV

Various technologies are required to implement a practical IPTV system. Many are common to other video over IP technologies discussed elsewhere in this book; however, several are used primarily for IPTV applications. In the following sections we'll begin with a description of the systems that are used to prepare incoming content for IPTV distribution. We'll follow this with a deeper look at video servers. Then, we'll conclude with a look at Multimedia Home Platform (MHP) and OpenCable Application Platform (OCAP), which are key technologies that support subscriber interactivity and the OSS functions required by service providers.

## Content Processing

The role of making content ready for immediate broadcast over an IPTV system falls to content processing systems. These devices accept real-time video signals from a wide variety of sources and make them suitable for transport over an IPTV system. The primary function of a content processor is to take incoming video signals and shape them into a consistent format so that the customer STBs can decode the signals and display them on the viewers' televisions. This process involves several functions, as described in Table 13-2.

Content processing can be performed on either a live stream, such as a live news or sporting event, or it can be done on content that is to be stored inside a video server for later playback. When content processing is done on a live stream that is already in a digital format, the process is called "digital turnaround." This would be used, for example, on news programming that was sent directly out to subscribers. When this process is performed on real-time content that is to be stored on a server before it is delivered to viewers, it is called "ingest." This process might be used, for example, to take a live video signal and store it for later viewing by subscribers as a form of VOD. Sometimes, ingest occurs on live video streams, but normally, ingest is done off-line with video content that has been delivered on tape or disk by content suppliers.

## Video Servers

Video servers are essential to any VOD system, because they create the actual video streams that are sent out to each viewer. These servers can range in size from very large to fairly small, and can be

**TABLE 13-2**

Content Processor Functions

- *Compression:* For analog video sources, digital compression is performed on each video signal before it can be transmitted on an IPTV system. Normally, this process involves feeding the video signal through some form of MPEG compression system. The compression parameters are strictly controlled to make sure that the resulting digital video stream will be compatible with the rest of the network. Items such as peak video data rate and packet length are made consistent between all of the different video sources to simplify the job of the transport and multiplexing functions. In this step, a unique program identifier is also added to each video stream so that the packets can be correctly identified later and delivered to the appropriate viewers.
- *Transcoding:* For video sources that are already in a digital format, it is sometimes necessary to convert them into the format that will be used by the IPTV system. This is done for a number of reasons, such as changing the MPEG profile or level of the incoming stream to one that is compatible with the STBs. Another possible conversion is to change from MPEG–2 to another format, such as MPEG–4.
- *Transrating:* Essentially, transrating is the process of changing the bit rate of an incoming digital video stream, generally in order to reduce the bit rate. This process is needed to take a digital video feed that may be operating at 4.5 Mbps and reducing it to, say, 2.5 Mbps for use in the IPTV system.
- *Program Identification:* Each video stream needs to be uniquely labeled within the IPTV system so that multiplexing devices and user STBs can locate the correct streams. Each audio or video program within each MPEG transport stream (using the PID mechanism discussed in Chapter 6) must be processed to ensure that all of the packets contain the correct label. Note that this label may change whenever a transport stream is broken apart or combined with other streams, and that these labels will change from system to system.

used for a variety of applications. In this section, we'll look at some of the different aspects of servers and how they are used for delivering content.

The role of a video server is to store content and to stream it out to viewer devices. The amount of storage can be large or small, and the number of streams supported can be large or small. These are not correlated; it is perfectly sensible to have a server with lots of storage and little streaming capacity, if it is being used to hold video content that is only rarely viewed. Conversely, it is also sensible to have a server with relatively little storage (say, 50–100 hours of video content) but very high stream capacity if it is being used to serve first-run Hollywood movies to many viewers simultaneously.

Many varieties of video servers are available. When you are purchasing a server, it is important to match the capabilities of the server to the task that needs to be performed. Video servers can be broken roughly into three categories, as follows:

- Production servers are used to store content for businesses that are engaged in the video production business, such as television networks and post-production houses. For these customers, a video server needs to handle a great deal of content, in a variety of formats, and rapidly deliver files containing the content to user workstations when it is needed. These servers typically do very little, if any, streaming. Instead, the focus on these devices is large capacity and good support for content searching, including tools that support the use of "meta-data" that describes the content. This is particularly important because of the need to track multiple versions of files as content moves through the production process.

- Personal and corporate servers are used in environments where a relatively few streams need to be delivered simultaneously, and the total amount of content is relatively low. One application for this would be a video server that was maintained by the training department of a medium-sized corporation, which would have a few dozen titles and usually no more than 5–10 simultaneous viewers. This class of server can be built with off-the-shelf hardware components and can possibly be implemented on a standard PC chassis with specialized software.

- Service providers need an entirely different class of video servers, which are capable of storing possibly thousands of hours of content and delivering video streams to hundreds or thousands of simultaneous viewers. For this application class, specially designed servers are required. These units typically have the capability to spread content across a large number of disk drives and to use multiple processors in parallel to format streams and deliver the content. The capacity of these systems is truly staggering; in order to supply 1000 simultaneous users each with a 2.5 Mbps stream, the server needs to be able to pump out 2.5 Gigabits of data every second. Since no single disk drive or processor in a typical server is capable of this amount of data, servers use load sharing among the devices. This means that each piece of content is spread out across multiple disk drives and that a high-speed backplane interconnects the different drives to the different processors.

One important constraint on a streaming video delivery system, such as IPTV, is that end-user devices (STBs) must be assumed to have a precisely defined amount of incoming signal buffer that they can use. If too much data is sent (causing a buffer overflow) or too little (causing an underflow), the video signal to the viewer will be interrupted. To prevent this, the video server is required to deliver a stream that will continuously arrive at the viewer's device at a rate that won't corrupt the buffer. Note that this is true whether we are talking about a single stream from one desktop PC to another or a home delivery system that sends hundreds of streams to STBs. This constraint dictates that streaming server hardware and software must be carefully designed to create streams that are well behaved.

Two main philosophies are used by service providers for server distribution in their networks, as shown in Figure 13-4. The first is centralized, where large, high-capacity servers are installed in central locations, and the streams for each viewer are delivered over high-speed communications links to each local service provider facility. The second is decentralized, where smaller servers are located at each facility and provide streams only to local viewers. A central library server provides content to the distributed servers whenever necessary. On one hand, the decentralized concept makes sense because it helps to reduce the amount of bandwidth needed between locations.

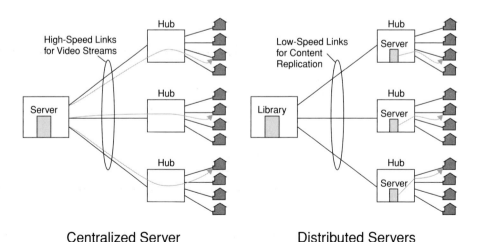

Centralized Server                    Distributed Servers

**FIGURE 13-4**  Centralized vs. Decentralized Video Servers

On the other hand, the centralized concept makes sense because it reduces the number of servers that must be installed and reduces the costs of transporting and storing copies of the content in each of the different locations. Overall, both centralized and decentralized systems are used in practice, depending on system architecture, capabilities, and user viewing habits that affect VOD traffic patterns.

## MHP and OCAP

MHP, which stands for Multimedia Home Platform, and OCAP, which stands for OpenCable Application Platform, are both software interface standards that have been developed for STBs. The Digital Video Broadcasting (DVB) Project based in Europe developed MHP, and CableLabs, a joint research and development group formed by members of the CATV industry in the USA, developed OCAP. To a great extent, OCAP is based on MHP. Both are open standards, which means they can be adopted by a variety of companies (although some license fees may need to be paid for intellectual property). Now, let's talk about why MHP and OCAP are important.

MHP functions as a standardized interface for "middleware." It provides a common interface between software applications and lower level software, such as operating systems and device drivers. It does not provide user interfaces, but it does provide a platform that user interfaces can be built upon. It is not an operating system; it defines a standard way that applications can access services provided by an operating system.

To understand why middleware is important, refer back to earlier in this chapter where we discussed the tremendous amount of operations support system (OSS) software needed to run a modern IPTV system. There are many vendors who have developed or who are developing STBs and other devices that need to interface with each provider's OSS. There are also a variety of IPTV system providers who are reluctant to develop specialized software that will run only on one vendor's STB equipment, since that vendor could possibly go out of business or no longer offer favorable pricing. Similarly, consumers would be reluctant to purchase a device such as an STB or a digital-cable ready TV unless they had confidence that the device could be used with their new CATV provider if they move to a new location. (This is one of the main goals of the OpenCable effort, and is being encouraged by the US government.) Finally, there are a number of software developers who would like to be able to create software for interactive TV without having to customize it for every different type of STB that arrives on the market. Taken together, all of these forces are a powerful incentive for hardware manufacturers, software developers, and IPTV system operators to agree on and implement the MHP and OCAP standards.

Table 13-3 defines some of the applications that MHP was designed to support. Table 13-4 defines some of the system resources inside an MHP device that applications can use to provide their intended functions.

Use of MHP greatly simplifies the task of application designers, by giving them a uniform platform to build upon. Once an application has been designed and tested to run on MHP, it should be able to run on MHP that is implemented on any of a variety of STBs from different manufacturers. This capability helps provide a greater market for these applications than what would be available if the application was tied to the products of a single STB vendor.

MHP also simplifies the tasks of STB vendors, because it allows them to deploy applications written by third parties. This can help reduce the software development costs for a new STB and allow products to reach the market more quickly.

Overall, MHP is designed to be a common interface for user interactivity applications and STBs, and it seems to be a fairly comprehensive approach. Huge gains in economy and efficiency should be

**TABLE 13-3**

MHP Application Examples

---

- User interface for electronic program guide/interactive program guide
- Home shopping
- Access to broadcast information services—news, weather, financial information (super teletext)
- Video games
- Applications synchronized to video content, such as sports scores, play-along games, audience voting/feedback
- Secure transactions—home banking

---

**TABLE 13-4**

Examples of Resources Available to MHP Applications

- Java virtual machine scripting
- MPEG stream control
- Text and graphics screen overlays
- Video and audio clip playback
- Program selector/tuner
- Communication protocols (e.g., TCP, UDP)
- Conditional access and encryption
- User mouse/keyboard/infrared remote control access
- Media storage and playback controls
- Internet access

possible if this standard is widely adopted, and a vigorous market for both applications and advance STBs should be a logical consequence of the use of this standard. Perhaps the only drawback to this standard is the need for a fairly powerful processor and a fair amount of memory to implement these functions in a low-cost STB. However, processors only get faster, and memory only gets cheaper. In the long run, anything like MHP or OCAP that can help drive software costs lower and provide truly open interfaces is good for service providers and, ultimately, consumers.

## DIGITAL SUBSCRIBER LINE VIDEO CASE STUDY

Now that we have discussed many of the technologies used in video over IP delivery to the home, let's look at an actual case study of a successful system. Kaplan Telephone is a local service provider located in south central Louisiana that has a long tradition of providing standard telephone service to a local area. When Kaplan made the decision to offer video services to its customers, DSL technology was selected. For established telephone companies, this is often the most economical choice, since it eliminates the need to build a second network based on fiber optic or coaxial cable technology to deliver video alongside the existing twisted pair network. This also helps reduce the upfront capital expense, because subscriber equipment in the home and the central office needs to be installed only as subscribers actually purchase service. Also, because DSL can provide data services alongside traditional subscriber line voice services, Kaplan can provide a full "triple play" of consumer services.

Kaplan selected Tut Systems of Lake Oswego, Oregon to provide the digital video head end for the DSL system. All video signals need to be converted into digital form because it is the only means of delivering video service over a digital subscriber line (DSL); analog video services simply won't flow over the twisted pairs connected to each household. IP video packet transport was chosen because of the simplicity of combining video and data services on the same distribution network.

The Astria® Content Processor is an integrated system that provides all of the necessary signal processing functions for a digital head end. This system is illustrated in Figure 13-5. To understand

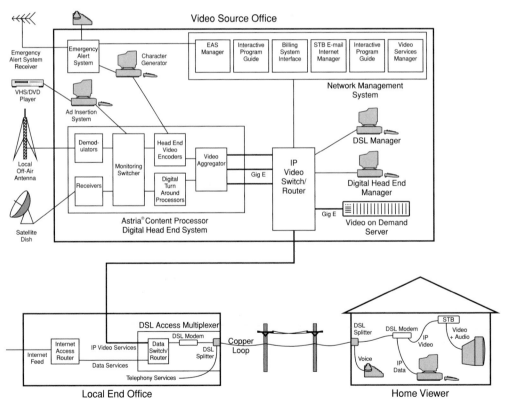

**FIGURE 13-5**  DSL Video System Example

these functions, let's look at how the different incoming signals are processed.

- Satellite signals normally arrive in digital format, often scrambled or encrypted to prevent unauthorized reception. Analog signals are still sometime used on satellites, but they are becoming increasingly rare. The satellite receiver is responsible for processing the signals from the satellite dish, which are normally in the form of high-frequency digitally modulated RF signals containing pre-encoded MPEG–2 signals delivered in a multi-program transport stream. The satellite receiver can either output this stream in DVB-ASI format or convert one or more programs into baseband digital or analog video signals. Receiver processing may include descrambling or decrypting the video signals.
- Local off-air video signals normally arrive as analog signals (at least for standard definition video), but they may also be broadcast in digital television format (particularly in the case of HD signals, but also increasingly for SD signals). The demodulator is responsible for taking the broadcast video signal and converting it into either a baseband analog or digital video signal.
- In many cases, local video service providers such as Kaplan are permitted to insert commercials into certain television channels at certain times. These local ad spots can come from a variety of sources; videotapes, DVDs, file transfers, etc. The spots are stored on a server, ready to play whenever they are required. The output of the server is fed into a monitoring switcher, where the commercials can be spliced into the video program streams as needed. Increasingly, digital ad splicing is being utilized that keeps both the primary stream and the ad content in the compressed domain.
- A legal requirement in the USA is the broadcast of Emergency Alert System (EAS) signals; similar requirements are present in many other countries. The EAS provides information to television viewers regarding severe weather events and other emergency situations. EAS signals are broadcast by official government agencies; local television providers are required to broadcast the EAS signals on the television channels that they are distributing. Many times, the EAS messages are text based and inserted into the bottom portion of the video screen. Suitable messages are created inside the character generator, and fed into

the MPEG encoders for the broadcast video channels. A recent extension of the EAS system has been able to incorporate the AMBER alert for missing children.

Inside the Astria® Content Processor based head end, a number of different functional blocks can be observed. On the input side, demodulators and receivers are used to convert incoming signals from their native format (RF television or satellite signals with various modulation schemes) into video signals that can be processed. These signals are fed into a monitoring switcher that allows local advertisements to be switched or digitally spliced into selected video streams and provides a method for personnel to tap into video streams as needed to observe their performance. Some of the signals flowing out of the monitoring switcher are baseband video; these signals need to be digitized and compressed by the head end video encoders. Other signals that flow out of the monitoring switcher are in digital format (DVB-ASI); they may need to be processed to make sure that they are digitally compatible with the DSL distribution network, by, for example, reducing their bit rate (transrating) to fit within system limits, or converting the content to a new compression format (transcoding). This latter process, called "digital turn around," is performed by specialized head end video stream processors. The final function is called video aggregation, in which many different video streams are multiplexed into large-capacity (Gigabit Ethernet) outputs. These signals flow out to the various DSL Access Multiplexers around the Kaplan network by way of high-speed switches/routers and a Gigabit Ethernet distribution network.

The main Operations Support System (OSS) for the Kaplan system covers a variety of functions, including the Emergency Alert System, the various video services offered to subscribers, the data interface to the subscriber billing system, the e-mail/Internet access system for subscriber set top boxes, and the interactive program guide. A separate system is used to manage the DSL hardware, and yet another to manage the Astria® Content Processor.

One point to keep in mind when reviewing the Kaplan system is the variety of different functions that must be accomplished, some of which are mandated by government regulations (such as the EAS) and others that are driven by economic realities (such as local ad insertion).

For an IPTV system to work properly and create an operating profit for the system owner, these various functions need to be efficiently and cost effectively delivered by the system provider(s). System owners need to consider not only the costs of the individual components, but also the costs associated with integrating all the components to form a working combined network. This is in addition to the costs of purchasing the rights to content and the costs of preparing the content for distribution. Typically, the costs of acquiring and installing all of the necessary hardware and software components can be substantial; these costs need to be amortized over a number of years with a substantial number of paying subscribers before economic breakeven can be reached. Modeling these cash flows can be tricky; however, it is an essential part of IPTV system planning.

## REVIEW AND CHECKLIST UPDATE

In this chapter, we covered IPTV services to the home. We began by looking at some of the market forces that are making a business out of this technology. We discussed Video on Demand (VOD) and some if its various flavors. Then, we examined the functions of the Operations Support Systems (OSS) that are crucial to large-scale deployment of any kind of video to the home system. A few applications were described, and we explored some of the key technologies for IPTV, including DSL, PON, and CATV transport; content processors; video servers; and the innovative middleware technology known as MHP and OCAP. Finally, we investigated a typical installation in detail.

### Chapter 13 Checklist Update

❑ Develop a business plan prior to deploying IPTV to the home. Make sure to include capital expenditures (hardware and software), installation costs, programming costs, and ongoing maintenance and customer support costs.

❑ Determine the level of viewer interactivity that will be supported.

❑ Determine how live content will be delivered to viewers. If digital turnaround will be used, determine the format of the incoming digital signals.

❏ Consider how this might change in coming years as HD content becomes more widespread and as content owners change their requirements.

❏ If Video on Demand is to be used, consider the following issues:

❏ Select a method for delivering VOD services: NVOD, pay-per-view VOD, or Subscription VOD. Make sure that systems are in place to support these functions if they are basic, "VCR-like," or content interactive.

❏ For large installations, select a video server deployment strategy: centralized, distributed, or a blend of the two.

❏ Calculate the total number of hours of programming that will need to be stored on each server, and ensure that adequate storage capacity is purchased.

❏ Determine how many simultaneous streams each server must deliver, and ensure that each server purchased has enough stream processing capacity.

❏ Make sure an ingest system is available to get pre-recorded content from a variety of sources onto the video servers.

❏ Select a supplier of electronic program guide data.

❏ For user software platforms (STBs and the systems that support them), consider using open standard middleware, such as MHP or OCAP.

# 14

## VIDEO FILE TRANSFER

Video file transfer is the process of transporting video and other content as data files, instead of as video streams. Commonly used during the production process, file transfer is similar to the process used daily by many IP network users when they send documents attached to e-mails. However, due to the extremely large size of many video content files, normal methods for file transfer (such as e-mail) won't work. In this chapter, we will discuss the specialized techniques that have been developed to transport large video files over IP networks.

## OVERVIEW

Some of the largest data files sent over IP networks today are those that contain video content. This is no accident; the sheer amount of data that is needed to faithfully reproduce a high-quality video image is much greater than the amount of data in voice conversations or even in graphic-intensive web pages. Even when video content is highly compressed, the amount of data needed to represent an image on the viewer's display that changes 25 or 30 times each second occupies megabytes of disk space for every minute of video.

Video content files even for routine video production can be very large indeed.[1] A simple uncompressed Standard Definition video file can occupy 2 Gigabytes of disk space for every minute of footage. When high definition video is being used, uncompressed video occupies over 11 Gigabytes of storage for each minute. Data files for movie production are even larger; 40 or 50 Gigabytes of data per minute of video are not unheard of, because movies are typically processed at resolutions much higher than HD television.

These large file sizes pose a problem for standard IP file transfer mechanisms. One commonly used data protocol (TCP) used on IP networks sends a few blocks of data and then waits for an acknowledgment before sending more data. In situations with long network delays, or with very large files, the total amount of waiting time can add up quickly. This has the effect of exponentially increasing the amount of time that it takes to transfer large files. For some applications, on certain types of networks, transfer times can be measured in terms of hours, if not days.

In order to overcome these problems, there are essentially two choices: change the devices at the ends of the network or change the network itself. One popular end-device technique involves temporarily storing (or "caching") the data inside a special device that then sends the data file out over a network connection with limited bandwidth. A network-based technique involves altering the protocols that are normally used to transmit data files so that they will operate more efficiently over networks with long delays. Both of these techniques can be used together, and both will be described later in this chapter.

---

1.  Note that in this chapter we will often discuss sizes of files and data transfer rates in terms of bytes, not bits. This is deliberate because data files are always measured in units of bytes.

## FILE TRANSFER APPLICATIONS

Video files are used throughout the video production and distribution industry. Because of the widespread use of digital video production and editing equipment, virtually all professionally produced video today spends at least part of its life as a file of one type or another. Table 14-1 lists some of the common uses of video files.

**TABLE 14-1**

Video File Transfer Applications

- *Video Capture:* When raw video from a camera or tape is transferred into a computer file that an editing or production system can manipulate, the process is called "video capture." Capture can be done directly from digital sources, such as digital video cameras or digital tapes. When analog video sources are used, the video signal must be digitized before it can be captured. Once the capture process is complete, the video data is stored in a computer-readable file, which can then be processed locally by the capture device or transferred to another workstation using file transfer technology.
- *Video Streaming:* Streaming servers transform video data files into live streams that are sent to users across a data network. These servers can contain a number of different content files, each of which needs to be loaded onto the server using file transfer technology. In most cases, a workstation (called an "authoring system") is used to prepare the content before it is loaded onto the hardware devices that perform the actual streaming. As a result, file transfer technology is needed to move content files from the authoring system to one or more streaming servers.
- *DVD Authoring:* As the business of producing and selling video content on DVDs has grown, a number of companies have gone into businesses that specialize in specific aspects of DVD production. Some companies specialize in converting film into digital formats, others specialize in compressing and formatting the content that will be used to create the master DVDs, and still others specialize in mass-producing finished DVDs for sale. Between each step in this process, large digital data files may need to be transferred between the different companies. Because of the large sizes of these files (finished DVDs can easily contain 9 Gigabytes or more of data) and the need to keep the content secure, special file transfer technology is required.
- *Film and Video Post Production:* As in the DVD production chain, various specialist companies have become involved in the creation of video content for broadcast and other applications. These companies range from boutiques that may be staffed with one or two specialists to large service bureaus with wide selections of equipment and talent. As a result of this diversity, and the time pressures involved with many video production projects, it is not uncommon for digital video content to be moved from one location to another several times during the production process.
- *Advertising:* Most television advertisements today are played out from files stored on specialized servers. This method is far simpler than the earlier tape-based systems that required special recording devices to prepare videotape with several hours' worth of commercials recorded in the proper sequence.

**TABLE 14-1** (*Continued*)

- *News:* Particularly in the audio realm, digital recorders and Internet file transfer have become the norm for reports from field correspondents. This trend is also taking hold in the video realm, although the larger file sizes are a challenge for many network connections in the field.
- *Download and Play:* Each day, new video content becomes available for consumers to view on their PCs or other playback devices. In many cases, this video content cannot be streamed to the viewer, because of inadequate networks between the video source and the viewers' devices. When streaming can't be used, download and play is the technology of choice, which is technically a file transfer application. For large download and play files, it is not unusual for special file transfer technology to be used. Often called a "download manager," this software provides functions including automatic recovery from interruptions, such as ones that can occur when a dial-up circuit suddenly disconnects in the middle of a download. When a broken connection is re-established, the download manager picks up the file transfer where it left off, rather than restarting the file transfer from the beginning.

Now, let's look at a couple of these applications in more detail.

## Post Production

Since the video production industry employs a great number of large video files that need to be transferred within a facility or from one facility to another, it makes sense for us to discuss the demands of this industry in more detail. For most of this book, we have been talking about delivering video in finished form: an edited product complete with a sound track, special effects, titles, and closing credits. To produce this final product, many hours typically go into scripting, filming, editing, and generating the final content. During the production process, a number of people with different talents and a wide variety of specialized equipment can all be called upon to work on a single project. This process can be thought of in terms of a chain, where each link is one task that needs to be completed to convert the raw video content into a finished product. This process is called Post Production because it occurs after the filming process but before distribution of the final product.

For a number of years, there was only one way to move content through the production chain: videotape transfers. After each step in the production process, a videotape of the result of that step was created that would be passed along to the next step. Due to the inevitable video quality losses during this process (caused in part by the conversion into and out of popular analog and digital tape formats), the number of steps had to be limited, so as to keep the quality of the finished product as high as possible. If different steps of production were done in different facilities, then videotapes had to be physically transported from one location to another, typically by use of a courier service.

As the technology of digital production progressed, many (if not all) of the production steps moved from specialized equipment to general-purpose workstations. Of course, these workstations have many special features, including high-quality input/output devices (pen tablets, video displays, etc.), huge amounts of disk storage and memory, and specialized video production software. Due to the costs of these workstations, the software that runs on them, and the talented person to operate them, production fees can easily run hundreds of dollars per hour on these machines. Because of these costs, and because of the proliferation of independent production companies, the need to rapidly and cost effectively move video content from one production step to the next has never been greater.

Fortunately, because most video production today is based on digital files, a solution is available: high-speed digital networks. With these networks, video files can be transferred directly from one workstation to the next with high quality and low cost. When the workstations are located inside a single facility, high-speed LANs operating at 100 Mbps or 1 Gbps can be used to transfer even the largest files in a matter of seconds or at most a few minutes. These networks are relatively low cost: Workstations can be equipped with Gigabit Ethernet LAN interface cards for less than $100 per workstation using today's technology.

When video content files need to be transferred between facilities, different economic trade-offs come into play. With these networks, even a common 1.5 Mbps T1 circuit is likely to cost a few hundred dollars per month for local service within a well-served metropolitan area, and more than that for long-distance and international service. Many of these networks are leased on a long-term basis, so the network is always on, whether or not data is being sent. Higher speed networks, operating at say 45 or 155 Mbps, are even more expensive. Even today, it is not uncommon, due to high costs for bandwidth, for files to be recorded onto digital tape and transferred using express delivery services.

Because of the costs involved, networks between facilities are commonly shared for multiple applications, including voice traffic, routine data traffic (e-mail, etc.), and video file transfer. This can mean that all of the bandwidth on the link is not available for video file transfer. Also, the bandwidth on these links has a relatively low upper limit, so even if there is a big file to transfer, the size of the data pipe can't be increased. Hence, for successful file transport, it is necessary to transmit the file out slowly enough to fit within the bandwidth that is available, so the devices that are used to provide this function need to be carefully configured.

## Advertising

Advertising is the lifeblood of many video broadcasting businesses, whether they are national or local in scope. Advertising funds many different types of programming, from sports to news to entertainment. Advertisers can choose to have individual 30- or 60-second advertising "spots" broadcast on specific programs on specific channels at specific times to specific audiences. Spots can be aired nationwide or to very specific viewing audiences, including specific neighborhoods in a city.

File transfer can play a major role in both the creation and delivery of advertising spots. During the creation process, advertisements can benefit from file transfer technology, which can be very useful for delivering approval copies of spots to advertising agency clients in order to cut down or eliminate the need to send videotapes out for review. During the delivery process, file transfer can be used to move spots to the locations where they will be needed for broadcast.

Many times, video file servers are used to play advertising spots each time they are needed during a broadcast. These servers can be located at a television network's main facility for ads that will play to all of the network's viewers, or servers can be located at different broadcast stations or cable television head ends to play ads that will be seen only in a specific region. File transfer is often used to deliver the appropriate spots to each of these servers in advance of the time that they will be broadcast. Sometimes, the transfer is done in parallel, where each file is delivered to many servers simultaneously using a multicast network (such as a satellite). Other times, the transfer is done individually for each server, using the technologies we will be discussing in the following section.

## FILE TRANSFER TECHNOLOGY

In order for file transfer to work properly between facilities, several technologies are used. Two of the more prevalent technologies are local caching and response spoofing. We'll look at how both of these technologies work in the following sections.

But first, a word of caution: Not all video files are interchangeable. In fact, many suppliers of editing workstations and software have developed their own proprietary file formats. This makes file transfers between dissimilar machines difficult at best. A variety of converters (sometimes called "file filters") are available. An industry group has also produced Media eXchange Format (MXF) standards that are intended to define a common file format to be used in transfers from one machine to another.

A popular application for transferring files is the File Transfer Protocol (FTP). FTP usually uses the TCP protocol for actual data transport; we will discuss TCP in more detail later in this chapter. One drawback to FTP is its lack of security: Passwords and file contents are not encrypted. Several new standards (several of which are confusingly called SFTP) and a flock of vendors have introduced products to address the shortcomings of FTP.

### File Caching

File caching operates by providing a local storage location that can be used to temporarily store (i.e., "cache," pronounced "cash") files before they are sent out over the network. The caching hardware could simply use random access memory (RAM), but for large video files, disk storage is the only cost-effective option. Special software is used to manage the cache.

Figure 14-1 shows a basic caching system in operation. In this example, User A-1 needs to send a file to User B-1 over the wide area network. Inside Facility A, all the workstations are connected with a high-speed LAN (say, 100 Mbps switched Ethernet). The caching device is also connected to this same network, again using a high-speed connection. In Facility B, the same architecture applies—a 100 Mbps LAN interconnecting all the workstations and the caching device.

The first step in the file transfer is for the file to be copied from User A-1's workstation to the cache device in Facility A. Since this process takes place over the high-speed network inside A, it happens rapidly. Then, the cache device A needs to make contact with cache device B. Once the connection is established between the two caches, then data transfer can begin. This may take awhile, because the amount of bandwidth that is available in the WAN between A and B limits the speed of the data transfer. After the transfer is complete, the file can be sent from cache device B to User B-1's workstation over the high-speed network inside Facility B. The cache device doesn't need to be a specialized piece of hardware; it can simply be a workstation equipped with at least two network interfaces and specialized software.

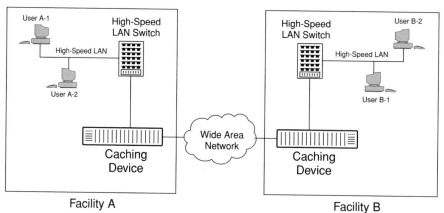

**FIGURE 14-1**   File Caching for Wide Area File Transfer

Note that in the preceding example, we discussed file transfer only from User A-1 to User B-1. Since most WAN technologies are bi-directional, it is perfectly logical for file transfers to take place in the opposite direction, say from User B-2 to User A-2. As long as the caching devices are set up to handle it, data transfer over the WAN (or the LANs for that matter) can take place simultaneously in both directions. Since most of the transit time in the network occurs due to the WAN bottleneck, allowing each cache device to both send and receive data can improve overall system operation.

Let's take a moment and think about some of the transactions that need to take place during this transfer. First of all, before the data can be transferred into cache A, the amount of available storage needs to be checked. If there is not enough storage for the entire file inside cache A, then the data transfer cannot take place until some room is freed up. Second, User A-1 needs to provide cache A with the ultimate destination of the data so that it can be forwarded properly over the WAN. Even though this example doesn't include multiple destinations, it is very common for the networks connecting the cache devices to support multiple destination devices. Third, cache B needs to have a mechanism to inform User B-1 that a file has arrived so that it can be transferred to the user's workstation. Finally, we have not discussed security arrangements for these file transfers, which are frequently quite important.

Many video content owners make rigorous demands on file transfer networks, particularly those used for original content that is intended for paying audiences. More than one production company has suffered lost business and litigation as a result of security lapses that allowed movie content to be released prior to movie release dates. Typically, the responsibility for encrypting the data falls to the cache on the data-sending side. Decryption becomes the responsibility of the cache on the receive side. For more information on encryption technology, please see Chapter 11.

## TCP Spoofing

TCP spoofing is a technique used to increase the throughput of TCP connections that may otherwise work poorly due to excessive delay on a link, or for other reasons. Spoofing operates by intercepting packets as they are transmitted and sending acknowledgments to the transmitter in advance of when they would normally be sent by the receiver. This is a useful technique for speeding up the transmission of large data files on links that have a significant delay.[2]

To get an appreciation of how spoofing works, we first need to get an understanding of how TCP makes sure that data gets from the data sender to the data receiver on an IP network. As we discussed in Chapter 6, TCP is a connection-oriented protocol. That means that the sender and the receiver communicate to set up a connection between the two ends of the network before any real data is sent.[3]

TCP uses "handshaking" to allow the two ends to communicate the success or failure of packet transfers. Handshaking means that the sender expects the receiver to acknowledge the receipt of data periodically. The sender uses these responses to gauge how quickly to send more data. A good analogy of this happens frequently when one person gives another person some specific information during a telephone conversation, such as a telephone number or a credit card number. Typically, one person will begin by saying the first three or four digits of the number and then pausing until the listener makes a suitable response. There are several different ways that the listener can make a response: He or she might say something non-specific such as "OK" or "Mm-hmm," or might read back the number the speaker just read, or something else. In any event, the listener indicates that he or she has heard what the speaker said and is ready for more data. After hearing this response, the speaker responds in turn by saying the next part of the number, pausing for another acknowledgment, and continuing this

---

2. It is very important to understand that the term "spoofing" has been used in other contexts to refer to certain types of malicious activities by hackers. For example, IP address spoofing can be used to make a data sender or receiver believe that it is talking to a different IP address than it really means to. The kind of spoofing we are talking about here is not malicious, and it can be very beneficial for transferring large data files across an IP network.

3. Now, of course, we use the term "connection" loosely here, because we are not talking about anything so drastic as setting aside part of the network bandwidth for the exclusive use of this TCP session. What we do mean by the term "connection" is that both ends of the network are aware that data is going to be sent over the link using the TCP protocol and that the two ends of the circuit will communicate to make sure that all of the data that is being sent is properly received.

process until the entire number is communicated. TCP handshaking is very similar to this process.

In TCP, each byte of data is assigned a sequence number as it gets sent. In each transmitted packet, the sequence number of the first byte of data contained in that packet is included in the packet header. This supports several very useful functions of TCP:

- The receiver can sort out any packets of data that have been delivered in the wrong order by looking at the sequence numbers.
- The receiver can detect whether any packets are missing by looking for gaps in the packet sequence numbers.
- The receiver can indicate to the sender which data bytes have been received and what is the next data byte that the receiver is ready to receive.

To accomplish this handshaking, each packet of data sent by the receiver back to the sender contains an acknowledgment sequence number. This number represents the sequence number of the next byte of data that the receiver is ready to accept. Figure 14-2 shows this process in action.

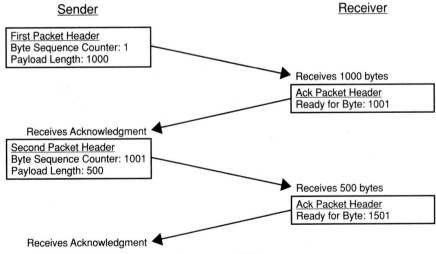

**FIGURE 14-2** Acknowledgment Handshaking in TCP

In the exchange shown in Figure 14-2, the sender begins by sending 1000 bytes of data, with a sequence number 1, to indicate that the first byte of data is contained in this packet. (In reality, the sequence number of the first byte is a pseudo-random number that is calculated from the internal clock of the sending system, to prevent packets from different sources all starting with the same sequence number.) The receiver processes this data and determines that it has received 1000 bytes of data, so it is now ready for byte 1001. The receiver sends a packet to the sender with that acknowledgment. When the sender gets the acknowledgment, it knows that it can now send the next packet of data, this time with 500 bytes. The sender uses sequence number 1001, because that is the first byte of this new packet. When the receiver gets the second packet, it calculates that it is now ready to receive sequence number 1501 and sends an acknowledgment stating so. When the sender receives this second acknowledgment, it knows that the first two packets have been received properly.

In reality, the sender is allowed to send several packets of data in a row without receiving an acknowledgment, but the total amount of data sent can't exceed a limit that is set by the receiver when the TCP connection is established. If, for example, this limit (called the "acknowledgment window") were set to 8000 bytes, the sender could transmit up to 8 packets that each contained 1000 bytes before it had to wait for an acknowledgment from the receiver.

### Acknowledgment Delay

Let's look at the impact of a long delay between the sender and the receiver. Such a delay can have a big impact on the speed of data transfer. For example, if the network delay between the sender and the receiver is 100 milliseconds, then the round-trip delay would be 200 milliseconds. Using an 8000-byte acknowledgment window, the sender could transmit only 8000 bytes of data at a time, before having to wait for the first acknowledgment, which would arrive just under 200 milliseconds later. Then, and only then, could data transmission begin again. Then, after another 8,000 bytes of data were transmitted, the sender would have to wait another 200 milliseconds for acknowledgment. In all, this process could be repeated up to five times in one second, allowing five batches of data to be sent. Since each batch is limited to 8000 bytes by the receive window limit, the maximum possible throughput on this link would be 40,000 bytes per second. Contrast this with the situation if the round-trip delay was only 10 milliseconds; in this case 100 round trips per second would be possible, increasing the total throughput to 800 kbytes/sec, an improvement by a factor of 20.

The role of the spoofing device is to send acknowledgments to the sender much more rapidly than what could be accomplished by the ultimate receiver in a long delay network. The spoofing device needs to pass along the outbound data immediately, but it also needs to keep a copy of the data in a local buffer. In the event that a data packet is lost between the spoofing device and the receiver, the missing data can be retrieved from the buffer and sent again. The buffer inside the spoofing device will need to be fairly large if the data transmission rate is high and the end-to-end delay is long.

### Slow Start Flow Control

Another built-in function of TCP is to provide flow control between a data sender and a data receiver. Flow control means making sure that the data flows out of the sender in a controlled manner, i.e., not in big lumps or at too high of a rate. This is important to avoid overcrowding networks and data receivers that may be busy with heavy loads from other data sources.

Flow control operates in the data sender and uses the acknowledgment information coming back from the receiver. Normally, TCP connections use a process called "slow start" where the sender transmits a small amount data and waits for an acknowledgment from the receiver. If the acknowledgment comes quickly, then the sender tries sending out a larger amount of data and continues ramping up the speed until the link is carrying as much traffic as can be reliably sent. This process is called "slow start" because the initial data rate is set low and increased only when it is determined that the link and the receiver are capable of handling a faster rate of data flow.

Slow start makes sense for normal, day-to-day operation of the Internet, but it can wreak havoc when large data files (such as video files) need to be transferred over an IP network. The problem is particularly acute when there is a large network delay time between the sender and the receiver, such as between locations that are far apart, or when a satellite, wireless, or other network segment that has long delays is included in the end-to-end data link.

To understand the issues with long transit times, let's think about what happens when a long time elapses between when data packets are sent and when they are received. Since we are using TCP, the sender needs to wait for acknowledgments from the receiver for the data packets that have been previously sent. When the acknowledgments arrive after a long delay, the sender has no way of knowing whether the delay is due to congestion on the network or due to a congested receiver, or due to a long delay from the sender to the receiver. Because of this uncertainty, the sender does not try to increase the data transmission rate and continues to send the data out very slowly. While this may not be a problem for normal web page transfers, it can be a big problem for video data files that may contain hundreds or thousands of megabytes of information that need to be transferred.

The spoofing device described previously solves the slow start problem as well, because it sends rapid acknowledgments to the transmitter, thereby circumventing the network delay.

There are some downsides to TCP spoofing. If the data channel between the sender and the receiver is error-prone, then packets will need to be re-transmitted periodically. This limits the benefits of spoofing. Additionally, spoofing introduces additional complexity to the file transfer mechanism, which may create incompatibilities with other software or devices that are part of the IP network. Accordingly, spoofing should be used only after careful testing of the transport network to make sure the error rate is low.

## Jumbo Frames

One way to make file transfer more efficient is to use jumbo frames, which are essentially large packets. Standard Ethernet packets are limited to 1,500 bytes in length; jumbo frames expand that limit to 9000+ bytes. This improves file transfer efficiency in two ways:

- Large packets mean a higher percentage of each packet is data, since the amount of header data is fixed regardless of the packet length.
- In protocols like TCP, the number of acknowledgments that need to be sent is reduced. This allows the acknowledgment window in the transmitter to be expanded, thereby improving end-to-end performance on networks with long round-trip delays.

Unfortunately, most networks, particularly wide area networks, do not support jumbo frames. For private or local area networks, this technology can be useful.

## REVIEW AND CHECKLIST UPDATE

In this chapter, we covered IP file transfer technology, with a particular focus on the large files that are common in video applications. We began by looking at why video applications tend to generate large data files. We discussed some of the applications of video file transfer, including video streaming, download and play, DVD authoring, and video production. We concluded the chapter by examining two different technologies for improving the performance of IP networks for handling large video files. This first, called caching, uses intermediate devices (called caches) to temporarily store video content while it is being sent over a long-distance IP network. The second, called TCP spoofing, changes the way in which acknowledgments are handled in file transfers that use the TCP protocol, helping to speed up the overall transfer time for large files.

### Chapter 14 Checklist Update

- ❏ If file transfer is to be used, determine the size range of the files, and estimate how often they need to be transferred.
- ❏ Make sure that the file formats are compatible between the source and destination machines, particularly if they use different editing software.
- ❏ Consider using caching when large files need to be sent over networks that have slow data transfer rates or long end-to-end delays.

❑ Consider using TCP spoofing to improve the performance of the standard TCP protocol for large data files as long as the network has a reasonably low error rate.

❑ Consider using low-resolution video (with less data per video frame) in place of large video files whenever possible.

❑ Strongly consider using a secure file transfer protocol in place of standard FTP.

# 15

# NETWORK ADMINISTRATION

"Network administration" is a catch-all term that refers to the procedures and technologies that are used to monitor and control a network. This term covers a variety of tasks, including installing and configuring new devices or users, configuring and monitoring network activity, detecting and repairing network congestion or failures, and managing the financial aspects of the network. Theses tasks can be performed manually using trained staff and procedures to perform them, or these tasks can be performed with the assistance of a variety of automated systems. Having a clearly defined network management strategy is essential for any viable video transport network.

Network management can range from complex to simple. In some cases (particularly for larger systems), network management is performed by a dedicated team of technicians supported by specialized hardware and software systems. In other cases (more commonly in smaller systems), network management tasks are performed on an ad-hoc basis by people with a variety of job titles. Also, different types of systems monitor different aspects of a network; some focus on hardware, some on the IP layer, and some on the applications software. No matter what, end users of the video network need to know what to do (or who to call) in the event of a network problem.

In this chapter, we will start by discussing the major network administration functions that need to be accomplished, whether they are done manually or are supported by an automatic network management system. We will then discuss several technologies that can be used for network management, including web-browser–based device management and the Simple Network Management Protocol (SNMP). We will also review an excellent example of an off-the-shelf application layer system for managing distance-learning networks. We will conclude with the final update to the checklist we have been creating throughout this book.

## MANAGEMENT TASKS

Any modern network, regardless of its level of complexity, requires a management system. We use the term "system" loosely here, because these functions can be manual, automated, or somewhere in between. Even the smallest networks (such as a home user with a dial-up Internet provider) need some management, even if the only tasks are initial network setup and responding to failures. Anyone who has spent the occasional hour or two on hold waiting for a service technician to answer his or her call could be considered to be a network manager, of sorts. This role can expand greatly, to the point where literally thousands of people are required to maintain the large, complex networks that make up a telephone company.

Video networks can present a challenge for network managers, particularly if video is being newly introduced into an existing data network. Not only are the bandwidths for video much larger than for most data flows, but also the impact of a momentary network glitch on a video signal can be much more immediate than on a routine data transmission. Of course, a number of networks carry time-critical data, but an unexpected delay of a few milliseconds in these networks generally doesn't cause the user application to fail. Contrast this with a video network, where even a short interruption of the video stream can cause video displays to go dark, or one lost IP packet can cause visible artifacts on the display. One compensating factor is that many video networks are used intermittently, particularly for contribution networks. When a network is not being used for live video traffic, it is very common to see video test patterns (such as color bars) being sent, as a way of confirming that the network is operational. These down times are also ideal for performing network maintenance.

The following sections describe some of the major tasks that need to be performed on an operational network. The tasks are grouped together here for ease of discussion. This is not meant to imply that separate systems are used for each function; quite the contrary—many automated systems include a wide selection of the tasks described in this chapter.

## Installation

Before a video network can begin servicing customers, it needs to be installed. This process can range all the way from a simple connection of a video device to an existing network to the complete construction of a residential video delivery network. In spite of these differences in scope and scale, many of the core functions are common to all video network installations. Table 15-1 lists some of the major tasks that need to be accomplished during system installation.

## Performance Monitoring

Performance monitoring is the process of observing the behavior of a network to determine whether it is operating properly. All sorts of behavior can be monitored, from counting the errors on a data link to tracking the number of simultaneous viewers for a piece of content. Many times, minimum performance levels are established, causing an alarm to be generated when the performance drops below this threshold. These alarms can be very useful as early predictors of network failures, particularly for systems such as an IP network that tend to degrade before completely failing.

Performance monitoring can begin as soon as the first network components are installed. Normally, monitoring is a shared responsibility,

**TABLE 15-1**

Typical System Installation Tasks

- *Address Allocation:* Each device in the network needs to be given an IP address, either upon installation or dynamically when connected. Typically, video sources are given fixed IP addresses so that the viewing devices can locate them. End-user viewing devices that do not generate any content are frequently given temporary addresses using the DHCP process, which gives each device an IP address only when it needs to connect to the network (see Chapter 5 for more detail on DHCP). Global IP addresses can be assigned to each network element, or the IP addresses can be restricted in scope to a single network segment.
- *Video Source Installation:* This task is normally performed early in the installation process, because there are typically fewer video sources than viewers, and these sources tend to be centralized and located near where the content is generated or stored. If the video signals are to be multicast, then the source may not need a very high bandwidth connection to the rest of the network. However, if the video signals are to be unicast, then the source must have at least enough bandwidth to send one copy of the video stream to each supported simultaneous viewer.
- *Client Installation:* Every person who wishes to become a user of the video network needs access to a viewing device, commonly called a "client device." This can take the form of either a software package that is downloaded onto an existing PC or a stand-alone device that is attached to a video display. Efficiently and cost effectively supplying and configuring these devices can be the key difference between success and failure for many video networks.

  Video delivery services (such as RealNetworks) which target PC users provide software download packages that contain their client software. These packages will automatically install on a viewer's PC once the package has been downloaded and launched. Other providers such as IPTV services supply specialized devices (such as set top boxes) that are given to each user. These client devices need to be properly configured before they can be connected to the network and to a television or other display device.

  The key to successful client installation is adequate preparation, with a particular focus on configuration control. The minimum requirements for a client PC must be well defined (this can include the processor speed, amount of RAM, and amount of free disk space, among other criteria). Sometimes, a special hardware accelerator or other video board needs to be installed in the client's PC; in these cases, lots of pre-deployment testing needs to be done to ensure that the devices will be compatible with all of the client PCs and software. For dedicated video networks (such as DSL video), the main concern of the network operator is the cost of each client device (set top box or equivalent), and the cost of the labor to install them. If thousands of devices are to be deployed, careful attention must be paid to minimize the cost of each box. Many video service providers also ask users to self-install the devices in their own home or business; this practice can save huge amounts of money and technical labor for the service provider, but the installation process needs to be very simple and well documented.
- *Configuring for Multicasting:* If multicasting is to be used, part of the installation process must be to verify that all of the networking equipment is capable of processing multicast streams. This may require software or possibly even hardware upgrades in network devices such as routers, because the processing burden on network devices is much greater in a multicast network than in a unicast-only network. (See Chapter 9 for more discussions on multicasting.)

**TABLE 15-1** (*Continued*)

- *Network Management Infrastructure Configuration:* One big advantage of IP-based video networks is that a single network can be used both for delivering the actual video content and for managing all of the network devices. The same physical network interfaces can be used to send and receive network management commands and transport video, as long as two-way capability is provided (which is the normal state of any IP network), and the network is not overloaded to the point where network management messages can't get through. Typically, the network management software inside each user device will communicate using a separate UDP port from the ones being used by the video content. As we will see later, devices may simply respond to external commands, or they can be configured to automatically report error conditions as soon as they are detected.
- *Managing Device Removal or Relocation:* Normally, when we discuss the tasks of device installation and configuration, thoughts go to new devices being added to a network. However, in many actual working networks, devices are constantly being removed and relocated. This is as much of a challenge for people management as it is for network management, because it is essential to update the system configuration whenever a device is moved from one location to another. Just think of the chaos that would result if an error report came in from a device with a fixed IP address that had just been moved across town to a new location without having the system configuration database updated!

where the individual devices gather statistical data about their own operations, and a central management system gathers this data periodically for analysis. Devices throughout the network are responsible for keeping track of a variety of performance data, such as the number of bit or packet errors detected in incoming signals. This information can then be used in several different ways, depending on the needs of the system operator. In some systems, the data is stored locally in each device and used only when a system technician decides to look at it. In other systems, data from multiple devices is gathered periodically by an automated system and shown on a system status display. In others, a central processor continuously analyzes incoming data and notifies technicians when equipment error counts have exceeded a specified threshold, and equipment needs to be tested and then possibly repaired or replaced.

Table 15-2 lists some of the types of data gathered and analyzed by performance monitoring systems.

**TABLE 15-2**

Typical Performance Monitoring Data

---

- *Bit Errors:* These errors can be detected in different ways. Many types of networks include a checksum or parity byte that will indicate whether any of the bits in a stream have become corrupted. In addition, many packet-based transport systems have a checksum in each packet so that bit errors that occur in a packet can be counted. Error counts can be accumulated in a variety of ways, such as a running total of errors during specific time periods.
- *Optical or Electrical Signal Levels:* Many signal receivers have the ability to measure the incoming signal. In the case of an optical network, this means that the intensity of the incoming light can be measured and reported.
- *Lost Packets:* As packet-based networks become more heavily loaded, congestion can occur on some routes. In the event of congestion, many network devices such as routers and switches will discard packets that cannot be sent over a network link in a reasonable amount of time. By monitoring the quantities of lost packets at various locations in a network, system operators can determine if more network capacity needs to be added, if alternate routes need to be placed into service, or if existing links need maintenance action.
- *User Statistics:* All kinds of data can be gathered about users, from a simple headcount to an analysis of usage patterns and favorite content sources. Knowledge of this information can help network managers determine if more capacity is needed for certain video titles, or if additional bandwidth or server capacity is required in certain locations. Usage statistics can also be analyzed to determine whether users are having problems with unexpected disconnections, which can be an early warning signal for network problems.
- *User Logon Behavior:* This can indicate that users are having problems getting access to the system or that user credentials have been misappropriated. The latter situation is quite evident when the same user is logged on to the system in several different locations at the same time.
- *Security System Monitoring:* By gathering data about the performance of security systems such as firewalls or invalid password attempts, system operators may be able to prevent security problems from occurring. This data can help to determine if firewalls are working properly or if network attacks are coming from inside or outside an organization, and it may provide early warning if a virus outbreak is occurring so preventative measures can be taken. This information can also be used after a security breach to determine how to prevent future security problems.

---

One drawback to performance monitoring is that it must operate while the network is up and running, so certain types of tests cannot detect all types of network errors. For example, consider a simplistic system that uses one parity bit for every 100 data bits. If one bit error occurs in the 100 bits, then one error is registered. If 10 bit errors occur in the 100 bits, then only one error is still registered. From a practical standpoint, this is not a significant problem, because multiple errors can be treated as one error for most purposes. However, it can make networks appear to be operating better than they actually are when error rates are high or bursty.

Performance monitoring works to prevent network failures because devices tend to exhibit degraded performance before they completely fail. For example, in an optical network, the output power of a laser will normally drop before it fails completely. If the optical power level is monitored at the receiver, repair technicians can be informed that a laser's output power is dropping, and it can be replaced before causing a major network outage. Similarly, a router might detect that an incoming stream has an increasing error rate, which could indicate that the source of the signal has a problem or that the data connection is degrading. In either case, early warning can mean that the problem can be repaired before the video traffic is severely affected.

There are limits to the effectiveness of performance monitoring. For instance a trade-off has to be made concerning the frequency of device polling: Poll too often and the system will be kept busy transmitting and processing the poll requests and burdened with data to be analyzed; poll too infrequently and transient errors can be overlooked. Also, as network complexity grows, the difficulty of analyzing the network increases exponentially. Finally, it is difficult for many organizations to devote resources to performance monitoring that might otherwise be occupied troubleshooting network failures or installing new equipment.

## Fault Management

If problems are detected, then fault management is used to mitigate the impact of the problems and to manage the network repair process. The main tasks that need to be performed by a fault management system are fault tracking, failure diagnosis, and fault workaround. We'll look at each area in more detail shortly.

Network problems can be detected in several different ways. A performance management system can detect them. An administrator using a web-browser management tool can discover them. An end user can call in a trouble report. No matter which method of detection is used, the fault management system plays an essential role in collecting the fault data and organizing it into a logical pattern. Records of network faults can also be stored in case they are needed for analyzing future trouble reports, or if they are needed to help in identifying long-term network performance trends in conjunction with user statistics and other performance data.

As failure data is collected, it needs to be analyzed. This process, called "root cause analysis," attempts to figure out the specific failure that could have caused the reported problems to occur. For example, consider some typical failures that might occur on a computer network. If only one user's PC is having trouble, it is logical to assume that the root cause of the problem has to do with that PC or its connection to the network. If a group of PCs that are all connected to the same Ethernet switch are experiencing problems, then it makes sense to examine that switch for problems, before checking into other possible failures.

One simple method for doing root cause analysis is to present a list of system failures to a network technician, who then determines where the failure has occurred. The technician will troubleshoot the network and try to come up with a repair strategy to correct the reported failures. This analysis may involve looking at the operating data for various devices on the network, connecting appropriate test equipment, or simply replacing devices until the problem goes away.

A second method for root cause analysis involves the use of software systems to analyze the reported failures and come up with a potential diagnosis. This requires the software system to have a detailed understanding of all the devices in the network and have an accurate description of the way they are interconnected. With this information, sophisticated algorithms can sometimes determine the root cause of a set of network problems. However, in reality, these systems can be enormously complex and costly to maintain. So, for most networks, humans are involved in the diagnosis process.

Sometimes, it might be possible to reconfigure the network to avoid most or all or the consequences of the failure. For instance, many high-speed telephone circuits (such as SONET links) have a main and a backup path. In the event of a failure on the main path, the backup is designed to take over operation within 50 milliseconds. In other cases, it may be possible for IP routers to send data along another route in place of one that has failed. These techniques, called "fault workarounds," are a powerful tool for improving network reliability.

## Repair Dispatch and Verification

Once a problem has been diagnosed, repairs are usually required. Dispatching repair technicians can be done manually or automatically. In a manual system, a dispatcher reviews a list of reported failures, prioritizes them, and then dispatches repair personnel to various locations. In an automatic system, this process is performed by a software package that looks at the same data. In either case, several rules apply. First, it is important to make sure that the technicians sent to address each failure have the proper training and the correct tools that will be needed to complete the diagnosis and fix the problem. If at all possible, it is also good to make sure that the technicians have replacement units for any modules or systems that might have failed.

Once a repair has been completed, it is critical to make sure that the repair has corrected the problem. Ideally, this needs to take place before the repair technician has left the work site, in order to avoid a second repair dispatch to correct a single problem. This will normally involve sending a test signal to or from the repaired or replaced device and verifying correct operation.

Another important consideration is to make sure that service restoration does not cause a problem with user video or data signals. This is particularly important on systems that use automatic protection switching to activate a standby circuit when the main circuit has failed. As mentioned previously, these systems can cause a brief interruption of service when the switchover takes place. If the circuit is carrying a live video feed, and if the circuit is switched from standby back to main during the repair process, then the live feed can be interrupted for the duration of the switchover, plus whatever time is necessary for the equipment to reset. This can cause the video users to become very upset and should, as a rule, be avoided. Professional video users prefer to be contacted whenever possible in advance of any switchovers so that each switchover can be scheduled when it will not affect the video feed (say, during a local affiliate commercial break).

## Accounting Issues

Accounting issues concern the collection of data that can be used to allocate the costs of a networking system, prepare bills for users, and calculate revenues from profit-making services. Many of the most useful video communication systems support users from different companies or organizations, so dividing up the costs or revenues that result from network activities can be a major responsibility for the network manager. In general, a network management system does not actually produce bills or modify a company's accounts; instead, the data is simply gathered by the network management system and reported for use by accounting systems.

A common accounting issue is tracking the amount of network usage from each user site, to allow a larger portion of the costs to be assigned to the more frequent system users. This can simply be a tally of the number of minutes of usage. More complicated schemes can be used when the system costs vary by site, such as when some users require more bandwidth or long-distance network connections. More detailed accounting, such as tracking individual users from each location, requires even more sophisticated software, and a means to identify which users are on-line at any point in time. Overall, it is important to balance the costs of gathering this data in terms of systems and people against the benefits of performing this accounting.

## CASE STUDY: ST. CLAIR COUNTY SCHOOLS

Let's look at one successful installation of a network management solution that operates at the application level. St. Clair County is located in the far eastern portion of Michigan and makes up part of the border between the USA and Canada. The St. Clair County Regional Educational Service Agency (SCCRESA) serves a population of approximately 28,000 students, ranging from Kindergarten (age 5) though High School (age 18). District network facilities are also used for higher education (by the St. Clair County Community College) and adult education.

SCCRESA first used interactive video distance learning in the late 1990's. The system has grown over time, reaching a total of 62 end-points in early 2005—15 units using MPEG-2 over IP technology operating at 5 Mbps and 47 units using H.323 technology operating between 384 and 1024 kbps. Connections are made over a private broadband IP network using RTP/UDP and multicasting technology. Typically, the conferences are configured to be 1x3, consisting of one main classroom where the instructor is located, and three remote classrooms. System usage has grown over time; in the last period measured, 14,000 conferences each lasting 1–3 hours were logged.

One interesting feature of this system is the gateway, which is used to make connections between classrooms that use incompatible technologies (H.323 and MPEG–2). Inside the gateway, three MPEG–2 over IP encoder/decoders are connected to three H.323 encoders/decoders by means of baseband audio and video circuits. Without this gateway, classrooms equipped with one technology could not communicate with classrooms employing the other technology even though both systems share the same IP network infrastructure.

Successful operation of this system requires system resources to be managed to prevent conflicts. For example, each classroom can participate in only one conference at a time. Similarly, the gateway is limited to supporting three different conferences at a time. The network links to each school must also be managed to ensure that each link's capacity is not exceeded by too many simultaneous conferences.

Managing this network requires a staff of three professionals and a sophisticated network administration software package supplied by Renovo Software of Edina, Minnesota (www.renovosoftware.com). The management console operates on a single web server platform and consists of an Oracle database with three main tools:

- Administration tool
- Scheduling tool
- Automation tool

The administration tool is used to enter and control the basic data that is required by the management system. The layout of the video network is defined using this tool, including descriptions of each video encoder/decoder location and data about each authorized user that is allowed to set up and reserve conferences. Descriptions are also required for each network link that connects between the sites; the administration system needs this information to make sure that network capacities are not exceeded when multiple simultaneous conferences use the same network links. The administration tool also manages data used by the conference scheduler, such as information about the school calendar.

The scheduling tool is accessed by authorized users such as instructors or school administrators to set up and schedule conferences. It is implemented as a web server, with the flexibility to give customized interfaces to different classes of users. Immediate feedback is one of the key features of this system so that users can find out right away if the conference that they are trying to schedule is allowed or denied due to a resource conflict (such as a classroom already reserved by another user or too many conferences on one network link). The scheduling tool also includes a notification module that can be used to send out reminders (in the form of e-mail or faxes) to conference participants or to technicians who may need to reconfigure a classroom for a particular conference, for example.

The automation tool is responsible for implementing all of the scheduled network connections on a timely basis. Each time a conference is started, the appropriate information needs to be loaded into each conference device. For example, IP source and destination addresses need to be given to each end device for formatting unicast packet streams. Other tasks include configuring the in-room equipment for each conference and connecting to the MPEG–2/H.323 gateway if necessary. The automation tool is typically configured to set up each conference five minutes before the scheduled start time, leaving a short time window for fault correction (if, for example, one of the required devices has been unintentionally powered down).

This software is a classic example of application-focused network management. It focuses on all of the tasks that are required to successfully manage an application (videoconferencing in this example), without having to manage all of the underlying networking hardware (IP routers and optical transmission equipment) that makes up the physical layer of the network, which is maintained by the companies that provide telecom services to SCCRESA.

## TECHNOLOGIES FOR NETWORK ADMINISTRATION

Various technologies are used in managing modern data and video networks. We'll look at two of the most popular ones in this section: web-browser based and SNMP systems. These two technologies provide some similar functions, but differ greatly in terms of the amount of effort required to install them and the functionality that they provide for a network manager. After discussing each technology, we'll summarize the differences between these two technologies.

### Web-Browser Device Management

Web-browser device management allows a networking device to be managed from another location through the use of a standard web browser. Information about the device is displayed in the browser window, and modifications to the device's operation or configuration can be made through the use of standard browser commands. Networking devices with this capability are available from a number of manufacturers, although it is up to each manufacturer to determine if and how they implement this function. Let's examine this technology in a little more detail.

Most modern networking devices contain a processor that is capable of a variety of tasks, such as controlling the operation of the device and communicating with the outside world. This communication can take many forms: It can be as simple as turning on a light on the front panel of the device or as complicated as an automatic alarm management and reporting system. Many devices that use IP interfaces for their standard operation are beginning to include a web server function. This built-in server allows remote web users to communicate with the device processor for a number of functions. (Note that in this context, the term "server" is not meant to imply that the device has a hard disk drive. Quite the contrary; many networking devices are specifically designed without using disk drives, which can be a potential source of reliability problems.) One of the most popular functions implemented in the web server is device management. Figure 15-1 shows how the different functions work together.

In Figure 15-1, the device on the right is a network element. This could be a variety of different devices, such as an MPEG video encoder with an IP network connection, or an IP switch with a management IP port, or any number of other devices. Software inside the device implements a web server function—that is, monitoring port 80 in the incoming side of the IP interface and processing HyperText Transfer Protocol (HTTP) requests as they come in. These requests can come from a number of different users with different levels of access permission. In response to these requests, the server will supply web pages that have been custom designed to allow the user to view important information about the device.

In the example given in Figure 15-1, three access classes are provided: network manager, maintenance technician, and authorized user. The network manager has full access to observe all aspects of the network element and is able to modify any portion of the device's configuration. The maintenance technician has the ability to observe all of the status and configuration of the device, but to modify only portions of the configuration. The authorized user may be given limited permission to observe the status of the device and is (in this example) required to ask either the network manager or a maintenance technician to make any required configuration changes. Different access classes are quite common for network devices and are commonly

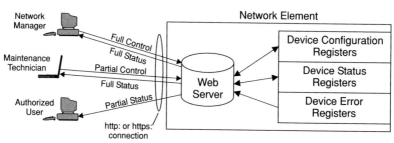

**FIGURE 15-1** Web-Based Device Management Architecture

implemented in the web-browser software through the use of account names and passwords.

Sometimes, the first page served up by the browser will identify the device and provide a request for the user to provide appropriate login information, such as user name and password.[1] Once satisfied that the user is authorized to view the device, the server may set up a secure HTTP (HTTPS) connection for all further communication. Using this secure connection, the user can then browse through the pages located on the device's web server to get the desired information, without disclosing this information to other network users.

The device's web pages typically have a fixed layout but can have rapidly changing information contained in them. One of the main functions of the web pages is to provide information about the current status of the device. This status information can be a complete display of all of the operating parameters of the device, or it can be limited to a subset. Many times, configuration data is also accessible, including such data as network addresses, active or inactive device features, optional cards that are present or absent, and a list of user names and passwords of those people who are allowed to access the device.

For example, think of the configuration options for a simple MPEG video compression device. Most likely, a web server in this device would allow the user to set the operating bit rate for the MPEG stream, the compression GOP, the number of active audio channels, plus a variety of other configuration data. (See Chapter 4 for more information on MPEG compression.) All this various information can be collected by the web server inside the device and served up to the user. In many instances, the user is given the ability to enter new data by using his or her browser; this information gets communicated to the device, which then modifies its configuration. When the web page is refreshed to the user's browser, the new configuration data should appear.

---

1.   In some devices, the amount of user authentication varies depending on the hardware port used to access the device. If the network port is used, then full authentication is required. If a local maintenance port is used, then little or no authentication could be required. This latter capability is intended to make it easier for on-site technicians to access the device when repairs are being made.

Web-browser–based management is very useful for managing a network that consists of a widely dispersed collection of devices, particularly when the video network manager does not have control of the network that is used to interconnect the devices. For example, consider a video-based training system that is implemented on a corporate data network. The head of the training department would be a logical choice for controlling the video devices, such as the video encoders, video servers, and any other classroom-based devices. However, the other equipment that provides the connectivity between these devices (such as IP routers and switches) might not be controlled by this manager. Instead, the corporate data networking department might be responsible for managing this equipment, particularly if there are a number of other applications and users on the network that are not involved in training activities. The relatively simple method of supplying the training manager with a web browser and connectivity to each video device might be the perfect network management solution for this type of application.

Some network management designs use both web-browser and SNMP technologies—SNMP for routine scanning and monitoring of a variety of different devices, and a web browser to perform detailed troubleshooting once a fault has been detected. It is also not unusual for different types of equipment to use different monitoring schemes. Physical layer parameters may be easier to manage with SNMP, whereas application layer software may be simpler to monitor with web browsers.

## SNMP

Simple Network Management Protocol (SNMP) is a simple but powerful protocol for monitoring and controlling devices, on both IP and non-IP networks. It is a well-specified, structured approach to defining all of the key parameters of a device that are related to the management function. SNMP was originally developed in 1988 for devices on an IP network but has since been adapted to a wide variety of devices and protocols. Various commercial tools are available for building SNMP systems.

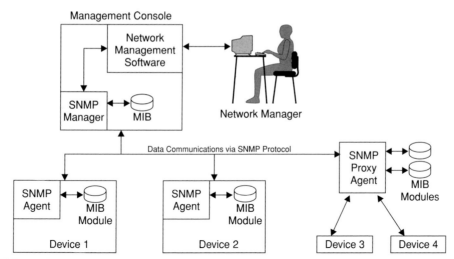

**FIGURE 15-2** SNMP Sample Network

At the most basic level, SNMP is a communication protocol that defines how system performance and operational data can be gathered from devices and how commands can be sent to these devices. Figure 15-2 shows the layout of a basic system. Table 15-3 describes the key components of this system.

One of the biggest benefits of an SNMP system is that the data-gathering and display functions can be automated, using a variety of off-the-shelf and custom-built tools. The key data from each device can be periodically gathered and displayed to a user for analysis and possible action. For example, it is quite common to see SNMP used in a network management system that was responsible for gathering network performance data, such as counts of lost packets, and displaying it to a person who was responsible for that network. In the event that congestion on a link between two routers exceeded a certain limit, the links might change color on the management console display and possibly start to blink. This would signal the network manager to investigate the cause of the congestion, and possibly take some corrective action, such as dispatching a repair technician or reconfiguring the network to send packets via a different route.

**TABLE 15-3**

SNMP Sample Network Description

---

- The *network manager* is a person who is responsible for the proper operation of a network, be it video or otherwise.
- This person is equipped with a *management console*, which is responsible for gathering information about the network, displaying it, and handling any commands that the network manager issues.
- *Network management software* runs on the management console to perform key tasks, including displaying network status, logging alarms, and sending manager commands to network devices. This software uses the SNMP manager to gather information from the various devices in the network.
- The *SNMP manager* is responsible for all management communications with the devices that are being managed and keeps a local record of the current status of the network in a master database called the *Management Information Base* (MIB).[2]
- *SNMP* is used to communicate with the various devices that make up the network, several of which are shown in Figure 15-2.
- *Devices 1 and 2* are both directly managed, because they are equipped with the intelligence to contain an *SNMP agent* and a local module of the MIB database. The SNMP agent inside these devices is responsible for gathering information from inside the device and storing it locally in the MIB module. The SNMP agent is also responsible for responding to requests from the SNMP manager for this information, and for processing commands received from the manager. In addition, the SNMP agent is able to generate special requests (called "traps") to the SNMP manager in the event of special events, such as when the device has encountered a situation that requires immediate attention—for example, a system reboot.
- *Devices 3 and 4* do not have the necessary intelligence to be directly managed or use a proprietary (non-SNMP) management protocol, so a specialized device called a *proxy agent* manages them. The proxy agent contains the SNMP agent software and a local MIB module that compiles data from the attached devices. Data must be gathered from each device using whatever means are possible, such as a serial port on the device, contact closure monitoring, or other methods that a device uses to report operational status data.

---

SNMP is implemented in a huge variety of network equipment, including devices used for normal data networking and those that may be targeted specifically for video applications. Since all these devices have different functions, the types of information gathered and displayed for each device will vary. Fortunately, the developers of SNMP came up with a method to represent all this different data in a systematic way—through the use of a Management Information Base, or MIB. Each manufacturer of network equipment that supports SNMP will develop and

---

2. Technically, a MIB is simply a format for a database, and not a database itself. However, for the sake of brevity, we will refer to the database that is formatted according to the MIB format as a "MIB."

publish a MIB for each device. Technically, the MIB in each device is just a portion of the global MIB that exists for the Internet, but in practical terms, each manufacturer can add functions to its device's private MIB as long as the resulting data is compliant with the standards and is well described to the user. A MIB can contain a wide variety of information including the name of a particular device, the name of the device's manufacturer, the number of seconds that a device has been active since it was last rebooted, the number of bad packets that the device has received since the last time the bad packet counter was reset, and so on. Some of the information in a device's MIB module is standard, and some is specific to that device. Each device's manufacturer should be able to supply a document describing the exact configuration of the data in its MIB. Note that translation tables may be required to allow data supplied by one manufacturer's equipment to be compared to data supplied by another manufacturer's equipment.

Setting up an SNMP system involves connecting all of the devices that are to be managed to a communications network that will support the SNMP protocol and then configuring the SNMP manager software. The key is to have a reliable, bi-directional network to support commands, responses, and traps to every device. Some consideration may be given to providing a mechanism to allow communication with devices in the event of a network failure. Alternative network routes and even dial-up communication links have been used successfully in many cases.

Before an SNMP system can operate, the SNMP manager software must be set up to handle all of the different types of equipment that need to be monitored. Configuring SNMP manager software is greatly eased through the use of standards. Each MIB module must be described using a highly structured specification language called ASN.1 (which stands for Abstract Syntax Notation One). In many cases, these descriptions can be automatically parsed by the SNMP manager software so that the data contained in the MIB can be understood and labeled on the management console display.

## Comparison of Web Browsing and SNMP

The technologies of web browsing and SNMP can be viewed as both substitutes and complements. They can substitute for each other because they have overlapping capabilities. They complement each other because one is better for overall management of a complicated network (SNMP), whereas the other is better for hands-on troubleshooting of network components (web browsing).

As a general rule, a web-browsing system is a low-cost solution for uncomplicated networks with relatively few network elements. Each device acts on its own, without a central management system to process data from a variety of sources. This system relies on the (human) network manager to identify, analyze, and diagnose system problems. No specialized hardware or software is required to operate this network management system; a simple PC with a standard browser will normally suffice.

SNMP systems are more suited for large, complex networks, with multiple vendors' equipment and where adequate funding is available to perform the necessary system integration. Because they can gather information from a variety of different devices, these systems can be made aware of the connections between the devices that they are monitoring. This, in turn, makes it possible to analyze individual error reports and determine the source of certain types of errors, although not all network management software provides this capability.

Table 15-4 shows a comparison of web browsing and SNMP for several aspects of network management installation and usage.

## REVIEW AND CHECKLIST UPDATE

In this chapter, we discussed the process of network administration, which grows in importance as the size of the video network increases, and as its proper operation becomes more essential to the user. We began our discussion with an analysis of the different network management tasks that need to be accomplished. They included installation, performance monitoring, fault management, repair dispatch/validation, and accounting issues. We discussed how these tasks can be performed using completely manual systems (i.e., paper, pencil, and telephone) or can be supported with automated systems. We then moved on to a discussion of two popular network management technologies. The first uses a web server in every managed device to provide information to the network manager who employs web browsing

**TABLE 15-4**

Web Browsing vs. SNMP Network Management

| | Web-Browsing Network Management | SNMP Network Management |
|---|---|---|
| *Device Configuration* | Very simple; a browser can be used on a stand-alone device before it is installed in a system or to change the configuration of a device once it has been installed. | Complex; configuration settings must be transmitted to a device using SNMP "SET" commands for each setting. This can be tedious, unless the process has been automated. |
| *System Setup* | May be required if web servers are to be accessed from a central location. Otherwise, little setup is needed. | Complex. Each device type must have its MIB processed by the network management software so that the alarms and status information for that device type can be recognized. |
| *Management Console* | Standard PC; adequate to operate browser software and communicate with devices on network. | High reliability system, with capacity to run network management software and communicate regularly with each device. Should also keep activity logs to allow analysis of long-term trends. |
| *Network Management Software* | None required. Standard browser software is used to check status of each device. | Off-the shelf or custom solutions can be used; configuration data for each managed device must be compiled and entered into system. |
| *Root Cause Analysis* | Essentially non-existent. When each device is managed separately, it is impossible to automatically compare alarms from different devices to find root causes. | Feasible, once appropriate software has been installed and configured on the management console. Proper analysis requires an accurate network connection map to be maintained. |
| *Management Information Network* | Must have enough bandwidth to support web pages as they are served from each managed device and prevent excessive delay. | Limited bandwidth, only as needed to send and receive SNMP packets (which are fairly small) periodically to each device. |
| *Support for Non-Intelligent Devices* | Limited to non-existent. A remote system could be installed to monitor these devices, but this could be hard to configure and manage. | Good with SNMP proxy agent. |
| *Vendor Specific* | High; no widely accepted standards exist for network management server page layout or content. | Moderate to low; major parts of many MIBs are standardized; however, vendor-specific portions of a MIB can vary widely. |
| *Continuous Monitoring* | Low to none; continuous display of device web status pages is possible, although it is rarely done. | High; most devices can be set to automatically report certain conditions, without waiting for a central system to poll. |

to monitor the health of the video system. The second uses specialized software in each device and a central management system that communicates using the SNMP protocol. We followed this discussion with a comparison of these two management technologies.

## Chapter 15 Checklist Update

❑ Develop policies and procedures for handling routine system management tasks, including the following items:
   ❑ System installation, for video sources and destinations
   ❑ New user setup, including software/hardware setup and user account information
   ❑ Equipment moves, changes, and re-installations
   ❑ Performance monitoring and trouble reporting
   ❑ System repair and repair verification
   ❑ Equipment tracking for units that have been removed from the system for vendor repair
   ❑ Usage tracking as needed for accounting purposes
❑ Determine which management functions will be performed manually and which will be supported by automatic systems.
❑ If automated systems are to be used, survey the management capabilities of the equipment that will be deployed in the video system. Typically, some devices will support web browsing, others will support SNMP, and many newer devices will support both.
❑ For simple systems, such as those where only video devices are the responsibility of the video network manager, consider using web-browsing device management.
❑ For complex systems, where multiple video and non-video devices need to be managed, consider using an SNMP-based management system.
❑ When purchasing new equipment, examine what types of network management tools are available from equipment vendors. Determine if there is a benefit in terms of network management of buying most or all equipment from a single vendor.
❑ Make sure that all elements of a network system have the flexibility to accommodate the needs of video transport, including high bandwidth, low latencies, accurate bandwidth allocation, and the ability to support video-oriented applications layer management.

# APPENDIX A

## THE DISCRETE COSINE TRANSFORM

The Discrete Cosine Transform, or DCT, is used throughout the MPEG standards as a way to provide video compression. This mathematical tool allows images to be represented with amazing visual accuracy (at least within the limits of human perception) with far fewer bits than those needed to create the original image.

The DCT used in MPEG operates on 8 pixel by 8 pixel blocks of image data. Luminance and the two color difference signals (see Chapter 3) are compressed separately by MPEG, but they use the same DCT principles. Figure A-1 shows a simple before-and-after picture of the DCT process. At the input to the DCT, an 8x8 block of pixel data is present. At the output from the DCT, an 8x8 block of data coefficients is present. The data contained in the output is a very accurate representation of the input; however, the transformation has made it easier to get rid of redundant information.

Let's take a closer look at the output of the DCT. First, it is important to understand that the DCT output is no longer a picture in any form

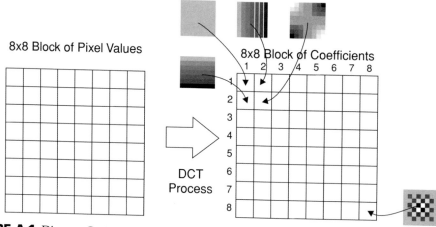

**FIGURE A-1** Discrete Cosine Transform (DCT) Input/Output Diagram

recognizable by a human. In order to create a recognizable picture, the DCT has to be run in reverse to create a block of pixels (this is part of what an MPEG decoder does). What the DCT output contains is a set of numbers that each corresponds to one aspect of the 64 input pixels. For example, the coefficient in the first column of the first row of the DCT output reflects the average value of all 64 input values. The next coefficient (in the second column of the first row of the DCT output) represents the relative intensity of the left four columns of the input as compared to the right four columns of the input. If the left four columns are brighter than the right four columns, then the coefficient that is stored in location (1,2) would be a positive number. If the left four columns are darker than the right four, then (1,2) would contain a negative value. In the third column of the first row of the DCT output [position (1,3)], a coefficient is stored that represents the brightness of the rightmost two columns and the leftmost two columns of pixels as compared to the middle four columns. Each additional coefficient in row 1 represents finer and finer detail of the original image, culminating in the coefficient in (1,8) that represents the relative brightness of the odd-numbered columns in the pixel block input as compared to the even-numbered columns. This same pattern is repeated in the vertical direction; the coefficient stored in row two, column 1 (2,1) of the output represents the relative brightness of the top four rows of input pixels as compared to the bottom four rows of input pixels.[1]

The astute reader might now be asking, "This is all very well and good, but what have we accomplished here? Haven't we just spent a lot of processing power to replace one table of 64 values (the input pixel data) with another table of 64 values (the DCT output coefficients)?" Well, in all truth the answer to this question is yes, that is all that we have done so far, but now let's look at what we can do to reduce the amount of data. To do this, we need to understand what the values in the DCT output matrix will look like for video signals that we are likely to encounter in the real world.

To begin with, let's look at the coefficient value that is likely to be in position (8,8) of the DCT output. This value represents the relative intensity of the odd-numbered pixels in the first row, the even-numbered pixels in the second row, the odd-numbered pixels in the third row, and so on, generating a pattern that would very closely resemble a checkerboard of alternating light and dark squares. Now, thinking about what we might see in a picture from the real world, ask yourself how likely it would be to see a picture with that amount of detail in a relatively small part of the screen. (Remember, we are talking about an area that is only 8 pixels wide by 8 pixels high.) The answer is "Not very likely," which in turn means that the value of this coefficient is likely to be close to zero, if not exactly zero. Consider what would happen if we were to simply set this value to zero and perform the inverse DCT to re-create the original picture: Chances are, a viewer would never notice the difference. This is the very goal we are striving toward with lossy perceptual coding—the ability to remove data and not affect the perceived picture quality.

We can continue this process and look at the coefficients in locations (7,8) and (8,7). As in the case for (8,8), chances are that these coefficients will be zero, or very close to zero. Again, if we simply set these coefficients to zero, chances are that a viewer would never notice.

---

1.  For anyone who has taken college-level math or science courses that discussed Fourier series, this may seem very familiar. In fact, this should, because the DCT is a special form of a Fourier series that is suited for image processing and compression.

This same argument can be made for many of the coefficients in the lower right corner of the DCT output. This is how compression works—by eliminating data that won't affect the perceived image in the eyes of the viewer.

Another benefit of the DCT process is that many of the coefficients in the output come out naturally to zero, particularly when the input block of pixels has a simple appearance (say, for example, a section of uniform blue sky). The compression engine takes advantage of this and removes all of the zero coefficients from the output. This achieves a great deal of compression on a video image. If more compression is needed, the compression engine can force some of the non-zero coefficients to be zero. It can also redefine the step sizes of the other non-zero values to use fewer bits; this process is called *requantization*.

The DCT is used in a huge number of popular image compression systems, including JPEG graphics; the H.260, H.261, and H.263 video-conferencing systems; all of the MPEG series systems; and also in some of the popular video streaming formats, including Apple's QuickTime. The popularity of this algorithm is understandable, given the ability to achieve compression ratios of 100:1 (which means that the output has 100 times fewer bits than the input) with acceptable perceptual video quality.

# APPENDIX B

## DIFFIE-HELLMAN KEY EXCHANGE

In 1976, Whitfield Diffie and Martin Hellman published a paper[1] that first described one of the key underlying technologies for exchanging cryptographic keys between two parties that wish to communicate. This process, which has come to be known as the Diffie-Hellman Key Exchange, is now in common use in throughout the Internet, particularly since the key US patents covering this technology expired in 1997. Since this is such an important technology, let's look at how it works.

Let's say two users, whom we'll call Bonnie and Clyde, are trying to exchange a secret message. Before they begin, they need to agree on two numbers: a prime number (p), and a second, smaller number called a generator (g).[2] For this example, let's say that they choose p = 19 and g = 2.

1. W. Diffie and M. E. Hellman, "New Directions in Cryptography," *IEEE Transactions on Information Theory*, vol. 22, no. 6 (1976): 644–654.
2. The number g needs to be a primitive root of p, such that when x goes from 1 to p − 1, then g raised to the x power (modulo p) goes through all the numbers 1 . . . (p − 1) in some order.

The first thing Bonnie does is choose her private key (a). Let's say she picks the number 7. Bonnie keeps this number secret but calculates her public number (x) by doing the calculation: $x = g^a$ modulo p, or $x = 2^7$ modulo 19. This gives her a public number $x = 14$, which she sends to Clyde.[3]

Meanwhile, Clyde picks his own private key (b). Let's say he picks the number 8. Clyde keeps this number secret but calculates his public number (y) by doing the following calculation: $y = g^b$ modulo p, or $y = 2^8$ modulo 19. This gives him a public number of 9, which he sends to Bonnie.

When Bonnie gets Clyde's public number (y), she needs to do another calculation. She already knows (g) and (p) because of her agreement with Clyde, and she knows (a) because it is her private secret. She needs to calculate the key (k), which is a shared secret between her and Clyde. To get the key, Bonnie does the calculation $k = y^a$ modulo p, or $k = 9^7$ modulo $19 = 4$.

Similarly, when Clyde gets Bonnie's public number (x), he needs to do another calculation. He already knows (g) and (p) because of his agreement with Bonnie, and he knows (b) because it is his private secret. He needs to calculate the key (k), which is a shared secret between him and Bonnie. To get the key, Clyde does the calculation $k = x^b$ modulo p, or $k = 14^8$ modulo $19 = 4$.

Now that both Bonnie and Clyde have a shared secret key ($k = 4$) that is a secret between only the two of them, they can use this value to encrypt data messages between them. Note that at no time did either Bonnie or Clyde have to tell the other party her or his private key (a and b), and they did not need to send the shared secret key (k) to each other; each one was able to calculate it herself or himself.

In practice, of course, much larger numbers are used. For example, one system for securing domain name servers uses a 768 bit prime

---

3. The *modulo* function returns the remainder of the result of dividing the first argument of the function by the second, i.e., (n) modulo (m) gives a value of the remainder when n is divided by m. For example, 27 modulo 4 is equal to 3 (3 is the remainder when 27 is divided by 4).

number for (p). The generator number (g) can be quite small (2 is a popular choice). With these values, and if Bonnie and Clyde also pick large numbers for their secret values (a) and (b), then it will be virtually impossible for a third party to figure out the common key (k), due to the amount of computing power that would be required by an attacker who knows only (p), (g), (x), and (y). It is interesting to note that it is also extremely difficult for either Bonnie or Clyde to determine each other's secret value (a and b).

# APPENDIX C

## VIDEO USER CHECKLIST

### Chapter 1: Overview of Video Transport

❑ *Source of Content:* Who will be supplying the content? Who owns the content? Are there any restrictions on use of the content? Can only certain users view the content? Will the content need to be protected against copying?

❑ *Type of Content:* What types of scenes are included in the content? How much detail is there? How much motion is present? Does the detail level of the content need to be preserved for the viewer?

❑ *Content Technical Requirements:* Does the content come from film, videotape, or a live camera? Is there a synchronized audio track? Is there more than one audio track (second language, commentary)? Is there any data that is included with the content, such as closed captioning, V-chip data, or program descriptions? Are there any limits mandated by the content owner on the amount or type of compression that can be used?

❑ *System Funding:* How will the content be paid for? How will the network usage be paid for? Will payments be required from each viewer? Will advertising be used?

❑ *Viewer Profile:* How many users will be viewing the content? Where will they be located? What equipment will they use to view the content?

❑ *Network Capabilities:* What bit rates will the network support? Will the network support multicasting? What security features does the network offer? Who owns the network?

❑ *Performance Requirements:* How much delay will be acceptable in this application? What video and audio quality levels will users accept? Will all users get the content at the same time? Will users be allowed to pause, rewind, and fast-forward the content? What is the financial impact of a service interruption?

## Chapter 2: Video Transport Applications

❑ If the application is entertainment television, determine if the network will be used primarily for contribution, distribution, or delivery.

❑ If the network will be used for contribution, determine the amount of processing that will be done to the video after the transport. As a rule, when more processing is done, higher-quality source video is needed. Consider using lightly compressed or uncompressed video signals for feeds where lots of post-production will be done.

❑ If the network is to be used for distribution, make sure that all categories of delivery providers can be reached as required by the application. Also, make sure that the network is reliable enough to handle this class of traffic.

❑ If the network is to be used for delivery, determine the number of subscribers that will be served simultaneously. Make sure that the chosen delivery system can scale up to this number. Also, consider the costs that will be incurred to equip each new viewer.

❑ For interactive video, make sure that the video quality is high enough to suit the application and that the delay is low. Generally, lower delay is more important than video quality, except for applications that require high image fidelity (e.g., telemedicine).

❑ For narrowcasting, determine if live feeds will be required, or if content can be stored and then streamed. If live feeds are required, then real-time video compression equipment will also be needed.

❑ For live narrowcasting, determine how many viewers will be served simultaneously, and select a mechanism to create an adequate number of streams for all the viewers.

❑ Determine if the application requires hard real time, or if soft real time or non-real time will be adequate. Also determine if real-time compression will be needed.

❑ When creating a business plan for a video delivery system, make sure that all the key factors are analyzed. Pay close attention to costs for obtaining necessary permits and the costs of controlling the ownership rights.

❑ Make sure that the costs of programming are included in any video delivery system business case.

## Chapter 3: Video Basics

❑ Determine the type of video signal that will be used: NTSC, PAL or SECAM; composite, S-video, component, SDI or HD.

❑ Determine the audio signal type: analog, digital stereo, digital multi-channel.

❑ Make sure that video and audio sources and destinations are configured for the correct signal types and that appropriate cables are used.

❑ If 270 Mbps SDI signals are used, check to see if the signals are 625/50 (PAL) or 525/60 (NTSC), since they are not compatible, even at the SDI level.

❑ If SDI or HD-SDI signals are used, determine whether audio signals will be embedded.

❑ Find out about any required or optional services that are being carried in the VBI, particularly closed captioning, V-chip, or other government mandates.

❑ If compression equipment is to be used, make sure that any required VBI signals are processed.

❑ Make sure that any video or audio switches include enough conductors to handle all the required signals, such as multiple channels of audio.

## Chapter 4: Video and Audio Compression

❑ Decide if compression will be used on video and/or audio content. If compression isn't going to be used, will all the networks that will be used have adequate bandwidth to handle the digital video content?

❑ Examine the devices that will be responsible for transmitting and receiving the video/audio content. Will they have adequate performance to encode and/or decode the video in addition to other required tasks?

❑ If desktop PCs will be used, will hardware encoders or decoders need to be added, or will software encoders and decoders be adequate?

❑ If stand-alone hardware devices are to be used (such as set top boxes), how will the users select programming and control other functions?

❑ Will the system connect to other video networks and devices? If so, what standards will be used to permit interoperability?

❑ When selecting a codec technology, make sure that both content sources and destinations can be equipped with compatible technology. Even when the chosen technology is based on published standards, it is important to make sure that each supplier has implemented a compatible set of features. Users of feature-rich technologies such as MPEG–4 need to be particularly careful in this area, because two suppliers can correctly assert that their products are both MPEG–4 compliant without being able to work together if the suppliers have implemented different portions of the standards.

❑ For MPEG systems, a fair amount of configuration of the units may be required. Make sure both encoder and decoder are configured to identical values for all parameters. Users must select a GOP length and pattern, a target video and audio bandwidth, a video resolution, a network interface bit rate, audio format, etc. Longer GOPs and those that include B frames mean better video quality at lower bit rates, but they introduce delay in the transport path. Lower video resolution also reduces bit rate but can result in smaller or blurrier images on the display.

❑ Make sure to evaluate compression systems in all critical areas, including
  ❑ Video Quality
  ❑ Audio Quality

❑ System Delay and Audio/Video (lip) Synchronization
❑ Compression Efficiency
❑ Make sure to use high-quality source material, displays, and speakers for evaluations. Make sure to use multiple people to evaluate the systems and score the results; different individuals will have different perceptions of compression artifacts.
❑ Make sure that the encoder and decoder correctly handle any required data contained in the VBI.
❑ Ensure that equipment and software vendors have paid the appropriate licensing fees for any technology products that are being purchased and that the proper fees are paid to all content rights holders.
❑ For applications in which viewers will be charged for video and audio content, determine whether royalties need to be paid on a per-stream or per-user basis for the compression technologies used, such as MPEG–4.
❑ If new networks are to be constructed, make sure that they can handle the full number of streams with each one operating at the maximum allowed bit rate.

## Chapter 5: IP Networking Basics

❑ What is the IP addressing scheme—private network or Internet compliant?
❑ For video sources, will NAT be used? If so, how will clients link to source?
❑ For video sources, DHCP may not be suitable.
❑ What types of networks will be used between the video source and video client? Will packet size limits cause fragmentation of IP datagrams?
❑ Will the Ethernet network have shared segments, or will each device have a dedicated switch port? Dedicated is preferred for high-bandwidth video.
❑ Will the Ethernet connections be half or full duplex? Full duplex is better for video, if available.
❑ Ensure that the network bandwidth is greater than the combined video/audio data rate and that there is enough bandwidth for other devices using the same network.
❑ Will wireless Ethernet links be used? If so, is the bandwidth sufficient, and will error correction be needed?

## Chapter 6: From Video into Packets

❏ Determine if long or short packets are going to be used for video transport, keeping in mind the pros and cons of each approach.

❏ Make sure that the selected packet length will not be so long as to cause fragmentation over the data networks that will be used.

❏ When choosing a stream format, keep in mind that transport streams have several functions that are specifically designed to operate in difficult environments, such as RS error correction, and a robust mechanism for handling the required clocks.

❏ Elementary streams should not, as a general rule, be used for video transport.

❏ If multiplexed DVB-ASI signals with multiple transport streams are used, make sure that the receivers are configured to process the correct stream, based on the PAT, PMT, and PID values.

❏ If non-MPEG streams are to be used, make sure that a mechanism exists to identify which audio and video content belongs to a given program, and that there is a way to synchronize the streams after they have been transported across a network.

❏ Use Reed-Solomon forward error correction and packet interleaving to make video streams less sensitive to transmission errors. When doing so, keep in mind the extra bandwidth required for the FEC data, and be careful not to allow packets to become so large that they cause fragmentation.

❏ If possible, choose RTP instead of TCP or plain UDP. TCP has some built-in behaviors that are great for data transfer but are not well suited for video transport. UDP alone lacks some of the nice features of RTP for real-time streams. RTP with UDP is well suited for video transport, provided the network devices support RTP.

❏ Keep in mind that RTP streams, which ride inside UDP packets, may be blocked by some firewalls. This should not be a problem for users with private networks (either physical or VPNs) but may be an issue if the streams are to be sent over the Internet.

## Chapter 7: Packet Transport

❏ Verify that the wide area network capacity and technology are suitable for the video traffic that is to be transported.

❏ Set up the video endpoint devices to handle impairments to the video stream. Consider the impact of packet loss, packet reordering, and jitter.

❏ Calculate the total bandwidth needed for the video signals, including any associated audio signals, ancillary data, MPEG overhead, and IP and Ethernet encapsulation overhead. Make sure the network can handle the peak bit rate expected.

❏ Make sure network delay is suitable for the application. For interactive video, one-way delay should be below 150 msec, and normally must be below 400 msec. For one-way applications, delay is not a significant factor.

❏ Consider using multiplexing to reduce the cost of bandwidth when multiple video signals are being transported.

❏ Ensure that network firewalls are configured correctly. In particular, make sure the necessary TCP or UDP ports are unblocked. Also, check whether UDP traffic is allowed to flow when RTP over UDP streams will be used.

❏ Decide whether the public Internet will be used. If so, ensure that video sources and destinations are configured to handle lost packets and large delay variation.

❏ If private networks will be used, determine whether different classes of service will be employed for video. Create policy for video QoS; make sure adequate bandwidth is available for non-video communications.

❏ Examine carrier SLAs. Will networks provide a suitable level of service for video?

## Chapter 8: Video Streaming and Media Players

❏ Determine the number of users who will want to view the content and determine the maximum number of simultaneous viewers permitted.

❏ Determine if public, private, or virtual private networks will be used (or some combination thereof). If video content is going to be delivered to the general public, then ensure that there is a mechanism for viewers to get the necessary viewer software and load it onto their personal computers.

❏ Select a video streaming format—download and play, progressive download, or true streaming—based on the application and the capabilities of the viewer devices.

❑ For live content, true streaming is used.

❑ Determine the requirements for a content preparation system. Will this system be used frequently or occasionally? All three major streaming format vendors offer free or very low cost software encoders for their own format.

❑ Capacity requirements can vary greatly for streaming servers, depending on the amount of content, the number of simultaneous viewers, and the speed of each created stream.

❑ Evaluate and select authoring tools to create the necessary compressed data files.

❑ If third-party content is to be used, ensure that reliable copy protection/encryption software is available for file creation, storage, and playback.

## Chapter 9: Multicasting

❑ Determine whether multicasting is possible. Are all viewers going to be satisfied with receiving the same video/audio at the same time?

❑ If a private network is used, will it be technically possible to enable multicasting on all of the network routers? If so, the router network layout should be reviewed to ensure that device performance will be adequate along all the major routes.

❑ If true multicasting isn't possible, it can be simulated using a unicast network or a CDN.

  ❑ Make sure that the stream bandwidth is calculated correctly, and determine how much total bandwidth is needed by multiplying the number of viewers by the bandwidth of the stream. Make sure to add some spare capacity to handle peaks, extra viewers, etc.

  ❑ Consider the use of a content delivery network provider for non-multicast applications that require very large numbers of viewers (thousands or more). Contract with a CDN provider to support reflected multicasts of the streamed content.

❑ For networks that won't allow multicasting, determine the maximum number of simultaneous users that will be connected at one time. Then, determine if more than one server will be required to create all of the required streams.

## Chapter 10: Videoconferencing Over IP

❑ Videoconferencing involves live, two-way transport of video and audio signals, and is a very popular application for IP networks. It is also one of the most delay-sensitive applications for video technology.

❑ Ensure that each videoconference location is properly equipped with cameras, microphones, and echo cancellers.

❑ Multipoint conferencing (with more than two parties involved in the conference) can be implemented in two different ways: switched video and continuous presence.

    ❑ Consider using switched video for applications with limited network bandwidth and where a central video switch (MCU) can be installed.

    ❑ Consider using continuous presence for high-bandwidth networks and for applications where users may be distracted by video switching (such as schoolchildren).

❑ If multicasting is to be used for continuous presence conferencing, make sure that all segments of the network are capable of supporting multicasts.

❑ Consider using H.323-based videoconferencing systems, which currently have a very large installed base of compatible systems, if videoconferences will frequently be held with parties that are outside the user's network.

❑ Consider using SIP-based videoconferencing systems when multiple types of media need to be involved during a conference, and the videoconferencing system will be built from the ground up, due to the greater flexibility of SIP and less complicated set of specifications.

❑ Before purchasing new systems, determine whether the supplier has a migration strategy for H.264.

❑ Many remote meeting needs can be handled with audio and data conferencing alone.

❑ If T.120 data conferencing is to be used, make sure that appropriate security measures and restrictions are put in place.

## Chapter 11: Content Ownership and Security

❑ Make sure that all video and audio content that is to be transmitted on a network is licensed for use on that network. Failure to do so can expose network owners and users to potential claims for royalties and lawsuits, and loss of access to content in the future.

❑ Consider using copy prevention circuits within video playback devices such as videotape players, DVD players, and STBs to make recording of the video content impractical or of exceedingly poor quality. Make sure copy prevention is also implemented in DVD players inside laptop and desktop computers.

❑ When authorized to use pre-recorded content from videotapes or DVDs, make sure that copy protection schemes won't interfere with the video capture or encoding process.

❑ Encryption or scrambling is normally required when transmitting valuable content over public or private networks with multiple users.

❑ Consider using automated key distribution. The biggest challenge for encryption and scrambling systems is ensuring that the proper keys are distributed to users whenever they have acquired the rights to view a piece of content.

❑ Smart card systems, with card readers at each viewer location, are a popular means for securely distributing descrambling or decryption keys to viewers. Many STB manufacturers have incorporated smart card readers into their products, and readers are also available for personal computers.

## Chapter 12: Transport Security

❑ Transport security can be supplied with private networking technology such as ATM, Frame Relay, leased line, and optical networks.

❑ ATM, Frame Relay, and leased line services can be obtained from most public network providers (telephone companies). Local and long-distance segments may need to be purchased from different suppliers, which may need user supervision.

❏ Optical networks are typically built to customer specification and may require the end user to purchase and maintain the necessary optical equipment. Obtaining fiber and associated rights of way can be expensive and difficult.

❏ Virtual Private Networks need to be configured properly to protect video content. A secure encryption scheme such as IPSec needs to be implemented to prevent content from being copied by others sharing the same network.

❏ Private networking technology does not prevent authorized viewers from making unauthorized copies of content (such as copying video being streamed over a private network). To prevent this, some form of copy protection is needed, as discussed in Chapter 11.

## Chapter 13: IPTV—IP Video to the Home

❏ Develop a business plan prior to deploying IPTV to the home. Make sure to include capital expenditures (hardware and software), installation costs, programming costs, and ongoing maintenance and customer support costs.

❏ Determine the level of viewer interactivity that will be supported.

❏ Determine how live content will be delivered to viewers. If digital turnaround will be used, determine the format of the incoming digital signals.

    ❏ Consider how this might change in coming years as HD content becomes more widespread and as content owners change their requirements.

❏ If Video on Demand is to be used, consider the following issues:

    ❏ Select a method for delivering VOD services: NVOD, pay-per-view VOD, or Subscription VOD. Make sure that systems are in place to support these functions if they are basic, "VCR-like," or content interactive.

    ❏ For large installations, select a video server deployment strategy: centralized, distributed, or a blend of the two.

    ❏ Calculate the total number of hours of programming that will need to be stored on each server, and ensure that adequate storage capacity is purchased.

❑ Determine how many simultaneous streams each server must deliver, and ensure that each server purchased has enough stream processing capacity.
❑ Make sure an ingest system is available to get pre-recorded content from a variety of sources onto the video servers.
❑ Select a supplier of electronic program guide data.
❑ For user software platforms (STBs and the systems that support them), consider using open standard middleware, such as MHP or OCAP.

## Chapter 14: Video File Transfer

❑ If file transfer is to be used, determine the size range of the files, and estimate how often they need to be transferred.
❑ Make sure that the file formats are compatible between the source and destination machines, particularly if they use different editing software.
❑ Consider using caching when large files need to be sent over networks that have slow data transfer rates or long end-to-end delays.
❑ Consider using TCP spoofing to improve the performance of the standard TCP protocol for large data files as long as the network has a reasonably low error rate.
❑ Consider using low-resolution video (with less data per video frame) in place of large video files whenever possible.
❑ Strongly consider using a secure file transfer protocol in place of standard FTP.

## Chapter 15: Network Administration

❑ Develop policies and procedures for handling routine system management tasks, including the following items:
❑ System installation, for video sources and destinations
❑ New user setup, including software/hardware setup and user account information
❑ Equipment moves, changes, and re-installations

❑ Performance monitoring and trouble reporting
❑ System repair and repair verification
❑ Equipment tracking for units that have been removed from the system for vendor repair
❑ Usage tracking as needed for accounting purposes
❑ Determine which management functions will be performed manually and which will be supported by automatic systems.
❑ If automated systems are to be used, survey the management capabilities of the equipment that will be deployed in the video system. Typically, some devices will support web browsing, others will support SNMP, and many newer devices will support both.
❑ For simple systems, such as those where only video devices are the responsibility of the video network manager, consider using web-browsing device management.
❑ For complex systems, where multiple video and non-video devices need to be managed, consider using an SNMP-based management system.
❑ When purchasing new equipment, examine what types of network management tools are available from equipment vendors. Determine if there is a benefit in terms of network management of buying most or all equipment from a single vendor.
❑ Make sure that all elements of a network system have the flexibility to accommodate the needs of video transport, including high bandwidth, low latencies, accurate bandwidth allocation, and the ability to support video-oriented applications layer management.

# GLOSSARY

**1080i** (1080 line interlaced)—High definition (HD) video format with 1080 horizontal lines using the interlaced scanning system.

**24P** (24 frames per second, progressively scanned video)—Video capture and recording format that is commonly used for theatrical movie production because the frame rate (24 frames per second) matches the frame rate of cinema production equipment and film projectors.

**3:2 Pulldown**—Process for converting 24 frames per second material (e.g., cinema films) into 30 frames per second material (e.g., NTSC television). Process involves converting movie frames into an alternating pattern of 3 video fields and 2 video fields, hence the name.

**4 CIF**—Video image with an image area that is four times larger than CIF resolution, or 704×576 pixels.

**5.1 Surround Sound**—Audio signal format consisting of 5 channels of audio (Left, Center, Right, Left Surround, Right Surround) plus a sixth low-bandwidth, low-frequency effects channel.

**720p** (720 line progressive scanning)—High definition (HD) video format with 720 horizontal lines using the progressive scanning system.

**AAC** (Advanced Audio Coding)—High-performance audio encoding format first developed for MPEG–2 and further enhanced for MPEG–4. Produces high-quality sound at reduced bit rates, plus offers efficient support for 5.1 surround sound. Also handles audio content that has a high sampling rate (96 KHz).

**AAF** (Advanced Authoring Format)—Industry standards that describe formats to be used for the exchange of video, audio, and related content between creators, as well as standards for the meta-data that describes the content for human and machine reading.

**AC-3**—A perceptual audio compression system that is often used to provide "5.1" channels of audio (called Left, Right, Center, Left Surround, Right Surround, and a low frequency sound effects channel ".1"). This audio format is commonly used on DVDs. Dolby AC-3 audio coding is also commonly known as Dolby Digital®.

**ADSL** (Asymmetric Digital Subscriber Line)—Technology that allows a standard telephone line to carry high-speed data in addition to normal voice telephony. Operates by using very high frequencies to carry data; requires DSL modem devices to be installed at customer premises and in provider facilities. Technology is termed "Asymmetric" because the data rate from the service provider to the end user is higher than the data rate from the user back to the provider.

**ASP** (Advanced Simple Profile)—Enhanced functionality version of MPEG–4 Simple Profile. Adds capability to do bi-directional (B) frames, ¼ pixel motion estimation, and handle interlaced video signals.

**Aspect Ratio**—Relationship between the vertical height and horizontal width of an image. For example, an image with a 16:9 aspect ratio has a width of 16 units and a height of 9 units.

**ATM** (Asynchronous Transfer Mode)—Digital multiplexing and networking standard that transports information in uniform size packets called "cells." Each cell contains 48 bytes of user data and a 5-byte header. Popularized in the 1990s for video and data transport.

**ATSC** (Advanced Television Systems Committee)—Industry consortium originally formed in 1982 to coordinate television standards across different media. ATSC was instrumental in developing standards for digital and high definition television broadcasts in the USA. Current standards cover many areas of digital broadcasting, including compression profiles, RF modulation techniques, and other areas needed to ensure compatibility between broadcaster and viewer equipment.

**AVC** (Advanced Video Coding)—Video compression system standardized in 2003 that provides significant improvement in coding efficiency over earlier algorithms. Also known as H.264 and MPEG–4 Part 10.

**AVI** (Audio Video Interleave)—File format developed by Microsoft for video and audio data. Supports a wide variety of video compression algorithms and can be converted to or from a variety of other video formats, including MPEG.

**Blowfish**—Public domain encryption algorithm used in a variety of applications as an alternative to DES encryption. Offers key lengths of from 32 to 448 bits.

**BNC**—A type of connector, normally used for terminating and connecting coaxial cables. Very common in video applications.

**Broadband**—Term used to describe signals or systems that cover a wide range of frequencies, usually more than several hundred MHz of signal bandwidth.

**CA** (Conditional Access)—Policies for controlling the access to video, audio, or other data files. User access, such as viewing or recording of video files, can be limited to specific categories of viewers that meet specific conditions, such as only those viewers who subscribe to a premium movie service.

**Cache**—Temporary storage location, used to place data for short-term storage. Commonly used in conjunction with disk drives and microprocessors to speed up data transfer by allowing larger blocks of data to be transferred in each read or write operation. Can also be used to simplify the connection between high-speed devices and low-speed networks.

**Caching**—Process of placing data into a cache, or temporary storage location.

**Capture**—Process of converting raw audio and video content into files that can be manipulated by computer-based editing, production, and streaming systems.

**CAS** (Conditional Access System)—Hardware and/or software system that enforces conditional access policies. Typically includes mechanism for scrambling or encrypting content prior to transmission, a mechanism to permit authorized user devices to descramble or decrypt content at the user's location, and a mechanism to securely distribute the required descrambling or decryption keys to authorized users.

**CAT5** (Category 5 Unshielded Twisted Pair Cable)—Type of data communication cable certified for use in 10BaseT and 100BaseT (Ethernet) network connections.

**CAT6** (Category 6 Unshielded Twisted Pair Cable)—Type of data communication cable certified for use in 1000BaseT (Gigabit Ethernet) network connections.

**CATV** (Cable Television or Community Antenna Television)—System that distributes video programming to subscribers through the use of broadband fiber and coaxial cables. Modern systems offer several hundred channels of broadcast and on-demand video programming as well as data and voice services.

**CDN** (Content Delivery Network)—Network of distributed servers used to deliver content such as web pages or video/audio files to users in multiple geographic areas.

**Cell Tax**—Networking community cliché for the amount of overhead data that is added to user data to form cells that are transported over ATM networks. In normal circumstances, each 48 bytes of data will have 5 bytes of header data added. This amounts to a "cell tax" of approximately 10.4%.

**Checksum**—Method for detecting bit errors on digital signals. In simplest form, a data sender adds up the values of all the bytes in a block of data (such as a packet header) and calculates the total. This total is sent along with the data, and called the check-sum. At the receiving end of the data, the same addition operation is performed on the data block, generating a received checksum. The received checksum is then compared with the checksum that was sent with the original data. If the two checksum values don't match, then at least one bit of the data block has changed value, and the data block will be designated as corrupted. Note that in most cases, a more complicated mathematical process is used instead of addition, so as to make the check-sum more robust.

**Chroma**—Portion of an analog video signal that carries the color difference signals. When a chroma signal is processed by a television display along with the luma signal, a full color image (with red, green, and blue pixels) can be created.

**CIF** (Common Intermediate Format)—Specialized video format used for videoconferencing. Picture is progressively scanned, has 352×288 pixels, and has a frame rate of 29.97 frames per second.

**Closed Captioning**—Process that adds text captions to video images that can be displayed on suitably equipped televisions. These captions are called "closed" because they are not visible on-screen unless the viewer chooses to display them. In many cases these captions will include descriptions of sound effects in addition to a text rendition of any spoken dialog.

**CO** (Central Office)—Facility used by a telephone company or other service provider to deliver signals to subscribers. Normally, a telephone CO will contain equipment that is used to process user telephone calls, and may contain data or video transport and processing equipment.

**Coaxial**—Cable or connector that contains two conductors, one in the center of the cable, and another that completely surrounds it, separated by an insulating layer. Coaxial cables are frequently used for video applications, because of their superior performance with both analog and digital video signals.

**Component**—Analog video signal in which different portions of the video signal are carried on separate conductors. Examples include RGB video, in which each of the three video image signals (red, green, and blue) is carried on a separate conductor, and the video signals delivered to most computer monitors.

**Composite**—Video signal in which all of the video information is combined into a single signal path, such as a coaxial cable. Contrast with Component and S-Video.

**CSS** (Content Scramble System)—Method used to scramble the content of DVDs and thereby prevent them from being duplicated or played on unauthorized playback devices.

**CSU/DSU** (Channel Service Unit/Data Service Unit)—Equipment located in a customer's premises that denotes the boundary between the carrier's network and the customer's network, used primarily for data circuits. Includes special circuitry that allows network on either side to be looped for diagnostic testing. In newer devices, the CSU/DSU function may be integrated into other networking equipment.

**DCT** (Discrete Cosine Transform)—Mathematical technique used in MPEG and other compression systems. Used to reduce the amount of data required to represent a block of pixels, while still allowing reconstruction of an image that is pleasing to viewers. (See Appendix A for more information.)

**DeCSS**—Software program designed to defeat the scrambling system (CSS) used on commercial DVDs.

**DES** (Data Encryption Standard)—US government–approved method for encrypting data.

**DHCP** (Dynamic Host Configuration Protocol)—Method for assigning an IP address to a device when it first joins a network. Allows scarce IP addresses to be reused and simplifies network administration, particularly for users with mobile laptop computers.

**Dolby Digital**®—High-quality digital audio format. See AC-3.

**DRM** (Digital Rights Management)—A generic term used to describe various mechanisms for controlling users' access to digital content. This can include a variety of functions, including encryption, scrambling, and copy protection, which are commonly applied to copyrighted or other proprietary works.

**DS1** (Digital Signal Level 1)—Standard North American signal for telephony networks; operates at a speed of 1.544 million bits per second.

**DS3** (Digital Signal Level 3)—Standard North American signal for telephony networks; operates at a speed of 44.736 million bits per second.

**DSL** (Digital Subscriber Line)—Popular mechanism for providing high-speed data connections to users over existing telephone wiring. Several different generations of technology have come to market, with varying combinations of speed and useful distance.

**DTH** (Direct-To-Home)—Satellite television broadcasting system in which programming is transmitted directly to antennas mounted on subscribers' premises. Differs from other satellite-based services that deliver programming to CATV, DSL, and terrestrial broadcasters who then distribute programming to viewers.

**DTV** (Digital Television)—System for broadcasting video using compressed digital signals. Can be either standard definition or high definition video images. Employs analog 6 MHz television channel that has been converted into a digital transmission channel capable of carrying 19 Mbps or more of data traffic.

**DVB** (Digital Video Broadcasting)—Organization formed in Europe to create standards for broadcasting digital television signals. Includes a variety of distribution methods (see immediately below) and formats that can be used in the content-creation process.

**DVB-C**—Digital Video Broadcasting standards for cable television applications.

**DVB-S**—Digital Video Broadcasting standards for satellite television applications.

**DVB-T**—Digital Video Broadcasting standards for terrestrial (land-based antenna) broadcast television applications.

**DVD** (Digital Versatile Disc)—High-density, removable storage medium commonly used for recording high-quality digital video and audio signals. Widely used for movie and other video content sales/rentals to consumers; has displaced VHS tapes as most popular format for new consumer purchases.

**DVI** (Digital Visual Interface)—Connector used to carry digital video signals between signal sources (PCs, DVD players, set top boxes) and displays of various types. Supports a protocol (High-bandwidth Digital Content Protection, or HDCP) that can be used to ensure that content is distributed only to proper display devices, and not to recording equipment that could be used to pirate video content. This 24-pin connector can now be found on many high-performance video displays.

**EAS** (Emergency Alert System)—Government-mandated system for broadcasters in the USA that is used for transmitting emergency alerts to the public in the event of a natural or man-made disaster or other emergency.

**Echo Canceller**—Device used to prevent the outputs from speakers in a videoconferencing room from being picked up by a microphone and retransmitted to other sites that are participating in the conference.

**Encryption**—Technique used to make data unreadable to parties other than the sender and intended recipients. Normally accomplished through the use of a mathematical operation performed on raw data in conjunction with a key known only to the sender and the recipients. Encryption algorithms are considered strong when third parties that do not have access to the key are unable to recover the original data.

**ES** (Elementary Stream)—Term used in MPEG systems to describe the raw compressed data that is fed into a video or into an audio decoder. These streams are converted into other forms for recording (see Program Stream) or transport (see Transport Stream).

**Feeder Plant**—Portion of a telephone network that transports signals between local central offices and remote terminals. Remote terminals are in turn connected by means of local loops to individual houses over twisted pair copper or other technology.

**Firewall**—Device used at junction point between two networks to ensure that certain types of data on one network do not get transmitted to the other network.

Commonly used when connecting private LANs to the Internet to protect the local users from harmful data or unwanted probes.

**FTTH** (Fiber To The Home)—System for distributing high-speed data and video services directly to customer premises using optical fiber for the entire link. Also known as Fiber To The Premises (FTTP). Contrast with DSL and HFC networks, both of which typically employ fiber in portions of the network, but use electrical cables for connection to customers.

**Full D1**—Digital video format with the full resolution of an SDI signal. For 525-line (NTSC) systems, Full D1 is at least 720×480 pixels; for 625-line (PAL/SECAM) systems Full D1 is at least 720×576 pixels. This format is commonly used in high quality video production.

**G.983**—Broadband Passive Optical Network point-to-multipoint data transport specification that handles multiple users with one wavelength in each direction (upstream and downstream) and employs a time-division multiple access system for bandwidth sharing.

**Gbps** (Gigabit per second)—Data transmission speed of 1 billion bits per second.

**GigE** (Gigabit Ethernet)—LAN data transmission standard operating at 1Gbps, standardized in IEEE 802.3

**Half D1**—Digital video format with half the horizontal resolution of a D1 signal (actually, slightly less than half). For 525-line (NTSC) systems, Half D1 is 352×480 pixels; for 625-line (PAL/SECAM) systems, Half D1 is 352×576 pixels. This format is commonly used in MPEG compression applications.

**Hard Real Time**—Video transport application in which the video destination is synchronized to the video source, and the end-to-end delay has to be kept to a minimum. Failure of the video signal to arrive on time could lead to the failure of the application, such as a videoconference.

**HD** (High Definition)—Video image with resolution greater than standard definition. Typical formats include 720-line progressively scanned images, 1080-line interlaced images, and many other formats. Many HD signals have an aspect ratio of 16:9.

**HD-SDI** (High Definition Serial Digital Interface)—Serial digital transmission interface for uncompressed high definition video signals, operates at a bit rate of 1.485 Gbps or 1.485/1.001 Gbps. Used to link cameras and other production equipment for HD signals by means of a single coaxial cable. Standardized in SMPTE-292M.

**HDTV** (High Definition Television)—Broadcast version of HD signal, typically compressed to 18 Mbps or lower to fit into single DTV broadcast channel.

**Head End**—In a CATV system, the source of video and other programming that is distributed to numerous subscribers.

**HFC** (Hybrid Fiber Coax)—Architecture commonly used in CATV distribution systems, in which fiber optic cable is used for long-distance connections from the head end into local areas and coaxial cables are used to distribute the signals into subscriber premises. This has the benefit of providing high-bandwidth, low-loss fiber optic transport for analog and digital signals over long distances without the expense of having to install fiber optic receivers in every customer's location.

**HTTP** (HyperText Transfer Protocol)—The primary protocol used on the World Wide Web to provide communications between clients and servers. Much of the information transported by HTTP consists of web pages and related data. Note that HTTP is stateless, meaning that each transaction is self-contained and that there is no built-in mechanism to connect a server to a particular client. To get around this limitation, many servers issue "cookies" to clients to allow the server to keep track of the status of different clients.

**Hub**—Data communications device used in twisted pair Ethernet networks to connect multiple circuits within the same collision domain.

**Hz** (Hertz)—Measurement unit representing the frequency of an electronic signal; 1 Hz corresponds to a frequency of 1 cycle per second. Commonly used for describing items such as stations on an FM radio dial (107.9 MHz is equivalent to a radio frequency of 107,900,000 cycles per second).

**IEEE** (The Institute of Electrical and Electronics Engineers)—Professional organization and standards setting body. Responsible for a number of data networking standards, including the 802 series that define Ethernet and other popular networks for IP data transport. For more information, go to www.ieee.org.

**IETF** (Internet Engineering Task Force)—Group of engineers that develop solutions and specifications needed to provide a common framework for the operation of the Internet. The IETF is responsible for creating the technical content of the RFCs that make up the standards that govern the operation of the Internet.

**Impulse PPV**—Method used by consumers to order Video on Demand (VOD) services that are offered on a pay-per-view (PPV) basis. With Impulse PPV, subscribers can simply use their remote control to order VOD content, with the charges normally being deducted from a pre-arranged account. This contrasts with the method used on many traditional PPV systems in which viewers call a telephone number displayed on their screen to order VOD content by speaking with a customer service agent.

**Interlaced**—Horizontal video scanning system that separates each video frame into two video fields, each of which is imaged at a distinct time. The contents of field 1 make up the odd-numbered lines $(1, 3, 5, \ldots)$ and those of field 2 make up the even-numbered lines $(2, 4, 6, \ldots)$ of the displayed video image. Interlaced scanning is used in both PAL and NTSC standard definition broadcast video signals. Contrast with Progressive.

**Internet**—Global network that provides interconnection among a large community of data providers and users. The Internet is used on a daily basis by millions of users for communication, reference, and entertainment; it provides a common medium for a diverse set of applications that allow many modern business, government, and personal activities.

**Inverse TeleCine**—Process for converting 30 fps (or 29.97 fps) video movie content into 24 fps (or 23.976 fps) video content. This is normally done prior to displaying or editing the content on a progressive scan display or workstation. Note that this process is sensible only for content that was originally in 24 fps movie format and was subsequently converted into 30/29.97 fps video using the 3:2 pulldown process (see above).

**IP** (Internet Protocol)—Standard set of rules for formatting and transporting data across the Internet and other networks that use packetized datagrams for communication. These rules include a standard format for headers that appear on each packet and a mechanism for addressing packets so that they can be sent from a source to a destination. The standard that we call IP today was defined in RFC 791 in September 1981 for the Defense Advanced Research Projects Agency of the US government; it is now part of the set of standards maintained by the IETF.

**IRD** (Integrated Receiver/Decoder)—Device used in satellite television systems to receive an incoming signal and decode it for display on a consumer television set. Often includes circuits necessary to descramble protected content and to convert digital satellite signals into analog video signals that are compatible with a consumer television set.

**ISO** (International Organization for Standardization)—International body made up of member organizations from around the world that defines and establishes international standards in a wide variety of areas.

**ISO/IEC**—The International Organization for Standardization and the International Electrotechnical Commission have a joint committee that is responsible for developing standards on information and communications technology. Many of the MPEG standards have been approved by this committee, and so carry the designation ISO/IEC before their number.

**ISP** (Internet Service Provider)—Company or group that provides network access to the public Internet for businesses and individuals, generally on a fee-for-service basis.

**ITS** (Intelligent Transportation System)—Program sponsored by the United States Department of Transportation that supports the addition of information technology to the country's roads and public transport systems. Video networking technology has a number of applications in ITS, including traffic monitoring, vehicle identification, and automated toll collection.

**kbps** (kilobit per second)—Data transmission rate equal to 1000 bits per second.

**kbyte** (Kilobyte)—1024 bytes of data.

**Key** (Encryption Key)—Secret digital value that is manipulated along with user data by an encryption algorithm to produce an encoded message. If only the sender and the receiver possess the key to an encoded message, then other parties will not be able to understand the message, provided the encryption algorithm has not been compromised.

**kft** (Kilofoot)—1000 feet (measure of distance). Commonly used to measure the length of copper telephone loops used by telephone companies in the USA.

**LAN** (Local Area Network)—Data communications network that covers a local area, such as a house, a business office, or a small building. Most LAN technologies are limited to transmission distances on the order of hundreds of meters.

**LCD** (Liquid Crystal Display)—Video display that uses specialized chemicals (liquid crystals) that can be made to be transparent or opaque under the control of an electric field. LCD displays differ from CRTs in that they are purely digital; each pixel in an LCD is individually controlled by the display processor.

**Lip-sync**—Property of video and audio signals in which both are aligned in time so that on-screen images of lip motions match the voice sounds. When lip-sync is not present, video programming can be annoying to watch.

**Loudspeaker**—Device used to convert electrical audio signals into sounds that can be perceived by the human ear.

**Luma**—Portion of an analog video signal that carries the brightness portion of the video image. When used by itself, a luma signal can be converted into a monochrome (black-and-white) video image. When a luma signal is processed by a television display in conjunction with a chroma signal, a full color image (with red, green, and blue pixels) can be created.

**Macroblock**—Fundamental working unit of the MPEG compression system that contains a 16×16 pixel portion of one frame or field of a video sequence. The term "macroblocking" is often used to describe a deteriorated MPEG image in which portions of the image have been replaced with single color blocks that occupy a 16×16 pixel portion of the displayed image; this is normally caused by missing or corrupt data in a compressed video stream that is being processed by an MPEG decoder.

**Mbps** (Megabit per second)—Data transmission rate equal to 1 million bits per second.

**Meta-data**—Literally, "data about data." Meta-data is used to describe the contents of digital files, with the goal of making the files easier to locate and work with. Meta-data about video content might include information such as the title of the work, the duration, the format, and other useful information. Often, some meta-data is inserted into the video stream itself (in the VBI, for example) to allow automatic identification of the content of the video. An analogy for meta-data would be a label on the outside of a videotape cassette, which allows a person to find a specific piece of material without needing to view the actual content of each tape.

**MHE** (Master Head End)—In a CATV system, an MHE is commonly used to receive signals from various sources and distribute them to head ends located within an

MSO's territory. It is not uncommon for one MHE to provide service to several hundred thousand subscribers.

**MHP** (Multimedia Home Platform)—Middleware standard developed by DVB that defines the interfaces between operating system software and user applications on set top boxes. Used to simplify the tasks of applications software developers and STB designers, and to provide a common platform for development and deployment.

**MIB** (Management Information Base)—Data structure that defines the management information that is available from a particular networking device, and also specifies the device functions that can be controlled by a management system. A MIB can include items such as a count of bad packets received by a device, or a control that can disable one of the inputs to a multiplexer prior to its being removed for servicing.

**Motion Estimation**—A key part of the compression process used in MPEG. Successive frames of video are analyzed and compared to determine if any portions of the image have moved. If so, the MPEG decoder can be instructed to simply move one or more macroblocks (of pixels) from one location in the image to another location in the following frame.

**Motion Vector**—This describes the motion of a macroblock from one position to another between two successive frames of a video image, including both direction and magnitude of the motion.

**MP@ML** (Main Profile at Main Level)—Common format for MPEG video compression, used for standard definition video images with interlacing (normal television broadcast signal). Color space is 4:2:0.

**MPEG** (Moving Pictures Experts Group)—A committee first formed in 1988 to develop international standards for video and encoding for digital storage. Numerous standards have been produced by this group, and given international approval by ISO/IEC. Today, the MPEG acronym is used to describe a wide range of different compression formats.

**MSO** (Multiple System Operator)—In CATV terminology, an MSO is a company that owns multiple cable television distribution systems. They can be in adjacent territories or spread out in different provinces or countries.

**Multicast**—Data transmission from a single source to multiple, simultaneous destinations. Contrast with Unicast.

**Musicam**—Another name for MPEG Layer 2 audio. This is used in DAB (Digital Audio Broadcasting) and DVB (Digital Video Broadcasting) systems in Europe.

**MXF** (Media eXchange Format)—Set of standards that have been developed to simplify the exchange of files containing video and audio content between different manufacturers of editing systems and software. SMPTE standard 377M specifies the overall file format defined by MXF, and many other documents describe the data/meta-data that is covered by this format.

**n+1**—System for deploying redundant equipment for protection against failures, where "1" standby unit is provided for every "n" active units.

**NTSC** (National Television System Committee)—Committee that in the early 1950s selected the color television broadcast standard for the USA. NTSC is often used as an abbreviation for the 525-line, 29.97 frame per second, interlaced video standard used in North America, Japan, and a number of other countries.

**NVOD** (Near Video on Demand)—Video delivery system that simulates some of the attributes of a Video on Demand system without the individual video stream control capabilities. One common form of NVOD is sometimes called "stagger-casting," in which multiple copies of a program are played starting at five-minute intervals, thereby limiting any individual viewer to no more than a five-minute wait before his or her program begins to play.

**OCAP** (OpenCable Application Platform)—Middleware interface standard developed by CableLabs to permit portability of software applications and STBs for cable operators in the USA. Based in part on MHP standards.

**PAL** (Phase Alternating Line)—Color video signal that is commonly used in Europe, where the individual lines alternate in phase from one line to the next. Also used as shorthand for the 625-line, 25 frame per second interlaced video standard used extensively in Europe and other countries around the world.

**PAT** (Program Association Table)—Data structure used in an MPEG transport stream to list all of the different programs that it contains. This is carried in PID 0 of every transport stream. Each entry in the PAT table is a pointer to a PMT for a single program.

**Parity**—Method for detecting bit errors on digital signals. In simplest form, one parity bit is added to each byte (8 bits) of user data. For odd parity, the extra bit is set to a "1" or a "0" so as to make the binary sum of all nine bits equal to "1." For even parity, the sum is made equal to "0." If any one of the nine bits is changed, the sum will no longer be odd or even, and the byte will be marked as corrupted.

**PC** (Personal Computer)—Generic term used to describe desktop and portable computers, generally those based on Intel/AMD processors and running an operating system supplied by Microsoft. Can also be used to describe Macintosh- and Linux-based computers in some contexts.

**PES** (Packetized Elementary Stream)—Term used in MPEG to describe an elementary stream that has been divided into packets, prior to further processing. PES packets can be hundreds of kilobytes long, so they typically need further processing into transport stream packets before they are sent over an IP network.

**PID** (Packet Identifier)—Method used to identify each of the different video and audio content streams contained in an MPEG Transport Stream. Each packet contained in a transport stream can have data from only one elementary stream, such as a video or an audio ES, and each packet has a single PID. A demultiplexer can easily locate the streams it desires by sorting the incoming packets by their PID.

**PMT** (Program Map Table)—Data structure used in MPEG to list all of the PIDs that make up a program. A typical PMT will have one PID for a video stream, another PID for an audio stream, and possibly other PIDs if different languages or data streams (such as closed captioning) are part of the program.

**PPV** (Pay-Per-View)—Method for charging viewers for the right to watch or listen to a specific piece of content for a specific time. Rights may be limited to a single showing of the content or may expire after a designated period of time (such as 24 hours).

**Progressive**—Horizontal video scanning system that displays each horizontal line of video in numerical order from the top to the bottom of the video display (1, 2, 3, 4, 5,...). Commonly used in computer displays and some forms of HD video.

**PS** (Program Stream)—An MPEG stream that contains one or more packetized elementary streams that have a common clock source. These streams can be different types (such as video and audio) and they can be played in synchronization. Program streams are not well-suited for transport, but do work well for recording purposes and disk storage, including DVDs.

**PVC** (Permanent Virtual Circuit)—In ATM, a circuit that is established by system configuration and remains available at all times. Note that a PVC does not require a fixed amount of bandwidth; it is very common for a PVC to occupy little or no network bandwidth if no data is currently flowing.

**PVR** (Personal Video Recorder)—Device that allows the recording and playback of content under the control of an end user; normally based on video compression and hard disk technology. TiVo was a pioneer in the development and sales of these devices, which can now be found from a number of manufacturers and in a variety of form factors.

**QCIF** (Quarter CIF)—Video image that is 176×144 pixels, equivalent to one-quarter of the CIF video image size.

**QSIF** (Quarter SIF)—Video image with resolution that is approximately one-quarter that of SIF, or 176×112 for 59.94 Hz video systems, and 176×144 for 50 Hz video systems.

**Quad Split Converter**—Device that takes 4 video pictures and combines them into one, by reducing each input to occupy one-quarter of the output video image. Can sometimes be found in videoconferencing applications where multiple images are present.

**Quantization**—Process of taking a continuously varying signal, such as a sound wave, and converting it into a numerical representation suitable for digital processing. Quantization can be uniform, in which each step in the digital scale is the same size, or it can be non-uniform, in which the size of the steps varies according to the magnitude of the input signal.

**Quantization Error**—Difference between the actual value of an input signal and the value that is assigned to represent it during the quantization process. Errors show up as distortions to a signal when it is converted back from a digital to an analog representation; large errors can introduce significant noise or other distortions to the converted signal.

**Return Path**—Communications channel flowing in the opposite direction to the principal flow of information. Term popularized in cable television applications in which many networks were originally constructed to operate in one direction only (from cable TV provider to subscriber homes). A return path is required for two-way applications such as data or voice communication.

**RF** (Radio Frequency)—High-frequency electrical signals that are capable of radiating from or being received by an antenna. A huge variety of devices use RF signals, including AM/FM radios, televisions, cellular phones, satellite receivers, and all modern computing devices.

**RFC** (Request for Comments)—Name given to documents that define the standards and protocols that govern the operation of the Internet. Documents produced by the IETF become RFCs once they have been approved by the Internet Engineering Steering Group, which is an arm of the Internet Society. RFCs can be experimental, informational, or they can be proposed or draft standards. In addition, RFCs can be updated, obsoleted, or designated historic.

**RJ-45**—Standard connector for 10BaseT and subsequent data communication standards that are commonly used for Ethernet communication. The RJ-45 connector is a small plastic clip with up to eight wires that is very similar in appearance to the four- or six-wire connectors that are widely used for connecting telephone sets to wall plugs. "RJ" stands for "Registered Jack."

**Round-Trip Delay**—Measurement of the amount of time a video image takes to complete the journey from the input at one end of a network to the far end and then back to the near end and then being displayed. Many things can affect delay, including the processing time of compression equipment and the distance that the signals must travel.

**Router**—(1) In IP networks, a device that is responsible for processing the headers on IP packets and forwarding them on toward their ultimate destination. (2) In video networks, a device that provides switching of connections between video sources and their destinations.

**Routing Switch**—(1) In IP networks, a switch (see below) that provides some processing of IP packet headers, although generally not with as much flexibility and functionality as a true router (see above). Typically, this processing is hardware-intensive, so the routing switch can operate at high speeds. (2) In video networks, a router (see above).

**RS-232**—Standard for low-speed, serial data transmission over short distances. Commonly used for low-cost data connections to PCs or other intelligent devices; rarely implemented at speeds exceeding 56 kbps.

**RS-530**—Standard for data transport, sometimes used in digital audio applications.

**RTCP** (Real Time Control Protocol)—Data transport control protocol that works in conjunction with RTP for transporting real-time media streams. Includes functions to support synchronization between different media types (e.g., audio and video) and to provide information to streaming applications about network quality, number of viewers, identity of viewers, etc.

**RTP** (Real Time Protocol or Real-time Transport Protocol)—Data transport protocol that is specifically designed for transporting real-time signals such as streaming video and audio. RTP is often used in conjunction with UDP, and provides important functions such as packet sequence numbering and packet time stamping. RTP is used in conjunction with RTCP.

**RTSP** (Real Time Streaming Protocol)—Protocol used to set up and control real-time streams. Commonly used to create links on websites that point to streaming media files.

**RU** (Rack Unit)—Standardized measurement for the height of electrical devices to be mounted in an equipment rack or cabinet; 1 RU is 44.45 mm, or 1.75 inches.

**SAP** (Secondary Audio Program)—Audio channels added to broadcasts in the USA to support alternative languages. Now more commonly used for video description.

**SAP** (Session Announcement Protocol)—Broadcast IP packets used to send out information about each of the multicast streams that are available on a network, along with information that user devices need in order to connect to a multicast.

**SD** (Standard Definition)—Video image with a resolution defined in standards popularized in the 1950s and widely used for television around the world. For 60 Hz NTSC systems, the video image is composed of 525 interlaced horizontal lines, of which 485 represent the actual image. For 50 Hz PAL systems, the video image is composed of 625 interlaced horizontal lines, of which 576 represent the actual image. Both of these standards use a 4:3 aspect ratio.

**SIF** (Standard Interchange Format)—A video signal with roughly one-quarter the resolution of SD that is commonly used in compression applications in which data rates are extremely limited, so reduced image resolution helps reduce the amount of data needed. For 59.94 Hz systems (NTSC), SIF resolution is 352×240, and for 50 Hz systems (PAL), SIF resolution is 352×288.

**SIP** (Session Initiation Protocol)—A signaling protocol used to set up multimedia sessions. Often used for voice over IP applications, and growing in use for videoconferencing over IP connections. SIP does not provide transport; that is the function of RTP and other transport protocols.

**SLA** (Service Level Agreement)—A contractual agreement between a carrier and a customer that specifies the level of network performance that the carrier will deliver to the customer. This often includes a set of network performance guarantees (minimum availability, maximum error rate, etc.) and a set of remedies (such as billing credits) if these minimums are not met.

**Smart Card**—Small plastic card or chip that contains a microprocessor and memory. Often used for storing and transporting decryption and authorization codes for devices such as set top boxes or mobile phones.

**SMPTE** (Society of Motion Picture and Television Engineers)—US based organization that, among other things, develops standards for movie and video technology. For more information, go to www.smpte.org.

**SNMP** (Simple Network Management Protocol)—Communication standard used for monitoring and controlling the operation of a wide variety of networking equipment, including end-user devices, routers, switches, fiber optic transmission equipment, and many other network components. Devices that offer SNMP functionality will have a well-defined MIB.

**Soft Real Time**—Video transport application in which the video signals are transported in the same amount of time as it takes to display them. Video signals may be live or pre-recorded for soft real time, and significant end-to-end delays are acceptable.

**SP** (Simple Profile)—MPEG compression performance profile, which requires less processing than other, more elaborate profiles. Does not allow the use of B frames, and is defined for use only at the main level of resolution. SP is useful for low-delay applications and for applications in which encoder and decoder implementations need to operate with minimal processing power.

**STB** (Set Top Box)—Device used in conjunction with video delivery systems that performs a variety of tasks, including signal processing, demodulation, decryption, and digital-to-analog conversion. STBs are normally required for DSL and DTH satellite television systems and are frequently required on CATV systems.

**STL** (Studio to Transmitter Link)—Signal transmission network used to deliver video and audio (and possibly other) signals from a broadcaster's production facility to a broadcast transmitter site. In most applications, high quality and high reliability are key STL requirements.

**Streaming**—Method for delivering video or other content over a network in a continuous flow at a rate that matches the speed at which data is consumed by the display device.

**Subtitles**—Text that is added to motion picture and television content for many purposes, including content display in another language. When content is subtitled, the text becomes part of the video image and is displayed to all viewers. Contrast this with closed captioning in the USA that can be displayed or hidden upon viewer command.

**Supertrunk**—High-performance link commonly used in CATV applications to transmit multi-channel signals from one head end to another. These signals can be either analog or digital, depending on the distances and the application.

**SVC** (Switched Virtual Circuit)—Type of ATM connection that is established just prior to data transmission and then disconnected after it is no longer needed.

**S-video**—Analog video signal in which the chroma and luma signals are carried over separate signal paths. This can improve video quality in comparison to a composite signal by eliminating the need to separate the chroma and luma signals in the television display, and can reduce or eliminate the visual image distortions than can be caused by the overlapping portions of the chroma and luma signals.

**Switch**—In Ethernet networks, a device that provides multiple ports that each have a separate logical and physical network interface. This feature eliminates the possibility of packet collisions between devices on separate ports of the switch, thereby improving overall system performance.

**T1**—Basic building block for the digital telephone system in North America. Overall bit rate is 1.544 Mbps, with a usable payload (after framing is removed) of 1.536 Mbps.

**TCP** (Transmission Control Protocol)—Reliable data transfer protocol used in IP networks that offers connection-oriented data transport, along with automatic data transfer rate control and re-transmission of corrupted packets. One of the most widely used data transport protocols, TCP is used throughout the public Internet. However, for live or streaming media signals, RTP over UDP is often a better choice.

**Teletext**—Method devised to support the broadcast of textual information inside the VBI of a video signal for display on specially equipped televisions. Lost popularity as other technologies grew to provide similar function, such as the World Wide Web.

**Trick Modes**—Non-standard video display modes, such as fast-forward, reverse, and fast or slow motion playback.

**Triple DES**—Data encryption algorithm that applies the DES encryption algorithm three times to each packet, generally with three different encryption keys.

**TS** (Transport Stream)—Standard method used in MPEG for converting PES streams into a stream of packets that can easily be transported, say, over an IP network, a satellite link, or over a digital television broadcast to a home. Each TS packet is a fixed 188 bytes long, although FEC data can be added, bringing the TS packet size up to 204 or 208 bytes. Note that MPEG IP packets generally contain multiple transport stream packets.

**Tunneling**—Process of sending a data stream through a network that is not normally designed to handle that type of stream. A classic example is sending private network data securely over the public Internet, without any exposure of the data to anyone other than the intended recipient.

**Unicast**—Data transmission from a single source to a single destination. Contrast with Multicast.

**UDP** (User Datagram Protocol)—Data transfer protocol used on IP networks that offers connectionless, stateless data transport. It is often used in video transport applications (along with RTP) because it offers low overhead and does not provide automatic rate reductions and packet re-transmissions (supplied by TCP) that can interfere with video transport.

**UTP** (Unshielded Twisted Pair)—Form of electrical cable used to transmit data signals, including a variety of forms of Ethernet.

**VBI** (Vertical Blanking Interval)—Portion of a normal video signal located between successive fields or frames that carries no image information (i.e., it is blank). In traditional CRT-based displays, this time interval was required to allow the electron gun to re-position from the bottom of the display to the top. Although some modern forms of display do not require this blanking time, the VBI is part of universal video standards. Ancillary data, such as audio signals, time codes, test signals, or other data, is often inserted into the VBI portions of video signals.

**VC1**—Video compression technique being standardized by SMPTE. Formerly known as Windows Media 9.

**VCR** (Video Cassette Recorder)—Videotape recording and playback device that became popular with consumers in the 1980s. The most popular tape format for consumers is VHS; a large number of professional tape formats are also widely used.

**VDSL** (Very high-speed Digital Subscriber Line)—Digital Subscriber Line technology that is capable of delivering a large amount of data in each second, typically defined as above 10 Mbps. Speeds in this range are generally required in order to deliver multiple simultaneous video streams to multiple television sets over a single DSL circuit.

**VOD** (Video On Demand)—Process for delivering video programming to viewers upon demand, i.e., when they want it. Commonly includes the ability to skip ahead (fast-forward) or rewind the video signal under user control. Contrast with NVOD.

**WAN** (Wide Area Network)—Network that connects two or more network segments across a significant geographic distance—between buildings, across a city, or around the world.

**WM9** (Windows Media Nine)—High-performance video compression system created by Microsoft that has been submitted to SMPTE for standardization. Renamed "VC1" for the purpose of creating standards.

**xDSL** (Digital Subscriber Line)—In this acronym "x" represents any one of a selection of words, including "A" for "Asymmetric" DSL, "H" for "High Speed" DSL, and others. xDSL is a generic term intended to mean "any of a variety of forms of DSL."

**Y/C**—Baseband analog video format used in S-video connectors. Here, Y stands for Luma (Luminance) and C stands for Chroma (Chrominance).

# INDEX